LEARNING BY EXPANDING, SECOND EDITION

First published in 1987, *Learning by Expanding* challenges traditional theories that consider learning a process of acquisition and reorganization of cognitive structures within the closed boundaries of specific tasks or problems. Yrjö Engeström argues that this type of learning increasingly fails to meet the challenges of complex social change and fails to create novel artifacts and ways of life. In response, he presents an innovative theory of expansive learning activity, offering a foundation for understanding and designing learning as a transformation of human activities and organizations. This second edition of this seminal text features a substantive new introduction that illustrates the development and implementation of Engeström's theory since its inception.

Yrjö Engeström is Professor of Adult Education and the director of the Center for Research on Activity, Development and Learning (CRADLE) at the University of Helsinki. He is also Professor Emeritus of Communication at the University of California, San Diego. His most recent book is *From Teams to Knots: Activity-Theoretical Studies of Collaboration and Learning at Work* (2008).

Learning by Expanding

AN ACTIVITY-THEORETICAL APPROACH TO
DEVELOPMENTAL RESEARCH

Second Edition

Yrjö Engeström
University of Helsinki

CAMBRIDGE
UNIVERSITY PRESS

University Printing House, Cambridge CB2 8BS, United Kingdom

One Liberty Plaza, 20th Floor, New York, NY 10006, USA

477 Williamstown Road, Port Melbourne, VIC 3207, Australia

314-321, 3rd Floor, Plot 3, Splendor Forum, Jasola District Centre, New Delhi - 110025, India

79 Anson Road, #06-04/06, Singapore 079906

Cambridge University Press is part of the University of Cambridge.

It furthers the University's mission by disseminating knowledge in the pursuit of
education, learning and research at the highest international levels of excellence.

www.cambridge.org
Information on this title: www.cambridge.org/9781107640108

First published 1987
Second edition 2015
First paperback edition 2019

A catalogue record for this publication is available from the British Library

Library of Congress Cataloging in Publication data
Engeström, Yrjö , 1948–
Learning by expanding : an activity-theoretical approach to developmental
research / Yrjö Engeström. – Second edition.
pages cm
Includes bibliographical references and index.
ISBN 978-1-107-07442-2 (hardback)
1. Active learning.   2. Learning, Psychology of.   I. Title.
LB1027.23.E55   2014
371.39–dc23   2014025980

ISBN 978-1-107-07442-2 Hardback
ISBN 978-1-107-64010-8 Paperback

CONTENTS

FIGURES

TABLES

PREFACE

This new edition of *Learning by Expanding* is essentially the same book that first appeared in 1987. The most important change is the inclusion of a new, rather substantial, introductory chapter, titled "Learning by Expanding: Origins, Applications, and Challenges." In this introductory chapter, I outline the development of the theory of expansive learning as it has unfolded after the initial publication of the book.

Besides this, the only changes in the original text are stylistic. These include formulating the references in accordance with APA rules, replacing the generic male "he" with "he or she" when possible, and adding an index at the end of the book.

In the original book, I named a long list of people to whom I was grateful for their inspiration and comments in the preparation of the book. I am still grateful to those people, but thanking them once was enough. More pertinently, I now see a much more complex and multilayered fabric of people who, directly or indirectly, have contributed to the formation of the ideas put forward in this book. It would be impossible to name all these people. It is sufficient to say that this book is a product and an instrument of cultural-historical activity theory understood as a living movement that does not recognize most of the conventional boundaries between nations, cultures, positions, and schools of thought.

I dedicate this new edition of *Learning by Expanding* to Annalisa Sannino and Jurij Enzo Engeström. Their collaboration and support truly made the completion of the job possible.

Sipoo, February 2014
Yrjö Engeström

LEARNING BY EXPANDING: ORIGINS, APPLICATIONS, AND CHALLENGES

Learning by Expanding was originally published in 1987. It was written in order to formulate a strong alternative to the dominant Cartesian views of cognition and learning that depicted the human mind as if it were a computer, isolated from the cultural context. In the 1980s, notions such as "everyday cognition" (Rogoff & Lave, 1984), "situated action" (Suchman, 1987), and "cognition in practice" (Lave, 1988) began to emerge and challenge the dominant views. *Learning by Expanding* was part of this emerging new groundswell.

The second motivation behind the book was methodological. Studies of cognition and learning were, and still are, predominantly observational and analytical. As Urie Bronfenbrenner (1977, p. 528) pointed out, "Most of our scientific ventures into social reality perpetuate the status quo; to the extent that we include ecological contexts in our research, we select and treat them as sociological givens rather than as evolving social systems susceptible to significant and novel transformation." Having grown up as an activist of the radical student movement, I was convinced that research needs to be actively involved in making the world better. *Learning by Expanding* built on an interventionist premise, well explicated by Bronfenbrenner.

> Naturalistic studies have the disadvantage of being limited to variations of macrosystems that presently exist or have occurred in the past. Future possibilities remain uncharted, except by hazardous extrapolation.... This foreshortened theoretical perspective was first brought to my attention by Professor A. N. Leont'ev of the University of Moscow.... "It seems to me that American researchers are constantly seeking to explain how the child came to be what he is; we in the USSR are trying to discover how he can become what he not yet is." ... Soviet psychologists often speak of what they call the "transforming experiment." By this term they mean an experiment that radically restructures the environment, producing a

new configuration that activates previously unrealized behavioral potentials of the subject. (Bronfenbrenner [1977, p. 527–528])

The third force behind *Learning by Expanding* was the discovery of cultural-historical activity theory as a potent framework for understanding and changing the world. In the Soviet Union, activity theory had a sixty-year history of original insights, groundbreaking research, and severe oppression. In the West, Vygotsky's work was found and promoted from the 1960s on in escalating steps by well-known North American scholars, such as Jerome Bruner (1962) and Michael Cole and Sylvia Scribner (1978). Activity theory, the most important heir and extension of Vygotsky's legacy, was primarily discovered by radical European scholars and students in the 1970s and 1980s mainly through the works of Leont'ev (1978). In the late 1970s the work of Vassily Davydov (1977, 1990) made a strong impression on me, and I was fortunate enough to persuade him to visit Finland in the early 1980s. The first international congress on activity theory was organized in West Berlin in 1986. *Learning by Expanding* is a fruit of that movement.

THREE GENERATIONS OF ACTIVITY THEORY

We may distinguish among three generations in the evolution of cultural-historical activity theory (Engeström, 1996a). The first generation, centered around Vygotsky, created the idea of *mediation*. This idea was crystallized in Vygotsky's (1997c, p. 86) triangular model of "a complex, mediated act," which is commonly expressed as the triad of subject, object, and mediating artifact.

The insertion of cultural artifacts into human actions was revolutionary in that the basic unit of analysis now overcame the split between the Cartesian individual and the untouchable societal structure. The individual could no longer be understood without his or her cultural means; and the society could no longer be understood without the agency of individuals who use and produce artifacts. This meant that objects ceased to be just raw material for the formation of the subject as they were for Piaget. Objects became cultural entities and the object orientedness of action became the key to understanding human psyche.

The limitation of the first generation was that the unit of analysis remained individually focused. This was overcome by the second generation, led and inspired by Leont'ev's work. In his famous example of "primeval collective hunt" Leont'ev (1981, p. 210–213) showed how *historically evolving division of labor* has brought about the crucial differentiation between an individual action and a collective activity. However, Leont'ev never graphically expanded Vygotsky's original model into a model of a collective activity system. In particular, the relationship between object-oriented production and communicative exchange between people remained somewhat unclear in Leont'ev's work. In Chapter 2 of *Learning by Expanding*, an effort was made to model the human activity system and to overcome the dualistic opposition between production and communication (see Figure 2.6).

The concept of activity took the paradigm a major step forward in that it turned the focus on complex interrelations between the individual subject and his or her community. In the Soviet Union, the societal activity systems studied concretely by activity theorists were largely limited to play and learning among children. Contradictions of activity remained an extremely touchy issue. Since the 1970s, the tradition has been taken up and recontextualized by radical researchers in the West. New domains of activity, including work, have been opened up for concrete research. A tremendous diversity of applications of activity theory began to emerge. The idea of internal contradictions as the driving force of change and development in activity systems, powerfully conceptualized by Ilyenkov (1977, 1982), began to gain its due status as a guiding principle of theoretical work and empirical research.

Ever since Vygotsky's foundational work, the cultural-historical approach has been very much a discourse of vertical development toward "higher psychological functions." Michael Cole (1988; see also Griffin & Cole, 1984) was one of the first to point out the deep-seated insensitivity of the second-generation activity theory toward cultural diversity. When activity theory became international, questions of diversity and dialogue between different traditions or perspectives became increasingly serious challenges. It is these challenges that the third generation of activity theory began to deal with.

The third generation of activity theory is developing conceptual tools to understand networks of interacting activity systems, dialogue, and multiple perspectives and voices. In this mode of research, the basic model is expanded to include minimally two interacting activity systems. This move toward networks of activities, while still in an embryonic form, was anticipated in the original text of *Learning by Expanding* (see in particular Figures 2.7 and 2.11).

Third-generation activity theory expands the analysis both up and down, outward and inward. Moving up and outward, it tackles multiple interconnected activity systems with their partially shared and often fragmented objects. Moving down and inward, it tackles issues of subjectivity, experiencing, personal sense, emotion, embodiment, identity, and moral commitment. The two directions may seem incompatible. Indeed, there is a risk that activity theory is split into the study of activity systems, organizations, and history, on the one hand, and subjects, actions, and situations, on the other hand. This is exactly the kind of split the founders of activity theory set out to overcome. To bridge and integrate the two directions, serious theoretical and empirical efforts are needed.

DEVELOPMENTAL WORK RESEARCH
AS AGENDA OF APPLICATION

The central ideas of this book may be condensed into the following five claims: (1) The object-oriented and artifact-mediated collective activity system is the prime unit of analysis in cultural-historical studies of human conduct; (2) historically evolving inner contradictions are the chief sources of movement, change, and development in activity systems; (3) expansive learning is a historically new type of learning, which emerges as practitioners struggle through developmental transformations in their activity systems, moving across collective zones of proximal development; (4) the dialectical method of ascending from the abstract to the concrete is the key for mastering cycles of expansive learning; and (5) an interventionist research methodology that aims at pushing forward, mediating, recording, and analyzing cycles of expansive learning in activity systems is needed.

At the time this book was initially written, my colleagues and I were taking the first steps toward constructing *developmental work research* as a systematic approach for applying activity theory and the theory of expansive learning in the world of work, technology, and organizations (e.g., Toikka, Engeström, & Norros, 1985; Engeström & Engeström, 1986; Engeström, 1991b, 1991c, 1993). Since then, a large number of studies and dissertations applying this framework have appeared (see Engeström, 2005a; Engeström, Lompscher, & Rückriem, 2005).

The focus of developmental work research is on the object of the activity (Engeström, Puonti, & Seppänen, 2003; Engeström & Blackler, 2005). The object is more than just a goal or product. Objects are durable concerns and carriers of motives; they are generators and foci of attention, volition, effort, and meaning. Through their activities people constantly change and create new objects. The new objects are often not intentional products of a single activity but unintended consequences of multiple activities. The object of an activity carries within it the foundational contradiction between the use value and the exchange value.

In our era of globalization and financialization, the use values of objects have become more difficult to grasp than perhaps ever before. But they have not vanished. The mission of developmental work research might be characterized as rediscovery and expansion of emancipatory use value in objects of human activity.

The expansion of the object proceeds in multiple dimensions. Engeström (2000b) and Hasu (2000) identified the social-spatial dimension ("Who else should be included?"), the anticipatory-temporal dimension ("What previous and forthcoming steps should be considered?"), and the moral-ideological dimension ("Who is responsible and who decides?"). Engeström, Puonti, and Seppänen (2003) compared three studies of expansive learning focusing on the sociospatial dimension, on the one hand, and the temporal dimension, on the other hand. They concluded that space and time are not the whole story; the moral-ideological dimension of power and responsibility is always also at stake. This third dimension was discussed by Puonti (2004) in her study of the investigation of economic crimes.

> A case under investigation consists of a constant interplay of the crime and its investigation. The case, however, is never merely unique: the crime under investigation constitutes a part of economic crime in general, and the investigation is part of economic crime prevention. The interplay between the crime and its investigation can be viewed at two levels: at the specific case level and at the general level. Expansion is a twofold movement: the crime is expanded by the criminal perpetrators, and the investigators have the opportunity to expand the object in their investigation. The self-movement of the object generates the potential for expansion, but the efforts to expand the object of investigation have remained insufficient....
>
> Expansion is commonly understood as positive development. My empirical setting, however, shows the dark side of expansion as well. It may be seen as a shift of a contradictory phenomenon from one developmental phase to another. There is a constant battle between the criminals and the authorities: Which side is able to move first to the next phase of development? The investigation is not merely in the hands of the investigators, but the crime "strikes back" and forces the investigators to adopt new ways of action. (Puonti, 2004, p. 82)

In the following sections, I briefly discuss experiences of and challenges to the theory of expansive learning that my research groups and colleagues around the world have encountered in studies and interventions in various activity systems during the years after this book was initially published. Much of the research based on the theory of expansive learning has been fairly thoroughly reviewed recently (Engeström & Sannino, 2010). Thus, I will concentrate on a few theoretical issues and refer to empirical studies only very selectively.

BEYOND UNIVERSALISM

The theory of expansive learning is a process or phase theory of learning. In other words, it proposes an ideal-typical sequence of learning actions that together make an expansive learning cycle. In this sense, the theory is prescriptive. A process theory tends toward orthodoxy if the sequence it promotes is taken as the universal and thus the only possible or desirable one.

Kruger and Tomasello (1998) and Tomasello (1999) forcefully demonstrate that human learning is to a large extent dependent on intentional instruction. The importance of this argument is that human learning is pervasively shaped according to normative cultural expectations. Such expectations are extremely diverse and they change historically. Thus, human learning processes are also very diverse and continuously changing. There is no single biologically determined universal, appropriate, or good way to learn among humans.

From this follows that a well-developed process theory of learning must denounce universalism and specify just what kind of learning it actually aims at describing, explaining, and promoting – and on what historical and cultural grounds. To preclude becoming a universalist orthodoxy, such a theory should make clear its own limits and engage in comparison and contrast with other theories of the learning process (Engeström & Sannino, 2012).

The theory of expansive learning builds on the idea of multiple types of learning, especially on Bateson's (1972) analysis of levels of learning (see Chapter 3). Expansive learning is defined as similar to Bateson's "Learning III." Such expansive learning is rare and risky: "Even the attempt at Level III can be dangerous, and some fall by the wayside" (Bateson, 1972, p. 305).

The historical emergence of expansive learning is discussed at length in Chapter 2 of *Learning by Expanding*. Three historical lineages of inner contradictions and potentials for the emergence of expansive learning are traced, namely, learning within school going, learning within work activity, and learning within science and art. The conclusion of the historical analysis is that "the ontogenetic emergence of [expansive] learning activity, at least in present-day capitalist societies, may with the highest probability take place in adulthood or adolescence, when the subject faces historically and individually pressing inner contradictions within his or her leading

activity – be it work, school-going, science or art." The historical emergence of expansive learning is connected to the increasingly rapid change
of overall concepts of production, business, and organization in all spheres
of economy and society (Pihlaja, 2005). Expansive learning is a type of
learning needed and generated in radical transformations of entire activity
systems and fields of activity. It is not a universal solution suitable for all
learning needs.

In empirical research, one way to combat the tendency of universaliza-
tion of a process theory of learning is to analyze one and the same set of
data with the help of two or more different process theories, thus comparing
and contrasting one's favorite theory with others. Such an analysis was
conducted in a study that examined the innovative learning processes in
two industrial team meetings, using the theory of expansive learning and
Nonaka and Takeuchi's (1995) theory of knowledge creation side by side
(Engeström, 1999c, 2008, pp. 118–168; see also Virkkunen, 2009).

To take seriously the intentionally instructed nature of human learning does not mean that we should return to the idea of complete instructional control over learning. In research and interventions, the assumption
of complete instructional control takes the insidious form of self-fulfilling
prophecy. If you have a strong universalistic theory of the process of learning, you will tend to impose it upon your data and examples so that you
will indeed find evidence confirming that your theory works in practice.
Correspondingly, if you have a strong universalistic theory of the optimal
process of learning guiding your intervention, you will tend to try to impose
it upon the learners. In both cases, you tend to get what you want.

But the very assumption of complete instructional control over learning
is a fallacy. In practice, such control is not possible to reach. Learners will
always proceed differently from what the instructor, researcher, or interventionist had planned and tried to implement or impose. You get what you
want only if you ignore this resistance to and deviation from the theory.

Therefore, we need to look at instruction and learning – the plans and
actions of instructors as well as the actions of learners – as dialectically intertwined. This means that the prescribed and planned process the instructor
is trying to implement must be compared and contrasted with the actual
process performed by the learners. The two will never fully coincide. The
gap, struggle, negotiation, and occasional merger between the two need to
be taken as key resources for understanding the processes of learning as
processes of formation of agency.

Analyses of different ways to articulate and bridge the gap –
contestations, negotiations, formation of dual objects, and creation of

"third spaces" – (Gutiérrez, Rymes, & Larson, 1995; Gutiérrez, Baguedano-López, & Tejeda, 1999) are a particularly promising direction of research. This line of research will put the formation of participants' agency in the center of expansive learning (see Engeström, Rantavuori, & Kerosuo, 2013).

LEARNING ACTIONS AND EXPANSIVE CYCLES

The theory of expansive learning is based on the dialectics of ascending from the abstract to the concrete. This is a method of grasping the essence of an object by tracing and reproducing theoretically the logic of its development, of its historical formation through the emergence and resolution of its inner contradictions. A new theoretical idea or concept is initially produced in the form of an abstract, simple explanatory relationship, a "germ cell." This initial abstraction is step-by-step enriched and transformed into a concrete system of multiple, constantly developing manifestations. In an expansive learning cycle, the initial simple idea is transformed into a complex object, into a new form of practice. Such a theoretically grasped practice is concrete in systemic richness and multiplicity of manifestations.

In this framework, abstract refers to partial, separated from the concrete whole. In empirical thinking based on comparisons and classifications, abstractions capture arbitrary, only formally interconnected properties. In dialectical-theoretical thinking, based on ascending from the abstract to the concrete, an abstraction captures the smallest and simplest, genetically primary unit of the whole functionally interconnected concrete system (see Ilyenkov, 1977; Davydov, 1990; also Falmagne, 1995).

The expansive cycle begins with individual subjects questioning the accepted practice, and it gradually expands into a collective movement or institution. Ascending from the abstract to the concrete is achieved through specific epistemic or learning actions. Together these actions form a cycle or a spiral that may be called learning activity or expansive learning. The process of expansive learning should be understood as construction and resolution of successively evolving contradictions in the activity system. The new concepts and practices generated by expansive learning activity are future-oriented visions loaded with initiative and commitment from below. They cannot be predefined and safely constrained by researchers or authorities.

According to Davydov (2008), an ideal-typical sequence of learning activity consists of the following six learning actions: (1) transforming the conditions of the task in order to reveal the universal relationship of the object under study; (2) modeling the identified relationship in a material, graphic, or literal form; (3) transforming the model of the relationship in order to study its properties in their "pure guise"; (4) constructing a system of particular tasks that are resolved by a general mode; (5) monitoring the performance of the preceding actions; and (6) evaluating the assimilation of the general mode that results from resolving the given learning task.

In subsequent years, the concept of expansive learning activity has been developed further, to deal with the challenges of learning outside the school and the classroom (Engeström, 1991d, 1999c). An ideal-typical sequence of epistemic actions in an expansive cycle may be described as follows (Engeström, 1999c, p. 383–384; Engeström & Sannino, 2010, p. 7):

- The first action is that of questioning, criticizing, or rejecting some aspects of the accepted practice and existing wisdom. For the sake of simplicity, I will call this action *questioning.*
- The second action is that of *analyzing* the situation. Analysis involves mental, discursive, or practical transformation of the situation in order to find out causes or explanatory mechanisms. Analysis evokes "Why?" questions and explanatory principles. One type of analysis is *historical-genetic*; it seeks to explain the situation by tracing its origins and evolution. Another type of analysis is *actual-empirical*; it seeks to explain the situation by constructing a picture of its inner systemic relations.
- The third action is that of *modeling* the newly found explanatory relationship in some publicly observable and transmittable medium. This means constructing an explicit, simplified model of the new idea that explains and offers a solution to the problematic situation.
- The fourth action is that of *examining the model,* running, operating, and experimenting on it in order to grasp fully its dynamics, potentials, and limitations.
- The fifth action is that of *implementing the model* by means of practical applications, enrichments, and conceptual extensions.
- The sixth and seventh actions are those of *reflecting* on and evaluating the process and *consolidating* its outcomes into a new stable form of practice.

These actions bear a close resemblance to the six learning actions put forward by Davydov (2008). Davydov's theory is, however, oriented at learning activity within the confines of a classroom, where the curricular contents are determined ahead of time by more knowledgeable adults. This probably explains why it does not contain the first action of critical questioning and rejection, and why the fifth and seventh actions, implementing and consolidating, are replaced by "constructing a system of particular tasks" and "evaluating" – actions that do not imply the construction of actual culturally novel practices.

The theory of expansive learning was initially applied to large-scale transformations in activity systems, typically spanning a period of several months, sometimes years. Subsequent studies have shown that large-scale expansive cycles involve numerous smaller cycles of learning actions. Such a smaller cycle may take place within a single encounter or meeting that involves intensive collaborative analysis and problem solving. Careful investigation may reveal a rich texture of learning actions within such temporally short efforts. But can such a miniature cycle be called expansive?

> Miniature cycles of innovative learning should be regarded as *potentially* expansive. A large-scale expansive cycle of organizational transformation always consists of small cycles of innovative learning. However, the appearance of small-scale cycles of innovative learning does not in itself guarantee that there is an expansive cycle going on. Small cycles may remain isolated events, and the overall cycle of organizational development may become stagnant, regressive, or even fall apart. The occurrence of a full-fledged expansive cycle is not common, and it typically requires concentrated effort and deliberate interventions. With these reservations in mind, the expansive learning cycle and its embedded actions may be used as a framework for analyzing small-scale innovative learning processes. (Engeström, 1999c, p. 385)

In a recent study (Engeström, Rantavuori, & Kerosuo, 2013), expansive learning actions and the relationship between large-scale cycles and miniature cycles were investigated in detail. The analysis shows that in a real-life intervention, expansive learning actions were accompanied by a fairly large number and diversity of nonexpansive learning actions. Each expansive learning action was found to have several subtypes. For example, the action of modeling (see previous discussion) manifested itself in five subtypes: sketching the initial idea of a model, exploiting existing models, naming and defining the model, fixing the model in material or graphic form, and varying and adapting the model. The analysis of cyclicity revealed an iterative loop within the overall cycle of expansive learning, indicating that smaller cycles are indeed part and parcel of the overall cycle of expansive learning.

Another recent study (Nummijoki & Engeström, in preparation) asks how the theory of expansive learning might be able to describe both learning actions that lead to virtuous expansive cycles and learning actions that lead to vicious defensive cycles. As the study analyzes learning in encounters between patients and their caregivers, it also asks how such learning episodes might be described as interplay between two cycles of learning, namely, between the patient's cycle and the caregiver's cycle. The study shows that it is indeed possible to extend the vocabulary of expansive learning to encompass actions of defensive or restrictive learning. The interplay between the patient's and the caregiver's learning cycles may take one of the four basic patterns, namely, + +, + −, − +, or − −, in which + stands for an expansive miniature cycle and − for a defensive or vicious miniature learning cycle.

As pointed out previously, expansive learning is a process of working out and resolving contradictions in the activity to be transformed. The activity-theoretical principle of contradictions has been used in a number of studies as a general explanatory lens (Murphy & Rodriguez-Manzanares, 2008). Recently a methodological framework was developed for systematic analysis of discursive manifestations of contradictions in the course of expansive learning as it unfolds in organizational change efforts and interventions (Engeström & Sannino, 2011). Four distinctive types of manifestations of contradictions were identified, namely, dilemmas, conflicts, critical conflicts, and double binds. Each type has its characteristic functions and linguistic cues. This framework enables the researcher to trace in detail the emergence and resolution of contradictions in the discourse of the participants going through an expansive learning cycle.

In expansive learning, new kinds of collective and transformative agency emerge (Virkkunen, 2006). Transformative agency may be defined as breaking away from the given frame of action and taking the initiative to transform it. The emergence of transformative agency is a stepwise process. To trace the steps of the process, a typology of six kinds of expressions of transformative agency has been developed (Engeström & Sannino, 2013). The six types of expressions are criticizing the existing activity and organization, resisting the interventionist or the management, explicating new possibilities, envisioning new patterns or models of the activity, committing to concrete actions aimed at changing the activity, and taking consequential actions to change the activity.

These recent methodological developments in the analysis of expansive learning enable researchers and interventionists to compare the detailed profiles of cycles of expansive learning conducted in different contexts and supported by different interventions. Expansive learning is not a uniform, mechanical process. Differences between expansive cycles reveal pitfalls and potentials that might otherwise not be detected and exploited in future efforts.

THE VERTICAL AND THE HORIZONTAL
IN LEARNING AND DEVELOPMENT

Activity theory is a child of Marxist scholarship. As such, it is influenced by Enlightenment thinking in which history and development are often depicted in vertical evolutionary terms, as progress that follows predetermined stages. A few years after the publication of *Learning by Expanding*, I explicated my standpoint on this as follows.

> From the viewpoint of historicity, the key feature of expansive cycles is that they are definitely not predetermined courses of one-dimensional development. What is more advanced, "which way is up", cannot be decided using externally given fixed yardsticks. Those decisions are made locally, within the expansive cycles themselves, under conditions of uncertainty and intensive search. Yet they are not arbitrary decisions. The internal contradictions of the given activity system in a given phase of its evolution can be more or less adequately identified, and any model for future which does not address and solve those contradictions will eventually turn out to be non-expansive.
>
> An activity system is by definition a multi-voiced formation. An expansive cycle is a re-orchestration of those voices, of the different viewpoints and approaches of the various participants. Historicity in this perspective means identifying the past cycles of the activity system. The re-orchestration of the multiple voices is dramatically facilitated when the different voices are seen against their historical background, as layers in a pool of complementary competencies within the activity system. (Engeström, 1991a, p. 14–15)

The acknowledgment of the horizontal or "sideways" movement in learning and development (Engeström, 1996b, 2003) calls attention to dialogue as discursive search for shared meanings in object-oriented activities. James Wertsch (1991) has done much to introduce Mikhail Bakhtin's (1981, 1986) ideas on dialogicality as a way to expand the Vygotskian framework. Ritva Engeström (1995) went a step further by showing a parallel between Bakhtin's ideas of social language, voice, and speech genre and Leont'ev's concepts of activity, action, and operation. One might say that activity theory, and developmental work research as its application, incorporated dialogue and discourse into their foundational repertoires in the 1990s. This move is anticipated toward the end of Chapter 4 in *Learning by Expanding*.

The horizontal aspect was conceptualized as boundary crossing, a powerful lens for analyses of sideways interactions between different actors and activity systems (Engeström, Engeström, & Kärkkäinen, 1995;

Tuomi-Gröhn & Engeström, 2003). Another step was the formulation of the idea of negotiated "knotworking" as an emerging mode of collaboration across organizational, professional, and cultural boundaries (Engeström, Engeström, & Vähäaho, 1999; Engeström, 2005b, 2008).

The analysis of types of interaction among the participants in expansive learning is a fruitful way to include the horizontal aspect of learning in concrete investigations. A framework of three basic types of interaction – coordination, cooperation, and reflective communication – has been effectively used to capture the dynamics of collaboration in processes of problem solving and learning (Engeström, 2008; see also Leadbetter, 2004; de Lange, 2011). This framework makes visible the shifts in participants' orientation toward one another and toward the object of their learning efforts simultaneously.

While it is important to recognize and theoretically understand the horizontal movement in learning, the vertical or hierarchical aspect of learning and development must not be overlooked (Engeström, 1995). Accounts of learning and innovation that only operate with horizontal or "flat" notions of cognition miss a crucially important resource in failing to explore the particular complementary potentials and limitations of different types of hierarchically arranged mediational means (Engeström, 2007a; Toiviainen, 2007), as well as the dynamics of power between hierarchically organized activity systems (Engeström, 2009a).

Arguments for the continuing importance of the vertical aspect have sometimes been interpreted as falling back to deterministic models of developmental stages leading to a fixed end point. For example, Klaus Holzkamp interpreted Bateson's (1972) levels of learning and my use of them in *Learning by Expanding* as "development depicted as learning passage through a logically pre-constructed matrix of stages of learning" (Holzkamp, 1993, p. 238).

Does an argument for a vertical aspect of hierarchical levels automatically imply a fixed course of development? Holzkamp overlooked here the dialectics of universality and context specificity in development. This very issue was discussed by Sylvia Scribner (1985) in her analysis of Vygotsky's uses of history.

But just as Vygotsky does not offer a "progression of cultural stages," he does not offer a stagelike progression of higher forms of behavior. One reason, I believe, is that he does not represent higher systems as general modes of thought or as general structures of intelligence in a Piagetian sense. *Vygotsky addressed the question of general processes of formation of particular functional systems, a project quite at variance from one aimed*

at delineating a particular sequence of general functional systems....
Vygotsky's comparisons are always made with respect to some particular
system of sign-mediated behavior – memory, counting, writing.... Each
of these systems has its own course of development; all of them ("higher"
or "cultural" by definition) advance from rudimentary to more advanced
forms. But there is no *necessity* in theory for all functional systems char-
acterizing the behavior of an individual, or behaviors in a given social
group, to be at the same level. (Scribner, 1985, p. 132, first italics added
by Y. E.)

In the context of my own argument, the spirit of Scribner's point trans-
lates as follows. I maintain that the Batesonian levels of learning represent
"general processes of formation of particular functional systems." As general processes or general mechanisms, they contain no fixed order of progression, nor a fixed end point. They are continuously present as resources
for the formation of specific innovations and transformations in specific
activities. It is characteristic of the levels of learning that they appear in various combinations and that there is continuous interplay among the levels.
In this sense, consider the levels as a kit of wrenches of successive sizes. The
kit itself is pretty general – it may be used in a tremendous variety of specific tasks. But it is always put into use in a particular context and situation.
There is definitely a hierarchy in the kit. Yet there is no inherent necessity
that the wrenches must be used in a specific order.

This insistence on working with both the horizontal and the vertical aspects, or more generally, with the spatial-social and the temporal-
historical, is also of serious practical consequence.

It is surely appropriate to avoid rigid, one-dimensional sequences being
imposed on social reality. But especially among Anglo-Saxon researchers
adhering to the ideas of Vygotsky, the standard alternative seems to be to
avoid history altogether. Differences in cognition across cultures, social
groups and domains of practice are thus commonly explained without seriously analyzing the historical development that has led to those
differences. The underlying relativistic notion says that we should not
make value judgments concerning whose cognition is "better" or "more
advanced" – that all kinds of thinking and practice are equally valuable.
While this liberal stance may be a comfortable basis for academic discourse, it ignores the reality that in all domains of societal practice those
very value judgments and decisions have to be made every day. People
have to decide where they want to go, which ways is "up". If behavioral
and social science wants to avoid that issue, it will be unable to work
out useful, yet theoretically ambitious intellectual tools for practitioners
making those crucial decisions. (Engeström, 1991a, p. 10)

The complementary relationship between the two aspects is highlighted in a recent study of expansive learning as collective concept formation (Engeström, Nummijoki, & Sannino, 2012). The analysis depicts ascending from the abstract to the concrete not simply as a vertical progression. Movement from an abstract germ cell toward the concrete is depicted as multidirectional, starlike expansion by means of trails in space. This view connects the dialectical theory of concept formation with the ideas of cognitive trails (Cussins, 1992; also Engeström, 2003) and lines of wayfaring (Ingold, 2007). Such a joining of ideas is, of course, also problematic and in need of further critical elaboration (Engeström, 2009b).

CRITIQUES OF THE THEORY

David Bakhurst's (2009) critical discussion of the current state of activity theory is a good example of criticism aimed at the ideas first formulated in *Learning by Expanding* (for a discussion of other critiques, see Engeström & Sannino, 2010, p. 16–20; Sannino, 2011, p. 577–580). Bakhurst argues that the triangular models of activity systems (see especially Figure 2.6 in this book) are not a theory but "a model or a schema that has minimal predictive power" (Bakhurst, 2009, p. 206).

> It is pretty much impossible to find something recognizable as an activity that does not fit the model. What is wrong with that?!, you might reply. Is not universality an advantage here? Not obviously so. The fact is that the model seems to work particularly well for the sorts of activity systems that activity theorists typically study: health care, work settings, some educational contexts; that is, where you have a reasonably well-defined object, a pretty good sense of desirable outcomes, a self-identifying set of subjects, a good sense of what might count as an instrument or tool, etc. It is much less plausible for activities like my writing and delivering this paper ... or for modest activities such as having dinner with colleagues, walking the dog, visiting one's invalid relative. The point is not that you cannot make the model fit these activities – you can. It is just that it has no explanatory value for activities like these: they need to be understood using methods that are remote from the conceptual apparatus suggested by the schema. This implies that what we have here is a universal, but generally vacuous schema, that turns out to be a useful heuristic in reference to certain kinds of activity. (Bakhurst, 2009, p. 206)

In this passage, Bakhurst argues that the model of activity presented in Figure 2.6 has no explanatory value for activities such as writing a paper, having dinner, or others he lists. However, from an activity-theoretical point of view, when a person writes a paper, has dinner, walks a dog, or visits a relative, we are not talking about relatively durable collective activities – we are talking about relatively short-lived individual or group actions or clusters of actions. In other words, by calling his examples "activities" Bakhurst mixes up key analytical categories in a way that may indeed lead to the notion that some "activities" are not analyzable with the help of the model. The distinction between activity and action is foundational for activity theory. Activities are realized by means of actions, and actions make sense when they are understood within the activities in which they emerge. Numerous studies, including some of my own (e.g., Engeström, 1989, 1996c, 2000a, 2000b; Hasu & Engeström, 2000), demonstrate that analyzing actions against the framework of the activity systems within which they arise can indeed have explanatory power. But this explanatory power is gained by the hard work of concrete analysis of data, not by proclamations.

Another criticism expressed by Bakhurst is the allegedly static structural character of the triangular model.

> The moral is that you must be very cautious about given, stable, structural representations where you aspire to understand dynamism, flux, reflexivity, and transformation. (Bakhurst, 2009, p. 207)

Activity theory does not see structure and dynamic transformations as mutually exclusive opposites. To the contrary, the founder of activity theory, A. N. Leont'ev, pointed out that "activity is not a reaction and not a totality of reactions but a system that has structure, its own internal transitions and transformations, its own development" (Leont'ev, 1978, p. 50). The triangular diagram is a tool for analyzing those transitions and transformations.

> I maintain that with the help of this model activity can be analyzed in its inner dynamic relations and historical change. However, this claim must be substantiated by using and transforming the model in the analysis of the development of concrete activities. (Engeström, 1987, p. 81–82)

Sannino clarifies this argument further:

> The triangle is a unit of analysis which discloses its analytical quality in the process of the analysis, but does not correspond to the analysis itself. The triangle operates as a germ cell whose dynamics are displayed not in its mode of representation, but in its use in analysis and in construction of new solutions. (Sannino, 2011, p. 578)

Bakhurst takes the liberty to tell us that Evald Ilyenkov would have been dismayed by much that passes for activity theory today.

> Finally, I am sure that Ilyenkov would have been critical of the preoccupation with schematizing activity that is so evident in the ubiquitous triangles that define the … approach. He would have said that they were tolerable as a heuristic, but it is crucial not to let these models acquire a kind of theoretical life of their own. (Bakhurst, 2009, p. 207)

Bakhurst is here attributing his own thoughts to a scholar who can no longer answer for himself. In other words, Bakhurst has no evidence for his claim. What we do have evidence of is that Bakhurst's own view of contradictions is in stark opposition to that of Ilyenkov. Defending the formal-logical law of noncontradiction, Bakhurst flatly rejects the idea of dialectical contradictions as the motor of self-development in real systems. He concludes that "Ilyenkov's account of dialectical contradictions is flawed" (Bakhurst, 1991, p. 170). With this, Ilyenkov's entire method of ascending from the abstract to the concrete becomes "murky and sometimes inscrutable" for Bakhurst (1991, p. 174). This would indeed have dismayed Ilyenkov.

In his rather quick rejection of dialectical contradictions, Bakhurst ignores the possibility that dialectical contradictions are foundationally different from the contradictions described in the formal-logical principle of noncontradiction. The latter assumes a fixed time, while dialectics sees the world in constant movement through time. As Wilde (1989, p. 104) puts it, "In analyses of systems in motion the principle of non-contradiction loses its prominence." If one says that "It is raining now" and, referring to the same time and place, "It is not raining now," the principle of noncontradiction applies just fine. We have no problem seeing that the two mutually exclusive claims make no sense – only one can be true at any given moment in any given place. But this has nothing to do with dialectical contradictions. They refer to concrete evolving systems, such as human activity systems, in which opposite forces or tendencies are effective simultaneously, as if pulling the system and its participants constantly toward opposite directions. In capitalism, commodities, including human beings, are contradictory unities of use value and exchange value.

Leont'ev (1981, p. 254) gave an example of how this foundational contradiction might operate in the activity system of a medical doctor.

> The doctor who buys a practice in some little provincial place may be very seriously trying to reduce his fellow citizens' suffering from illness, and may see his calling in just that. He must, however, want the number

of the sick to increase, because his life and practical opportunity to follow his calling depend on that.

Leont'ev (1981, p. 255) added that "to ignore these peculiarities and remove
them from the context of psychological research is to deprive psychology of
historical concreteness, converting it into a science solely of the psyche of
an abstract man, of 'man in general.'" This is what inevitably happens when
dialectical contradictions are ignored or rejected.

Andy Blunden (2010) offers another example of critiques of the triangular model of activity developed in this book. For Blunden, the triangular
model presented in Figure 2.6 simply "cannot be a unit of analysis," apparently because it is a system made up of too many components.

> The idea of pairs or triplets of concepts which are *mutually constitutive*,
> being a differentiated unity, has a long pedigree, but a set of *seven* mutu-
> ally constitutive concepts is not really tenable, and Engeström surely
> doesn't mean it that way. (Blunden, 2010, p. 231)

Well, I actually do mean it just that way. Human activity is a complex systemic formation. Why would three mutually constitutive components be
allowed but not seven? Is there some hidden universal law that forbids it?
Blunden does not tell us. I suspect that the complexity represented in the
model of Figure 2.6 seems just too laborious.

TOWARD A METHODOLOGY OF FORMATIVE INTERVENTIONS

The best way to respond to critiques is to demonstrate and develop further
the power and potential of the theory in empirical research and living practice. Chapter 5 of *Learning by Expanding* is titled "Toward an Expansive
Methodology." The chapter formulates a first draft for what is today called
the methodology of formative interventions.

The historical legacy of cultural-historical activity theory is one of
theoretically and methodologically argued interventionism. Vygotsky (e.g.,
1997b, p. 68; 1997c; 1999, p. 57–59) used various terms to characterize this
methodological orientation, including "experimental-genetic method,"
"instrumental method," "historical-genetic method," and "method of
double stimulation." Davydov and his followers use the term "genetic modeling experiment" (Tsuckerman, 2011). This interventionist legacy has
been picked up and systematically developed further in a few places in
today's world, including Helsinki, Paris, and San Diego (for an overview,
see Sannino, 2011). At the CRADLE research center in Helsinki, we use

the term *formative intervention* (Engeström, 2011). The idea of formative interventions is being adopted in various educational research communities internationally (e.g., Anthony, Hunter, & Thompson, 2014; Bronkhorst, Meijer, Koster, Akkerman, & Vermunt, 2013; Eri, 2013).

Formative interventions differ from traditional interventions, and from most of the work done within the framework of design experiments (Brown, 1992) or design-based research (Kelly, Lesh, & Baek, 2008). I have characterized these as linear interventions. Key differences between formative and linear interventions may be listed as follows.

1. *Starting point:* In linear interventions, the contents and goals of the intervention are known ahead of time by the researchers, and the intervention itself is commonly detached from vital life activities of the participants. In formative interventions, the participants (whether children or adult practitioners, or both) face a problematic and contradictory object, embedded in their vital life activity, which they analyze and expand by constructing a novel concept, the contents of which are not known ahead of time to the researchers.

2. *Process:* In linear interventions, the participants, typically teachers and students in school, are expected to execute the intervention without resistance. Difficulties of execution are interpreted as weaknesses in the design that are to be corrected by refining the design. In formative interventions, the contents and course of the intervention are subject to negotiation and the shape of the intervention is eventually determined by the participants. Double stimulation as the core mechanism implies that the participants gain agency and take charge of the process.

3. *Outcome:* In linear interventions, the aim is to complete a standardized solution module, typically a new learning environment, that will reliably generate the same desired outcomes when transferred and implemented in new settings. In formative interventions, the aim is to generate new concepts that may be used in other settings as frames for the design of locally appropriate new solutions. A key outcome of formative interventions is agency among the participants.

4. *Researcher's role:* In linear interventions the researcher aims at control of all the variables. In formative interventions, the researcher aims at provoking and sustaining an expansive transformation process led and owned by the practitioners. (Engeström, 2011, p. 606)

Research done using formative interventions focuses on transformations and learning embedded in object-oriented activities (Greeno &

Engeström, 2014), often outside schools, in workplaces and communities (e.g., Mukute & Lotz-Sisitka, 2012). The object of these activities is not self-evident; it is typically at risk or in crisis, ambiguous, fragmented, and contested. The object is rediscovered as a result of historical and empirical work of data collection and analysis with the help of conceptual models by the participants, supported by researcher-interventionists. The object is inherently contradictory from the beginning. Negotiations emerge as shared tools and concepts are built to depict and handle the contradictory object and the conflicting motives related to it. The emphasis is on the creation and implementation of foundational germ cell models for new patterns of the activity. These are usually first constructed by a pilot group, then disseminated, implemented, and generalized.

The methodology of formative interventions is built on two epistemological principles, namely, (1) the principle of double stimulation and (2) the principle of ascending from the abstract to the concrete (Sannino, 2011). The first one was formulated and implemented by Vygotsky and his colleagues (e.g., Vygotsky, 1997b). The second one stems from the classic works of Hegel and Marx, was incorporated in activity theory by the philosopher Ilyenkov (1982), and was systematically implemented as the foundation for a theory of learning and instruction by Davydov (1990).

The principle of double stimulation, in its full Vygotskian version, regards the formation of higher mental functions as a process in which the subject faces a paralyzing conflict of motives (first stimulus). The conflict is resolved by discovering an artifact that is filled with meaning and turned into a sign (second stimulus). This new mediating instrument enables the subject to redefine the situation and to take volitional action to break out of it. Vygotsky's favorite example of this principle was the experiment of a meaningless situation.

> In experiments involving meaningless situations ... the subject searches for some point of support that is external to him and he defines his own behavior through this external support. In one set of experiments, for example, the experimenter left the subject and did not return, but observed him from a separate room. Generally, the subject waited for 10–20 minutes. Then, not understanding what he should do, he remained in a state of oscillation, confusion and indecisiveness for some time. Nearly all the adults searched for some external point of support. For example, one subject defined his actions in terms of the striking of the clock. Looking at the clock, he thought: "When the hand moves to the vertical position, I will leave." The subject transformed the situation in this way, establishing that he would wait until 2:30 and then leave. When

the time came, the action occurred automatically. By changing the psychological field, the subject created a new situation for himself in this field. He transformed the meaningless situation into one that had a clear meaning. (Vygotsky, 1987, p. 356)

The principle of ascending from the abstract to the concrete was described earlier. It depicts developmentally valuable learning as transforming a problematic situation to discover and model an initial "germ cell" abstraction that is then applied and implemented to construct a complex new concreteness. A formative intervention typically aims at generating and supporting a cycle of expansive learning.

Since 1995, the methodology of formative interventions has been implemented and developed in practice by means of a toolkit called the Change Laboratory (Engeström, Virkkunen, Helle, Pihlaja, & Poikela, 1996; Engeström, 2007b; Virkkunen & Newnham, 2013). The Change Laboratory is used when an activity system or a cluster of activity systems faces an uncertain but necessary transformation riddled with conflicting motives and energized by a possibility of reaching a qualitatively new, emancipated mode of activity. The Change Laboratory process consists of a series of sessions in which practitioners of an organization (or several collaborating organizations) analyze the history, contradictions, and zone of proximal development of their activity system; design a new model for it; and take steps toward the implementation of the model. The Change Laboratory sessions are regularly videotaped to secure rich and comprehensive data for analysis.

The first stimulus in a Change Laboratory intervention consists of so-called mirror materials presented to the participants in the form of videotaped disturbances at work as well as interview excerpts, statistics, and other data that reveal recurring problems and tensions in the activity. The initial second stimulus is usually the triangular model of activity (Figure 2.6), which the participants fill with contents specific to their own activity systems as they analyze the present troubles and past development of their activities. As the expansive learning process moves forward, the initial second stimulus is usually replaced with models and emerging concepts constructed by the participants themselves.

In Change Laboratories the practitioners, sometimes also including students or patients or clients, take over the leading role in designing their future. The taking over is a crucial feature of a formative intervention. The very point is to generate the unexpected – learning what is not yet there. This does not mean that the interventionists do not introduce their own ideas and aims. Such interventions are based on introduction and collaborative application of new tools – literally on *remediation* or *reinstrumentation*. This is more than opportunistic, casual, and informal dialogue; the researcher has a substantive contribution and must often be very determined and systematic in offering that contribution. The dynamism of the intervention stems in part from the tension and interplay between the interventionists' and the practitioners' ideas and intentions.

Previous Vygotskian theorizing and research have mainly focused on a single individual or a dyad of two subjects using a single, well-defined mediating tool or artifact. Language as mediator has required a more complex approach – but studies of semiotic mediation have commonly excluded material instruments and tools. In interventionist studies of expansive learning, the mediational setup is complex and multilayered both semiotically and instrumentally, yet the crucial events are temporally and spatially constrained so as to allow the collection of comprehensive high-fidelity data by means of videotaping. Analysis of such data forces the researcher to adopt a new view of mediation: Instead of single instruments, one has to analyze a whole interconnected *instrumentality* (Engeström, 2007a; see also Grismshaw, 1981, for an earlier, more restrictively discursive notion of instrumentality). The concept of instrumentality implies that the instruments form a system that includes multiple cognitive artifacts and semiotic means used for analysis and design, but also straightforward primary tools used in the daily practice and made visible for examination, reshaping, and experimentation.

This type of design requires a bold experimental attitude rather than the outlook of a casual observer and facilitator. Bringing about and traversing collective zones of proximal development (see Chapter 3) is experimentation with activity systems. When practitioners face a mirror depicting their own disturbances, they often experience them as personal failures or even crises. Powerful and unpredictable cognitive, emotional, and social dissonances are triggered. The Change Laboratory is a microcosm that allows such processes to surface in a relatively safe and supportive context. The formative interventionist needs to record, analyze, and support these processes, including the interventionists' own actions and interactions.

The Change Laboratory process is typically carefully planned. Each session is aimed at fostering some specific expansive learning actions. There is a script that the interventionists strive to follow. In a study of a Change Laboratory process conducted among the staff and clients of an academic library (Engeström, Rantavuori, & Kerosuo, 2013), two types of gaps between the interventionists' script and the learners' actions were identified. These were called action-level deviations and object-level deviations. The former were bounded episodes in which the learners took one or more actions that deviated from the script – but the process then resumed following the initial script. The latter were episodes in which the learners took actions that redefined and transformed the initially planned object of the learning effort, thus changing the entire course of the process and forcing the interventionists to redefine their script. Importantly enough, these object-level deviations energized rather than blocked expansive learning.

THE FUTURE OF THE THEORY

Learning by Expanding is a theoretical framework and an agenda for interventionist research in concrete human activities undergoing historical transformations. It is an ambitious research program both theoretically and practically. Changes in the world of work and other activities require that the theory be continuously reexamined and developed to meet new challenges.

In November 2013 I and my coworkers at our research center, the CRADLE, received the following message from a colleague, Marco Querol, who recently received his Ph.D. in our doctoral program and now works as a professor at a university in his home country, Brazil.

Dear colleagues,

Today I had a meeting to plan an intervention for developing accident prevention in an airport construction. The challenge is that the activity is conducted through projects, which last only months. The projects are conducted by a consortium of companies. The combination of companies changes in each project. It means that the staff and workers are changing all the time. Moreover, the consortium hires dozens (sometimes more than a hundred) of outsourced companies for doing the work.

The challenge for the interventionist is that expansive learning may take time. But how to go through the cycle in a situation that the staff (companies, managers and workers) are changing all the time? One thing that is stable is the Public Ministry, responsible for workers' health. Even if we manage to convince a manager to participate in a Change Lab, the short duration of the project and the change of the staff put at risk the expansion process.

Is this phenomenon also taking place in Finland? How to make an intervention sustainable in such a fast changing situation? Do you know some similar cases? How have they managed to deal with the change of the staff? How to make a sustainable learning activity in fast changing networks?

Best regards,
Marco

The message exemplifies challenges of third-generation activity theory. Activity systems are increasingly interconnected and the combinations of actors keep changing rapidly. This is the type of challenge that generated the concept of negotiated knotworking. Knotworking is being appropriated in the Finnish construction industry, which struggles with challenges very similar to those described by Marco, plus with the challenge of implementing new collaborative technologies such as the Building Information Modeling (BIM) tools (Kerosuo, Mäki, & Korpela, 2013).

Knotworking is more than a technique; it is a deep and pervasive cultural transformation in work organizations, involving new tools and rules for rapidly pulsating renegotiation of the object. Such a transformation typically requires expansive learning. But one cannot expect that expansive learning cycles proceed smoothly and continuously. They will be interrupted. Such interruptions may lead to dead ends, but they can also be bridged (Engeström, Kerosuo, & Kajamaa, 2007).

On the horizon of third-generation activity theory, there are big issues that will increasingly challenge and stimulate the development of the theory and practice of expansive learning. The first of these is the emergence of large "runaway objects" (Engeström, 2009a) or "hyperobjects" (Morton, 2013), objects so massively distributed in time and space as to transcend localization, such as climate change or pandemics. Runaway objects have the potential to escalate and expand up to a global scale of influence. They are objects that are poorly controlled and have far-reaching, unexpected effects. Such objects are often monsters: They seem to have a life of their own that threatens our security and safety in many ways. Runaway objects are contested objects that generate opposition and controversy. They can also be powerfully emancipatory objects that open up radically new possibilities of development and well-being. There are typically numerous activity systems focused on or affiliated with a runaway object. But the object is pervasive and its boundaries are hard to draw. Thus, the positions of the activity systems are ambiguous and they often seem to be subsumed to the object rather than in control of it.

Another challenge is what I call "wildfire activities" and mycorrhizaelike forms of organizing (Engeström, 2009b). Wildfire activities, for example birding, skateboarding, or volunteer disaster relief work, offer little monetary reward but are very highly motivated. These activities, sometimes characterized as forms of "gift economy," have strong object and use-value orientation and resistance to thorough commercialization. They can pop up in unexpected locations at unexpected times and expand very rapidly. They also seem to become extinguished from time to time, yet they reappear and flare up again. These activities show remarkable resilience and expansion in spite of a number of severe adversities and constraints. They are constantly learning to transcend the constraints and overcome the adversities – in other words, to renew themselves without much deliberate and centrally organized effort. Communities associated with wildfire activities are hybrid and poorly bounded; in them, the center does not hold. They resemble mycorrhizae, the invisible undergrowth of fungi.

A third challenge consists of local, regional, and global social movements. Today social movements are forming transnational and global alliances, with the result that "one sees the emergence of more horizontal, 'polycentric'... social movements that at the same time struggle to construct coherent coordinative structures for greater vertical integration" (Borras, 2008, pp. 259–260). Although many social movements have led to durable cultural innovations and new types of organization (Rao, Morill, & Zald, 2000), social movements are often relatively short-lived. The ephemeral character of social movements may, however, be partly a misconception that results from viewing social movements in isolation from the networks and organizational fields in which they are embedded. As Soule (2012, p. 1721) points out, "Social movement organizations are not bounded entities; rather they are embedded in a web of connections to other organizations (both within the movement and outside the movement)." One might argue that today's social movements are increasingly driven by runaway objects and taking the shape of wildfire activities and mycorrhizae organizations.

The very idea of social movements is transformation and generation of qualitatively new forms of practice and culture. Thus, expansive learning is an inherent potential of social movements. One might say that all expansive learning processes have characteristics of a social movement – but not all social movements accomplish expansive learning. There is an obvious need for rigorous studies of expansive learning in and by social movements (see Krinsky, 2007, 2008; Krinsky & Barker, 2009, as promising openings).

1

Introduction

In his standard textbook *The Conditions of Learning*, Robert Gagné (1970) identifies eight hierarchically organized types of learning. The highest, cognitively most advanced type is called problem solving. In problem solving, "two or more previously acquired rules are somehow combined to produce a new capability that can be shown to depend on a 'higher-order' rule" (Gagné, 1970, p. 64). Problem solving is dependent "on the *store of rules* the individual has available" (Gagné, 1970, p. 223).

Although Gagné's position was first presented quite a while ago, it has not really been surpassed or superseded by more recent theorizing within cognitive psychology. For example, Donald Norman in his textbook *Learning and Memory* (1982) identifies three basic types of learning: accretion, structuring, and tuning. His structuring is a fairly close counterpart of Gagné's problem solving. It implies the formation of a new conceptual structure or schema on the basis of previously acquired knowledge and experience. As a typical example, Norman reports his own learning of the Morse code. Having trained himself a long time to receive individual letters in the Morse code, not improving noticeably in speed, he was advised to focus on words and phrases instead of letters. A dramatic improvement occurred.

> I already had a solid base of performance on the individual letters, and so I was able to benefit from the advice to enlarge the unit size – to restructure my knowledge. (Norman, 1982, p. 83.)

The similarity between Norman's structuring and Gagné's problem solving is obvious. The jargon has changed, but the substance remains the same.

At the first sight, problem solving or structuring seems to be a satisfactory characterization of the uppermost reaches of human learning. What

1

more can one expect than insightful solutions to problems through a novel structuring of the subject's mental model or cognitive schema?

The problem is that problem solving and structuring are essentially *reactive forms of learning*. Both presuppose a given context that presents the individual with a preset learning task. Learning is defined so as to exclude the possibility of finding or creating new contexts. However, it is *this* very aspect of human performance – or rather the lack of it – that is becoming the central source of uneasiness and trouble in various fields of societal practice. In general terms, troubles of this type may be named the *difficulty of anticipating, mastering, and steering qualitative changes* in individual lives, in families and organizations, and in the society as a whole.

Symptomatically enough, Norman ends his book with a tirade on how badly modern technology matches human capabilities. According to him, system designers misuse and ignore the users: "They start with the machine, and the human is not thought of until the end, when it's too late: witness the control panels in the nuclear power plants" (Norman, 1982, p. 115). Norman's solution is that technological systems should be designed so as to make learning easier.

Pleas like this follow the traditional patronizing approach: The poor learners must be helped to cope with the tasks *given* to them. The approach is self-defeating. Norman himself points out that it takes a long time to learn the mastery of a complex skill. At the same time, the contexts of the tasks and skills are going through profound qualitative changes, which often render previous tasks and skills obsolete. Norman himself says, "when it's too late." This lag can never be overcome by patronizing, by asking designers to plan more "user-friendly" systems. It can only be overcome by enabling the users themselves to plan and bring about the qualitative changes (including the design and implementation of technologies) in their life contexts.

If learning has nothing to offer in this respect, we have good reason to talk about the futility of learning. Both in theory and in practice, human learning actually seems to be doomed to the role of running after those qualitative changes in people's life contexts. While the learners are engaged in diligent problem solving and structuring in order to cope with changes that have shaken their lives, there are already new qualitative changes quickly ripening to fall on them. This stance is documented by Gagné as follows:

> A great scientific discovery or a great work of art is surely the result of problem-solving activity.... Nothing ... supports the idea that there is anything very different about the problem solving that leads to discoveries of great social import.... But the major discovery, in contrast to the common garden variety, involves a feat of generalizing that goes far

beyond what may be expected in the usual learning situation. There is an "inductive leap," a combining of ideas that come from widely separated knowledge systems, a bold use of analogy that transcends what is usually meant by generalizing within a class of problem situations. (Gagné, 1970, p. 227–228)

Here we have two assertions. First, great creative achievements are based on the same kind of inductive, combinatorial problem solving as any common act of learning by problem solving. Second, usual acts of learning by problem solving have practically nothing in common with truly creative discoveries because in the latter the "inductive leap" is so much greater. In other words, Gagné first denies that creation has anything qualitatively special in it. Immediately thereafter he points out that creation is indeed qualitatively special because it transcends the context given.

The outcome is rather gloomy for learning.

Because it is a method rich in reinforcement value, the solving of problems within structures of intellectual skills to be learned may create a love of learning, a "thirst for knowledge" in the individual learner. But it is a vastly different thing to suppose that this kind of learning will necessarily predispose the individual to become a "creative" thinker, capable of making great contributions to science or art. To be sure, the variables that produce genius are surely not entirely innate and must prominently include factors in the individual's experience, arising from his environment. But except as a method for acquiring prerequisite intellectual skills, "practicing discovery" seems an unlikely choice of antecedent variable to be involved in the production of genius. (Gagné, 1970, p. 229)

This is a specimen of self-defeating circular reasoning. First, the author tacitly assumes that the highest form of learning is practicing inductive combinatorial problem solving, which by definition does not transcend the context given. Then the author triumphantly concludes that learning by problem solving does not lead to true creativity, that is, to transcending given contexts.

In this book, I shall examine whether learning really is doomed to futility or whether this is a historical artifact of only limited and temporary validity, both in theories of learning and in the societal practices involving learning.

More specifically, I shall argue (a) that the conception of creation as inductive combinatorial generalization (albeit in magnified scale) is fundamentally false and (b) that the conception of the highest form of learning as inductive combinatorial problem solving or structuring is also fundamentally false.

PROBLEM TWO: THE ELUSIVENESS OF EXPANSION

The alternative to reactive forms of learning is expansion, which transcends the context given. Because of its elusiveness, expansion is traditionally not considered a proper object of scientific investigation. It has very much remained a domain of mysticism.

C. G. Jung made one of the important early attempts to incorporate expansion into psychological theory. For him, the key concept was the *collective unconscious.*

> From this point of view the conscious personality is a more or less arbitrary segment of the collective psyche. It consists in a sum of psychic facts that are felt to be personal. The attribute "personal" means: pertaining exclusively to this particular person. A consciousness that is purely personal stresses its proprietary and original right to its contents with certain anxiety, and in this way seeks to create a whole. But all those contents that refuse to fit into this whole are either overlooked and forgotten or repressed and denied. This is one way of educating oneself, but it is too arbitrary and too much of a violation.... Hence these purely "personal" people are always very sensitive, for something may easily happen that will bring into consciousness an unwelcome portion of their real ("individual") character. (Jung, 1966, p. 157)

According to Jung, psychoanalysis may lead to annexing deeper layers of the collective unconscious, a process that produces an enlargement of the personality leading to the pathological state of "inflation."

> It occurs whenever people are overpowered by knowledge or by some new realization. "Knowledge puffeth up," Paul writes to the Corinthians, for the new knowledge has turned the heads of many, as indeed constantly happens. The inflation has nothing to do with the *kind* of knowledge, but simply and solely with the fact that any new knowledge can so seize hold of a weak head that he no longer sees and hears anything else. He is hypnotized by it, and instantly believes he has solved the riddle of the universe. But that is equivalent to almighty self-conceit. This process is such a general reaction that, in Genesis 2:17, eating of the tree of knowledge is represented as a deadly sin. (Jung, 1966, p. 156)

On the other hand, expansion may lead to self-knowledge and truly widened consciousness.

> The more we become conscious of ourselves through self-knowledge, and act accordingly, the more the layer of the personal unconscious that is superimposed on the collective unconscious will be diminished.

In this way there arises a consciousness which is no longer imprisoned in the petty, oversensitive, personal world of the ego, but participates freely in the wider world of objective interests. This widened consciousness is no longer that touchy, egotistical bundle of personal wishes, fears, hopes, and ambitions which always has to be compensated or corrected by unconscious counter-tendencies; instead, it is a function of relationship to the world of objects, bringing the individual into absolute, binding, and indissoluble communion with the world at large. The complications arising at this stage are no longer egotistic wish-conflicts, but difficulties that concern others as much as oneself. (Jung 1966, p. 178)

For Jung, expansion is achieved through the collective unconscious, which in turn is reached with the help of psychoanalytic therapy. The conception is somehow very static: The collective unconscious *resides* somewhere deep beneath more superficial layers. The task is to get into touch with it, to seize some of its immense power. But how did the collective unconscious emerge in the first place? How does it develop? Can the individual participate in creating new forms of the collective unconscious? And above all: Is the collective unconscious only a mental, spiritual layer, or does it have some kind of material basis and embodiments in people's societal and productive practice?

As long as these questions remain unasked and unanswered, the Jungian theory remains mystical.

In recent psychological theorizing, some attempts have been made to reintroduce expansion as a scientific concept. In his "transgressive model of man," Jozef Kozielecki (1986) distinguishes between protective and transgressive behavior. The latter "allows for moving forward: the person is capable of exceeding the boundaries of his or her material or symbolic achievement, that is, capable of creating or assimilating new values" (Kozielecki, 1986, p. 90). Transgressive behavior is further divided into two types, expansion and creation. The former consists in the acquisition and assimilation of existing material or symbolic values (commodities, business, power, influence, knowledge). The latter entails the solution of new, unconventional problems.

Kozielecki gets into trouble when he tries to apply these distinctions in concrete cases.

There should be no difficulty in classifying Columbus's voyage or Einstein's discoveries as typical instances of transgressive behavior. We are apt to hesitate, however, when asked to decide if the solving of the Missionaries and Cannibals puzzle is a case of transgression or not. Similar problems in classification crop up in every other domain of psychology, of course. (Kozielecki, 1986, p. 92)

To preclude such difficulties, Kozielecki puts forward a definition as broad as possible.

> Any intentional action whose outcome transgresses the subject's past achievements is seen as a case of transgressive behavior. (Kozielecki, 1986, p. 92)

In other words, if the subject could not previously solve the Missionaries and Cannibals problem – and then finally solves it – this should obviously be accepted as a case of transgression. In effect, there is no clear difference between any kind of problem solving or structuring and transgression. The difference between a problem and the context producing the problem is blurred – or rather, contexts are not considered. Notice that Kozielecki speaks of transgression only in terms of an intentional and individual-psychological process, as "exceeding the boundaries of *his* or *her* achievement." Jung's powerful though opaque idea of the *collective* and often not very intentional character of expansion is given up without discussion. Notice also the circularity of Kozielecki's definition: What transgresses is transgression. Very little explanatory power is left in our hands.

Another recent attempt is provided by Karsten Hundeide (1985). His key concept is *perspective*. Using a spatial metaphor, Hundeide introduces a general theoretical idea of two developmental principles, expansion and contraction. When one is located in a definite position, there are certain things one can see directly. They occupy a central position in the field of vision. Other things are in the periphery, and still others are outside one's field of vision or perspective.

Correspondingly, when one is in a definite interpretive position, there are certain conclusions, judgments, and insights that can be immediately seen as plausible and evident. Others are impossible, irrelevant, or implausible. Thus, in order to arrive at a definite conclusion or insight, one must be in the right position. If one is in a "false position" in relation to a certain conclusion or insight, there is little point in elaborating alternatives from that position. Instead, one must redefine the situation or "restructure the field," as Gestalt psychologists put it. Such a redefinition of one's position may be of an expansive character.

> This expansion may result from a *confrontation* between positions, between *the recurrent alternative one takes for granted* and *a contrasting alternative*. In order to solve this conflict, the person may have to "move back" to the more detached and abstract position....From this position both conflicting perspectives may be integrated and united....

> There is also the opposite movement.... I call this the *contraction of perspective*. This term was chosen because it is a movement from a wider more inclusive position to a narrower one with fewer options. Contraction of perspective may take place under conditions of monotony, reduced variation, or the absence of contrasting alternatives. (Hundeide, 1985, p. 314–315)

Hundeide is very conscious of the difference between problem and context. He also recognizes a specific type of problems, namely, conflicts or contradictions, as the source of expansive recontextualization. However, his expansive recontextualization suffers from the same weakness as Kozielecki's whole conception. It is reduced to an individual and mental process. Thus, it is one-sidedly attributed the flavor of abstraction and detachment. Jung's insight into the collective nature of expansion effectively counteracts this type of cognitivist impoverishment of human development.

> The collective dream has a feeling of importance about it that impels communication. It springs from a conflict of relationship and must therefore be built into our conscious relations, because it compensates these and not just some inner personal quirk.
>
> The processes of the collective unconscious are concerned not only with the more or less personal relations of an individual to his family or to a wider social group, but with his relations to society and to the human community in general. The more general and impersonal the condition that releases the unconscious reaction, the more significant, bizarre, and overwhelming will be the compensatory manifestation. It impels not just private communication, but drives people to revelations and confessions, and even to a dramatic representation of their fantasies. (Jung, 1966, p. 178–179)

So Jung sees new kinds of communication as necessarily involved in expansion. But are only cognition and communication reorganized? Does the material practice remain intact?

In this book, I shall argue that it does not. To the contrary, true expansion is always both internal and external, both mental and material. More specifically, I shall argue (a) that expansive processes can indeed be analyzed and modeled; (b) that the gateway to understanding expansion is neither the concept of collective unconscious nor that of perspective but the concept of *activity*; (c) that expansive processes are becoming integrated into processes of learning, that is, that a historically new advanced type of learning – learning by expanding – is currently emerging in various fields of societal practice.

THEORETICAL RESEARCH AS EMPIRICAL RESEARCH

This book is a report of extended theoretical research. For many people, theory construction is *either* inductive generalization from so-called empirical facts *or* purely speculative reasoning. In my view, theoretical research in its mature form is neither one nor a combination of these two.

I agree with Klaus Holzkamp's (1983) characterization of theoretical research. He differentiates between what he calls the level of categories and the level of specific theories. Categories are basic concepts with which the scientific paradigm or school defines its object, its inner structure and boundaries. Such categories "always include certain *methodological* conceptions about how one shall proceed scientifically in order to grasp the object adequately" (Holzkamp, 1983, p. 27–28). The research reported in this book belongs to the level of category construction.

> Whereas the construction of categories as basic theoretical concepts may be regarded from a bourgeois point of view mainly as a question of arbitrary definitions and conceptual fixations, the *"historical"* *category analysis* we are proposing is a procedure based on *empirical* material ... in which *scientific rationality* is extended to a problem field which used to be closed to it: the *formation of basic psychological concepts.* The methodological difference between research on the level of specific theories and research on the level of analysis of categories is thus not that the former is "empirical" but the latter "speculative", merely "deductive", or the like. To the contrary, *both research types are empirical*, but the material collected and used is in the first case of an *"actual*-empirical" and in the second case of an *"historical*-empirical" nature. (Holzkamp, 1983, p. 50)

So the research reported in this book is theoretical research aimed at the construction of categories, using a specific type of empirical data. This specific type of data typically consists of *propositions and findings of previous analyses,* or, more generally, of previous representations of the object of research.

Such data may be predominantly either object-historical or theory-historical. Object-historical data consist of propositions and findings describing the development of the object of the research – in this book, the historical development of human learning and expansion. Theory-historical data consists of theories or theoretical propositions concerning the object, considered in their historical origination and succession – in this book, theories related to human learning and expansion.

In the construction of categories, actual-empirical data are also often useful and necessary. But here Holzkamp's distinction between the level of category construction and the level of constructing specific theories is essential. In research aimed at a specific theory, actual-empirical data are an indispensable and integral element of the research project. In research aimed at category formation for an entire paradigmatic orientation, actual-empirical data may play a suspended and more mediated role, as if gradually growing into (and simultaneously altering) the suggested categories from various concrete projects.

In any theoretical investigation moving on the level of categories, three methodological questions must be implicitly or explicitly answered. These three questions are (1) how to *select* the data, (2) how to *process* the data into categories, (3) how to place the categories developed in fruitful *contact with practice*.

In the following sections, I shall address these three questions, using two very different examples of theoretical research as points of comparison. The first example is the short but pathbreaking paper "Toward a Theory of Schizophrenia" (Bateson, 1972, p. 201–227), written by Gregory Bateson, Don Jackson, Jay Haley, and John Weakland in 1956. The second example is the much discussed two-volume work *The Theory of Communicative Action* by Jürgen Habermas (1981; in English 1984 [vol. 1]).

Incidentally, both examples are concerned with the theme of communication. However, the paper by Bateson and associates is aimed at a reconceptualization of the theory of schizophrenia, while Habermas's book aims at formulating a comprehensive theory of communicative action in general. It may appear that the paper by Bateson et al. would be quite specific and not belong to the level of category construction at all. However, its theoretical kernel, the single central category generated by the authors in that paper, has had an impact that far exceeds the limits of a specific subtheory. It has been instrumental in the reorientation of the entire field of family therapy (see Hoffman, 1981), and it has inspired a variety of novel theoretical openings in other fields.

HOW TO SELECT THE DATA

In theoretical research, as in all empirical research, the selection of data is crucial for the credibility of the outcome. Two dangers are constantly present. The first danger is data selection through blind chance or intuition without articulated justification. The second danger is the subordination of data selection to predetermined outcomes, that is, use of data as mere illustration of conclusions fixed by the researcher in advance. In both cases, the typical critique focuses on the questionable representativeness or comprehensiveness of data.

At the beginning of their paper, Bateson and his collaborators explicate their database as follows.

> The theory of schizophrenia presented here is based on communications analysis, and specifically on the Theory of Logical Types. From this theory and from observations of schizophrenic patients is derived a description of, and the necessary conditions for, a situation called the "double bind" – a situation in which no matter what a person does, he "can't win." ...
>
> Our research in this field has proceeded by discussion of a varied body of data and ideas, with all of us contributing according to our varied experience in anthropology, communications analysis, psychotherapy, psychiatry, and psychoanalysis. We have now reached common agreement on the broad outlines of a communicational theory of the origin and nature of schizophrenia; this paper is a preliminary report of our continuing research. (Bateson, 1972, p. 201–202)

The data demonstrated in the paper itself consist mainly of (1) the philosophical Theory of Logical Types (adapted from Whitehead & Russel's *Principia Mathematica)*, as applied to communication, and (2) observations of schizophrenogenic family situations and schizophrenic patients. However, the data are presented in a rather brief and condensed manner. The whole paper consists of twenty-seven pages in the 1972 book version. It contains sixteen footnotes (of which two refer to personal communications). No attempt is made at representativeness of data. The choice of data seems to stem from the authors' personal inspirations rather than from any systematic analysis of previous theories or of the history of schizophrenia. The whole paper bears the characteristics of a lucky hybrid: a good idea that emerged in a group versatile, sophisticated, and unconventional enough to embark on a challenging intellectual adventure. The credibility of the category generated (double bind) lies less in its database than in its immediately fascinating heuristic power and in the visions it opens.

Habermas's voluminous work is completely different in its relation to data. Thomas McCarthy, the translator of Habermas, gives the following characterization.

> He develops these themes [of communicative action; Y. E.] through a somewhat unusual combination of theoretical constructions with historical reconstructions of the ideas of "classical" social theorists.

The thinkers discussed – Marx, Weber, Durkheim, Mead, Lukacs, Horkheimer, Adorno, Parsons – are, he holds, still very much alive. Rather than regarding them as so many corpses to be dissected exegetically, he treats them as virtual dialogue partners from whom a great deal that is of contemporary significance can still be learned. The aim of his "historical reconstructions with systematic intent" is to excavate and incorporate their positive contributions, to criticize and overcome their weaknesses, by thinking with them to go beyond them. (McCarthy, 1984, p. vi–vii)

In fact, Habermas pours a massive cavalcade of theories and concepts onto the canvas of his book. More specifically, it draws together "the theories of action, meaning, speech acts, and other similar domains of analytic philosophy" (Habermas, 1984, p. xxxiv), on the one hand, and classical sociological theories, on the other hand. In the 1,174 pages of the book, there are 1,242 footnotes (original German version; Habermas, 1981). The reader is subjected to a virtual bombardment of sources. The credibility of the argumentation is very much based on the data. But it is not based on the professed representativeness of the data, rather on the internal connections and "plots" found between and within the various sources.

In the present book, I follow neither Bateson and colleagues nor Habermas in my selection of data – and I follow both in certain respects.

I shall use three principal types of data in this book. The *first type* of data consists of *theories and theoretical propositions* pertaining to human learning and expansion. This type of data has the dominant role in the present work. In the selection and presentation of this data, I am following certain structural steps or stages of argumentation.

First of all, in each chapter (except Chapter 5, which is actually a methodological postscript), the construction of categories begins with an identification and characterization of the most advanced state of theorizing within the *currently dominant paradigm*. With "the most advanced" I refer to theorizing that either crystallizes the dominant conception in a very clear fashion *or,* in its aspiration to go further, tendentially exceeds the conceptual and methodological boundaries of the dominant paradigm and thus makes those boundaries or limits visible. However, such theorizing is also acknowledged as advanced within the paradigm – it is not generally disregarded as merely an eccentric curiosity. Given the object of this book, the dominant paradigm is the cognitive psychology of learning and development. As its representatives, I am using Gagné, Norman, Kozielecki, and Hundeide in Chapter 1; Bereiter, Langley & Simon, and Klix in Chapter 2; Baltes et al.; Brown, Riegel, Bronfenbrenner, Lerner, and Buss in Chapter 3;

Hallpike, Dreyfus & Dreyfus, Brehmer, Bruner, Miller, and Simon – and later a long list of others – in Chapter 4.

Second, to counter and problematize the propositions of cognitive psychologists, I examine and employ certain *classical theories* that present the problem of the chapter in question in a more penetrating light. The task of these sources is to enforce a deepening of the analysis so as to identify the long lineages or historical "red threads" of category formation. These classical theories were chosen on the basis of their known general characteristics, but in the course of the investigation, each one of them turned out to be a well of surprises. In Chapter 1, I use the theory of C. G. Jung. In Chapter 2, three classical lineages are examined: the semiotic and epistemological lineage from C. Peirce to K. Popper, the lineage from the symbolic interactionism of G. H. Mead to modern interactionist developmental psychology, and the lineage of cultural-historical psychology from Vygotsky to Leont'ev. In Chapter 3, the work of G. Bateson is used. And in Chapter 4, the theories or J. Dewey, M. Wertheimer, and F. Bartlett are examined.

Third, to develop the argument further, I take up and analyze the ideas of the *cultural-historical theory of activity* in its modern form. This is the line of thought I try to continue and develop further. For that purpose, it is necessary to explicate the relevant insights produced within or close to this school of thought. In Chapter 2, I discuss especially the analyses presented by A. N. Leont'ev and E. V. Ilyenkov, but also those of V. P. Zinchenko, L. A. Radzikhovskii, and D. B. El'konin. In Chapter 3, I continue employing the work of L. S. Vygotsky, A. N. Leont'ev, and their students, but related Western works by M. Wartofsky, R. Harré & al., I. Prigogine, M. Cole, S. Scribner, K. Holzkamp, and others are also drawn upon. In Chapter 4, especially the work of E. V. Ilyenkov and V. V. Davydov on concept formation and dialectics is discussed, as well as the related ideas of M. Bakhtin on the dialogical nature of thought. And in Chapter 5, the methodological ideas of L. S. Vygotsky, S. Scribner, and M. Cole are considered, along with the more specific suggestions of G. Altshuller and B. Fichtner. In general, this third step is not carried out in a dogmatic manner. Often in this stage of the analysis I take up theoretical insights that have not originated within the confines of any strictly delimited school – or have originated within schools of their own. Usually those insights are, however, based on philosophical and methodological assumptions that are substantively very much akin to those that have inspired the cultural-historical school founded by Vygotsky, Leont'ev, and Luria.

In all three steps, I approach and use theory-historical data much in the same manner as Habermas approaches his data. The theories considered are taken as live discussion partners. While criticizing and often plainly rejecting them, I try to incorporate some of their wisdom into my further argumentation. Criticism for criticism's sake would not make much sense.

The *second type* of my data consists of *general historical accounts* of the development of human learning and expansion. Such data are mainly used in Chapter 2, in the sections concerning the evolution of activity and the cultural-historical evolution of human learning.

The section on the evolution of activity is a condensed systematic reconstruction based on the evolutionary and anthropogenetic data presented in works of Keiler, Leakey, Lewontin, Reynolds, and Schurig. This section does not intend to display an extensive variety of data because the subtle disagreements and variations in the interpretation of anthropogenesis are not relevant for my argument. My conclusions rest on fairly generally accepted main features of anthropogenesis. The end part of that section is based on the analysis of human societal production provided by Marx in *Grundrisse*.

The large section on the cultural evolution of human learning is divided into three subsections. The first one is a systematic reconstruction of the historical development of learning within schooling. In this subsection, I rely on data on the development of literacy and schooling, presented by such researchers as Fichtner, Ong, Scribner & Cole, and others. The second subsection is a reconstruction of the development of learning within work, this time restricted to the era of capitalism. This section begins with the data provided by Marx in *Capital*, then goes on to discuss the effects of Taylorist rationalization, countering Braverman's linear deskilling thesis with a case provided by Hirschhorn. Finally, the third subsection discusses the development of learning within science and art. Studies by Zilsel, Lefèvre, Malinowski, Bronowski, Vygotsky, and Wartofsky are used as material in the reconstruction.

All three subsections, as well as the section on the evolution of activity, bear the character of *historically informed sketches,* limited in scope and coverage. They are not object-historical investigations in themselves. They are sketches in the sense of *working out a preliminary basis for hypothetic categories.* Object-historical material is used much in the same way as the Theory of Logical Types was used by Bateson et al., namely, as a heuristic gateway (or a shortcut, or perhaps a crutch) for reaching the formulation of a hypothetic novel category. That is why secondary object-historical sources, used almost in an anecdotal fashion, are considered sufficient in this book. On the other hand, the gateway is here grounded in and preceded by the larger theory-historical discussion.

The *third type* of my data consists of accounts of *specific historical cases* in the development of human learning and expansion. These cases serve as test material to which I apply the categories formulated. At the same time, the analyses of the cases produce findings that enable me to develop the categories further. There are two types of main cases and additional subsidiary cases.

The two types of main cases are (a) literary cases and (b) cases from the history of science. Two cases of both types are analyzed. In Chapter 3, I analyze the literary cases of *The Adventures of Huckleberry Finn* by Mark Twain and *Seven Brothers* by Aleksis Kivi. In Chapter 4, I analyze Mendeleev's *discovery of the periodic law of elements*, described and documented by B. F. Kedrov, and the *discovery of nuclear fission*, which led to the construction of the atom bomb, as described and documented by R. Jungk. All four cases are examples of expansive developmental transitions.

The reason for using literary fiction as data on developmental transitions is the following. Expansive developmental transitions are relatively long in duration. They are complex collective dramas in which both the context and the actors are profoundly changed. Such processes are difficult to document, especially if one wants to catch the psychological aspects of the process. Classic developmental novels are often excellent reconstructions of such processes, "viewing the individual in movement, in constant development, as a necessary condition of his existence" (Bratus, 1986, p. 95). Their validity and "truthfulness" may of course be questioned. Surely they are not simple descriptions or direct recordings of events that have "really happened." But they have become classic for the very reason of expressing and reflecting, and indeed breeding and promulgating, something essential and concretely general in the expansive processes emerging in and typical of a certain culture and certain historical period.

The use of accounts of important scientific discoveries, on the other hand, is justified by the increasing societal impact of such expansive processes. Also there exist some relatively well-documented cases, such as the two I am using. In the case account on Mendeleev's discovery, Kedrov has had exceptionally complete archive material at his disposal. Mendeleev had the habit of recording even the small events and thoughts that occurred to him, and he stored all these written documents with great care. In the case account on the discovery of nuclear fission and on the subsequent construction of the atom bomb, Jungk had the opportunity of not only going through extensive written materials, including private correspondences, but also interviewing personally an impressive number of the central personalities directly involved in this historical process.

Besides these four main cases, a few subsidiary cases are taken up and analyzed more superficially. These include Hirschhorn's account of the accident in the nuclear power plant on the Three Mile Island (Chapter 2) and Grünewald's account of the Children's Campaign for Nuclear Disarmament (Chapter 3), as well as some other minor cases, presented mainly for the purpose of illustration and concretization of the argument.

It may be asked why I have not used a single comprehensive report of my own concrete research as data. The answer is that the expansive developmental research methodology outlined in this book, especially in Chapter 5, requires a complex and extensive report to be understood. I found it impossible to incorporate such a report without either making the book unbearably voluminous or severely mutilating the concrete research report. This may be due to the fact that I am still too close to and too involved in the concrete projects I could in principle have used as sources of data. In the text, I have also refrained from referring to any other publications of my own.

HOW TO PROCESS CATEGORIES OUT OF DATA

In the presentation of a theory, that is, in the outcome of theoretical research, the emergence of the categories may look simple, as if they had appeared from the "pure thought" of the author. This kind of presentation is deceptive. It only reveals that the author him- or herself is not conscious of the path he or she has traveled. The more this path of processing categories out of data is brought into the open, the greater is the possibility that the reader may become involved in the theory as an active discussion partner and contributor to its further development. The theory becomes a processual entity and an instrument of its own development.

On the other hand, if the path or the process of derivation and critical analysis becomes the sole central focus, the outcome itself may get lost. When nothing seems to get fixed into clear-cut categories, the reader has little to cling to in his or her own efforts of reconstruction, application, and critique. Theory becomes a stream in which the reader tries to hold his or her head above the surface without quite knowing where he or she is floating.

In the paper by Bateson and associates, the new category (double bind) is presented immediately after the discussion of the use of Logical Types in communication. The category is first provisionally defined with the help of a series of six necessary ingredients. Then the effects of a double bind are characterized in general terms. After that, the category is concretized by embedding it into the context of the family situation, and further concretized by presenting illustrations from clinical data. The procedure is rather *deductive and straightforward.*

Strangely enough, unlike in so many deductive theories, the whole argumentation does not appear to be a finished and frozen structure. To the contrary, it evokes (and has indeed evoked) a host of questions, counterarguments, application ideas, and so on. How is this possible?

I think that the reason is twofold. Firstly, about halfway in the middle of the paper, the authors specify their database in an important way:

> The theoretical possibility of double bind situations stimulated us to look for such communication sequences in the schizophrenic patient and in his family situation. Toward this end we have studied the written and verbal reports of psychotherapists who have treated such patients intensively; we have studied tape recordings of psychotherapeutic interviews, both of our own patients and others; we have interviewed and taped parents of schizophrenics; we have had two mothers and one father participate in intensive psychotherapy; and we have interviewed and taped parents and patients seen conjointly. (Bateson, 1972, p. 212)

It seems obvious that these data have actually not only been used *after* the category was found and formulated theoretically, as if for verifying and concretizing them only – although this impression is built into the deductive structure of the paper. Clearly the kinds of object-historical and actual-empirical data characterized earlier have played an important role in the very finding and formulation of the category. This conclusion is further supported by a footnote where the authors refer to one of the most famous firsthand object-historical sources on schizophrenia, namely, *Perceval's Narrative* of 1830–1832. My argument is that Bateson and coworkers succeeded so well in hitting the core of their research object, or in finding something like its germ cell, not only because they had become acquainted with the philosophical Theory of Logical Types (as the paper implies), but because they actually had done and were doing very demanding object-historical and actual-empirical analysis of their object. The Theory of Logical Types probably functioned as more of a springboard, a novel analogy needed for the breakthrough to take place.

The second reason for the liveliness of the theory of Bateson et al. is simply its incomplete and open-ended nature. Unlike the classical deductive theory, the paper stops short before even starting to deduce subcategories from the central category of the double bind. The paper provides barely enough concretization by clinical illustrations to set off the reader's own thought experiments. This has been a source of much frustration and much creative effort.

If Bateson et al. develop their category with one piercing sting, the method employed by Habermas is more like spinning and weaving a complicated conceptual texture or web. The entire texture is extremely demanding for the reader because of the multitude of excursions and sidetracks. But on the whole, the chain of argumentation is logical.

Habermas's starting point is an explicit shift from the paradigm of consciousness to the paradigm of *language* as speech. The goal-directed actions of different individuals are socially coordinated, and language is the means of *coordinating* them. The fundamental category of *communicative action* is established on this basis: It is a coordinating action aimed at "reaching understanding in the sense of a cooperative process of interpretation" (Habermas, 1984, p. 101). On this basis, the category of *communicative competence* is derived. This in turn implies a general category of *rationality* as achieving mutual understanding in communication that is free of coercion. The category of communicative action is used to analyze "whether and in what sense the modernization of a society can be described from the standpoint of cultural and societal rationalization" (Habermas, 1984, p. 6). The categories of *modernity* and *rationalization* are analyzed with the help of the categories of *lifeworld* and *system*, which together form Habermas's two-level concept of society. Modernity is analyzed as rationalization and colonization of the lifeworld, or as the decoupling of lifeworld and system.

All these categories are worked out and elaborated through the theory-historical data provided by the classical sociological theories of Weber, Lukacs, Adorno, Mead, Durkheim, Parsons, and Marx.

This chain of categories – coordination-language-communicative action-communicative competence-rationality-modernity-rationalization-lifeworld-system – is not linear or deductive in any simple sense. The links of the chain, that is, the chapters and sections of the book, are in themselves relatively independent cycles of argumentation and analysis. Still the chain is a logical whole. It follows a complex and bouncy logic of interconnections and mutual transitions that is not very clearly explicated by the author. The reader has to reconstruct the logic for him- or herself with great effort. This is obviously the intention of the author. The ideal reader dwells in the book, moves back and forth, discovers new connections and ideas by diving into the texture time and again. Of course, the problem is that there may not be very many such ideal readers. Many a reader will drown in the conceptual stream, never reaching the point of constructing his or her own vessels for sailing.

In the present book, too, the central chapters are relatively independent cycles of analysis and category construction. Each one of Chapters 2, 3,

and 4 follows roughly the same logic. At first, the problem is presented
by introducing certain antinomies or conceptual troubles within cognitive psychology. Second, the problem is elaborated using theory-historical
data. Third, the new categories are provisionally characterized, defined, and
modeled. Fourth, the new categories are tested and further elaborated using
general object-historical accounts or specific object-historical cases as data.
Fifth, some implications are discussed and an intermediate balance is drawn
as a preparation for the next round of category construction. The sequence
may be partially repeated and the order of some steps may be changed, but
this is the general logic of the argumentation.

In Chapter 2, the task is to find the initial abstraction, *the germ-cell
category that can mediate between learning and expansion*. The analysis proceeds through the five steps named previously in the following manner: (1)
The problem is presented as the "learning paradox" of Bereiter and as the
problem of the evolution of learning as posed by Klix. (2) The problem is
elaborated using theory-historical data from three lineages that have taken
the system of man-in-society or individual-in-context as their basic unit of
analysis. (3.1) The *general category of activity* is defined and modeled. (4)
Three historical lines of the cultural evolution of human learning are interpreted with the model of activity. (3.2) The *germ-cell category of learning
activity*, or *learning by expanding*, is defined and modeled as the outcome
of the preceding step. (5) Two sets of implications are discussed, namely,
those concerning the subject of learning activity and those concerning the
emergence of learning activity in the ontogenesis.

In Chapter 3, the task is to find the *mechanism of transition from learning
to expansion*, from everyday individual actions to novel collective activity.
(1) The problem is presented as the dilemma of learning versus development and as the dilemma of individual versus societal development. (2)
First, Bateson's work, then more recent activity-theoretical and related
works are employed as theory-historical data to elaborate the problem. (3.1)
The category of the *zone of proximal development* is defined as the solution to the problem. (4) Two historical case accounts of expansive transition
(classic developmental novels) are analyzed with the help of the category of
the zone of proximal development. (3.2) The analyses yield a more detailed
picture of the phases or steps within the zone of proximal development –
the stepwise structure is modeled. (5) Instructional implications of the
category are discussed.

In Chapter 4, the task is to find the *central instruments needed for the
mastery of expansive transitions*, or zones of proximal development. (1.1) The
problem is presented in the form of three dichotomies in cognitive theories

of thinking. (2.1) The ideas of Dewey, Wertheimer, and Bartlett are analyzed as theory-historical data to elaborate the problem. (1.2) The dilemma of advanced cognitive theories of concepts is taken up as an extension of the initial problem. (2.2) Activity-theoretical ideas of concepts are analyzed as theory-historical data to elaborate the problem further. (3.1) Three basic types of secondary instruments of expansive transitions are defined: *springboards, models,* and *microcosms.* (4) Two historical case accounts of expansive transition (scientific discoveries) are analyzed and the secondary instruments employed in the cases are identified. (2.3) Theories of dialectical and dialogical thinking are analyzed as further theory-historical data. (3.2) A provisional definition of *dialectics* as the tertiary instrument of expansion is suggested. (5) Implications for concrete research methodology are pointed out.

My way of processing categories out of data in these three chapters has certain affinities both with Bateson and associates and with Habermas. I try to share with Bateson et al. the way of defining the novel categories found in a relatively unambiguous and systematic manner. This entails a certain risk of rigidity. On the other hand, I share with Habermas the aspiration to proceed through a chain of cyclic analyses of theory-historical data where theories are treated as live discussion partners. This entails a certain risk of drowning the reader in theories. In the worst case, these risks reinforce each other. In the best case, they balance and neutralize each other.

There are further two specific features of presenting and processing data in this book. The first one is the extensive use of quotations from the theoretical sources discussed and analyzed. The second one is the almost equally extensive use of graphic models.

All theories have a dual character. They are simultaneously fixed conceptual structures and living processes of continuous concept formation. The continuous development of the theory is possible only from within it, through its immanent contradictions and gaps. The more polished and closed the appearance of the theory, the harder it is for the reader to enter the immanent process of its critical elaboration. Glazman (1972, p. 204) points out that scientists may more or less consciously construct "windows" in their theories. These windows are gaps, inconsistencies, or ambivalent formulations that invite the reader to engage in immanent polemics with the author.

In this book, I use quotations as windows into the innermost movement and dynamics of my theory construction. In theoretical research, the difference between displaying original quotations and only the author's own interpretations of the given theoretical sources is much the same as the difference between displaying original interview protocols and only questionnaire data in actual-empirical research. In other words, the quotations serve in theory as what in empirical anthropology would be called "thick description" (Geertz, 1973).

An original quotation, when it is not mishandled and mutilated so as to be totally subordinated to the single-minded purpose of the author, represents a *voice* and a *language* of a researcher other than the author. It represents a dynamism of its own, never perfectly in line with the author's intentions. It allows for a variety of interpretations and associations, not only the ones the author employs in his or her line of reasoning. The intentional use of multiple voices and multiple languages is called *heteroglossia*.

> Heteroglossia ... is *another's speech in another's language,* serving to express authorial intentions but in a refracted way. Such speech constitutes a special type of *double-voiced discourse.* It serves two speakers at the same time and expresses simultaneously two different intentions: the direct intention of the character who is speaking, and the refracted intention of the author. In such discourse there are two voices, two meanings and two expressions. And all the while these two voices are dialogically interrelated, they – as it were – know about each other ...; it is as if they actually hold a conversation with each other. (Bakhtin, 1982, p. 324)

For example, in this quotation, Mikhail Bakhtin is speaking about heteroglossia in the novel, not in scientific theorizing. I am using *his* voice to express, in a refracted form, *my* intentions and arguments about heteroglossia in theoretical research. But his voice does not yield to my purposes without simultaneously producing what Bakhtin (1982, p. 325) calls "dialogized ambiguity."

Quotations are *not* primarily used for illustrative purposes in this book. To the contrary, quotations function here as pieces of a puzzle or a mosaic. The overarching theme and conceptual pattern of this book emerge *through* the quotations. The dialectical derivation of categories demands that the research become "sunk into the material in hand," "following the course that such material takes" (Hegel, 1966, p. 112). The aim is that "by this process the whole as such, surveying its entire content, itself emerges out of the wealth wherein its process of reflection seemed to be lost" (Hegel, 1966, p. 113).

My extensive use of graphic models serves a twofold purpose. First, it aims at making the central categories found transparent and compact. This is the *representation* function of the models. But I use the graphic models in series of successive variations, not just as singular representations. The series of successive variations serve the *instrumental* or *processual* function of the models. With the help of such variations, I try to demonstrate how the models can depict movement and change. The reader is invited to formulate and test his or her own variations.

HOW TO MAKE THE CATEGORIES REACH REALITY

A theory is a potential instrument for dealing with practice. Within theories of man and society, such as those discussed in this book, different intended practice relations are embedded. The practice relation built into traditional theories is that of speaking to *academic empirical researchers* who will verify and concretize the theoretical categories. In such traditional theories, the societal practice remains a distant testing ground, used mainly (a) as source of ex post facto data or of data abstracted via experimental designs (see Maschewsky, 1977), and (b) as object of benevolent recommendations based on the findings gained in research.

There are at least two more radical and direct ways of building the practice relation into the theory. One alternative is to speak directly to *professional practitioners* in the field the theory is concerned with, that is, to prompt them to act as experimenters in their practical contexts. Another alternative is to speak to *social movements* concerned with the problems the theory is trying to illuminate. The classical example is of course the theoretical work of Karl Marx and Friedrich Engels.

The paper by Bateson and colleagues quite clearly speaks to professional practitioners in the field of psychotherapy.

> The understanding of the double bind and its communicative aspects may lead to innovations in therapeutic technique.... Double bind situations occur consistently in psychotherapy. At times these are inadvertent in the sense that the therapist is imposing a double bind situation similar to that in the patient's history, or the patient is imposing a double bind situation on the therapist. At other times therapists seem to impose double binds, either deliberately or intuitively, which force the patient to respond differently than he has in the past.... Many of the uniquely appropriate therapeutic gambits arranged by therapists seem to be intuitive. We share the goal of most psychotherapists who strive toward the day when such strokes of genius will be well enough understood to be systematic and commonplace. (Bateson et al., 1972, p. 225–227)

The practice relation built into Habermas's work is more ambiguous. Habermas emphasizes that he has written his book for researchers, "for

those who have professional interest in the foundations of social theory"
(Habermas, 1984, p. xlii). On the other hand, he points out that new kinds
of conflicts and social movements have developed in advanced Western
societies during recent years.

> They do not flare up in areas of material reproduction; they are not
> channeled through parties and associations; and they are not allayed by
> compensations that conform to the system. Rather, these new conflicts
> arise in areas of cultural reproduction, of social integration and of
> socialization; they are carried out in subinstitutional, or at least extra-
> parliamentary, forms of protest.... It is not primarily a question of com-
> pensations that the social-welfare state can provide, but of protecting
> and restoring endangered ways of life or of establishing reformed ways
> of life. (Habermas, 1981, vol. 2, p. 576)

Here, toward the end of his book, Habermas is increasingly speaking to
the "new social movements." He mentions such phenomena as the ecology and antinuclear movements, the limits-to-growth debate, the peace
movement, the women's movement, experiments with communal and rural
living, liberation movements of various minority groups, conflicts over
regional and cultural autonomy, protests against "big government," religious
fundamentalism and the proliferation of religious sects, the multifarious
"psychoscene," the proliferation of support groups, and the like. Most of
these are purely defensive; only some (like feminism) have forward-oriented
features grounded in modernity. Habermas summarizes his message to such
movements: "Restricting the growth of monetary-administrative complexity is by no means synonymous with surrendering modern forms of life.
In structurally differentiated lifeworlds a potential for reason is marked
out that cannot be conceptualized as a heightening of system complexity"
(Habermas, 1984, p. xlii). The perspective offered in this message is vague
optimism, promising some room for the movements with their emancipatory and defensive communicative actions in the enclaves of the modern
rationalized society.

In the present book, I am speaking to *both researchers and practitioners,*
whether the latter be professional or blue-collar, or engaged in activities
entirely other than wage labor. The methodology of expansive research
sketched in Chapter 5 is necessarily a joint venture. The researcher (or
rather, the team of researchers) has the task of pushing the cycle of expansive transition forward and introducing instruments or components for
new instruments into it. The practitioners have the task of facing and solving the contradictions of their activity system as they are identified and

intensified along the voyage through the zone of proximal development. In this process, the practitioners tendentially become subjects – or rather a collective subject – of their evolving new activity system, thus also subjects of analysis and intervention.

In other words, the methodology proposed in Chapter 5 is not only a methodology of research but also a methodology of practical societal transformation. This means that I am also speaking to *social movements*. But social movements are not taken as something given. Rather, they are conceived of as something *potentially emerging,* something in the process of becoming, within any real societal activity system.

Here I disagree with Habermas, who seems to see hope only outside the system of production and administration. I contend that such a stance indicates a lack of intimate knowledge of the inner contradictions and emancipatory dynamics within the world of wage labor, be it in production or administration. In the heart of modern production and administration, the hidden powers of qualitative change are also greatest. Retreat into the safe world of academic discourse is today almost a guarantee of distorted observation. The naive optimism of Bateson et al., prophesying "innovations" in professional therapeutic work, has a deeper historical truth in it than the wordy roundabouts of Habermas.

SUMMING UP THE INTENTIONS

The problems motivating this inquiry are (1) the increasingly recognizable futility of learning in its standard reactive forms, and (2) the elusive and uncontrollable nature of expansive processes where human beings transcend the contexts given to them. The hypothesis guiding the further course of my study is that learning and expansion are becoming integrated, forming a historically new type of activity.

Thus, the present study falls into the category of general developmental and educational theory. For reasons that will become clear in Chapter 2, I see the central fields of application of this theory in the life practices of adults and adolescents, especially in the interrelations of work and learning.

The method used in this study employs dialectical derivation and construction of categories. Each substantive chapter is a relatively independent cycle of analysis and construction, following roughly the same logical sequence as the others: (1) The problem is presented by introducing certain antinomies or conceptual troubles within cognitive psychology. (2) The problem is elaborated using theory-historical data. (3) The new categories are provisionally characterized, defined, and modeled. (4) The new categories are tested and further elaborated using general object-historical accounts or specific object-historical cases as data. (5) Some implications are discussed and an intermediate balance is drawn as a preparation for the next round of category construction.

The outcomes of the study are condensed into a series of graphic models. Since these models are instruments of thought and practice, they are best understood by following their creation and by applying them in activity.

2

The Emergence of Learning Activity as a Historical Form of Human Learning

AT THE LIMITS OF COGNITIVISM

Within developmentally oriented cognitive psychology, the unsatisfactory state of learning theory has recently evoked attempts at serious reconceptualization. One such attempt is Carl Bereiter's (1985) discussion on the "learning paradox." Another is Friedhart Klix's (1982) treatment of the evolutionary nature of learning processes. In an exemplary manner, these two attempts manifest the qualitative difference – or the paradigmatic boundary – between cognitivism and the cultural-historical approach to human development. They do this in spite of their advanced striving for ecological validity, and precisely because of it. By stretching the limits of cognitivism, attempts like these make the limits visible.

Bereiter illustrates the "learning paradox" as follows.

> What needs explaining from the standpoint of the learning paradox is not only how the child learns to test theories but also how the child acquires the theories to be tested. Statements to the effect that the child "learns from experience" ... dodge the issue and are often not very plausible. Out of the infinitude of correspondences that might be noticed between one event and another, how does it happen that children notice just those ones that make for simple theories about how the world works – and that, furthermore, different children, with a consistency far beyond chance, tend to notice the same correspondences? (Bereiter, 1985, p. 204)

The author then formulates the "learning paradox" on the metatheoretical and theoretical levels. Metatheoretically, the problem is "How can a structure generate another structure more complex than itself?" Theoretically, the problem is "How can the development of complex mental structures be accounted for by mechanisms that are not themselves highly intelligent or richly endowed with knowledge?" In other words, how is progress toward higher levels of complexity possible without there "already being some ladder or rope to climb on" (Bereiter, 1985, p. 204–205).

Bereiter correctly points out that the learning paradox "descends with full force on those kinds of learning of central concern to educators ... – the kinds of learning that lead to understanding core concepts of a discipline, mastering more powerful intellectual tools, and being able to use knowledge critically and creatively" (Bereiter, 1985, p. 202). He also notes that problems very similar to the learning paradox occur in efforts to explain intuition and creativity (Bereiter, 1985, p. 205–206).

The author then proceeds to consider culture as an explanation, offered notably by Vygotsky.

> Following Vygotsky (1978), for instance, one might formulate the following explanation: Learning does, indeed, depend on the prior existence of more complex cognitive structures, but these more complex cognitive structures are situated in the culture, not in the child. The child acquires them through interaction with adults, who help the child do things that it could not do alone. Through such shared activities the child internalizes the cognitive structures necessary to carry on independently. Such an explanation, satisfying as it may appear, does not eliminate the learning paradox at all. The whole paradox lies in the word "internalizes." How does internalization take place? ... Solving that problem means confronting, not circumventing, the learning paradox. (Bereiter, 1985, p. 206)

After this rather brief rebuttal to the cultural-historical approach, Bereiter goes on to present what he calls "10 theoretical principles that seem to hold promise as contributions to a theory of how bootstrapping can occur in cognitive development" (Bereiter, 1985, p. 208). At the core of the ten principles, there are "field facilitation," "imitation," "learning support systems," and "concrete behavior settings." All these are actually different aspects of the idea of exploiting the "more complex cognitive structures situated in the culture," both in material artifacts and in patterns of social interaction. In other words, Bereiter is presenting a list of possible explanatory mechanisms that might account for the processes of internalization.

One is tempted to point out that a list is not a theory (especially as no attempt is made to "deal with the overlap or potential connections among principles" [Bereiter, 1985, p. 208]). One is also tempted to point out that during the fifty years that have passed since Vygotsky's death, voluminous work has been done (and published even in English) by Vygotsky's followers – especially by Leont'ev, Luria, Gal'perin, El'konin, Davydov, and Meshcheryakov – to grasp theoretically and practically the very essence of internalization. But these arguments would be beside the point.

The heart of the matter is, Does the whole paradox really lie in the word "internalizes"? Can the learning paradox really be solved by finding out how internalization takes place?

Here we find a curious anomaly in Bereiter's discussion. On the one hand, he repeatedly speaks of the higher forms of learning as "creation." But, on the other hand, creation for him seems to mean only creation of new cognitive structures *subjectively, "in the head" of the individual.* Thus, learning is effectively reduced to internalization – even if internalization is considered as a process of creative restructuring.

Can creation really be understood as internalization only? If that is so, how can we explain the emergence and renewal of external culture? Does it have nothing to do with learning? Or is it just a self-evident consequence or by-product of internalization?

This is the first complex of questions motivating my quest in this chapter. To formulate the second complex, I now turn to an article by Friedhart Klix (1982).

First, a prelude: A year before Klix published his article, Pat Langley and Herbert Simon (1981, p. 378) argued that *"assuming learning is invariant* is a useful research strategy for the immediate future" (italics in the original).

Klix starts out by questioning the assumption that learning is invariant, that is, that the laws of learning are in principle the same in all organisms. He points out that there are two qualitatively different broad classes of learning performances in animals and man, namely, the class of *conditioning* and the class of *reasoning* or *cognitive learning.* These originate on different levels of evolution. In other words, learning processes are not an evolutionary invariant.

Within the class of conditioning, the subclasses of habituation, conditioned reflex, and instrumental (operant) conditioning are mentioned. Within reasoning, the subclasses of hypothesis formation, inductive and deductive inferences, analogical reasoning, and rule learning (heuristic techniques) are mentioned. The essential qualitative difference between the two basic classes lies in the main information source for decision making. In conditioning, the source is "environmental properties." In reasoning, the source is "long-term-memory properties: concepts, relations, procedures" (Klix, 1982, p. 389). In other words, "insight is not entirely mediated by perceptual information but rather based on mental or cognitive operations which become applied to stored knowledge" (Klix, 1982, p. 388). With cognitive learning, "an increasing independency of any specific environment comes into being"; cognitive learning is "nonspecialized adaptive behavior" (Klix, 1982, p. 389).

According to Klix (1982, p. 386), "early modes of inferential (or cog-nitive) learning may be found among pre-human primates," in a limited sense (hypothesis checking) even among dogs. Thus, the class of reasoning or cognitive learning in no principled way distinguishes man from other mammals.

For the theoretical understanding and practical mastery of human learning, it would be essential to know whether humans have some evo-lutionary qualities that make their learning potentialities qualitatively different from those of other species. Klix's analysis indicates that this is not the case. It indicates that the essence of human (and of all cognitive) learning is just the fact that it is cognitive, that it relies on the properties of long-term memory. To put it in simple terms, human learning is essentially learning "within the head" of the individual – it often allows the individual to "predict and derive the right decision without any overt false trial" (Klix, 1982, p. 388).

Is the evolution of learning essentially a story of progressively enlarged capacity for internal individual processing of information? Is man finally leaving behind the restrictively specific influence of environmental proper-ties? Is man's crucial feature simply the fact that he thinks more than his evolutionary predecessors?

This is the second complex of problems. In order to tackle the two com-plexes, I will first consult P. I. Zinchenko for methodological advice.

ZINCHENKO'S CONTRIBUTION

In 1939, P. I. Zinchenko published an important long paper titled "The Problem of Involuntary Memory." This work has immediate bearing on the analysis of learning undertaken in the present chapter.

Zinchenko tackles the problem of the evolution of memory.

> The position that involuntary memory is the first genetic stage in the development of memory is beyond dispute in both classical and contem-porary psychology. In both the historical development of human con-sciousness and the development of the child's consciousness, the initial forms of memory are involuntary. Of course, in animals, involuntary memory is not merely the first but the only form of memory....

> In spite of the extreme diversity of current views on the nature of mem-ory, involuntary memory is consistently characterized as *mechanical memory*.... Here, there is a division of memory into mechanical and log-ical forms, forms that are understood as two sequential, genetic stages in the development of memory. (Zinchenko, 1983–1984, p. 56–57)

Zinchenko argues that this kind of interpretation of the evolutionary nature of memory is fundamentally distorted and false. It actually reproduces both of the two classical cul-de-sacs of traditional psychology. Firstly, it reproduces associationism and mechanistic materialism by treating involuntary memory as something purely mechanical and physiological. Second, it reproduces intellectualism and idealism by treating voluntary memory as something purely logical and mental.

To overcome this position, it is necessary to grasp that involuntary memory is not the same as mechanical memory. Involuntary memory may be defined as follows.

> It is characterized by the fact that remembering occurs within an action of a *different* nature, an action that has a definite task, goal and motive and a definite significance for the subject, but that is not directly oriented toward the task of remembering. (Zinchenko, 1983–1984, p. 77)

Examples of involuntary memory are common in everyday situations: We remember many things that are embedded in some actions that are significant for us without ever consciously trying to remember them. According to Zinchenko, "None of these forms of memory can be reduced to the laws of associative or conditioned-reflex connections, since these are always external to the actual content of the action" (Zinchenko, 1983–1984, p. 77). In other words, involuntary remembering changes and develops along with changes in the subject's activity and actions within which it occurs. It is literally a by-product and by-process – but not a simple and mechanical one.

Correspondingly, even though voluntary memory is clearly a later and thus higher evolutionary form, it is by no means necessarily logical or non-mechanical. Voluntary remembering is simply a special action devoted to remembering; "The subject is consciously aware of the object of the action as an object of remembering" (Zinchenko, 1983–1984, p. 78). As a matter of fact, voluntary memory quite often takes the form of mechanical memorizing.

> In our view, what is referred to as mechanical memory is not a stage in the genesis of memory: it is a special form of memory that tends to occur when conditions make it difficult for the subject to carry out the meaningful activity required in a particular situation. The resulting memory is "mechanical" in the sense that an object is remembered under conditions in which its meaning or significance is not apparent to the subject. It is important to emphasize, though, that even this kind of memory is psychological rather than physiological. It is not, in the final analysis, "nonmeaningful"; and it is not a function of mechanical impressions

made on a passive subject. It is the result of the subject's activity, activity
that realizes the subject's relationship to a given object. When remembering is mechanical, however, this relationship is not adequate to the
situation in which the activity is carried out. (Zinchenko, 1983–1984,
p. 108–109)

Similarly, so-called logical memory, employing logical operations, may be
either voluntary or involuntary.

Zinchenko sums up his article with a merciless verdict.

The division of memory into mechanical and logical forms, as if these
were two genetically consecutive stages, is false. This perspective is linked
to a tendency to identify and contrast the mental and the physiological,
a tendency to identify and contrast the essence of mind and its material
basis. (Zinchenko, 1983–1984, p. 108)

There are three important lessons to be drawn from Zinchenko's
contribution.

First, the manner in which Klix treats the evolution of learning matches
perfectly with the criteria of false analysis worked out by Zinchenko. In evolutionary terms, it is illegitimate to treat earlier or lower types of learning
as "conditioning" and later or higher types as "reasoning." Various forms of
reasoning are to be found in quite early evolutionary forms of learning –
and vice versa (a point partially demonstrated by Klix himself).

Second, in evolutionary terms, the initial form of learning is that of
incidental (or involuntary) learning operations that take place as a tacit and
casual by-product and by-process of other activities and actions. *Conscious,
goal-directed learning actions* are a later and higher formation (though I
would not go so far as to restrict them to the human species only, a reservation substantiated in Chapter 3).

Third, to understand the structure and dynamics of different forms of
learning, whether incidental or conscious, we have to study them as parts
or aspects of concrete historical activities with specifiable subjects, objects,
and instruments, within specifiable contexts.

The third lesson implies that we must have some conceptual means with
which activities can be analyzed. The next sections aim at deriving such conceptual means. Only after that can we return to the analysis of learning.

THE TRIANGLES OF ACTIVITY

In the nineteenth century, philosophy, biology, and social sciences experienced fundamental conceptual and methodological breakthroughs that

were more or less directly intertwined with the huge development of the productive forces and global commerce through industrial capitalism. In philosophy, the breakthrough was realized above all by Hegel. In biology, it was realized by Darwin. And in social sciences, it was realized by Marx.

Two fundamental features are evident in these breakthroughs. *First,* they meant that organism and environment, man and society, were no more seen as separate entities but as integral systems within which retroactive causality and internal dynamic transitions prevail. *Second,* these breakthroughs meant that organism and environment, man and society, could no more be understood as stable, unchanging entities but only as something characterized by qualitative transformations requiring a historical perspective.

Each of the three breakthroughs had its specific content and impact. In the most general terms, Hegel's contribution may be summarized as follows.

> Basing himself on the solid national tradition (the German enlightenment, Kant, Fichte, Schelling), Hegel from the outset links the activeness of human consciousness not with the peculiarities of man's bodily, natural organization, but with the process of each individual's active assimilation of the spiritual wealth accumulated by previous history, and with the realization of what he has assimilated in his own activity that overcomes the resistance of object. (Mikhailov, 1980, p. 87)

Hegel was the first philosopher to draw attention to the role of material, productive activity and the instruments of labor in the development of knowledge. He clearly enunciated the theory that individual consciousness is formed under the influence of knowledge accumulated by society and objectified in the world of things created by humanity.

> The individual possesses consciousness (spirit) insofar as the spirit of history has possessed him, insofar as history acts in him and through him. (Mikhailov, 1980, p. 92; for an interpretation of Hegel's psychological importance, see Marková, 1982)

It was Charles Darwin who laid the natural-scientific, empirical foundation for the systemic and historical conception of man.

> By coordinating the opposing forces of internal structure and external environment, Darwin eliminated the need to appeal to supernatural forces in scientific explanation. He created the first powerful model of a natural, self-contained system that changed progressively. (Richards, Armon & Commons, 1984, p. xx)

As Howard Gruber (1974, p. 71) notes in his excellent *Darwin on Man,* Marx and Engels greeted *The Origin of Species* enthusiastically when it appeared.

Marx and Engels combined the insights of Hegel and Darwin. More than that, they put forward a conception whereby man was not only a product of evolution and an assimilator of culture but a creator and transformer.

> The chief defect of all previous materialism ... is that things *[Gegenstand]*, reality, sensuousness are conceived only in the form of the *object, or of contemplation,* but not as *sensuous human activity, practice,* not subjectively. Hence, in contradistinction to materialism, the *active* side was set forth abstractly by idealism – which, of course, does not know real, sensuous activity as such....
>
> The materialist doctrine concerning the changing of circumstances and upbringing forgets that circumstances are changed by men and that the educator must himself be educated. This doctrine must, therefore, divide society into two parts, one of which is superior to society.
>
> The coincidence of the changing of circumstances and of human activity or self-change can be conceived and rationally understood only as *revolutionary practice.* (Marx, 1976, p. 615–616)

These famous lines from *Thesis on Feuerbach* set the standard for my further inquiry. The problem is that the human sciences of the twentieth century, especially psychology and education, have not yet met the challenge of constructing coherent theoretical instruments for grasping and bringing about processes in which "circumstances are changed by men and the educator himself is educated." Yet, as Bibler (1970, p. 157) points out, the conceptual upheaval foreseen by Hegel and Marx "now takes hold of productive activity in general, becomes a logical necessity."

Though the challenge of the nineteenth century breakthroughs has not been met yet, it was faced and dealt with by certain lineages of thought in the twentieth century. These lineages have taken seriously the idea of man as a systemic and historical being. On this basis, they have produced attempts at modeling the basic structure of human activity.

I will limit my search for a viable root model of human activity with the following initial delimitations. *First,* activity must be pictured in its simplest, genetically original structural form, as the smallest unit that still preserves the essential unity and quality behind any complex activity.

Second, activity must be analyzable in its dynamics and transformations, in its evolution and historical change. No static or eternal models will do.

Third, activity must be analyzable as a contextual or ecological phenomenon. The models will have to concentrate on systemic relations between the individual and the outside world.

Fourth, specifically human activity must be analyzable as a culturally mediated phenomenon. No dyadic organism-environment models will suffice. This requirement stems already from Hegel's insistence on the culturally mediated, *triadic* or *triangular* structure of human activity.

The first delimitation excludes, among other theories, the work of Habermas from the present discussion. Instead of the original inner unity, Habermas takes the division of action into labor and interaction as his starting point (see Giddens, 1982).

The last delimitation makes it unnecessary, for example, to consider here Piaget's concept of activity (see Piaget, 1977 and Gallagher, 1978; for insightful criticism see especially Damerow, 1980; Wartofsky, 1983).

Prerequisites for a theory of human activity that fulfill these four requirements may be found in three broad research traditions. The first one is the theorizing on signs, meanings, and knowledge, beginning with Peirce[*] and extending through Ogden and Richards all the way to Popper's evolutionary epistemology. The second one is the study of the genesis of intersubjectivity, founded by G. H. Mead and finding continuity in studies of infant communication and language development. And the third one is the cultural-historical school of psychology, starting with Vygotsky and maturing in Leont'ev. In all these theories, the concept of mediation, of thirdness or triangularity, is seen as the constitutive feature of human activity. This idea is frequently expressed, developed, and applied in the form of graphic models.

The First Lineage: From Peirce to Popper

C. S. Peirce, one of the founders of semiotics, built his theory of mediation on the idea of a triadic relationship among an object, a mental interpretant, and a sign.

> A *Sign,* or *Representamen,* is a First which stands in such a genuine triadic relation to a Second, called its Object, as to be capable of determining a Third, called its *Interpretant,* to assume the same triadic relation to its object in which it stands itself to the same Object. (Peirce, 1902, cited in Parmentier, 1985, p. 27)[*]

The triadic relation is not reducible to independent dyads. Otherwise, the dynamic character of the triad is destroyed and "there is no interpretation

---

[*] For the sake of clarity, Peirce's excessive and often opaque work (see Peirce, 1931–1935) is here discussed only through the concise but balanced interpretation of Parmentier (1985); see also the related volume of Pharies (1984).

or representation by the resultant moment of the earlier moment; no symbolic or conventional relations exist among the elements; and no thought, idea, or meaning is embodied and transmitted in the process" (Parmentier, 1985, p. 26).

There are two vectors in this dynamism. First, there is the vector of *representation* pointing from the sign and interpretant toward the object. Second, there is the vector of *determination* pointing from the object toward both sign and interpretant.

> This interlocking of the vectors of representation and determination implies that the three elements in the sign relation are never permanently object, representamen, and interpretant, but rather each shifts roles as further determinations and representations are realized.... Semiosis is, thus, an 'infinite process' or an 'endless series' in which the interpretant approaches a true representation of the object as further determinations are accumulated in each moment. (Parmentier, 1985, p. 29)

Besides purely logical and linguistic entities, Peirce applied his conception to human actions, too.

> In all action governed by reason such genuine triplicity will be found; while purely mechanical actions take place between pairs of particles. A man gives a brooch to his wife. The merely mechanical part of the act consists of his laying the brooch down while uttering certain sounds, and her taking it up. There is no genuine triplicity here; but there is no giving either. The giving consists in his agreeing that a certain intellectual principle shall govern the relations of the brooch to his wife. The merchant in the Arabian Nights threw away a datestone which struck the eye of a Jinnee. This was purely mechanical, and there was no genuine triplicity. The throwing and the striking were independent of one another. But has he aimed at the Jinnee's eye, there would have been more than merely throwing away the stone. There would have been genuine triplicity, the stone being not merely thrown, but thrown *at* the eye. Here, *intention*, the mind's action, would have come in. Intellectual triplicity, or Mediation, is my third category. (Peirce, 1902, cited in Parmentier, 1985, p. 41)

This citation reveals the first fundamental problem in Peirce's conception. The mediating sign is here, in the context of human action, treated as something purely mental and intentional. It thus loses its potentially anti-Cartesian, cultural quality and reverts to individualism and rationalism.

> Although Peirce often made clear that his notion of representation included everything, mental as well as nonmental, that possesses attributes, he gave little attention to the sensible or material qualities of signs

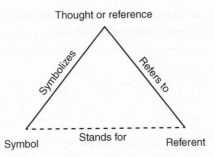

FIGURE 2.1. Meaning as the triad of thoughts, words, and things (Ogden & Richards, 1923, p. 11).

in the nonmental category, or what he later termed the representamen. In fact, the need for some "medium of outward expression" is admitted only as something that may be necessary to translate a "thought-sign" to another person; and these material qualities are, in themselves, only a residue of nonsemiotic properties of the sign that play no positive role in the sign's representative function. (Parmentier, 1985, p. 33)

The second problem in Peirce's thought became dominant toward the end of his productive career. This problem is the strict separation of the form from the content of the signs and the exclusive interest in the pure form. The contents in no way contributed to the determination of the form, and sign forms became "blind vehicles for communicating meanings that they do not influence" (Parmentier, 1985, p. 45).

In their seminal work on the meaning of meaning, Ogden and Richards (1923) present a triangular diagram (Figure 2.1) as their point of departure.

The authors point out the specific nature of the bottom line of the triangle, that is, the relation between symbol (word) and referent (thing).

Between the symbol and the referent there is no relevant relation other than the indirect one, which consists in its being used by someone to stand for a referent. Symbol and Referent, that is to say, are not connected directly ... but only indirectly round the two sides of the triangle. (Ogden & Richards, 1923, p. 11–12)

This means that there is no direct correspondence between the symbol and the thing it symbolizes, or between words and things. Their relation is always *constructed* by man and thus historically changing.

We shall find, however, that the kind of simplification typified by this once universal theory of direct meaning relations between words and

things is the source of almost all the difficulties which thought encounters. (Ogden & Richards, 1923, p. 12)

So meanings are constructions. The construction of meaning is the specifically human type of activity.

But Ogden and Richards, much in the manner of Peirce, conceive of the
construction of the relation between symbol and referent purely and exclusively as a *thought process,* as a mental act of *the individual.* Furthermore,
they see meaning embedded and embodied exclusively in symbols and language, not in material things and artifacts in general. This renders them
rather helpless in the face of the problem of the origination of thought, symbols, and language.

It is also symptomatic that Ogden and Richards restrict the indirect,
mediated nature to the bottom line of the triangle. The other two relations,
that between thought and symbol and that between thought and thing, are
seen as "more or less direct" (Ogden & Richards, 1923, p. 11).

Can these two relations really be direct? Consider first the relation
between thought and symbol. Symbols are sociohistorically produced and
transmitted artifacts. They are abstracted and generalized from the production and use of material tools and objects. The relation of an *individual* to a
symbol *appears* direct. But the cultural development of symbols can never
be understood in direct individual terms. It is a superindividual, collective
process, based on the mediated, indirect interaction of subjects with symbols via objects (referents). Also the individual grasp and use of symbols
originate from practical encounters with the world of objects, which the
symbols represent and from which they stem.

This origination of words and symbols from practical material actions
is pointed out by Malinowski in his supplement to the book of Ogden and
Richards.

> Thus, when a savage learns to understand the meaning of a word, this
> process is not accomplished by explanations, by a series of acts of apper-
> ception, but by learning to handle it. A word *means* to a native the proper
> use of the thing for which it stands. (Malinowski, 1923, p. 321)

> The real knowledge of a word comes through the practice of appropri-
> ately using it within a certain situation. The word, like any man-made
> implement, becomes significant only after it has been used and properly
> used under all sorts of conditions. (Malinowski, 1923, p. 325)

Historically and theoretically this theme has been elaborated by Leont'ev
(1981, especially p. 219–220), Leroi-Gourhan (1980, especially p. 147–153),
and Tran Duc Thao (1984). Within cognitive psychology, David McNeill

(1985) has recently discussed the common origins of gestures and speech. The most convincing experimental material is provided by Meshcheryakov (1979) from his work with the education of deaf-blind children. Meshcheryakov's reappraisal of Helen Keller's development, often characterized as the unfolding of the inner spiritual essence dormant within, is refreshing in its own right.

> By the time her teacher appeared on the scene Helen could find her way about the house easily, also in the orchard, vegetable garden and the whole of the immediate vicinity of the house. She was familiar with many household objects, kitchen utensils and garden implements, she knew what many of the objects around her were used for and was able to use them properly. She used a well-developed language of gestures which she made wide and systematic use of.... Indeed, there are definite grounds for maintaining that Helen Keller's first teacher was the little black girl Martha Washington. It was she who first began to break down the wall isolating the little deaf-blind girl, and it was thanks to her contact with Martha that Helen started to evolve her language of gestures. It should be pointed out that neither Anne Sullivan, nor those specialists who later attempted to analyze Helen's instruction from the psychological angle, attached any particular, let alone decisive importance to this period of Helen's life. (Meshcheryakov, 1979, p. 60)

The relation between thought and thing may be analyzed in a similar vein. Things are not just there, to be thought about and referred to. They are produced and used by human beings in their collective life activities, in their practice. This does not take place directly but always with the (visible or invisible) help of symbols, that is, of tools and models, concerning the qualities and behavior of the things. Again, as we look at an individual referring to a material object, it appears that he or she has a direct relation to that object. But the referring is always done with some means – gestures, pictures, words, other objects – that must be communicable and understandable to at least some other individuals. The act is not direct, not even when it proceeds automatically. The mediating cultural instrument is there, whether the subject is conscious of it or not.

In the triangle of Ogden and Richards, the prime mover is the uppermost corner, the *thought*. But the subject not only – and not primarily – thinks. Above all, he or she acts practically, molds the material environment. And the subject does this cooperatively, not alone.

Among modern epistemological theories, Karl Popper's (1972) conception of the three worlds is certainly the most well-known version of triplicity. The basic position is the following.

> First, there is the physical world – the universe of physical entities …; this
> I will call "World 1." Second, there is the world of mental states, including
> states of consciousness and psychological dispositions and unconscious
> states; this I will call "World 2." But there is also a *third* such world, the
> world of the contents of thought, and, indeed, of the products of the
> human mind; this I will call "World 3." (Popper & Eccles, 1977, p. 38)

In his World 3, Popper includes stories, explanatory myths, tools, scientific
theories, scientific problems, social institutions, and works of art. These entities may and often do exist in material form. But the material aspect is not
essential. World 3 entities can also exist in a nonmaterial, unembodied form.
The prime example of such entities are scientific and other *problem situations.*
Problem situations, according to Popper, exist objectively within the mass of
knowledge, regardless of whether men have become conscious of them or
 not. The task is to discover them. Popper contends that grasping World 3
objects is totally independent of the material embodiments of those objects.

> Both … theories and their logical relations are World 3 objects, and in
> general it makes no difference, neither to their character as World 3
> objects nor to our World 2 grasp of them, whether or not these objects
> are embodied. Thus a not yet discovered and not yet embodied logical
> problem situation may prove decisive for our thought processes, and may
> lead to actions with repercussions in the physical World 1, for example to
> a publication. (Popper & Eccles, 1977, p. 46)

But certainly even problems and logical possibilities have to be fixed in
some kind of language. Popper readily admits this. But still these entities
are unembodied – because language itself is.

> *Language is non-material,* and appears in the most varied physical
> shapes – that is to say, in the form of very different systems of physical
> sounds. (Popper & Eccles, 1977, p. 49; italics added)

In other words, Popper insists on the absolute separation of content and
form, of the immaterial substance and the material vehicle, much in the
manner of the late Peirce (whom he considers to be "one of the greatest phi-
losophers of all time" [Popper, 1972, p. 212]). Time and again, this leads him
to statements upholding the independent and discrete nature of each of the
three worlds. Again, Helen Keller's development is a case in point.

> All normal men speak; and speech is of the utmost importance for them;
> so much so that even a deaf, dumb and blind little girl like Helen Keller
> acquired with enthusiasm, and speedily, a substitute for speech through
> which she obtained a real mastery of the English language and of literature.

Physically, her language was vastly different from spoken English; but it had a one-to-one correspondence with written or printed English. There can be no doubt that she would have acquired any other language in place of English. *Her urgent though unconscious need was for language – language in the abstract.* (Popper & Eccles, 1977, p. 49; italics added)

Would Popper hold that even Helen Keller's early, gestural language, with its inseparably intertwined earthly contents and forms, was "immaterial"? Probably.

According to Popper (1972, p. 155), "the three worlds are so related that the first two can interact, and that the last two can interact." In other words, he postulates discontinuous relations among the three worlds. He *reduces the triangle into two dyads* – something that Peirce considered legitimate only within the sphere of purely mechanical actions, such as the movement of billiard balls (Parmentier, 1985, p. 25–26).

This dyadic reductionism actually destroys the intended interactionist or systemic character of Popper's theory. Instead of mediation as real practical movement, as activity, we have three worlds living their autonomous lives and entering into the familiar dualistic subject-object relations with one of the other worlds at a time. Thus, the theories of World 3 not only exist but also act autonomously: "They create new, unintended and unexpected problems, autonomous problems, problems to be discovered" (Popper, 1972, p. 161). In other words, problem situations are situated – one could say stored – in World 3.

From the point of view of activity, this makes no sense. Problem situations are not statically situated or stored; they are rather one essential form of the movement of the triangle, being constructed and appearing in and between all the three "corners."

Popper does speak of activity – *"the activity of understanding consists, essentially, in operating with third-world objects"* (Popper, 1972, p. 164). This dyadic conception fails to explain how World 3 objects are *created*. Understanding becomes receptive intellectualism, not just in the ordinary sense of being detached from World 1, but in the more important sense of being unable to grasp practically the productive nature of the continuous triplicity of activity.

The biologist and epistemologist R. C. Lewontin cogently summarizes Popper's position of "evolutionary epistemology."

For Popper, science and nature, the individual and the real world, are each alienated from the other. ... Each has its autonomous processes. The external world is in part a fixed reality with eternal laws of nature, but in part evolves by physical processes of cosmic and terrestrial evolution.... Living beings, on the other hand, have an autonomous process of variation, the throwing up of novelties, of "conjectures". Their generation has no particular connection with external nature, except, of course, that they are manifestations of universal molecular and physical forces. The autonomous variation of organisms and the autonomous states of external nature are then connected to each other by a unidirectional process in which the organism adapts to outer nature by the differential survival of variations. So, too, individual psyches generate conjectural novelties which are then refuted by the outer world. (Lewontin, 1982, p. 163–164)

What remains after the critique? The first lineage leading to the theory of activity has provided us with the fundamental idea of *knowledge and meaning as mediated construction*. Even Popper testifies to that.

According to my view, we may understand the grasping of a World 3 object as an active process. We have to explain it as the making, the recreation, of that object. In order to understand a difficult Latin sentence, we have to construe it: to see how it is made, and to re-construct it, to re-make it. (Popper & Eccles, 1977, p. 44)

But the theories of the first lineage narrow human activity down to individual intellectual understanding. They provide little cues for grasping how material culture is created in joint activity.

The Second Lineage: From Mead to Trevarthen

The second lineage toward the theory of activity was initiated by G. H. Mead's "social behaviorism." Mead's theory was aimed at overcoming individualism and intellectualism.

We are not, in social psychology, building up the behavior of the social group in terms of the behavior of the separate individuals composing it; rather, we are starting out with a given social whole of complex group activity, into which we analyze (as elements) the behavior of each of the separate individual composing it....

In social psychology we get at the social process from the inside as well as from the outside. Social psychology is behavioristic in the sense of starting off with an observable activity – the dynamic, on-going social process, and the social acts which are its component elements – to be studied and analyzed scientifically. But it is not behavioristic in the sense of ignoring the inner experience of the individual – the inner phase of that process or activity. On the contrary, it is particularly concerned with the rise of such experience within the process as a whole. It simply works from the outside to the inside instead of from the inside to the outside. (Mead, 1934, p. 7–8)

Mead's approach is commonly called "symbolic interactionism" or a theory of "symbol-mediated interaction" (Joas, 1980). One central tenet of this approach is the priority of social objects and social consciousness to physical objects.

> The social process, as involving communication, is in a sense responsible for the appearance of new objects in the field of experience of the individual organisms implicated in that process. Organic processes or responses in a sense constitute the objects to which they are responses; that is to say, any given biological organism is in a sense responsible for the existence (in the sense of the meanings they have for it) of the objects to which it physiologically and chemically responds. There would, for example, be no food – no edible objects – if there were no organisms which could digest it. And similarly, the social process in a sense constitutes the objects to which it responds, or to which it is an adjustment. That is to say, objects are constituted in terms of meanings within the social process of experience and behavior through the mutual adjustment to one another of the responses or actions of the various individual organisms involved in that process, an adjustment made possible by means of a communication which takes the form of a conversation of gestures in the earlier evolutionary stages of that process, and of language in its later stages. (Mead, 1934, p. 77)

This social, interactive construction of physical objects takes place through symbols.

> Symbolization constitutes objects not constituted before, objects which would not exist except for the context of social relationships wherein symbolization occurs. Language does not simply symbolize a situation or object which is already there in advance; it makes possible the existence or appearance of that situation or object, for it is a part of the mechanism whereby that situation or object is created. The social process relates the responses of one individual to the gestures of another, as the meanings of the latter, and is thus responsible for the rise and existence of new objects in the social situation, objects dependent upon or constituted by these meanings. (Mead, 1934, p. 78)

Thus, a triadic definition of meaning is worked out.

> This threefold or triadic relation between gesture, adjustive response, and resultant of the social act which the gesture initiates is the basis of meaning; for the existence of meaning depends upon the fact that the

adjustive response of the second organism is directed toward the resultant of the given social act as initiated and indicated by the gesture of the
first organism. The basis of meaning is thus objectively there in social
conduct, or in nature in its relation to such conduct. (Mead, 1934, p. 80)

Now there seem to be four basic elements in Mead's reasoning about activity: the individual, the other(s), the symbol, and the object. The intriguing
question is that of the origin of symbols. According to Mead, symbols grow
out of gestures.

> The primitive situation is that of the social act which involves the inter-
> action of different forms, which involves, therefore, the adjustment of the
> conduct of these different forms to each other, in carrying out the social
> process. Within that process one can find what we term the gestures,
> those phases of the act which bring about the adjustment of the response
> of the other form....
>
> The vocal gesture becomes a significant symbol ... when it has the same
> effect on the individual making it that it has on the individual to whom
> it is addressed or who explicitly responds to it, and thus involves a refer-
> ence to the self of the individual making it. The gesture in general, and
> the vocal gesture in particular, indicates some object or other within the
> field of social behavior, an object of common interest to all the individuals
> involved in the given social act thus directed toward or upon that object.
> The function of the gesture is to make adjustment possible among the indi-
> viduals implicated in any given social act with reference to the object or
> objects with which that act is concerned; and the significant gesture or sig-
> nificant symbol affords far greater facilities for such adjustment and read-
> justment than does the non-significant gesture. (Mead, 1934, p. 45–46)

But where do gestures originate? For Mead, they are something originally
given in both human and animal behavior. However, significant or conscious gestures are found only among humans (Mead, 1934, p. 81). How
these significant or conscious gestures arise is not explained.

It is instructive to compare Mead's conception with those of Leont'ev and
Tran Duc Thao. These authors agree with Mead on the constructed nature of
objects. But they disagree with Mead on the interpretation of construction
as mere communication and symbolization. For them, the construction of
objects is above all sensuous, material construction by means of tools, that
is, production. Communication and symbolization are seen as derivative,
though organically intertwined aspects of production.

According to Leont'ev, conscious gestures originated as people experienced that even when a work movement did not lead to its practical result
for some reason or other, it was still capable of affecting others involved in

production. It could, for example, draw them into the fulfillment of a given action.

> Movements thus arose that preserved the form of the corresponding work movements but lacked practical contact with the object, and consequently also lacked the effort that converted them into real work movements. These movements, together with the vocal sounds that accompanied them, were separated from the tasks of acting on an object, and separated from labor activity, and preserved in themselves only the function of acting on people, the function of speech intercourse. In other words, they were converted into gestures. A gesture is nothing else than a movement separated from its result, i.e. not applied to the object at which it is aimed. (Leontyev, 1981, p. 219)

Tran Duc Thao elaborates this line of reasoning in detail. He sees the precursor of language in the prehominid indicative sign.

> Most likely from the very beginning of the prehominid development, in the cognizance of the indicative sign, the original form of the circular arc gesture was transmuted into the straight line form. Yet if, by virtue of the excitation of collective work, the straight line indicative gesture is prolonged for an instant, *the prehominid necessarily follows the object in its motion:* for example, the game that is fleeing or falls down, or the bone fragment or piece of wood which pierces the animal like a beak or a dagger. The gestural sign developed in this way is reinforced each time by a *diffuse sound,* of emotional origin, but which is now related to the tendential image projected by the gesture, and in this way obtains value as a *word* with an objective meaning: "*this here* in a motion in the form of distancing, overturning, piercing", etc.... It is evident that the communication of such a meaning content allows a coordination of collective labor by far superior to the simple concentration of the forces of the group on the object indicated as the "this here!" (Tran Duc Thao, 1984, p. 56)

Both Leont'ev and Tran Duc Thao stress the genetic connection of gestures and tool-mediated work on material objects. Their point of departure is the original unity of instrumental and communicative aspects of activity. Therefore, signs and symbols are seen as derivative instruments of productive activity that necessarily has an interactive, communicative form. For Mead, the original situation is that of interaction, of a "social process" with only secondary and abstract presence of material objects. For him, symbols are not primarily instruments for mastering tool-mediated procedures on objects.

> A symbol is nothing but the stimulus whose response is given in advance. That is all we mean by a symbol. There is a word, and a blow. The blow is

the historical antecedent of the word, but if the word means an insult, the response is one now involved in the word, something given in the very stimulus itself. That is all that is meant by a symbol. Now, if that response can be given in terms of an attitude utilized for the further control of action, then the relation of that stimulus and attitude is what we mean by a significant symbol. (Mead, 1934, p. 181)

Control of action means here control of interaction between people. Objects to be worked on and molded into useful artifacts by means of instruments play an accidental role, if any.

Mead does discuss material production. He takes it up toward the end of his *Mind, Self, and Society* (1934, p. 248–249 and p. 363). He points out that a human act "has this implemental stage that comes between the actual consummation and the beginning of the act" (Mead, 1934, p. 248). The human hand is the fundamental tool and implement of material production. Mead (1934, p. 363) appreciates its cognitive importance by noting that "man's manual contacts, intermediate between the beginnings and the ends of his acts, provide a multitude of different stimuli to a multitude of different ways of doing things, and thus invite alternative impulses to express themselves in the accomplishment of his acts, when obstacles and hindrances arise."

But this instrumental line of thought remains more or less a separate sidetrack in Mead's work. Communicative and instrumental aspects of activity do not form a unified system. Their interrelations are not worked out in any recognizable manner.

Hans Joas, a connoisseur and proponent of Mead's legacy, has one important reservation concerning the theory of symbol-mediated interaction, namely, "that Mead's concept of action is oriented too much toward a model of adaptive intercourse and too little toward objectification and material production of the new" (Joas, 1980, p. 231). It is easy to sympathize with this assessment. However, it is hardly a question of "too much" or "too little." What is lacking are dynamic relationships between the two.

Mead's ideas have experienced a revival in recent research on infants' communicative development (see Lock, 1978; Bullowa, 1979). One of the most inventive attempts in this direction is the work of Colwyn Trevarthen on what he calls secondary intersubjectivity in small children.

According to Trevarthen, a fundamental qualitative change takes place in human communication about forty weeks after birth, well before speech begins.

The most important feature of the new behaviour at 9 months is ... its systematically combining of interests of the infant in the physical, privately-known reality near him, and his acts of communication addressed to persons. A deliberately sought sharing of experiences about events and things is achieved for the first time. Before this, objects are perceived and used, and persons are communicated with – but these two kinds of intention are expressed separately. Infants under 9 months share themselves with others but not their knowledge or intentions about things. (Trevarthen & Hubley, 1978, p. 184)

The authors point out that "once free interaction between communicative and praxis modes of action is achieved, the infant suddenly shows behaviour that is unique to man in its complexity" (Trevarthen & Hubley, 1978, p. 213–214). This formation of secondary intersubjectivity links *"mother, infant and object on an equal plane of importance"* (Trevarthen & Hubley, 1978, p. 214; italics added). This is illustrated with the help of a series of diagrams (Figure 2.2). Halliday (1975) and Nelson (1979) present analyses along similar lines, though locating the coordination of the social and object spheres at later points in ontogenesis.

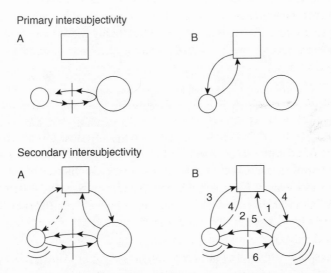

FIGURE 2.2. Primary and secondary intersubjectivity exemplified (adapted from Trevarthen & Hubley, 1978, p. 215).
Primary intersubjectivity: (A) Communicating: baby and mother interact face to face; no interest in object. (B) Acting on an object: baby acts; mother watches.
Secondary intersubjectivity: (A) Baby gives object and shows pleasure when it is accepted. (B) Full person-person-object fluency: mother shows baby how to do a task (1 + 2), baby accepts (3 + 4), then looks at mother and both are pleased (5 + 6).

The transition from primary to secondary intersubjectivity takes place through games, described in detail by Trevarthen. Trevarthen's results seem to establish something that was lacking in Mead, namely, the relationship between communicative and instrumental aspects of activity. But here we should hesitate for a moment. Trevarthen speaks about a praxis mode of action, not about an instrumental one. As a matter of fact, he gives no serious consideration to the role of instruments or tools as something essentially different from and yet intrinsically related to the objects to which they are applied. In this respect, Trevarthen's model of secondary intersubjectivity is entirely compatible with Mead's conception of intersubjectivity.

There is, however, another element that Mead considers essential but is not incorporated in Trevarthen's model – the symbol. Symbols represent for Mead the universal or public dimension of interaction. As we saw, they are dissociated from instruments and procedures of material production – but they are definitely societal and historical. This sociohistorical aspect is no more present in Trevarthen's model.

John R. Morss's recent critique of the basic assumptions of what he calls the neo-Meadian school is interesting against this background. According to Morss, the neo-Meadians have a fundamentally flawed interpretation of Mead's theory.

> Mead places great emphasis on the "generalised other" as the *personification* of group values, but it must be emphasised that this entity is a highly abstract one. As in early role-playing, social meaning is *not* tied to specific individual others: the generalised other is actually a *general* other. Mead's concern is therefore with the individual in his relationships with a community, not with specific other individuals. The neo-Meadian emphasis on dyadic interaction in general, and on the mother-infant dyad in particular, thus deviates radically from Mead.... The neo-Meadian view does not appear to question the equation of "social" with "interpersonal" (nor, indeed, the reduction of "interpersonal" to "dyadic"). (Morss, 1985, p. 168)

Morss argues that this reduction leads to a view of knowledge opposite to that of the original Mead. For Mead, the social character of knowledge meant that knowledge is above all public, impersonal. For the neo-Meadians, the social character of knowledge means that knowledge is interpersonal.

> That is, it can be interpreted to require fully cognisant individuals who set out to establish contact with one another. Interpersonalism in this

sense is merely an elaboration of personalism – as it were, a pluralistic personalism. (Morss, 1985, p. 171; see also the ensuing debate between Shotter, 1986 and Morss, 1986)

This means that the neo-Meadians end up in a new version in individualism or privatism as they tacitly set aside the truly societal, public dimension of Mead's theory.

If the first lineage from Peirce to Popper provided us with the idea of activity as individual construction of knowledge, what has the second lineage to offer? Mead obviously extends the picture, giving us the social, interactive, symbol-mediated construction of reality. But this construction is still conceived of as construction for the mind, not as practical material construction.

The Third Lineage: From Vygotsky to Leont'ev

In 1930, L. S. Vygotsky, the founder of the Soviet cultural-historical school of psychology, sketched his idea of mediation as follows.

> Every elementary form of behavior presupposes *direct* reaction to the task set before the organism (which can be expressed with the simple S – R formula). But the structure of sign operations requires an intermediate link between the stimulus and the response. This intermediate link is a second order stimulus (sign) that is drawn into the operation where it fulfills a special function; it creates a new relation between S and R. The term "drawn into" indicates that an individual must be actively engaged in establishing such a link. The sign also possesses the important characteristic of reverse action (that is, it operates on the individual, not the environment).
>
> Consequently, the simple stimulus-response process is replaced by a complex, mediated act, which we picture as:

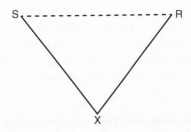

FIGURE 2.3. The structure of the mediated act (Vygotsky, 1978, p. 40).

In this new process the direct impulse to react is inhibited, and an auxiliary stimulus that facilitates the completion of the operation by indirect means is incorporated.

Careful studies demonstrate that this type of organization is basic to all higher psychological processes, although in much more sophisticated forms than that shown above. The intermediate link in this formula is not simply a method of improving the previously existing operation, nor is a mere additional link in an S-R chain. Because this auxiliary stimulus possesses the specific function of reverse action, it transfers the psychological operation to higher and qualitatively new forms and permits humans, by the aid of extrinsic stimuli, *to control their behavior from the outside.* The use of signs leads humans to a specific structure of behavior that breaks away from biological development and creates new forms of a culturally-based psychological process. (Vygotsky, 1978, p. 39–40)

Vygotsky distinguished between two interrelated types of mediating instruments in human activity: tools and signs. The latter belonged to the broader category of "psychological tools."

The tool's function is to serve as the conductor of human influence on the object of activity; it is *externally* oriented; it must lead to changes in objects. It is a means by which a human external activity is aimed at mastering, and triumphing over, nature. (Vygotsky, 1978, p. 55)

Psychological tools have a different character.

They are directed toward the mastery or control of behavioral processes – someone else's or one's own – just as technical means are directed toward the control of processes of nature.

The following can serve as examples of psychological tools and their complex systems: language; various systems for counting; mnemonic techniques; algebraic symbol systems; works of art; writing; schemes, diagrams, maps, and mechanical drawings; all sorts of conventional signs; etc. (Vygotsky, 1981, p. 137)

Both technical tools and psychological tools mediate activity. But only psychological tools imply and require reflective mediation, consciousness of one's (or the other person's) procedures. Vygotsky (1978, p. 54) describes these two types of instruments as *parallel,* as "subsumed under the same category" of mediated activity. However, a little later in the same text he characterizes their relation in *hierarchical* terms.

The use of artificial means, the transition to mediated activity, fundamentally changes all psychological operations just as the use of tools limitlessly broadens the range of activities within which the new psychological functions may operate. In this context, we can use the term *higher* psychological function, or *higher behavior* as referring to the combination of tool and sign in psychological activity. (Vygotsky, 1978, p. 55)

The latter, hierarchical characterization is essential. In my interpretation, we may actually distinguish between two levels of mediation: the primary level of mediation by tools and gestures *dissociated from one another* (where gestures are not yet real psychological tools), and the secondary level of mediation by tools *combined with* corresponding signs or other psychological tools. The acquisition and application of new tools *broaden* the sphere of influence. The acquisition and application of new psychological tools *elevate* the level of influence (potentially; the result is actually achieved only when the tool and the psychological tool meet each other).

The essence of psychological tools is that they are originally instruments for cooperative, communicative, and self-conscious shaping and controlling of the procedures of using and making technical tools (including the human hand). This original function is well demonstrated in Tran Duc Thao's (1984) analysis of the emergence of developed indicative gestures and first representations among prehominids. I would contend that this formation of psychological tools (= secondary instruments) through the combination of previously separate gestures and technical tools (= primary instruments) is actually the essence of what Mead called the emergence of "significant gestures" or "significant symbols" and of what Trevarthen calls "secondary intersubjectivity."

The idea of primary and secondary instruments is clearly expressed by Marx Wartofsky.

> What constitutes a distinctively human form of action is the creation and use of artifacts, as tools, in the production of the means of existence and in the reproduction of the species. *Primary* artifacts are those directly used in this production; *secondary* artifacts are those used in the preservation and transmission of the acquired skills or modes of action or praxis by which this production is carried out. Secondary artifacts are therefore *representations* of such modes of action, and in this sense are *mimetic,* not simply of the *objects* of an environment which are of interest or use in this production, but of these objects as they are acted upon, or of the mode of operation or action involving such objects. Canons of representation, therefore, have a large element of convention, corresponding to the change or evolution of different forms of action or *praxis,* and thus cannot be reduced to some simple notion of "natural" semblance or resemblance. Nature, or the world becomes a world-for-us, in this process, by the mediation of such representations. (Wartofsky, 1979, p. 202)

Wartofsky calls secondary artifacts "reflexive embodiments." He points out that their mode may be gestural, oral, or visual, but "obviously such that they may be communicated in one or more sense-modalities" (Wartofsky, 1979, p. 201). These representations "are not 'in the mind', as mental entities"; they are "externally embodied representations" (Wartofsky, 1979, p. 202; see also Keiler & Schurig, 1978, p. 146–147).

For me, Wartofsky's secondary artifacts and Vygotsky's psychological tools are essentially the same thing. Vygotsky's intellectualist bias (see Leontiev & Luria, 1968, p. 354–355) led to a somewhat one-sided emphasis on signs and word meanings. The broader category of psychological tools, as well as the exciting relations between technical and psychological tools, were not elaborated concretely by Vygotsky. Ironically, the activity-oriented approach in Soviet psychology after Vygotsky tried to get rid of Vygotsky's intellectualism by neglecting the problem of signs and psychological tools in general: "If the polemic with concrete works of Vygotsky on the problem of the sign was necessary and natural, the removal of this problematic – in principle – led only to a substantial 'narrowing' of the theory of activity" (Davydov & Radzikhovskii, 1985, p. 60). In the recent revival of Vygotskian studies, signs may again be treated too much "on their own," separated from the spectrum of psychological tools and their relations with primary tools. This danger seems to lure in even outstanding analysis, such as that of Wertsch's (1985b) work on Vygotsky's concept of semiotic mediation.

According to Vygotsky, the instrumentally mediated act "is the simplest segment of behavior that is dealt with by research based on elementary units" (Vygotsky, 1981, p. 140). On the other hand, as V. P. Zinchenko (1985, p. 100) demonstrates, in concrete research, especially in *Thinking and Speech,* Vygotsky used another basic unit of analysis, namely, that of meaning or word meaning.

V. P. Zinchenko (1985, p. 100) argues that meaning "cannot be accepted as a self-sufficient analytic unit since in meaning there is no 'motive force' for its own transformation into consciousness." Only the cognitive aspect of thinking is fixed in meaning; the affective and volitional aspect is left unexplained.

The author then suggests that the adequate unit is tool-mediated action – which is actually the same thing as Vygotsky's instrumental act. Furthermore, as V. P. Zinchenko (1985, p. 103) correctly states, "One can consider tool-mediated action as being very close to meaning as unit of analysis" because "of necessity, tool-mediated action gives rise both to object meaning and to categorical meaning."

But V. P. Zinchenko fails to demonstrate how the suggested unit of tool-mediated action will overcome the limitations inherent in the unit of meaning. Tool-mediated action in no way solves the problems of motivation, emotion, and creation. To the contrary, it seems that both meaning and tool-mediated action are formations of the same structural level. This is the level of goal-directed individual cognition, the "rational level" of human functioning. The problems of motivation, emotion, and creation seem to be unanswerable on this level. They belong to a higher, collective and – paradoxically – less conscious level of functioning. Shoots of this line of analysis are visible in Vygotsky's insistence on the concept of *higher* psychological functions. But this hierarchical aspect of Vygotsky's conception is left undeveloped by V. P. Zinchenko.

As a matter of fact, P. I. Zinchenko (father of V. P. Zinchenko) came close to this problem is his 1939 article. In a critical review of Vygotsky's ideas of the instrumental act, he wrote the following rather opaque lines.

> But, in Vygotsky's thinking, the relationship of the means to its object was divorced from the subject's relationship to reality considered in its actual and complete content. In the strict sense, this relationship between the means and the object was a logical rather than a psychological relationship. But the history of social development cannot be reduced to the history of the development of culture.... The history of cultural development must be included in the history of society's social and economic development; it must be considered in the context of the particular social and economic relationships that determine the origin and development of culture. (Zinchenko, 1983–1984, p. 70)

However, the problem of a level of functioning beyond separate actions is also present in the most thoughtful cognitivist analyses – if only in the form of an intriguing mystery. Thus, V. P. Zinchenko ends his article by taking up the notion of "liberated action."

> According to specialists in the prevention of aviation catastrophes, in complex flying conditions humans and machines turn out to be, as it were, outside of time (we have in mind here the 'time' of consciously controlled decisions and actions). It is precisely this fact that provides the potential for avoiding catastrophes. But where does this potential originate? Or must we assume in such cases, as a minimum, a double reading of time – that is, actual situational time and a suprasituational time that flows in the space of the activity itself? And must we also assume their coordination? But by whom are they coordinated? Is there a subject who is responsible for this act of coordination?

The obvious precondition here is the subject's loss of self-control (i.e., the separation of the personal "I" from the situation and, consequently, its separation not only from the time of objects but from the time of the subject as well). This means that the "I" is "outside of time." This kind of "switching off" may not affect the possibility of self-reflection on the actions being performed. But the subject does not plan or control their realization. It is the subject's observing beyond himself or herself that may give him or her the possibility of fixing actions in memory....

In fact, we find that in such situations we are faced with liberated or unloosed action. And as the ancients said, a liberated person does not make mistakes....

The timelessness of liberated action in situations that are critical for the subject is like the timelessness of acts of creation, acts of brutality, and acts of discovery. In all of these the necessary condition is the liberation or unfettering of the subject, the repudiation of strict subjectivity. (Zinchenko, 1985, p. 112–114)

Zinchenko's lines remind us of Jung's concept of the collective psyche (Chapter 1). It is more than a mere coincidence that Sir Frederic Bartlett (1941) took up the same question of a superior level of functioning using the same example of extreme situations in flying. While Zinchenko discusses instances when the individual performance goes beyond the expected, Bartlett, as reported by Broadbent, discussed cases when the individual performance deteriorates dramatically.

The Cambridge laboratory had been looking at the breakdown of skill in RAF pilots flying on a simulator. The full task was to control height, course, and air speed as well as to undertake peripheral functions. Bartlett quotes data showing that prolonged performance of one part of the task by itself showed no decline in efficiency; but that when all the parts were being done together, there was such a drop. Instead of attributing the drop to over-loading of a single level, he says, "It is not the local response that has lost its accuracy or its power. It is the central control which has functionally, but without knowledge, expanded the limits of its indifference range." Not the isolated tasks, but the way they fit together. He notes that conscious verbal report comes only from one of the levels involved; he discusses the fact that the pilots were frequently quite unaware that their skills had deteriorated, and rather blamed the experimenter or the apparatus for any apparent error. (Broadbent, 1977, p. 183)

The problem with both Zinchenko and Broadbent (of Bartlett I am not sure; see Edwards & Middleton, 1986) is that they are seeking the explanation to essentially superindividual phenomena within the individual head. Flying typically is an activity with an elaborate "infrastructure" of interaction and division of labor (between the pilot and the ground control, especially) – though it looks like a lonely job. Both the extraordinary performances and the unexpected breakdowns might be fruitfully analyzed from that angle. Zinchenko's timeless subject might also acquire some flesh and blood that way.

The problem of levels in human functioning was theoretically worked out by A. N. Leont'ev, a collaborator and pupil of Vygotsky.

> When a member of a group performs his labour activity he also does it to satisfy one of his needs. A beater, for example, taking part in a primaeval collective hunt, was stimulated by a need for food or, perhaps, by a need for clothing, which the skin of the dead animal would meet for him. At what, however, was his activity directly aimed? It may have been directed, for example, at frightening a herd of animals and sending them toward other hunters, hiding in ambush. That, properly speaking, is what should be the result of the activity of this man. And the activity of this individual member of the hunt ends with that. The rest is completed by the other members. This result, i.e., the frightening of game, etc., understandably does not in itself, and may not, lead to satisfaction of the beater's need for food, or the skin of the animal. What the processes of his activity were directed to did not, consequently, coincide with what stimulated them, i.e., did not coincide with the motive of his activity; the two were divided from one another in this instance. Processes, the object and motive of which do not coincide with one another, we shall call "actions". We can say, for example, that the beater's activity is the hunt, and the frightening of game his action. (Leontyev, 1981, p. 210)

> What unites the direct result of this activity with its final outcome? Obviously nothing other than the given individual's relation with the other members of the group, by virtue of which he gets his share of the bag from them, i.e., part of the product of their joint labor activity. This relationship, this connection is realised through the activity of other people, which means that it is the activity of other people that constitutes the objective basis of the specific structure of the human individual's activity, means that historically, i.e., through its genesis, the connection between the motive and the object of an action reflects objective social connections and relations rather than natural ones. (Leontyev, 1981, p. 212)

These lines, originally published in 1947, demonstrate the insufficiency of an individual tool-mediated action as a unit of psychological analysis. Without consideration of the overall collective activity, the individual beater's action seems "senseless and unjustified" (Leontyev, 1981, p. 213). Human labor, the mother form of all human activity, is cooperative from the very beginning. We may well speak of the activity *of the individual,* but never of *individual activity;* only actions are individual.

Furthermore, what distinguishes one activity from another is its object. According to Leont'ev, the object of an activity is its true motive. Thus, the concept of activity is necessarily connected with the concept of motive. Under the conditions of division of labor, the individual participates in activities mostly without being fully conscious of their objects and motives. The total activity seems to control the individual, instead of the individual's controlling the activity.

Activities are realized by goal-directed actions, subordinated to conscious purposes. These are the typical objects of the cognitive psychology of skills and performances, whether they are motor or mental.

But human practice is not just a series or a sum of actions. In other words, "activity is a molar, not an additive unit" (Leont'ev, 1978, p. 50).

> Correspondingly, actions are not special "units" that are included in the structure of activity. Human activity does not exist except in the form of action or a chain of actions. (Leont'ev, 1978, p. 64)

On the other hand, one and the same action may accomplish various activities and may transfer from one activity to another. And one motive may obviously find expression in various goals and actions.

Finally actions are carried out in variable concrete circumstances. The methods with which the action is accomplished are called operations. Actions are related to conscious goals, operations to conditions not often consciously reflected by the subject. Tools are crystallized operations.

> Thus in the total flow of activity that forms human life, in its higher manifestations mediated by psychic reflection, analysis isolates separate (specific) activities in the first place according to the criterion of motives that elicit them. Then actions are isolated – processes that are subordinated to conscious goals, finally, operations that directly depend on the conditions of attaining concrete goals. (Leont'ev, 1978, p. 66–67)

The hunting example demonstrates the development from activity to actions as the consequence of division of labor. There is also the opposite direction of development, often neglected in the interpretation of Leont'ev's work. Actions may develop into an activity.

> These are the ordinary cases when a person undertakes to perform some actions under the influence of a certain motive, and then performs them for their own sake because the motive seems to have been displaced to

their objective. And that means that the actions are transformed into activity. (Leontyev, 1981, p. 238)

In a pathological case, some separate actions become the meaning and motive of the whole life of an individual – be they drinking or preaching (see Leont'ev, 1978, p. 112–113). This implies that the tasks or actions (including their objects) themselves are not objectively transformed. They are attributed an overwhelming illusionary importance and often a repetitively increased volume. This is the kernel of Jung's concept of "inflation," discussed in Chapter 1.

In the expansive case, the actions themselves are objectively transformed.

Motives of activity that have such an origin are conscious motives. They do not become conscious, however, of themselves, automatically. It requires a certain, special activity, some special act. This is an act of reflecting the relation of the motive of a given, concrete activity to the motive of a wider activity, that realises a broader, more general life relation that includes the given, concrete activity. (Leontyev, 1981, p. 238)

I shall later substantiate the proposal that in this very passage, pointing out the necessity of some "special activity," Leont'ev actually foresees the psychological core of what will be the concept of learning activity, or learning by expanding.

For Leont'ev, activity is a systemic formation in constant internal movement.

In this process man's cognition of the objects takes place, exceeding the possibilities of direct sensory reflection. If in direct action, "subject-object," the latter discloses its properties only within limits conditioned by the kind and degree of subtlety that the subject can sense, then in the process of interaction mediated by an instrument, cognition goes beyond these limits. Thus, in mechanical processing of an object made of one material with an object made of another, we carry out an unmistakable test of their relative hardness within limits completely inaccessible to our organs of skin-muscle sensitivity: On the basis of the change of form of one of the objects, we draw a conclusion about the greater hardness of the other. In this sense the instrument is the first real abstraction. (Leont'ev, 1978, p. 23)

In activity there does take place a transfer of an object into its subjective form, into an image; also in activity a transfer of activity into its objective results, into its products, is brought about. Taken from this point of view, activity appears as a process in which mutual transfers between the poles "subject-object" are accomplished. (Leont'ev, 1978, p. 50)

Hans Joas (1980), Klaus Ottomeyer (1980), and some other interaction-
ists criticize Leont'ev and his followers for a one-sided emphasis on the
instrumental-productive aspect of activity and for a neglect of the social
and communicative aspect. The preceding citations seem to support this
criticism.

But a fair reading gives a more sophisticated picture.

> Another condition [besides the instrumental; Y. E.] is that the individ-
> ual's relations with the world of human objects should be mediated by
> his relations with people, and that these relations should be included in
> a process of intercourse. This condition is always present. For the notion
> of an individual, a child, who is all by itself with the world of objects is a
> completely artificial abstraction.
>
> The individual, the child, is not simply thrown into the human world; it
> is introduced into this world by the people around it, and they guide it in
> that world. (Leontyev, 1981, p. 135)
>
> Only through a relation with other people does man relate to nature itself,
> which means that labour appears from the very beginning as a process
> mediated by tools (in the broad sense) and at the same time mediated
> socially. (Leontyev, 1981, p. 208)

And Meshcheryakov, a disciple of Leont'ev, calls the unit of analysis "shared
object activity" (Meshcheryakov, 1979, p. 294).

> A kind of vicious circle develops: in order to know how to act with the
> tool the child has to know it, and in order to know the tool it is essential
> that the child act with it. The vicious circle is broken when the adult
> begins to teach the child to act with the tool in the process of satisfying
> its needs. This instruction is only possible in the form of joint object
> action shared between the adult and the child. (Meshcheryakov, 1979,
> p. 296)

The problem is that the instrumental and the communicative aspect of activity were not merged into a unified complex model by Leont'ev. Vygotsky's
model of the instrumental act (Figure 2.3) was not graphically superseded
in Leont'ev's work.

This incomplete unification of the two aspects of activity in Leont'ev's work
provided room for Lomov's (1980) attempt to separate activity and communication as the two spheres of the life process of the individual. According to
Lomov, activity should be understood as the relation subject-object, while
communication comprises the relation subject-subject. This dualistic conception was heavily criticized by A. N. Leont'ev's son, A. A. Leont'ev. According

to him, activity cannot be legitimately characterized as individual; rather it is social in all its components (A. A. Leontjew, 1980, p. 527).

> Thus, when we are dealing with joint activity, we can with full justification speak of a *collective subject* or of a total subject of this activity, whose interrelation with the "individual" subjects can only be comprehended through a psychological analysis of the structure of the joint activity. (A. A. Leontjew, 1980, p. 530)

Thus, communication for A. A. Leontev is an integral aspect of every activity. On the other hand, communication may also differentiate into its own specialized activity system – very clearly in various forms of mass communication, for example. But in this case, it retains all the basic elements of activity (including the aspect of internal communication within it).

A. A. Leontev's point is convincing enough. But he, too, refrained from producing a more adequate unified model of activity. In other words, the essential elements and inner relations of activity were not comprehensively analyzed and modeled by either the older or the younger Leontev.

Symptomatically, this problem was more recently taken up in Soviet discussion, this time by Radzikhovskii (1984).

> This morphological paradigm [of A. N. Leontev; *Y. E.*] does not ... explain very well why activity should change as a consequence of the real or imagined presence of other people; nor does it answer the question of wherein, from the psychological point of view, lies the qualitative difference between "another" person and any other physical object, e.g., questions associated with communication, interaction, etc.... The social nature of motives and means of activity is by no means reflected in a specific structure of activity; this social nature is invariant relative to this structure. (Radzikhovskii, 1984, p. 37)

Radzikhovskii's most important argument is that "the genesis of activity itself is not illuminated, i.e., the structural-genetic original unit from which the structure of activity ... unfolds is not demonstrated" (Radzikhovskii, 1984, p. 40). The author proposes "social action" or "joint action" as the alternative unit of analysis.

> Concretely, we are saying that the general structure of ontogenetically primary joint activity (or, more accurately, primary joint action) includes at least the following elements: subject (child), object, subject (adult). The object here also has a symbolic function and plays the role of the primary sign. In fact, the child's movement toward, and manipulation of, an object, even when he is pursuing the goal of satisfying a vital need,

is also simultaneously a sign for an adult: to help, to intervene, to take part.... In other words, true communication, communication through signs, takes place here between the adult and the child. An objective act is built up around the object as an object, and sign communication is built up around the same object as the sign. Communication and the objective act coincide completely here, and can be separated only artificially. (Radzikhovskii, 1984, p. 44)

The unit defined above should be seen as genetically earlier (in ontogeny), as determining the basic internal sign structure of human activity, and, finally, as a universal unit and a component of individual activity. (Radzikhovskii, 1984, p. 49)

At first glance, Radzikhovskii is merely adopting the neo-Meadian conception of activity, exemplified in Trevarthen's model of secondary intersubjectivity (Figure 2.2). However, Radzikhovskii's account of the genesis of "primary joint action" differs substantially from those of Mead and Trevarthen. For Radzikhovskii, the use of the sign in the primary joint action is nonconscious and completely fused into the action on the object. For Mead, this kind of sign usage is something that precedes the specifically human stage of conscious "significant gestures." And Trevarthen's elaborate data show that up to nine months the infant's gestures and object actions are *separate,* not fused. Their combination (not merger) is a developmental achievement, signifying a new level in the child's self-consciousness.

Actually this very same principle was formulated by El'konin in 1971. El'konin pointed out that the dominant thought form in psychology splits development into two mutually disjointed spheres: the need-motivational sphere, on the one hand, and the cognitive-instrumental sphere, on the other hand. The former represents the "world of people," the latter the "world of things." This dichotomous thought form is by no means merely a subjective fancy. It reflects rather accurately, though nonconsciously, the historical division of labor within class societies, "rearing certain children primarily as performers of the operational and technical aspects of labor while educating others chiefly as bearers of the objectives and motives of that activity" (El'konin, 1977, p. 552).

If things are viewed as physical objects and other people as random individuals, then the child's adaptation to these "two worlds" actually does seem to proceed along two parallel, fundamentally independent lines. (El'konin, 1977, p. 547)

If we look at the formation of personality in the system "child in society," we can see how the links in the systems "child-thing" and "child-individual

adult" assume a radically different character. They change from two independent systems into one unified system. And, as a result, the content of each
system is essentially changed. When we examine the system "child-thing"
we now see that things, possessing definite physical and spatial properties, appear to the child as social objects: it is the socially evolved modes of
action with these objects that predominate. (El'konin, 1977, p. 549)

It almost seems that Radzikhovskii's description of the "primary joint
action" might correspond to the actual structure of animal activity preceding humanity in evolutionary terms. Radzikhovskii's nearly total neglect of
the role of material production and material instruments (and their relations to signs and other "psychological tools") supports this conclusion.

In spite of its rather regressive outcome, Radzikhovskii's attempt is a
symptom of the existence of an unsolved problem in the Vygotsky-Leont'ev
tradition.

This third lineage, from Vygotsky to Leont'ev, gives birth to the concept
of activity based on material production, mediated by technical and psychological tools as well as by other human beings. This is the lineage I will
try to continue and develop. The next task is to derive a model of the structure of human activity through genetic analysis.

THE EVOLUTION OF ACTIVITY

The general mode of biological adaptation as the animal form of activity
may be depicted as follows (Figure 2.4).

A central tenet embedded in this model is the immediately collective
and populational character of animal activity and species development (see
Jensen, 1981). Species is seen as a systemic formation, as a "methodology
of survival," produced to solve the contradiction between population and
nature. In this formation, the prototype and the procedure define each
other in a complementary manner.

The adaptive nature of animal activity does not mean passive acquies-
cence in the demands and pressures of nature. As Lewontin (1982, p. 160–
161) shows, organisms and environments always penetrate each other in
several ways.

> The importance of these various forms of dialectical interaction between
> organism and environment is that we cannot regard evolution as the
> "solution" by species of some predetermined environmental "problems"
> because it is the life activities of the species themselves that determine
> both the problems and the solutions simultaneously.... Organisms

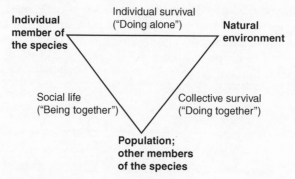

FIGURE 2.4. The general structure of the animal form of activity.

within their individual lifetimes and in the course of their evolution as species do not *adapt* to environments; they *construct* them. (Lewontin, 1982, p. 162–163)

On higher levels of animal evolution, we witness ruptures in each of the three sides of the triangle depicted in Figure 2.4. The uppermost side of "individual survival" is ruptured by the emerging utilization of tools, most clearly demonstrated by the anthropoid apes (see Schurig, 1976). The left-hand side of "social life" is ruptured by collective traditions, rituals, and rules, originating at the crossing of adaptation and mating. The right-hand side of "collective survival" is ruptured by division of labor, influenced by the practices of breeding, upbringing, and mating and appearing first as the evolving division of labor between the sexes.

These ruptures cannot be comprehended "simply as a linear process of higher development, but rather as a process in which, under the influence of various different evolutionary factors, differing competing lines of development may have emerged" (Keiler, 1981, p. 150). Anthropoid apes are the prime example of the rupture by tools. Dolphins, with their extraordinary "capacity to organize many individuals into a system which operates as a whole" (Keiler 1981, 151), may be a prime example of the ruptures in "doing together" and "being together."

This stage of "ruptures" is actually the still quite dim transitional field between animal and man. It may be depicted with the help of Figure 2.5.

Anthropoid apes do not make and preserve tools systematically. Tool making and tool utilization are still exceptional rather than dominant forms of their activity. The activity of dolphins may be assessed analogously.

The fact ... that the transition from animal psyche to human consciousness is not completed in the case of the dolphins is ... to be explained by

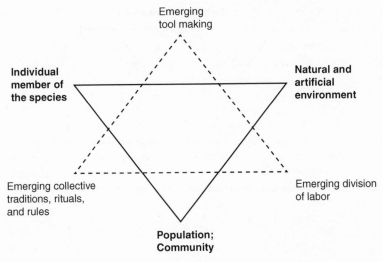

FIGURE 2.5. Structure of activity in transition from animal to man.

the circumstance that there is no active, instrumentally mediated, appropriation of material reality within the social behavior of dolphins parallel to the use and preparation of external aids for the completion of operations such as is found in the phylogenetic line of the apes, and which can be seen as an anticipation of human productive (that is, mediated by tools) activity at the animal level. However complex the social life of dolphins may be, the relationships that arise within it are not coordinated by "the activity of production", they are not determined by it and do not depend upon it. (Keiler, 1981, p. 153)

The breakthrough into human cultural evolution – into the specifically human form of activity – requires that what used to be *separate ruptures* or emerging mediators become *unified determining factors*. At the same time, what used to be ecological and natural becomes economic and historical.

Since intentional action is frequently co-operative and socially regulated in non-human primates, it makes more sense to derive co-operation from social interactions where it already exists than from object-using programs where it does not. Consequently, a theory of the evolution of human technology should place less emphasis on differences in the tool-using capacities between human and apes (important as they are) but ask instead how emergent tool-using capacities become integrated into the domain of intentional social action. (Reynolds, 1982, p. 382; see also Reynolds, 1981)

Richard Leakey and Roger Lewin propose an elegant sketch of this original integration. They point out that humans are the only primates who *collect* food to be eaten later. In their mixed economy, the early humans did this both by gathering plants and by scavenging and hunting meat. However, "sharing, not hunting or gathering as such, is what made us human" (Leakey & Lewin, 1983, p. 120).

> The invention of a primitive container – the first carrier bag – transformed the early hominids' subsistence ecology into a food-sharing economy. The digging stick may have come before or after the carrier bag, but, important though it was, it lacked the social impact of the container: the digging stick may have made life easier, but it didn't usher in an entirely new life-style. (Leakey & Lewin, 1983, p. 127)

Another point of integration was the emergence of collectively organized tool making, concentrated on steady campsites (Leakey & Lewin, 1983, p. 83; 128).

The paleoanthropological ideas of Leakey and Lewin correspond to the philosophical point made by Peter Ruben.

> Every social system is faced with the analytical problem of dividing the total product into necessary and surplus product. And the regulations created for distribution of these products provide the norms for "justice" in each system. So the existence of a surplus of labor beyond necessary labor is given *a priori* in every system of labor, and one can say that sociality, in contrast to individuality, is perceivable exactly in this surplus product.... It is the struggle for the surplus product that constituted sociality! ... Thus, a social mechanism that is especially a mechanism of political domination ... does not serve as a genetical precondition for bringing about the surplus product, but as a means for its quantitative expansion. (Ruben, 1981, p. 128–129)

The whole structure of activity is thus reorganized (Figure 2.6).

The model depicted in Figure 2.6 is a logical continuation of the transitional model depicted in Figure 2.5. What used to be adaptive activity is transformed into consumption and subordinated to the three dominant aspects of human activity – production, distribution, and exchange (or communication).

The model suggests the possibility of analyzing a multitude of relations within the triangular structure of activity. However, the essential task is always to grasp the systemic whole, not just separate connections. Here the analysis provided by Karl Marx in the introduction to *Grundrisse* is essential.

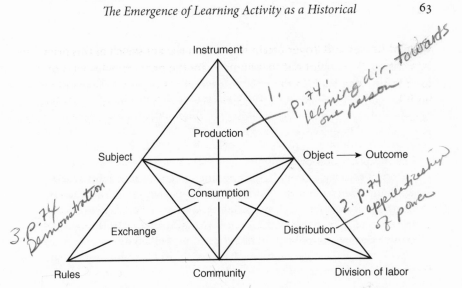

FIGURE 2.6. The structure of human activity.

> Production creates the objects which correspond to the given needs; distribution divides them up according to social laws; exchange further parcels out the already divided shares in accord with individual needs; and finally, in consumption, the product steps outside this social movement and becomes a direct object and servant of individual need, and satisfies it in being consumed. Thus production appears to be the point of departure, consumption as the conclusion, distribution and exchange as the middle. (Marx, 1973, p. 89)

Marx goes on to show that matters are not so simple as this. Production is always also consumption of the individual's abilities and of the means of production. Correspondingly, consumption is also production of the human beings themselves. Furthermore, distribution seems to be not just a consequence of production but also its immanent prerequisite in the form of distribution of instruments of production and distribution of members of the society among the different kinds of production. Finally, exchange, too, is found inside production, in the form of communication, interaction, and exchange of unfinished products between the producers.

Does this mean that the boundaries between the subtriangles of Figure 2.6 are blurred and eventually given up?

> The conclusion we reach is not that production, distribution, exchange and consumption are identical, but that they all form the members of a totality, distinctions within a unity. Production predominates not only over itself, in the antithetical definition of production, but over the other

moments as well. The process always returns to production to begin anew. That exchange and consumption cannot be predominant is self-evident. Likewise, distribution as distribution of products; while as distribution of the agents of production it is itself a moment of production. A definite production thus determines a definite consumption, distribution and exchange as well as *definite relations between these different moments.* Admittedly, however, *in its one-sided form,* production is itself determined by the other moments. For example if the market, i.e., the sphere of exchange, expands, then production grows in quantity and the divisions between its different branches become deeper. A change in distribution changes production, e.g., concentration of capital, different distribution of the population between town and country, etc. Finally, the needs of consumption determine production. Mutual interaction takes place between the different moments. This is the case with every organic whole. (Marx, 1973, p. 99–100)

Marx's notions of "the antithetical definition of production" and of production "in its one-sided form," especially when applied to the earliest simple forms of societal organization, seem to refer to the double existence of production as *both* the whole activity system of Figure 2.6 *and* the uppermost subtriangle or action type of that system.

Take the primordial gatherer-hunters described by Leakey and Lewin. The total practice of their life may be called production in the broad sense. On the other hand, they used only a certain amount of time in gathering and hunting – these may be called *production* in the narrow sense. The sharing of the food produced was a distinctive part of their daily life – it may be called *distribution.* Having obtained their shares of the food, they ate them – *consumption.* Finally, there was "a good deal of spare time" (Leakey & Lewin, 1983, p. 126) used in various forms of social interaction – *exchange.*

In other words, each subtriangle in Figure 2.6 is potentially an activity of its own. Within the total practice of the society, the subtriangles are initially only actions since their *object* is still a relatively undifferentiated whole (mainly food) and the temporal, spatial, and social boundaries between them are fluid. As Leakey and Lewin (1983, p. 109) point out, "There are no separate living areas and 'workshop' areas" and, likewise, "no specialists in gatherer-hunter communities." However, demanding tasks such as hunting very early acquire a division of labor of their own and become relatively independent activities, as was shown in Leont'ev's hunting example earlier in this chapter.

In a more complex and differentiated society, there exist a multitude of relatively independent activities, representing all the subtriangles. But within any such relatively independent activity system, we find *the same internal structure* as depicted in Figure 2.6. Thus, an activity representing, for example, exchange within the total societal practice (e.g., a leisure time hobby activity) has within it the subtriangles of production, distribution, exchange, and consumption. This has the important implication that *there is no activity without the component of production;* only actions may be void of it.

The specificity of human production is that it yields more than what goes into the immediate reproduction of the subjects of production. One part of this "more" is the surplus product that leads to sharing and sociality, discussed by Leakey and Lewin and Ruben previously. The other part is the tools and instruments created for and within the process of production.

> From them the process of labor can begin each time anew, and in such way that it is not only a repetition of the same process but a repetition on the basis of changed conditions, i.e., of conditions created and extended by the subjects themselves. ... With regard to the specificity of the human labor process, this means that it is a process of tendentially extended reproduction. (Damerow, Furth, Heidtmann & Lefèvre, 1980, p. 238)

In a complex society, "the antithetical definition of production" refers primarily to the simultaneous existence of productive activity (1) in the form of the total practice of the society *and* (2) in the form of the numerous specific productive activities within the same society. Damerow, Furth, Heidtmann, and Lefèvre (1980, p. 241) call the former "the concrete general labor" and the latter "the concrete specific labor."

The model of Figure 2.6 may now be compared with the four criteria of a root model of human activity, set forth earlier in this chapter.

First, I argue that the model is actually the smallest and most simple unit that still preserves the essential unity and integral quality behind any human activity. The simpler models presented in Figures 2.1 to 2.5 have been shown to be either oversimplifications or representations of genetically earlier forms of activity. Such simplifications may naturally be useful when applied in contexts demanding focusing on or abstraction of certain aspects of human activity. However, reduction requires conscious justification in order not to become distortion.

Second, I maintain that with the help of this model activity can be analyzed in its inner dynamic relations and historical change. However, this claim must be substantiated by using and transforming the model in the analysis of the development of concrete activities. In this chapter, the cultural evolution of learning will serve as such a developmental problem. In

Chapters 3 and 4, four historical cases of activity development are analyzed. Before these analyses can be carried out, the concept of *inner contradictions* must be introduced as the source of dynamics and development in human activity (next section).

With regard to the *third* and *fourth* criteria (activity as a contextual and ecological phenomenon; activity as a mediated phenomenon), the status of the model of Figure 2.6 is rather evident.

INNER CONTRADICTIONS OF HUMAN ACTIVITY

The basic internal contradiction of human activity is its *dual existence* as the total societal production *and* as one specific production among many. This means that any specific production must at the same be *independent of and subordinated to* the total societal production (see Damerow, Furth, Heidtmann & Lefèvre, 1980, p. 240–241). Within the structure of any specific productive activity, the contradiction is renewed as the clash between *individual actions and the total activity system*. This fundamental contradiction acquires a different historical form in each socioeconomic formation.

The fundamental contradiction arises out of the division of labor.

Division of labour in a society, and the corresponding tying down of individual to a particular calling, develops itself ... from opposite starting points. Within a family, and ... within a tribe, there springs up naturally a division of labour, caused by differences of sex and age, a division that is consequently based on a purely physiological foundation, which division enlarges its materials by the expansion of the community, by the increase of population, and more especially, by the conflicts between different tribes, and the subjugation of one tribe by another. On the other hand, ... the exchange of products springs up at the points where different families, tribes, communities, come in contact; for, in the beginning of civilization, it is not private individuals but families, tribes etc. that meet on an independent footing. Different communities find different means of production, and different means of subsistence in their natural environment. Hence, their modes of production, and of living, and their products are different. It is this spontaneously developed difference which, when different communities come in contact, calls forth the mutual exchange of products, and the consequent gradual conversion of those products into commodities. Exchange does not create the differences between the spheres of production, but brings what are already different into relation, and thus converts them into more or less interdependent branches of the collective production of an enlarged society. In the latter case, the social division of labour arises from the exchange between spheres of production, that are originally distinct and independent of each other. In the former, where the physiological division of labour is the starting point, the particular organs of a compact whole grow loose and break off, principally owing to the exchange of commodities with foreign communities, and then isolate themselves so far, that the sole bond, still connecting the various kinds of work, is the exchange of the products as commodities. In the one case, it is the making dependent what was before independent; in the other case, the making independent what was before dependent. (Marx, 1909, p. 344–345)

The two directions or "opposite starting points," *from within* an activity and *from between* two activities, are essential for the emerging concept of expansion, as will become clear in Chapter 3. Here, I shall focus on the dialectic between independency and subordination.

In precapitalist socioeconomic formations, the basic contradiction, the subordination of individual producers to the total system of production, took the form of immediately visible *personal suppression by force,* be it exercised by slave owners or feudal lords.

> The less social power the medium of exchange possesses (and at this stage it is still closely bound to the nature of the direct product of labour and the direct needs of the partners in exchange) the greater must be the power of the community which binds the individuals together, the patriarchal relation, the community of antiquity, feudalism and the guild system.... Relations of personal dependence (entirely spontaneous at the outset) are the first social forms in which human productive capacity develops only to a slight extent and at isolated points. (Marx, 1973, p. 157–158)

In capitalism, the contradiction acquires the general form of *commodity.* Commodity is an object that possesses *value* (i.e., *exchange value),* not only and not primarily *use value.* The value of the commodity is basically determined by the average necessary amount of social labor needed for its production. This entails "the reduction of all phenomena to 'labor in general', to labor devoid of all qualitative differences" (Ilyenkov, 1982, p. 97).

> As a general rule, articles of utility become commodities only because they are products of the labour of private individuals or groups of individuals who carry on their work independently of each other.... Since the producers do not come into social contact with each other until they exchange their products, the specific social character of each producer's labour does not show itself except in the act of exchange.... It is only by being exchanged that the products of labour acquire, as

values, one uniform social status, distinct from their varied forms of existence as objects of utility. This division of a product into a useful thing and a value becomes practically important only when exchange has acquired such an extension that useful articles are produced for the purpose of being exchanged, and their character as values has therefore to be taken into account, beforehand, during production. From this moment the labour of the individual producer acquires socially a two-fold character. On the one hand, it must, as a definite useful kind of labour, satisfy a definite social want, and thus hold its place as part and parcel of the collective labour of all, as a branch of a social division of labour that has sprung up spontaneously. On the other hand, it can satisfy the manifold wants of the individual producer himself, only in so far as the mutual exchangeability of all kinds of useful private labour is an established social fact, and therefore the private useful labour of each producer ranks on an equality with that of all others. (Marx, 1909, p. 44)

In capitalism, all things, activities, and relations become saturated by the dual nature of commodity – they become commodified. The relation between individual actions and collective activity, between specific productions and the total production, is transformed accordingly.

The reciprocal and all-sided dependence of individuals who are indifferent to one another forms their social connection. This social bond is expressed in *exchange value*, by means of which alone each individual's own activity or his product becomes an activity and a product for him; he must produce a general product – *exchange value*, or, the latter isolated for itself and individualized, *money*. On the other side, the power which each individual exercises over the activity of others or over social wealth exists in him as the owner of *exchange values*, of *money*. The individual carries his social power, as well as his bond with society, in his pocket. Activity, regardless of its individual manifestation, and the product of activity, regardless of its particular make-up, are always *exchange value*, and exchange value is a generality, in which all individuality and peculiarity are negated and extinguished....

The social character of activity, as well as the social form of the product, and the share of individuals in production here appears as something alien and objective, confronting the individuals, not as their relation to one another, but as their subordination to relations which subsist independently of them and which arise out of collisions between mutually indifferent individuals. The general exchange of activities and products, which has become a vital condition for each individual – their mutual interconnection – here appears as something alien to them, autonomous, as a thing. In exchange value, the social connection between persons is

selfish

transformed into a social relation between things; personal capacity into objective wealth. (Marx, 1973, p. 156–157)

The essential contradiction is the mutual exclusion and simultaneous mutual dependency of use value and exchange value in each commodity. This *double nature* and inner unrest are characteristic of all the corners of the triangular structure of activity. They penetrate the subject and community corners because labor force itself is a special kind of commodity.

Leont'ev recognized this contradiction as a necessary precondition for a scientific study of activity in capitalism.

Everything acquires a dual aspect under the dominance of private ownership of the means of production, viz., both man's own activity and the world of objects around him....

The doctor who buys a practice in some little provincial place may be very seriously trying to reduce his fellow citizens' suffering from illness, and may see his calling in just that. He must, however, want the number of the sick to increase, because his life and practical opportunity to follow his calling depend on that....

The penetration of these relations into consciousness also finds psychological reflection in a "disintegration" of its general structure characterized by the rise of an estrangement between the senses and meanings in which the world around man and his own life are refracted for him. (Leontyev, 1981, p. 254–255)

This is not just a subsidiary aspect for Leont'ev.

To ignore these peculiarities and remove them from the context of psychological research is to deprive psychology of historical concreteness, converting it into a science solely of the psyche of an abstract man, of "man in general."(Leontyev, 1981, p. 255)

Moreover, it is a question of a real contradiction, not of one-dimensional repression and alienation. In other words, there are competing opposite forces within the capitalist labor activity – positive as well as negative.

(a) It [labor, *Y. E.*] is positive as the means of his activity. They constitute real wealth, the "technical" side, so to speak, of his life; it is the wealth of knowledge, skills and know-how that he must possess in order to perform his labour activity.

(b) It is positive as a condition of the enriching of his life with a new content quite different to that proper of his alienated activity, but nevertheless engendered precisely by it. The worker in a capitalist mill not only alienates his labour; he enters into relations with other people in that way. (Leontyev, 1981, p. 256)

Marx points out this positive perspective in a more global fashion.

Since ... the autonomization of the world market (in which the activity of each individual is included) increases with the development of monetary relations (exchange value) and vice versa, since the general bond and all-round interdependence in production and consumption increase together with the independence and indifference of the consumers and producers to one another; since this contradiction leads to crises, etc., hence, together with the development of this alienation, and on the same basis, efforts are made to overcome it: institutions emerge whereby each individual can acquire information about the activity of all others and attempt to adjust his own accordingly, e.g. lists of current prices, rates of exchange, interconnections between those active in commerce through the mails, telegraphs etc. (the means of communication of course grow at the same time).... Although on the given standpoint, alienation is not overcome by these means, nevertheless relations and connections are introduced thereby which include the possibility of suspending the old standpoint. (Marx, 1973, p. 160–161)

Marx goes on to emphasize that the objective social bond of exchange value and market is a historical product brought about by the individuals. It is a necessary intermediate stage, producing not only alienation of the individual from himself and from others, but "also the universality and the comprehensiveness of his relations and capacities" (Marx, 1973, p. 162). Thus, it would be ridiculous romanticism to yearn for a return to an imaginary "original fullness."

Internal contradictions find their outward expressions in external ones. The latter are no less real, but derivative in genetic terms (see Ilyenkov, 1977, p. 334–335). In the analysis of human activity, four levels or layers of contradictions may be discerned. These levels may be illustrated with the help of Figure 2.7, an elaboration of the model of activity depicted in Figure 2.6.

The primary contradiction of activities in capitalist socioeconomic formations lives as the inner conflict between exchange value and use value within each corner of the triangle of activity.

The secondary contradictions are those appearing between the corners. The stiff hierarchical division of labor lagging behind and preventing the possibilities opened by advanced instruments is a typical example.

The tertiary contradiction appears when representatives of culture (e.g., teachers) introduce the object and motive of a culturally more advanced form of the central activity into the dominant form of the central activity. For example, the primary school pupil goes to school in order to play with his mates (the dominant motive), but the parents and the teacher try to

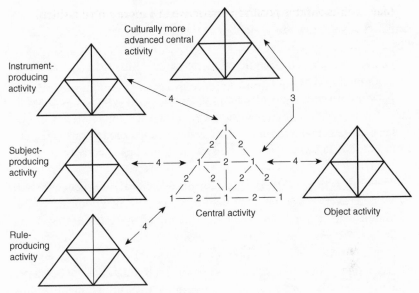

FIGURE 2.7. Four levels of contradictions within the human activity system.
Level 1: Primary inner contradiction (double nature) *within* each constituent component of the central activity.
Level 2: Secondary contradictions *between* the constituents of the central activity.
Level 3: Tertiary contradiction *between* the object/motive of the dominant form of the central activity and the object/motive of a culturally more advanced form of the central activity.
Level 4: Quaternary contradictions *between* the central activity *and* its neighbor activities.

make him study seriously (the culturally more advanced motive). The culturally more advanced object and motive may also be actively sought by the subjects of the central activity themselves.

The quaternary contradictions require that we take into consideration the essential "neighbor activities" linked with the central activity that is the original object of our study.

The "neighbor activities" include *first* of all the activities where the immediately appearing objects and outcomes of the central activity are embedded (let us call them object activities). *Second,* they include the activities that produce the key instruments for the central activity (instrument-producing activities), the most general representatives being science and art. *Third,* they include activities such as education and schooling of the subjects of the central activity (subject-producing activities). *Fourth,* they include such activities as administration and legislation (rule-producing activities). Naturally the "neighbor activities" also include central activities that are in some other way, for a longer or shorter period, connected or related to the given central activity, potentially hybridizing each other through their exchanges.

Now the quaternary contradictions are those that emerge between the central activity and the neighboring activity in their interaction. Conflicts and resistances appearing in the course of the "implementation" of the outcomes of the central activity in the system of the object activity are a case in point.

The work activity of physicians in primary medical care (general practitioners) may serve as an illustration of the four levels of contradictions.

The primary contradiction, the dual nature of use value and exchange value, may be analyzed by focusing on any of the corners of the "central activity" of the doctor. For example, *instruments* of this work activity include a tremendous variety of medications and drugs. But they are not just useful preparations – they are above all commodities with prices, manufactured for a market, advertised and sold for profit. Every doctor faces this contradiction in his or her daily decision making.

A typical secondary contradiction in this work activity would be the conflict between the traditional biomedical *conceptual instruments* concerning the classification of diseases and correct diagnosis, on the one hand, *and* the changing nature of the *objects,* namely, the increasingly ambiguous and complex problems and symptoms of the patients. These problems more and more often do not comply with the standards of classical diagnosis and nomenclature. They require an integrated social, psychological, and biomedical approach that may not yet exist.

A tertiary contradiction arises when, say, the administrators of the medical care system order the practitioners to employ certain new procedures corresponding to the ideals of a more holistic and integrated medicine. The new procedures may be formally implemented, but probably still subordinated to and resisted by the old general form of the activity.

Suppose that a doctor, working on such a new holistic and integrated basis, orders or suggests that the patient accept a new habit or conception and change his way of life in some respect. The patient may react with resistance. This is an instance of the quaternary contradictions. The patient's way of life or his "health behavior" is here the object activity. If patients are regarded as abstract symptoms and diseases, isolated from their activity contexts, it will be impossible to grasp the developmental dynamics of the central activity, too.

Contradictions are not just inevitable features of activity. They are "the principle of its self-movement and ... the form in which the development is cast" (Ilyenkov, 1977, p. 330). This means that new qualitative stages and forms of activity emerge as solutions to the contradictions of the preceding stage or form. This in turn takes place in the form of "invisible breakthroughs."

> In reality it always happens that a phenomenon which later becomes universal originally emerges as an individual, particular, specific phenomenon, as an exception from the rule. It cannot actually emerge in any other way. Otherwise history would have a rather mysterious form.

> Thus, any new improvement of labor, every new mode of man's action in production, before becoming generally accepted and recognized, first emerges as a certain deviation from previously accepted and codified norms. Having emerged as an *individual exception* from the rule in the labor of one or several men, the new form is then taken over by others, becoming in time a new *universal norm*. If the new norm did not originally appear in this exact manner, it would never become a really universal form, but would exist merely in fantasy, in wishful thinking. (Ilyenkov, 1982, p. 83–84)

After this important conclusion, Ilyenkov proceeds by pointing out that in thinking, a truly developed concept "directly includes in it a conception of the dialectics of the transformation of the individual and the particular into the universal" (Ilyenkov, 1982, p. 84). Recall here Leont'ev's point about the development of individual actions into activity. Leont'ev spoke of "reflecting the relation of the motive of a given, concrete activity to the motive of a wider activity." This kind of "reflecting" is actually the same as Ilyenkov's "developed concept." They are both preliminary formulations of the psychological and epistemological substance of learning activity.

In Chapter 3, I shall elaborate further on the analysis of contradictions as successive forms of the expansive development of a new activity.

ON THE CULTURAL EVOLUTION OF HUMAN LEARNING

"Learning activity" cannot be invented or simply be found by chance and afterwards be shaped into systematic theoretical concepts.

Nor does "learning activity" represent a pedagogical idea as such, that can be explained in terms of the history of pedagogical thinking, for instance in terms of "self-activity" in Renaissance pedagogy.

> Nor is "learning activity" being developed out of learning in school in some evolutionary and immanent way, as for example out of growing complexity of the organization and institution of instruction and school.
>
> "Learning activity" rather represents a fundamentally new type of learning in school, being fundamentally opposite to a thousand-year-old tradition of learning in school. (Fichtner, 1985, p. 47)

In other words, the concept of learning activity can only be constructed through a historical analysis of the inner contradictions of the presently dominant forms of societally organized human learning.

The original forms of human learning are those in which learning appears predominantly as an unintentional and inseparable aspect of the basic work activity (Alt, 1975; Wilhelmer, 1979). In terms of activity theory, this kind of incidental learning consists of nonconscious *learning operations*, embedded in the daily participation in joint work.

The emergence of first distinct, specialized forms of transmission of knowledge and experience brings about the first conscious *learning actions*. Three such early forms of transmission may be identified.

The first is situated in the uppermost subtriangle "production" within the structure of Figure 2.6. Fichtner (1985, p. 49) calls it "the transmission of handicrafts." It is embedded in the immediate context of productive work and directed to the single person, the individual apprentice. The second form of early transmission is situated in the subtriangle "distribution." It is essentially learning to divide and control the production and distribution of surplus; it could be called "the apprenticeship of power" – not surprisingly the least well known of the three forms of primitive transmission. Finally, the third form of early transmission is situated in the subtriangle "exchange." Initiation ceremonies are a typical example of this form.

> Here, systematic instruction is disconnected from "seriousness" and from any connection to everyday life and working in a spatial and temporal way.... Nothing is produced here, there is only demonstration of how to behave. This "demonstrating" can appear in quite different ways, but it is always directed to behavior in its social dimension ... never orientated to a single person but always to the whole group. (Fichtner, 1985, p. 49–50)

These three early forms of transmission generate such specific learning actions as "conscious imitation," "conscious memorizing," and "conscious trial and error." This does not mean that such "higher-order" cognitive performances as forming and testing hypotheses do not exist. They do take place (see Leakey & Lewin, 1983, p. 102–105), but not as actions aimed specifically at learning. Rather, they appear as actions aimed at solving problems of the production, distribution, and exchange themselves – not as actions aimed at *learning* to solve those problems. Specific learning actions are actions in which "the subject is consciously aware of the object of the action as an object of learning," to paraphrase Zinchenko. Thus, learning actions (even those of the first form of transmission) are already "off-line" from the viewpoint of the immediate aims of work activity. For that very reason, they remain relatively simple. Complicated reflective actions may be necessary in exceptional situations of the work activity. But it would be irrational to train novices with learning tasks of such an exceptional kind.

From this point on, the cultural evolution of human learning must be analyzed in a differentiated manner. The prerequisites of the emergence of learning as an independent activity system may be found by tracing the formation of learning actions within historically earlier types of societal activity. In the preceding sections, I sketched three theoretical lineages leading to the concept of activity. In the following, I shall consider three activity types as practical lineages leading to the formation of learning activity. These three are the activity of school going, the activity of work, and the activities of science and art.

School is the central socially organized institution that proclaims human learning as its objective. Schooling, or school going, as I shall here call it, is therefore an obvious candidate for the birthplace of learning activity.

However, as I pointed out earlier, learning originally takes place as an unintentional and inseparable aspect of the basic work activity. Learning at the workplace has continued its own line of development relatively independently of formal schooling. The historical transition from craft apprenticeship to industrial wage labor is often regarded one-dimensionally as gradual elimination of the learning potential of work. Yet recent empirical studies have seriously challenged this view, making work activity another candidate demanding closer analysis.

Learning has been characterized as a search for truth and beauty. On the other hand, science and art define themselves as activities dedicated to the search for those very same values. The difference between science/art and learning is commonly seen in that the former *produce* truth and beauty while the latter *reproduces* them. In the ideal case, it is said, learning also reproduces in essence the course of scientific/artistic production. This implies that human learning at its best is a simplified reproduction of scientific research and artistic creation. This gives us sufficient grounds to consider science and art as the third candidate for the birthplace of learning activity.

The First Lineage: Learning within School Going

The early forms of transmission are not yet schools. We know that during the past two thousand years or so, school has been the increasingly dominant organizational form of human learning. Two questions arise. First: What made schooling necessary? Second: What is the relationship between schooling and learning activity?

To understand the emergence of schooling, we must return to the difference between primary and secondary instruments. As long as the secondary instruments – those "used in the preservation and transmission of the acquired skills or modes of action" (Wartofsky 1979) – remain *specific* representations, their transmission and acquisition can be carried out by means of discrete learning actions of the types named previously. But the situation changes dramatically as soon as a truly *general* secondary instrument appears. Written language, more specifically that based on the phonetic alphabet, is such a general instrument.

> Using a phonetic alphabet, writing was radically separated from each figurative symbolism. It has become a system of signs, no longer representing things but words in such a way that words are visually present all at once, can be divided into segments and be put together again.... The letters of the phonetic alphabet no longer are symbols for facts, objects of a natural, social or divine order, but they are symbols for a process, namely symbols for the process of human speech.
>
> So there is no object being expressed but a relation to an object. Now it is possible to note down anything you can talk about. In principle, the system gets constructive by this simple possibility to combine. (Fichtner, 1985, p. 50)

Schools do indeed appear wherever people start reading and writing. In their very generality, reading and writing are such abstract or indirect instruments that they cannot be learned by simply participating in work activity. Writing seems to have been invented to help debit deliveries, register credits and compensations, stockpile and determine quantities of goods, and record capacities, volumes, amounts, sizes, incomes, and so on (see Schmandt-Besserat, 1978).

> Writing and reading soon grow to an administrative skill which can no longer be learnt spontaneously.... "Workshops for writing and reading" very early develop into writers' schools and then into writing schools which then do not only give instruction in the skilled techniques of reading and writing but also – to a certain extent – their contents.... To a

remarkable extent, instruction and school emerge, being fully developed and perfected, at the very same time as do written language and the necessity of its transmission. (Fichtner, 1985, p. 49)

Much good research has been done on the psychological consequences of literacy (e.g., Coulmas & Ehlich, 1982; Havelock, 1976; Olson, Torrance & Hildyard, 1985; Ong, 1982; Scribner & Cole, 1981). Research of this kind has revealed impressive powers peculiar to written language. In contrast to oral culture, written language entails a distinct tendency to decontextualization, to definiteness and explicitness. Language acquires an autonomous, self-sufficient mode of existence – it becomes text. The storing, transport, and transmission of knowledge are greatly enhanced. Phonetic writing opens up the metalinguistic function of language. Because of its fixed nature, text brings forth reflective awareness and analysis of language. This property makes possible important strides in the development of logical thinking.

One could think that such a powerful instrument would make schools centers of critical, productive, and experimental activity – that all doors would be opened for imagination and reflective thinking. But this was not the case. Learning remained "reproductive and receptive" (Fichtner, 1985, p. 51).

> Neither the traditional wisdom peddled by the rhetoricians, nor the theoretical analysis of the philosophers, could contribute at all usefully to the solution of contemporary problems.... Except for the fact that it guaranteed literacy and certain habits of industry and ordered thought, education impeded rather than helped its possessors in the world of affairs.... They [the Athenian educators; Y. E.] remained blind to the fact that the continued existence of their world turned upon the effective exercise of many skills; they overvalued the politician's arts and under-estimated the growing consequence of administrative, economic, and technical achievement. (Bolgar, 1969, p. 48–49)

But this "betrayal" of the potentialities of text was not restricted to the schools of the Hellenistic age. It was not caused only by conditions "external" to the instrument of written language. To the contrary, the subsequent history of schooling in the Middle Ages testifies to the double-edged character of the text itself.

> The concentration of the "humaniora" on grammar, rhetoric and – above all – on dialectic, that is, the concentration on the most general level of language seems very formal and to be supported by a concept of knowledge to which all reality is text. I would like to regard this as the kernel of the Middle Ages' literacy. It forms a tight, figurative unity of formal

symbols, the content and the analogies connecting these symbols and the objects. In this figurative unity, knowledge is – in principle – static and non-changeable analogies.

For the Middle Ages, the identity of knowledge and text at the same time is the adequate form of the obligations of knowledge itself. What really happened in instruction, especially in the faculty arts, seems to correspond to this static conception. In the European Middle Ages, knowledge is understanding texts. Getting to know reality means to learn what authorities wrote about it. The recitation of texts is the most important means of communication of scientific knowledge.

It forces a memorizing of what has been heard and enormous techniques of recollection, especially when it wasn't allowed to make notes. Learning is a continuous memorizing of given patterns, a molding of an exemplary universality on the single, individual intellect: Learning is "imitatio". The constancy of knowledge is equivalent to a likewise non-developability of the learning person.... The central principle in the medieval instruction, "simultaneity", is an expression of just this non-developability of both, subject and object of learning. (Fichtner, 1985, p. 53–54)

Written text thus becomes the central pillar of a static, hierarchical worldview, somehow very foreign to the critical potentialities of written language listed earlier.

The paradox lies in the fact that the deadness of the text, its removal from the living human lifeworld, its rigid visual fixity, assures its endurance and its potential for being resurrected into limitless living contexts by a potentially infinite number of living readers. (Ong, 1982, p. 81)

In a similar vein, Leroi-Gourhan (1980, p. 264) speaks of the tendency of written text to "narrow down the images, to linearize the symbols rigorously," which eventually also means "an impoverishment of the means for expressing irrational moments."

It may be argued that the emergence of modern science, of the printing press, and of capitalism changed everything. According to Fichtner, the essential revolution was that of "setting free" the medieval signs, the decomposition of the seemingly absolute identity of sign and the denotation, of knowledge and the way it is represented.

In a way, signs now have their new positions again and again, and that happens by active cognition.... Signs become means to develop ideas and – more important – means to shape ideas. On the other hand, reality as such can be organized in a quite new constructive way: as empiricism.... The manifold forms of standardizing knowledge enable and facilitate its development. Tables, schedules, curves, maps, diagrams and models allow – to a previously unknown extent – to detect contradictions, to discover and record relationships but also to make changes and supplements, to clear off open points and errors. (Fichtner, 1985, p. 55)

Fichtner (1985, p. 54) argues that this implies a general change in the attitude toward knowledge. Knowledge becomes something to be developed, implying "a concept of cognition as a process of knowledge-construction."

It seems to me that accounts like that of Fichtner are basically correct with regard to the rather narrow "learned communities" of science and letters. But I think these accounts underestimate the inertia inherent in text, especially as it continues to function within the schooling of populations. This point is rather nicely summarized by Elizabeth Eisenstein in her discussion on the printing press as an agent of change.

Image worship gave way to bibliolatry among the masses of faithful in Protestant lands. At the same time, men of learning (whether Protestant or Catholic) often became less certain than earlier scholars had been about the literal meaning of the sacred word. (Eisenstein, 1985, p. 21)

Thus, if we consider the basic forms of organized *learning*, not primarily scientific and artistic activities, a different picture emerges. "Bibliolatry" is a fitting term in this context.

Catechisms and textbooks presented "facts" or their equivalents: memorizable, flat statements that told straight-forwardly and inclusively how matters stood in a given field. (Ong, 1982, p. 134)

No doubt the emergence of general obligatory school systems in the nineteenth century signaled a major change in the nature of education and school learning. School going became an activity required of every new member of the society. Instead of church and religion, education oriented to *science* emerged as the integrating force of society, as the new and higher form of generality. This meant that, for the first time in history, all people had to learn to carry out certain voluntary and disciplined learning actions.

Still I maintain that the general transition to modernity and public schooling has *not* been a qualitative breakthrough into *learning activity*. The seemingly endless stream of literature on the crisis and obsolescence of school learning should be taken as a first symptomatic indication in favor of this claim.

But it would also be incorrect to blame the inherent properties of text for the quality of schooling. Scribner and Cole (1981) have convincingly demonstrated that literacy, mastery of written language, may be acquired also without school going, and literacy alone does not have the same cognitive consequences as literacy through schooling. So far, I have merely endeavored to point out the double-edged nature of text as an instrument. The task is now to place this instrument in the general context of the activity of school going.

According to Sharp, Cole, and Lave (1979), the cognitive effects of schooling are found in tasks emphasizing paradigmatic relations between words and demanding readiness to solve problems "for their own sake," independently of their relationship to problem solving outside the school. This conclusion is substantiated by recent studies comparing people's performances in everyday problem tasks and in schoollike tasks with analogous structure.

> There appear to be discontinuities between problem-solving in the supermarket and arithmetic problem-solving in school. School problems seem designed primarily to elicit the learning and display of procedures, using set inputs. School lessons are fraught with difficulty and failure for many students. On the other hand, extraordinarily successful arithmetic activity takes place in situations outside school.... Researchers in the Adult Math Project discovered that *all* participants had poor opinions of their arithmetic practices in everyday settings. They apologized for not doing what they called "real math" – the math taught in school. This is especially interesting in the face of their extraordinary arithmetic efficacy in kitchen and supermarket. (Lave, 1985, p. 174)

The essential peculiarity of school going as the activity of pupils is the strange "reversal" of object and instrument. In societal practice, text (including the text of arithmetic algorithms) appears as a general secondary instrument. In school going, text takes the role of the object. This object is molded by pupils in a curious manner: The outcome of their activity is above all the same text reproduced and modified orally or in written form (summarized, classified, organized, recombined, and applied in a strictly predetermined manner to solve well-structured, "closed" problems). As Gladwin (1985, p. 209) says, "School takes away the sense of problem and substitutes hierarchies of abstraction."

> On the whole, the general scheme of such education is the same as that of the Middle Ages when a literate master transferred his utilitarian skills to his apprentices. Generally, the master himself did not realize in what way these skills *appeared*, on what basis they can be actually universal and applicable in all the situations, or how to find the possibilities of application of these skills in unexpected situations unlike those in which they had been mastered. As for the pupils, they received from their teacher

the ready form of notions and skills without asking themselves about the universal premises of their emergence and formation. Besides, they master these notions by way of continuous exercises, adapting themselves to their ready models....

Such education is a form of *practical* interaction of children and adults oriented to mastering ready utilitarian results of previous human activity. Naturally, the very means of obtaining these results, the very means of comprehending the condition of their origin and further formation remain outside both teacher's and pupil's consciousness and outside the real educational process. (Davydov, 1982, p. 39)

This has two important implications. First, since the dominant task is to reproduce and modify the given text, the role of the text in the societal practice, in the activity systems where it is created and used, is necessarily of peripheral importance. In other words, text becomes a closed world, a dead object cut off from its living context. Second, since text is not employed as instrument, a chronic "instrumental poverty" arises in school going. Dominant primary instruments are pencils and pens, erasers and notebooks. Dominant secondary instruments are formal study techniques. If texts were treated as living object systems (as in literary criticism and historical research, for example), the ridiculous inadequacy of these instruments would be readily transparent.

In capitalism, these features of the activity of school going are further determined by the primary contradiction of this socioeconomic formation, the double nature of commodity as a unity of value and use value. The constituent elements of this activity appear to the pupil in two competing forms. Thus, the object "text" has a twofold meaning. First of all, it is a dead object to be reproduced for the purpose of gaining grades or other "success markers" that cumulatively determine the future value of the pupil him- or herself in the labor market. On the other hand, text tendentially also appears as a living instrument of mastering one's own relation to society outside the school. In this respect, the school text possesses potential use value. As the object of the activity is also its true motive, the inherently dual nature of the motive of school going is now visible.

The structure of the activity of school going in capitalism may be depicted with the help of a diagram (Figure 2.8). Notice that when I here and later speak of capitalism, I do not imply that analogous contradictions would disappear in socialism. But I do imply that we cannot dump these two socioeconomic formations under one rubric of "industrialized societies." The inner contradictions of activities in socialism require their own analysis.

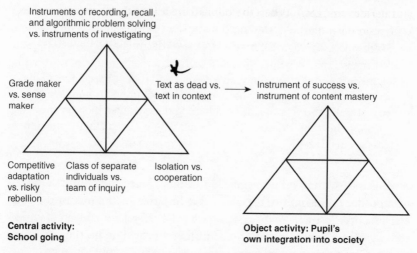

Instruments of recording, recall, and algorithmic problem solving vs. instruments of investigating

Grade maker vs. sense maker

Text as dead vs. text in context

Instrument of success vs. instrument of content mastery

Competitive adaptation vs. risky rebellion

Class of separate individuals vs. team of inquiry

Isolation vs. cooperation

Central activity: School going

Object activity: Pupil's own integration into society

FIGURE 2.8. The primary contradiction of the activity of school going.

In the activity of school going, certain learning actions are cultivated systematically. But as a whole, school going is a far cry from learning activity. Pupils remain subjects of separate learning actions, not of a whole system of learning activity.

The essential difference is to be found in the object. My contention is that the object of learning activity cannot be reduced to text. Such a reduction normally leads to the minimization of the productivity of learning (text as a dead object), and even in the best case to the narrowing down of productivity into intellectualism (production of text only).

But who says learning should or could be productive? Is it not enough that we solve the problem of internalization, as Bereiter urges us to do? Are there really some objective grounds or forces that justify the claim that a new productive type of human learning is about to emerge? And if so, what will be the object of this new learning activity?

The inner contradiction of school going, depicted in Figure 2.8, also continuously produces "deviant" pupil actions toward the use value aspect of this activity. The history of the school is also a history of inventing tricks for beating the system, and of protesting and breaking out. But although these actions are age-old, they have not expanded into a new type of activity – into learning activity. No doubt the inner contradiction of school going becomes increasingly aggravated as today's pupils are at an early age intensively drawn into the market as relatively independent consumers, even as producers of exchange values (as computer hackers, as sports stars and performers, etc.). When the pupils' direct participation in the societal production is intensified, the "holding power" of the school is endangered. In this respect, school going may well be approaching a crisis of new qualitative dimensions. Whether this will mean a breakthrough into learning activity in school – that remains to be seen.

The contradictions and forces leading to learning activity obviously cannot be found exclusively within school going. The school does not have a monopoly of organized human learning. To the contrary, the preceding analysis indicates that learning within school has remained and is likely to remain with remarkable persistence a series of more or less disconnected though systematically repeated learning actions (for a nice historical specimen on the persistence of recitation, see Hoetker & Ahlbrand, 1969; for a general historical account, see Cuban, 1984). These are complemented by equally disconnected "deviant" and emancipatory actions. The symptoms of a deeper qualitative change in school learning are still premature.

Learning actions appear with increasing frequency within other activities, too. Two such fundamental activity types are *work* activity, on the one hand, and the activities of *scientific research* and *artistic creation*, on the other hand.

The Second Lineage: Learning within Work Activity

While schools are organized around the instrument of written language, learning continues within work practice, too. Learning on the job is usually considered inferior to learning in school: more restricted, even crippling in its adherence to fixed routines. This conception gains impetus as industrialization, mechanization, and Taylorization wipe out the traditional hand workers' craftsmanship.

> Not as with the instrument, which the worker animates and makes into his organ with his skill and strength, and whose handling therefore depends on his virtuosity. Rather, it is the machine which possesses skill and strength in place of the worker, is itself the virtuoso, with a soul of its own in the mechanical laws acting through it.... The worker's activity, reduced to a mere abstraction of activity, is determined and regulated on all sides by the movement of the machinery, and not the opposite. The science which compels the inanimate limbs of the machinery, by their construction, to act purposefully, as an automaton, does not exist in the worker's consciousness, but rather acts upon him through the machine as an alien power, as the power of the machine itself. (Marx, 1973, p. 692–693)

In the sociology of work, theories of alienation, deskilling, and polarization of the labor force gradually became the dominant credo, presented masterfully in Braverman's *Labor and Monopoly Capital* (1974) – with the telling subtitle *The Degradation of Work in the Twentieth Century.*

Theories of dequalification and polarization are based on the tacit assumption that the qualifications of different kinds of work can be compared and quantitatively measured with a common universal yardstick. Thus, it is always a question of "higher" or "lower," "more" or "less" qualified work. In closer scrutiny, the criterion of measurement (often characterized as "autonomy" or "variety of tasks") turns out to be taken from the ideal model of handicraft. Against this background, it is naturally found that in the modern mechanized or automated factory the workers' qualifications are "lower" than in handwork. In other words, there really is very little left of the original quality of handicraft. In that meaning, work has indeed been "degraded." But this argumentation is based on a rear-mirror perspective. The qualification comparisons and prognoses remain abstract and hollow, and very vulnerable empirically. They have about the same theoretical status as a comparison stating that medieval serfs were "more free"/"less free" than ancient Roman slaves. The possibility that something *qualitatively new* might be developing in the new form of industrial work, replacing the vanishing handwork qualifications, is tacitly set aside. What really would be needed is a qualitatively new yardstick for the new type of work.

This new yardstick is to be found in the radically increased *societal character* and productivity of work. In terms of activity theory, this means that in industrial capitalism it is increasingly difficult for the individual worker to grasp and master the total work activity in which he or she performs only comparatively small subordinated actions. The sheer volume as well as the technological, economic, and organizational complexity of the production process of the plant or firm seems to be absolutely overwhelming for an individual. The whole machinery seems to run by itself, directed by scientific management and planning far beyond the reach of the worker. This immediate appearance gives plenty of nourishment for theories of dequalification.

But strangely enough, theories of deskilling and polarization have all but collapsed in the 1980s.. Ten years after Braverman's book, the so far leading European proponents of polarization theory, Horst Kern and Michael Schumann, after a new cycle of comprehensive empirical data collection, made a full break with their earlier stance and published a book named *The End of Division of Labor?* (1984). And this is not a lonely phenomenon, rather a symbol of the general turn of the tide, started already a few years earlier (see Wood, 1982; for a review of literature, see Wood, 1987). What has caused this change?

To the degree that large industry develops, the creation of real wealth comes to depend less on labour time and on the amount of labour employed than on the power of the agencies set in motion during labour time, whose 'powerful effectiveness' is itself in turn out of all propor-tion to the direct labour time spent on their production, but depends rather on the general state of science and on the progress of technol-ogy, or the application of this science to production.... Labour no longer appears so much to be included within the production process; rather, the human being comes to relate more as watchman and regulator to the production process itself. (What holds for machinery holds likewise for the combination of human activities and the development of human intercourse.) No longer does the worker insert a modified natural thing [*Naturgegenstand*] as middle link between the object [*Objekt*] and him-self; rather, he inserts the process of nature, transformed into an indus-trial process, as a means between himself and inorganic nature, mastering it. He steps to the side of production process instead of being its chief actor. In this transformation, it is neither the direct human labour he himself performs, nor the time during which he works, but rather the appropriation of his own general productive power, his understanding of nature and his mastery over it by virtue of his presence as a social body – it is, in a word, the development of the social individual which appears as the great foundation-stone of production and of wealth. The *theft of alien labour time, on which the present wealth is based,* appears as a miserable foundation in face of this new one, created by large-scale industry itself. As soon as labour in the direct form has ceased to be the great well-spring of wealth, labour time ceases and must cease to be its measure, and hence exchange value [must cease to be the measure] of use value. The *surplus labour of the mass* has ceased to be the condi-tion for the development of general wealth, just as the *non-labour of the few,* for the development of the general powers of the human head. With that, production based on exchange value breaks down.... Capital itself is the moving contradiction, [in] that it presses to reduce labour time to a minimum, while it posits labour time, on the other side, as sole mea-sure and source of wealth.... On the one side, then, it calls to life all the powers of science and of nature, as of social combination and of social intercourse, in order to make the creation of wealth independent (rela-tively) of the labour time employed on it. On the other side, it wants to use labour time as the measuring rod for the giant social forces thereby created, and to confine them within the limits required to maintain the already created value as value. (Marx, 1973, p. 704–706)

This aspect of Marx's visionary analysis is regularly neglected by theorists of dequalification. Is there any real basis to it?

Consider the nuclear power plant accident at Three Mile Island in 1979.

> A nuclear reactor has been described as a very complicated way to boil water. One of the key problems is controlling the immense heat generated by nuclear fission. A nuclear power plant therefore is an elaborate plumbing system of intricate water and steam pipes designed to draw off the excess heat not used to drive the steam turbine and generate electricity.
>
> The accident at Three Mile Island began when two water pumps failed, causing water temperature and pressure inside the reactor to soar. A feedback device correctly shut down the reactor, but the excess heat triggered several other breakdowns that intensified the threat to the entire system. A relief valve, which automatically opened to vent excess steam, remained stuck in the open position. Inside the reactor core, steam was interfering with the primary cooling system, leaving the hot core partly uncovered, and threatening the ultimate disaster, a meltdown.
>
> All of these events happened within the first few minutes of the accident. This was an entirely unanticipated emergency of multiple, accelerating breakdowns involving *high* temperature and *low* pressure. It overwhelmed both the computer and the human workers in the TMI control room. More than a hundred different alarm lights lit up the control board, each signaling a different malfunction. By midmorning, the computer had a three hour backlog of data waiting to be printed out, which workers desperately needed in order to determine the cause of the breakdown, the extent of the damage, and the corrective measures that were still possible. At one point, the computer began printing out question marks. Workers frantically leafed through the "Emergency Procedures" manuals, but this particular emergency had not been foreseen. It was several hours before workers and engineers sorted out what had happened. (Hirschhorn, 1982, p. 42–43)

 One clear conclusion from the accident is that "insufficient, rote training produced workers" who could not adapt to the demands of an emergency which the system did not anticipate" (Hirschhorn, 1982, p. 44).

> Workers in cybernated systems cannot function as passive machine tenders, looking to instruction manuals for the appropriate response. This suggests an entirely new definition of work in a post-industrial setting. Skills can no longer be defined in terms of a particular set of actions, but as a general ability to understand how a system functions and to think flexibly in trying to solve problems.

At Three Mile Island, of course, workers were inflexible in their conceptual approach, because they had been trained to be inflexible. Notwithstanding the new technology and new demands on the workforce, managers and engineers in traditional industries remain highly reluctant to introduce workers to questions of system design, or to train workers to think conceptually beyond a limited list of specified responses to anticipated problems....

Real accidents, however, often proceed through a train of events, a set of interdependent failures (where one failure increases the probability that another will occur) and in interaction with the workers. (Hirschhorn, 1982, p. 45)

What is the general weight of an argument based on such an extreme case? Hirschhorn (1982, p. 46) points out two pertinent facts. First, "increasingly, manufacturing is placing workers in the control room rather than on the assembly line." Second, "just as workers must respond to emergencies, so must they be ready to control the controls when new machinery is introduced or new products are manufactured."

This kind of development raises the inner contradictions of work to the surface.

The logic of the post-industrial workplace leaves both management and labor in a paradoxical position. Management's traditional interest in keeping control requires workers with limited skills and aspirations. But to protect their machinery, management needs highly skilled workers who are trained to think independently....

Effective training might require teams: in a crisis like the Three Mile Island emergency, for example, where the crucial need is accurate diagnosis, each worker needs to have some familiarity with the tasks and skills of other workers. Otherwise the diagnostic process breaks down.... But work teams tend to flatten hierarchy and challenge traditional management notions of supervision and control.

Like managers, trade unionists also find themselves in a contradictory position. Worker solidarity requires unions to emphasize the class divide that separates workers and managers, but in doing so unions underplay the professional character of control room work. At the same time, unions need to protect the skills and increase the competence of workers to prevent demoralization and vulnerability in the face of technological change. (Hirschhorn, 1982, p. 46–47)

Marx pointed out that labor time "appears as a miserable foundation" in conditions of automation. The idea of cost-effectiveness, of squeezing out more "output" per hour, is indeed a miserable foundation for managing production processes like the one at Three Mile Island.

The release of methyl isocyanite (MIC) at the Union Carbide plant in Bhopal, India, on the night of December 2, 1984, killed and blinded thousands of people. This catastrophe makes it abundantly clear why the saving of labor time is such a miserable foundation in automated production.

> When the plant was started up,... only individuals with university degrees or technical school diplomas were hired as operators – and "subjected to six months' theoretical training and then trained on the job." By the time of the accident, operators had been taken on without academic science backgrounds – some were simply transferred in from other units or plants – and nobody was being given the original rigorous training.

> The size of the staff was also reduced.... Initially, the crew included twelve operators, three supervisors, and two maintenance supervisors; a superintendent responsible for about half the operations at the plant was also on duty during each shift. In December 1984, the MIC crew included six operators and one supervisor. There was no maintenance supervisor on the night shift, and the superintendent on duty had responsibility for the entire plant. (Krigman, 1985, p. 13)

Hirschhorn's argumentation is further enriched by the findings of Jens Rasmussen, one of the most prominent researchers of human error reports.

> What bothers me is that the explanations of major industrial incidents in terms of human errors are often based on superficial analysis which result in *ad hoc* changes of the system and, almost invariably, in recommendations for better training together with "stricter administrative control of the adherence to instructions". Needless to say, we have good evidence that this will not solve the problem – especially when at the same time the acceptable probability of the release of potential accidents is steadily decreasing. (Rasmussen, 1980, p. 97–98)

Rasmussen presents data on the character of two hundred reports of "operational problems" in nuclear power plants. The error modes to which Rasmussen ascribes greatest substantial importance are those of inadequate consideration of latent causes and inadequate consideration of side effects in selecting procedures.

> These two kinds of error are very probably related to difficulty of the human mind to keep track of the spread of events in the complex causal net of a technical system. Constructive recall of a procedure, or modification of a procedure to fit special circumstances, demands

simultaneous consideration of several potential causal conditions and possible side effects of the intended actions. This is difficult for unsupported, linear natural language reasoning due to the limitations of working memory....

In large installations, we also have to consider rare events for which operators cannot be prepared by trained procedures. In such cases, the operator has to generate proper procedures by functional evaluation and causal reasoning based on knowledge about system properties. (Rasmussen, 1980, p. 105–106)

Rasmussen's conclusion touches the core of the contradiction.

> The essence of this argument is that the development towards large, centralized installations has now reached a state where the design and operation of many systems can no longer be considered separate activities which are effectively decoupled by a commissioning test period. Effective feed-back of operational experience, especially concerning the co-performance of system and staff during the entire plant life is important for acceptable systems design.... To cope with unplanned situations and to co-operate effectively with automatic instrumentation and control functions, operating staff needs much more systematic access to the information base, performance criteria and decision strategies used by designers. (Rasmussen, 1980, p. 112–113; see also Rasmussen, Duncan & Leplat, 1987)

Very similar analyses have recently been presented by specialists in other branches of industrial production, including small batch production with numerically controlled (NC) machines (Brödner, 1985) and flexible manufacturing systems (FMS) (Köhler, Schultz-Wild & Lutz, 1983; Toikka, Hyötyläinen & Norros, 1986). Cherns (1980, p. 264) summarizes the argumentation by pointing out a general shift of skills "away from deciding *how to act in this situation* towards deciding *what kind of situation* this is"; in other words, "as in modern medicine, treatment becomes routine, diagnosis becomes the key."

The primary inner contradictions of modern work, situated within the corners of the structure of activity and stemming from its dual commodity character, may now be sketched with the help of the familiar diagram (Figure 2.9).

The two poles of the contradiction within each corner of the model suggest two competing alternative strategies both for the management and for the trade unions. Brödner (1985) has identified these two strategies as the strategy of "the unmanned factory" and the strategy of "skill-based production." It should be noted that, contrary to the single-minded optimism

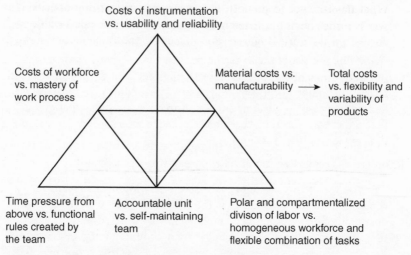

Costs of instrumentation
vs. usability and reliability

Costs of workforce
vs. mastery of
work process

Material costs vs.
manufacturability ⟶

Total costs
vs. flexibility and
variability of
products

Time pressure from
above vs. functional
rules created by
the team

Accountable unit
vs. self-maintaining
team

Polar and compartmentalized
divison of labor vs.
homogeneous workforce and
flexible combination of tasks

FIGURE 2.9. The primary contradiction of modern work activity.

of some representatives of the sociotechnical school (e.g., Cherns, 1980; Davis, 1980), we are dealing here with real contradictions, that is, with developments in which both sides of the contradiction coexist, struggle, and penetrate each other.

In terms of activity theory, we may say that there is, on the one hand, the *object activity* (appearing in the form of market demands) requiring high quality, flexibility, variability, and short delivery times from the *products*, which in turn require complex programmable cybernated *instruments*. However, there is an acute conflict between these factors and the striving for immediate cost efficiency, manifested above all in the polar and compartmentalized *division of labor.* In effect, industrial capitalism has split the work activity into two basic layers of *actions,* those of operating or performing and those of design and management.

The increasingly societal nature of work processes, their internal complexity and interconnectedness as well as their massive volumes in capital and capacity, are making it evident that, at least in periods of acute disturbance or intensive change, no one actually quite masters the work *activity* as a whole, though the control and planning of the whole are formally in the hands of the management. This creates something that might be called "grey zones" (Projekt Automation und Qualifikation, 1981), areas of vacuum or "no man's land," where initiative and determined action from practically any level of the corporate hierarchy may have unexpected effects.

What has this got to do with the emergence of learning activity? The answer is rather obvious. There is an objective pressure, manifesting itself in various forms, toward *placing the mastery of the whole work activity* in the hands of the people who participate in that activity. This pressure is felt on both sides of the primary contradiction. Both the strategy of "the unmanned factory" and the strategy of "skill-based production" require, in opposite ways, major qualitative change and expansion in the practical and cognitive steering of work. The former strategy promises practically to exclude the unreliable and costly human operator. The latter builds on the flexibility and inventiveness of the very same operator.

To gain mastery of the whole work activity means to move from actions to activity in the sense tentatively characterized by Leont'ev and Ilyenkov. As I pointed out earlier, the expansive form of this transition implies that the actions themselves are objectively transformed. Moreover, such a transition requires "reflecting the relation of the motive of a given, concrete activity to the motive of a wider activity" (Leont'ev). In other words, the subjects must become aware of the contradictory nature of their present work activity and relate it to a future form of the work activity "that realizes a broader, more general life relation that includes the given, concrete activity" (meaning that the given form of work is not eliminated or replaced at once). This is a tall order that cannot be accomplished without "a certain, special activity" of a new type – learning activity.

The argument presented so far might be interpreted to indicate that the shoots of learning activity emerge within work activity only on the soil provided by advanced automation. I contest this conception, widespread among the "postdequalification" sociologists of work. The contradictions of work activity described previously have in principle existed since the maturation of capitalism. New cybernated technologies have aggravated those contradictions and made them visible. But, as Figure 2.9 implies, changes in the objects, market conditions, and products may be of equal or greater importance in this aggravation. It is systemic and holistic change, not a monocausal one.

> Firms following this strategy [of "the unmanned factory"; Y. E.] would suffer from relative inflexibility with respect to both alteration of batches and process innovation. This is due to the fact that every change of a customer order or a piece of production equipment has first to be modeled in the computer system. In the long run the firm might even loose its innovative capability, since production knowledge and creativity on the human side have been wasting away over time. All this is in contrast to market requirements. (Brödner, 1985, p. 2)

This means that the pressure and demand for learning activity are not necessarily restricted to work activities employing costly advanced technologies. Other work activities facing new kinds of market conditions and product demands may well contain similar possibilities of breakthrough. This is demonstrated by Donald Schön for professional work.

> In such fields as medicine, management, and engineering, for example, leading professionals speak of a new awareness of a complexity which resists the skills and techniques of traditional expertise. As physicians have turned their attention from traditional images of medical practice to the predicament of the larger health care system, they have come to see the larger system as a "tangled web" that traditional medical knowledge and skill cannot untangle. How can physicians influence a massively complex health care system which they do not understand and of which only a very small fraction is under their direct control? ...
>
> The situations of practice are not problems to be solved but problematic situations characterized by uncertainty, disorder, and indeterminacy. (Schön, 1983, p. 14–16)

The Third Lineage: Learning within Science and Art

In the centuries from 1300 to 1600, three layers of intellectuals could be identified in European culture: the university scholars, the humanists, and the skilled artisans (engineers, artists, healers, navigators, and the like). The university scholars and humanists were trained in logical thinking, but they despised handwork and experimentation.

> Thus the two components of scientific method were separated by a social barrier: logical training was reserved for the learned of the upper class; experimentation, causal interest and quantitative methods were more or less left to the plebeian artisans. Science was born as, along with technological advance, the experimental method finally overcame the social prejudices against handwork and was taken over by rationally educated scholars. This was accomplished around 1600 (Gilbert, Galilei, Bacon)....
> The whole process was embedded in the development of early capitalism which weakened the collective consciousness, magic thinking and belief in authority, pushing forward secular, causal, rational and quantitative thinking. (Zilsel, 1976, p. 49)

But what is the difference between science and handwork?

> As long as natural forces are used in work as effects and properties of certain natural objects, not scientific cognition but knowledge about the

things and their properties ... is required as the intellectual moment of work. In contrast, scientific cognition is required when it is a question of using natural forces in their *general* form. (Lefèvre, 1978, p. 23; italics added)

This implies that the object of science is not the external world of natural and cultural objects or events as some kind of self-sustained virgin raw material. Such a virgin material does not exist. As Wartofsky (1979, p. 206) notes, nature becomes transformed, not only in the direct practical way of becoming cultivated, or shaped into objects of use, "it becomes transformed as an object or arena of action, so that the forest or the river itself becomes an 'artifact' in this ramified sense." Already by observing and describing an object, humans incorporate it into the sphere of their cultural construction. Without these acts, it does not exist for them as an object.

We never make concrete occurrences *as such* the object of explanation, rather it is always a question of occurrences considered through a certain *description*. Instead of mere spatio-temporal chunks, we try to explain ones *described* in a certain way. (Jensen, 1978, p. 27)

The true object of science is the *general* in nature and culture – or in culturally penetrated nature and naturally penetrated culture. As Malinowski (1944, p. 11) observes, "We find, first and foremost, the isolation of the real and relevant factors in a given process." Scientific activity begins with the isolation of the general, although "often in spite of the conscious logical precepts and maxims that its representatives profess" (Ilyenkov, 1977, p. 361). We can say with Peter Ruben (1978, p. 20) that science is "universal labor" that "makes objects isolated from the surrounding world into models of general determinations."

Science tries to capture and fixate the general into models. Models are simultaneously secondary instruments and outcomes of science. But science cannot be understood without the sensitive link of transmission and translation of scientific models into secondary instruments of work or other productive practice outside science – something Malinowski (1944, p. 11) calls the necessary ingredient of "control of academic discourse by practical application."

The object of science is the general, but the general is not directly available. It must be constructed through a complex series of actions, beginning with preliminary isolation and description of "a field for experiment or observation" (Malinowski, 1944, p. 11). This is the paradox of science: Its object is and is not there. This slippery, transitional character of the object of science is in fact the very essence of this activity. It is a special kind of *indirectness*. The object must be "fetched" from the world, as it were, but it only becomes an object after being transferred into the reflective system of science – and back again. The problem in true research is that the researcher does not exactly know what he or she is looking for before finding it. If one knew it at the beginning, nothing new would be discovered. Of course, this aspect of unexpectedness resides in any productive work activity, too – but only as an aspect. In science it is the dominant motive force.

The general is slippery, first of all, because it is relational.

> The general is anything but continuously repeated similarity in every single object taken separately and represented by a common attribute and fixed by a sign. The universal is above all the regular connection of two (or more) particular individuals that converts them into moments of one and the same concrete, real unity.... Here the general functions as the law or principle of the connection of these details in the make-up of some whole, or totality. (Ilyenkov, 1977, p. 350)

Moreover, the general would not be general if it remained isolated and static. The general contains the expansive movement of "becoming" from the isolated to the interconnected, from the simple relation to the complex system.

> The general includes and embodies in itself the whole wealth of details, not as the "idea" but as a quite real, particular phenomenon with a tendency to become general, and developing "from itself" (by virtue of its inner contradictions) other just as real phenomena, other particular forms of actual movement. (Ilyenkov, 1977, p. 369)

Jacob Bronowski expresses the same expansive idea of science in more familiar words.

> A theory does not simply state the facts: it shows them to flow from an inner order and imaginative arrangement of a few deep central concepts. That is the nature of a scientific theory, and that is why I have called it the creation of the human mind. Of course a good theory has practical consequences, and forecasts true results, which go beyond the facts from which it started. But these successful forecasts do not make the theory true – they only show that it was even wider that its creator supposed. (Bronowski, 1978, p. 31)

In a similar vein, Lefèvre (1978, p. 115) points out that as modern natural science emerged, it only superficially seemed to divorce itself from practice. Actually it *ran ahead* of practice, anticipating and paving the way for "a stage of practice whose realization in material production required still more than a hundred years of development."

But science itself has been industrialized and commodified. It is increasingly organized into large research centers with intricate division of labor. Research operates with costly complex primary instruments, but secondary instruments (models and theories) seem to fall into myriad disconnected microtheories. The objects of science appear in the form of separate "problems" or "tasks" given from outside. Above all, science is tendentially reduced to its immediate products or results possessing exchange value in the "science market" and being essentially *known or fixed in advance* (as "customer's orders" or promises from the researchers).

This commodification is experienced among the practitioners or "users" of scientific results, too.

> They gape at the discovery from the outside, and they may find it strange or marvelous, but their finding is passive; they do not enter and follow and relive the steps by which the new idea was created. But no creative work, in art or in science, truly exists for us unless we ourselves help to recreate it. (Bronowski, 1978, p. 23)

The contradiction inherent in this development is manifested in the poor productivity or "problem-solving capacity" of science as the tasks exceed certain limits in complexity. Various attempts to find relief in "holistic" philosophies (Bohm, 1980) and cosmology (Toulmin, 1982) bear witness to the uneasiness felt with this state of science. These attempts typically do not deal with the contradiction but rather paint pictures of harmonious alternatives and utopias.

The essence of the contradiction is the tension between the *fixed, reified, predetermined* nature of the exchange-value aspect of scientific objects, on the one hand, and the *transitional, expansive, unexpected* nature of their use-value aspect, on the other hand. This may be expressed with the help of a diagram (Figure 2.10).

Here again, it is not a question of "choosing" the more appealing alternative within each corner of the model. One has to take both. The contradiction cannot be swept away by moral decisions.

There is a fairly obvious kinship between science and art. Both are specifically indirect modes of imaginative, experimental practice, aimed at producing "alternative worlds."

> On this reconstruction, we may speak of a class of artifacts which can come to constitute a relatively autonomous "world," in which the rules, conventions and outcomes no longer appear directly practical, or which,

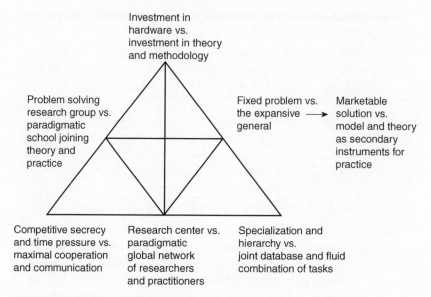

FIGURE 2.10. The primary contradiction of the activity of science.

indeed, seem to constitute an arena of non-practical, or "free" play or game activity.... So called "disinterested" perception, or aesthetic perception, or sheer contemplation then becomes a possibility; but not in the sense that it has *no* use. Rather, in the sense that the original role of the representation has been, so to speak, suspended or bracketed....

The construction of alternative imaginative perceptual modes, freed from the direct representation of ongoing forms of action, and relatively autonomous in this sense, feeds back into actual praxis, as a representation of possibilities which go beyond present actualities. (Wartofsky, 1979, p. 208–209)

But art is not science. Artistic activity has its own peculiar object. According to Wartofsky (1979, p. 357), art "takes *itself* as its own object."

Art represents its own process of coming into being and ... exemplifies and objectifies the distinctively human capacity of creation. It is in the self-recognition of this creative capacity that human beings come to know themselves as human, in the specific sense that they come to know themselves as creators or as artists. Thus it is not *what* is portrayed, or depicted which provides the humanizing content of the artwork, but rather the reading back of the very process of its genesis which makes the artwork an objective representation of human creativity. Art thus exemplifies or symbolizes the activity of art. The artist thus becomes a model of the potentialities of human nature, of human creativity. (Wartofsky, 1979, p. 357)

Art is a continuous indirect reflection of the creative core of productive practice. Both science and art "fetch" the substance of their objects from human productive practice (from the "central activity" of Figure 2.7). Science enters this substance from the "object" corner; art enters the same substance from the "subject" corner. Both construct their objects in a "distanced" or "disinterested" manner, within their own systemic structure. And it is a matter of life and death for both to transfer the object back into productive practice.

It must be kept in mind that "it is not the product – the artwork, the completed and dead image – which is the mirror of human nature, but rather the process of artistic creation itself, *and* the process of *re*creation in the act of aesthetic appreciation" (Wartofsky, 1979, p. 362). This processual nature of the object of art is not linear. As Vygotsky pointed out, it is characterized by qualitative expansion and transformation.

> Art would have a dull and ungrateful task if its only purpose were to infect one or many persons with feelings. If this were so, its significance would be very small, because there would be only a quantitative expansion and no qualitative expansion beyond an individual's feeling. The miracle of art would then be like the bleak miracle of the Gospel, when five barley loaves and two small fishes fed thousands of people, all of whom ate and were satisfied, and a dozen baskets were filled with the remaining food. The miracle is only quantitative: thousands were fed and were satisfied, but each of them ate only fish and bread. But was this not their daily diet at home, without any miracles? ...
>
> The miracle of art reminds us much more of another miracle in the Gospel, the transformation of water into wine. Indeed, art's true nature is that of trans-substantiation, something that transcends ordinary feelings; for the fear, pain, or excitement caused by art includes something above and beyond its normal, conventional content. This "something" overcomes feelings of fear and pain, changes water into wine.... Initially, an emotion is individual, and only by means of a work of art does it *become* social or generalized. (Vygotsky, 1971, p. 243)

The learning actions inherent in scientific and artistic activity are those of learning to imagine, learning to "go beyond the given," not in the privacy of the individual mind but in public, material objectifications.

> A physicist experiments with material situations whose properties he does not wholly know, and a poet tries to find his way through human

situations which he does not wholly understand. Both are learning by experiment. (Bronowski, 1978, p. 22)

However, art, too, has become commodified. Wartofsky has an interesting characterization of the effects of this process.

> When the activity becomes ritual or automatic; when the object comes to be seen only in its surface appearances – e.g., as description or portrayal, as thematic content, or even as sheer aesthetic surface,... or as form alone – the human content of the artwork becomes transparent and redundant: it is seen through but not realized. In this case, one may speak of an alienated aesthetic consciousness, a fetishism of the artwork, in which the object is taken as an autonomous and independent reality. (Wartofsky, 1979, p. 366–367)

It is easy to see the similarity of this phenomenon with the phenomena brought about by the industrialization of science. In both cases, the counterreaction is visible. As Wartofsky (1979, p. 368) notes, "The newer art forms focus on a return to the process: but perversely." What in science takes the form of search for holism may be observed in art in the form of "institutionalized despair." The learning actions of experimentation and imaginative world making, the most sophisticated techniques and skills of art and science, turn out to be insufficient for the purpose of *taking hold of the activity of art or science itself as a whole, in its own commodified contradictoriness.* For this, "a certain special activity" of reflecting is required.

THE STRUCTURE OF LEARNING ACTIVITY

The argument presented so far may be summarized in the following theses.

1. Human learning begins in the form of learning operations and learning actions embedded in other activities, phylogenetically above all in work.
2. Learning activity has an object and a systemic structure of its own. Its prerequisites are currently developing within earlier activity types: school going, work, and science/art. In the network of human activities, learning activity will mediate between science/art, on the one hand, and work or other central productive practice, on the other hand (Figure 2.11).
3. The essence of learning activity is production of objectively, societally new activity structures (including new objects, instruments, etc.)

out of actions manifesting the inner contradictions of the preceding
form of the activity in question. Learning activity is *mastery of expansion from actions to a new activity*. While traditional school going
is essentially a subject-producing activity and traditional science is
essentially an instrument-producing activity, learning activity is an
activity-producing activity.

But what is the specific object of learning activity? What is its
structure like?

The object of learning activity is the societal productive practice, or the
social life-world, in its full diversity and complexity. The productive practice, or the central activity, exists in its presently dominant form as well
as in its historically more advanced and earlier, already surpassed forms.
Learning activity makes the interaction of these forms, that is, the historical
development of activity systems, its object.

This object appears to the subject first in the form of discrete tasks, problems, and actions. As Michael Cole (1983, p. 51) notes, "Discovery of the
goals is essential to true activity." Learning activity (a) *analyzes* and *connects*
these discrete elements with their systemic activity contexts, (b) *transforms*
them into contradictions demanding creative solution, and (c) *expands* and
generalizes them into a qualitatively new activity structure within societal
productive practice.

According to V. V. Davydov (1982, p. 39), the motive of learning activity is *theoretical relation to the reality*. In other words, the components (a),
(b), and (c) result in a theoretical reconstruction of the object. The concept
of theoretical relation to reality shall be subjected to closer elaboration in
Chapter 4.

By what means does this theoretical reconstruction take place? The
essential instruments of learning activity are models. With the help of
models, the subject fixes and objectifies the essential relations of the object.
However, the construction of theoretical models is accomplished with the
help of a more general instrument – a methodology. Learning activity may
be conceived of as expansive movement from models to the methodology
of making models – and back.

Theoretical models and methodologies are entities typically produced
by science and art. These instruments, however, cannot be directly taken
over from science and art. Activity types differ from each other in the extent
and intensity to which they produce their own instruments. Science and art
are activities strongly oriented toward producing their own instruments.
Although work activities do also mold and produce their own instruments,

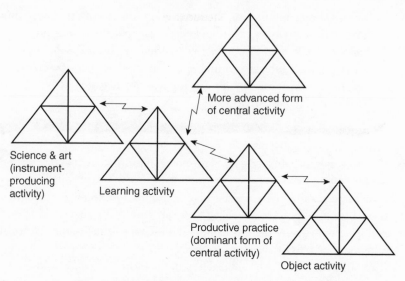

Science & art
(instrument-
producing
activity)   Learning activity

More advanced form
of central activity

Productive practice
(dominant form of
central activity)

Object activity

FIGURE 2.11. The place of learning activity in the network of human activities.

they do it less intensively and are more dependent on instruments produced by other activities.

Learning activity occupies the place between these two. It uses the products of science and art, but they become usable for learning activity only as they are recreated and reworked into more economical, as if stylized, representations than the original products of science and art. And this is not a question of mere popularization or simplification for illustrative purposes. Learning activity has much of the quality of play, "dissociating means and ends to permit exploration of their relation to each other" (Bruner, 1985, p. 603). But learning activity is more than this. It is true development of instruments: "purification" by elimination of secondary or accidental features, variation and enrichment, testing novel connections and disconnections. By moving the products of science and art into a new type of formative contact with productive practice, learning activity introduces a new creative moment into the activities of science and art themselves. In other words, learning activity never leaves its instruments qualitatively intact. It is not just consumption of instruments given from outside.

The structure of learning activity may now be presented in diagrammatic form (Figure 2.12). The diagram shows the essential quality of learning activity, namely, its transitional and expansive character.

But what kind of a subject is required and produced by learning activity? This is very much a question of the quality of consciousness associated

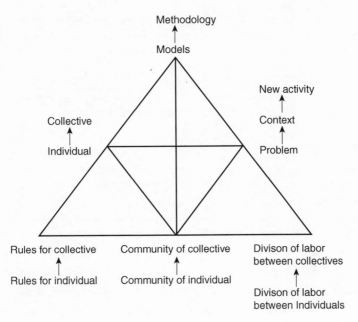

FIGURE 2.12. The structure of learning activity.

with learning activity. The problem of consciousness in learning, in turn, is currently discussed under the conceptual umbrella of "metacognition."

METACOGNITION AND THE SUBJECT OF LEARNING ACTIVITY

According to Flavell (1976, p. 232), metacognition "refers to one's knowledge concerning one's own cognitive processes and products or anything related to them, e.g., the learning-relevant properties of information or data." Brown and DeLoache (1978) present a list of basic metacognitive skills. These include predicting the consequences of an action or event, checking the results of one's own actions, monitoring one's ongoing activity, reality testing, and performing a variety of other behaviors for coordinating and controlling deliberate learning and problem solving.

In another paper, Brown (1978) names the basic metacognitive skills of checking, planning, asking questions, self-testing, and monitoring.

Perhaps it would be possible to train the child to stop and think before attempting a problem, to ask questions of himself and others to determine if he recognizes the problem, to check his solutions against reality by

asking not "is it right" but "is it reasonable," and to monitor his attempts
to learn to see if they are working or are worth the effort. (Brown, 1978,
p. 139)

More recently Brown, Campione, and Day (1982) developed further the idea
of metacognition as the basis of "learning to learn." They use a four-factor
model of the learning situation as their point of departure.

> In order to become expert learners, students must develop some of
> the same insights as the psychologist into the demands of the learn-
> ing situation. They must learn about their own cognitive characteris-
> tics, their available learning strategies, the demands of various learning
> tasks and the inherent structure of the material. They must tailor their
> activities finely to the competing demands of all these forces in order to
> become flexible and effective learners. (Brown, Campione & Day, 1982,
> p. 16–17)

In other words, the authors have realized that the metacognitive skills do
not exist and function in a vacuum. But this realization is formal. Regardless
of the context and contents, the metacognitive skills remain qualitatively
the same – it is just a question of using them in varying situations. A case
in point is the skill of "reality testing" (asking, "Does this make sense?"),
mentioned by Brown. What does it mean to "make sense"? Brown and
her colleagues (Brown, Campione & Day, 1982, p. 20) stress the arbitrary
character of the criterial tasks or objectives of learning and the need to
"tailor efforts accordingly." But what if the *goal or task given to the learner*
does *not* make sense to him or her? This possibility is not discussed by the
authors. To the contrary, since verbatim learning of texts, for example, is
often demanded by the school, it must be considered "a worthwhile activity" (Brown, Campione & Day, 1982, p. 16). What first appears to be the
optimally self-directed and self-conscious learner is actually the maximally
flexible individual, finding the most successful technique of *adaptation in
any situation given by the authorities*.

Thus, my first critique of Brown's approach is directed against the use of
the *situation* as the unit of metacognition. Situations are defined by tasks.
They are typical action-level units, portraying human behavior as rational
adaptive choice and cognitive calculation. The possibility that the learner
might him- or herself *create new situations* is tacitly ruled out.

My second critique concerns the undialectical conception of learning
situations and tasks presented by Brown and her colleagues. According to
them, the four factors (characteristics of the learners, learning strategies, criterial tasks, and structure of the materials) must be considered in a balanced

manner. But there is no awareness of the possibility that the tasks themselves might be inherently contradictory. Consider the following example.

> I observed the professor in one class beginning the term by explaining that the students were expected to be creative and involved; in short, they were to be engaged. They would have the opportunity to take intellectual risks, to make mistakes.... Five weeks later the first quiz was given. The students found they were asked to return a large amount of information that they could only have mastered by memorization.... In spite of the professor's opening pronouncements, the hidden but required task was *not* to be imaginative or creative but to play a specific, tightly circum-scribed academic game. The consequences for the students varied: some became cynical and said, "Okay, if that's the way you play the academic game, if that's what he really wants, I won't make the same mistake again. Next time I'll memorize the key points." (Snyder, 1971, p. 16–17)

The students quoted by Snyder display the awakening of a kind of meta-cognition in Brown's terms – metacognition for successful adaptation to the exchange-value aspect of studying. But how about the students' nag-ging feeling of missing something beyond the game of success – the feeling that knowledge should be acquired and used to master reality, to master societal productive practice? If a student protests and eventually becomes a "troublemaker," is his or her metacognition poorly developed?

The essential question is, *What* is to be metacognitively controlled and monitored? It would probably be fairly easy to obtain handsome results and transfer effects by teaching students such metacognitive skills as "how to fool the teacher," "how to get good grades with minimum effort," "how to cheat successfully." The substantive logic of these skills corresponds to the dominant exchange-value logic of schooling.

It follows from these two critical points that a truly high level of meta-cognitive awareness in learning requires (a) conscious analysis and mastery of not just discrete learning situations but of the continuous activity context in which the situations are embedded (whether they are situated within school going, work, science, art, or some other activity), (b) not just bal-ancing the components of the learning situation but "seeing through" the inherent contradictoriness of the learning tasks, that is, their double nature as unities of exchange value and use value.

These are the two essential prerequisites for the emergence of the subject of learning activity. As indicated in Figure 2.12, this subject is a transitional being, beginning in individual and developing into collective subjectivity. Its first spontaneous indications probably appear in the form of disturbing questions, counterarguments, attempts to break away, and the like.

[handwritten margin note, top right: ontogeny = development/course of development, esp of an individ. organism]

THE EMERGENCE OF LEARNING ACTIVITY
IN THE ONTOGENESIS —

[handwritten margin note, left: Motivation]

Leont'ev (1981, p. 401–404) discusses the transition from one leading activity to another in the ontogenesis. He uses the transition from play to study as the example. In his example, a pupil in the first grade cannot be made to do his homework. The pupil knows well that the homework must be done; it is a duty that he accepts in principle. But this "understandable motive" is not effective: "Another motive, however, is really effective, namely to get permission to go out and play" (Leont'ev, 1981, p. 402).

Now, the child is told that he may go out to play only after he has finished his homework. That does the trick and the pupil does his homework.

[handwritten margin note, left: transformation of motive]

> Once, while copying something out, it suddenly stops and leaves the table, crying. "Why have you stopped working?" it is asked. "What's the good," it explains, "I'll just get a pass or a bad mark; I've written very untidily."

> This case reveals a new effective motive for its homework. It is doing its lessons now because it wants to get a good mark....

> The really effective motive inducing the child to do its homework now is a motive that was previously "only understandable" for it.

> How does this transformation of motive come about? The question can be simply answered. It is a matter of an action's result being more significant, in certain conditions, than the motive that actually induces it.... A new "objectivation" of its needs comes about, which means that they are understood at a higher level. (Leont'ev, 1981, p. 402–403)

Leont'ev's account may be systematically presented as a sequence of four steps.

1. Along with the subject's dominant activity (for example, play), there is a culturally valued motive for a more advanced activity (for example, studying). In the subject's consciousness, the latter exists as an "understandable" motive only.

2. The representatives of culture induce by some means (e.g., rewards) the subject to engage in selected actions or components of the more advanced activity within the motivational framework of the earlier activity.

3. The "understandable" motive of the more advanced activity begins to be "effective" as the selected actions representing it begin to produce results that exceed the limits of the motive of the earlier activity. This transition manifests itself in disturbances – for example, the selected

actions are temporarily terminated because the subject senses acutely their inadequate quality in relation to the emerging more advanced motive.

4. Eventually, the new motive and activity take over the leading role.

Leont'ev seeks the mechanism of emergence of new activities in the contradiction *between* the motive of the previous activity and the motive of the new, more advanced activity. The problem is the external character of this contradiction. It seems as if the seed of the conflict, the new motive, were "transplanted" from outside, by the wise men of the culture. In his account Leont'ev fails to penetrate the inner contradiction *within* the previous activity.

This problem is visible in the characterization of the new, more advanced activity of Leont'ev's example. The new motive is supposed to be "to get a good mark." This would correspond to the exchange-value aspect of the motive of school going. The whole inner contradictoriness of this motive is here set aside.

The idea of inner contradictions of the existing dominant activity as the dynamic source of transition to the new activity was formulated by El'konin (1977). He postulated two phases within the development of each leading activity in the ontogenesis. In the first phase, the socioemotional and motivational aspects of activity (the relations between the subject and the others) dominate. Gradually, the mastery of the operational-technical aspect (the relations among the subject, the instruments, and the objects) improves, becoming dominant in the second phase. The contradiction arises as the operational-technical possibilities acquired by the subject exceed the limits of the motive of the activity.

> The transition from one period to the next is marked by a discrepancy between the child's operational and technical capacities and the tasks and motives that constitute the fabric of which these capacities are woven. (El'konin, 1977, p. 560–561)

Davydov, Markova, and Shumilin (1980) have applied this principle to the analysis of the ontogenetic emergence of learning activity in early school age. According to them, play produces the means and operations of imagination and symbolic transformation.

> Developed imagination and symbolic transformation start gradually to miss comprehensive and wide contents which could offer the child a possibility to use the hidden potentials of these abilities. But play in itself cannot offer such contents to the child. (Davydov, Markova & Shumilin, 1980, p. 11)

The problem with this formulation is its ahistorical nature. Inner contradictions of activities always take a form peculiar to the given socioeconomic formation. In the conceptions cited previously, the inner contradiction of play becomes abstract and universal.

What would be the quality of the inner contradiction of play activity peculiar to capitalism? If the object of play is imaginary practice, the contradiction must exist in the double nature of this very object. Symptomatically, the words "play" and "imagination" awaken associations of futility and escape, on the one hand – and of creative construction, on the other hand.

In her critique of the theories and practices of role playing, Frigga Haug (1977) argues that in capitalist society role playing is effectively reduced to pure interaction. It is socialization into flexible role exchange and intrinsic motivation *without objects and instruments*. This abstract aspect of role play would be motivated simply by the peer contacts and release of energy offered in play situations.

The relative poverty of the objective and instrumental aspect of play would mean that the inner contradiction of play activity often remains latent and inarticulate – manifesting itself mainly in complaints like "Mother, I don't know what to play." In the sphere of imaginary production, this would explain the prevalence of flat stereotypical reproductions of the models given by mass media and entertainment industry. This peculiar *underdevelopment of the inner contradiction of play* would also explain the relatively weak spontaneous aspiration for initial forms of learning activity found among primary-school children.

Jerome Bruner suggests that the mechanism behind this impoverishment of the objective-instrumental aspect of play is the general estrangement of industrialized man from the contents of work. According to him, "The young become more and more remote from the nature of the effort involved in running a society" because "vocation, competence, skill, sense of place in the system ... become more and more difficult for the young to fathom" (Bruner, 1976, p. 55.) As a consequence, the fulfillment of play is postponed to youth.

> Now "the play of the babes" has become separate from, dissociated from, the adult community and not understood by that community any better than the young comprehend or accept the ideals of the adult community.
>
> A place is made automatically, perhaps for the first time in our cultural tradition, for an intermediate generation, with power to model new forms of behavior. Their power comes precisely, I think, from the fact that they offer deep play. (Bruner, 1976, p. 59)

The developers of the theory of learning activity in the Soviet cultural-historical school, especially El'konin and Davydov, concentrated their theoretical and experimental efforts on primary school children. Learning activity was supposed to emerge directly after the dominance of role play, within the administrative and physical framework of school going (Davydov, 1982, p. 37). Against the background of my conceptualization of learning activity, this means that the primary object of learning activity in that age is the development of learning activity *itself*. In other words, the primary school pupils' task is to expand the discrete, internally contradictory learning actions occurring within the activity of school going into the objectively new system of learning activity. The motive of this activity is to learn how to acquire skills and knowledge and solve problems *by expanding the tasks into objectively novel activity systems,* resulting eventually not just in acquiring and solving the given, but in creating tasks and problems out of the larger activity context.

But learning activity cannot be acquired and developed "in general." Even if it is its own primary object, it simultaneously requires an object activity (or several activities) outside itself. In primary school, such object activities are reading, writing, and communicating with language; mathematics; rudiments of natural and social sciences; music; and so forth. Can pupils of that age really enter these varied and complex societal activity systems and take them to a historically new developmental stage? Hardly. What they perhaps can do is develop human learning into an objectively new qualitative stage – the stage of learning activity.

Thus, the object systems of language, mathematics, and so on, function here as secondary, derived objects, as "demonstration samples" for the methodology of learning activity. To take them as such requires a well-developed instrumentarium of play, enabling the pupils to see through this "demonstration sample" character of the school subjects and yet tackle them with full vigor. Using Bateson's (1972, p. 185) cryptic terminology: "In primary processes, map and territory are equated; in secondary processes, they can be discriminated," but "in play, they are both equated and discriminated."

Provided that the inner contradiction of play activity is more developed than it presently is in capitalist societies, this is a reasonable task. Indeed, there is some evidence of substantial differences between play activities in socialism and capitalism (Helenius, 1982). However, it would be unfounded to delimit the possibility of the ontogenetic emergence of learning activity to the confines of primary school years. At least in capitalism, *the inner contradictions of school going, work, and science/art seem to be more developed and mature than the inner contradiction of play.* This is not surprising, for the intensive commodification of play is of relatively recent origin. As play is commodified, it is, paradoxically, rearmed with instruments with which one may be able to penetrate the abstract societal practices and create imaginary ones. I refer to the emerging sophisticated general-purpose toys, ranging from Lego blocks to microcomputers. But this development has barely begun.

In conclusion, I suggest that the ontogenetic emergence of learning activity, at least in present-day capitalist societies, may with the highest probability take place in adulthood or adolescence, when the subject faces historically and individually pressing inner contradictions within his or her leading activity – be it work, school going, science, or art.

THE FIRST INTERMEDIATE BALANCE

In this chapter, the concept of learning activity has been derived from the evolution of the general concept of activity, on the one hand, and the cultural evolution of learning within other, historically earlier activities, on the other hand.

The concept of learning activity proposed here may be crystallized as *learning by expanding*. This formulation evokes several questions. What exactly is the relation of learning activity to other, supposedly "lower" forms of human learning? What is the relation of learning activity to development? And, above all, how and through what steps does the proposed learning activity proceed in practice? I will turn to these questions in Chapter 3.

3

The Zone of Proximal Development as the Basic Category of Expansive Research

TWO CLASSIC DILEMMAS OF DEVELOPMENTAL PSYCHOLOGY

Within modern developmental psychology, two classic dilemmas persist. The first is the problematic relationship between learning and development. The second is the equally problematic relationship between individual and societal development.

The first dilemma may be provisionally formulated as follows.

> The central question for our purposes is whether learning is identical to development or, at least, whether development can be conceptualized as consisting of some kind of accumulation of units of learning. (Baltes, Reese & Nesselroade, 1977, p. 208)

Another way of stating the problem is found in the work of Ann L. Brown. For her, development is essentially the process of going from the specific and context-bound to the general and context-free.

> Basically, the problem is how does the learner go from specific learned experiences to the formulation of a general rule that can be applied to multiple settings.... How does the learner come to use knowledge flexibly? How do isolated skills become connected together, extended and generalized? (Brown, 1982, p. 107)

The second dilemma has been formulated by Riegel in a polemical manner.

> Although they [developmental psychologists; Y. E.] study developmental differences (and sometimes changes), they eliminated, with few exceptions, any consideration of history. For example, young and old persons tested at one particular historical time differ widely in regard

to the social-historical conditions under which they grew up. Although the impact of historical changes during an extended period, for example, in education, health care, nutrition, communication, etc., is often much more dramatic than any differences in performance between young and old persons, this factor is generally disregarded in developmental studies. (Riegel, 1979, p. 21)

Bronfenbrenner states the same argument in poetic terms.

It would appear that, over the decades, developmental researchers have been carrying on a clandestine affair with Clio – the muse of history.... I suggest that, after so many years, the developmental researcher's illicit liaison with Clio is no longer a tenable arrangement; it is time we embraced her as a legitimate partner in our creative scientific efforts. (Bronfenbrenner, 1983, p. 176)

Bronfenbrenner notes that development takes place like in a moving train. One can walk forward and backward through the cars, but what really matters is where the train is going (Bronfenbrenner 1983, p. 175). The train metaphor exemplifies the central problem embedded in most of the available societally and ecologically oriented analysis of development, including his own (Bronfenbrenner, 1979). The environments or societal contexts are seen as historically changing, but not as being constructed and reconstructed by the people living in these contexts. Contexts are imposed upon, not produced by humans. Nobody seems to be driving the train, not to mention building and repairing it. Within the Riegelian tradition, there are attempts to turn this determination upside down and picture "individuals as producers of their own development" (Lerner & Busch-Rossnagel, 1981). This time, individual life choices are interpreted as decisive constituents of the historically changing societal context – an attempt not much more convincing than that of the ecologists. Buss (1979, p. 330) correctly notes that there has been a lot of loose talk within the life-span developmental literature about the individual-society dialectic as involving mutual or reciprocal determination – but little concrete analysis of what this really means. Regrettably, Buss himself offers merely a continuation of the loose talk.

What makes the individual-society dialectic a dialectic is that a given level of development on one side of the relationship is dependent upon, while at the same time is a condition for, that same level of development on the other side of the relationship. (Buss, 1979, p. 331)

A glance at recent discussions concerning these two classical dilemmas reveals a characteristic gap. Solutions to both dilemmas are sought *either* by reducing and subjugating one side of the dilemma to the other *or* by postulating a formal "reciprocal" relationship between the two sides of the dilemma. In both cases, no mediating "third factor" with which the connection of the two sides could be made concrete and alive is found.

In the following sections, the concept of activity is employed and further developed as such a mediating factor. On the basis of this mediating tool, the analysis of the two dilemmas will produce a deeper and more concrete problem, namely, *how the new is generated* in human development.

LEVELS OF LEARNING

In 1942, Gregory Bateson introduced the concept of "deutero-learning" to denote the processes of learning to learn. According to Bateson, learning to learn means the acquisition of certain abstract habits of thought like "'free will', instrumental thinking, dominance, passivity, etc." (Bateson, 1972, p. 166). As Bateson further noted, "Even within the duration of the single learning experiment we must suppose that some deutero-learning will occur" (Bateson, 1972, p. 169). Deutero-learning often takes place as tacit acquisition of nonconscious apperceptive habits.

In 1969, Bateson presented a more sophisticated version of his learning theory. He worked out a complex hierarchy of the processes of learning, based upon "an hierarchic classification of the types of error which are to be corrected in the various learning processes" (Bateson, 1972, p. 287). He summarized the hierarchy as follows.

> *Zero learning* is characterized by *specificity of response*, which – right or wrong – is not subjected to correction. *Rote*
>
> *Learning I* is *change in specificity of response* by correction of errors of choice within a set of alternatives.
>
> *Learning II* is *change in the process of Learning I*, e.g., a corrective change in the set of alternatives from which choice is made, or it is a change in how the sequence of experience is punctuated.
>
> *Learning III* is *change in the process of Learning II*, e.g., a corrective change in the system of *sets* of alternatives from which choice is made. (We shall see later that to demand this level of performance of some men and some mammals is sometimes pathogenic.)
>
> *Learning IV* would be *change in Learning III*, but probably does not occur in any adult living organism on this earth. Evolutionary process has, however, created organisms whose ontogeny brings them to Level III. The combination of phylogenesis with ontogenesis, in fact, achieves Level IV. (Bateson, 1972, p. 293)

According to Bateson, Learning I comprises the forms of learning treated by various versions of connectionism: habituation, Pavlovian conditioning, operant conditioning, rote learning, extinction. "In Learning I, every item of perception or behavior may be stimulus or response or reinforcement according to how the total sequence of interaction is punctuated," Bateson (1972, p. 292) notes. On the other hand, Learning II or learning to learn (deutero-learning) means the acquisition of the context or structure of some type of Learning I. Thus, common descriptions of a person's "character" are actually characterizations of the results of Learning II. "It follows that Learning II acquired in infancy is likely to persist through life" (Bateson, 1972, p. 301)

The outcomes of Learning II, the habits or the "character," save the individual from "having to examine the abstract, philosophical, aesthetic, and ethical aspects of many sequences of life" (Bateson, 1972, p. 303). Learning III, on the other hand, is essentially conscious self-alteration: It will "throw these unexamined premises open to question and change" (Bateson, 1972, p. 303). Learning III is a rare event, produced by the contradictions of Learning II. On Level III, the individual learns to control, limit, and direct his or her Learning II. One becomes conscious of one's habits and their formation. "Certainly it must lead to a greater flexibility in the premises acquired by the process of Learning II – a freedom from their bondage" (Bateson, 1972, p. 304).

The power of Bateson's argument has been amply testified by a number of eloquent analyses of the "hidden curriculum" in school learning (see especially Levy, 1976) as well as by works like those of Argyris and Schön (1974; 1978) on "single-loop learning" and "double-loop learning" in organizations and professions. The unconscious learning to learn, acquiring the context of "how to make it" in school and work, is a fact readily observable every day. Learning III seems indeed a rare event.

Bateson's conception cannot, however, be reduced to this. Otherwise he would not really be a groundbreaking thinker, richer than copies and followers. There are two major aspects that make his analysis distinctive. First, his hierarchy is not based on observation and classification but on evolutionary and historical analysis. Second, Bateson is not satisfied with presenting the situation as a stable picture. Instead of moral pleas for "changing the situation," he probes into the inner contradictions in Learning II that generate Learning III.

In 1956, Bateson and his colleagues worked out a general description of these inner contradictions and named it the *double bind*. In double bind situations, the individual, involved in an intense relationship, receives two messages or commands that deny each other – and the individual is unable to comment on the messages; that is, he or she cannot make a metacommunicative statement.

> If you say this stick is real, I will strike you with it. If you say this stick is not real, I will strike you with it. If you don't say anything, I will strike you with it. (Bateson, 1972, p. 208)

In a thoughtful discussion of the interpretations of the double bind, Paul Dell clarifies the concept as follows.

> The double bind is not done to someone, it resides in the "interaction-over-time" by which *"important basic relationships are chronically subjected to invalidation through paradoxical interaction."* (Dell, 1980, p. 325; see also Berger, 1978; Sluzki & Ransom, 1976)

The outcomes of Learning II, the unconscious habits, frequently and necessarily lead the individual to double bind situations. The habit once learned becomes self-defeating in a superficially similar but structurally altered social context; or two mutually exclusive habits seem to be required at the same time. Bateson reports an ingenious experiment with a porpoise. The animal was trained to demonstrate "operant conditioning" to the public. First, for a certain movement she received reinforcement (food). The next time, the previous movement did not yield reinforcement – but as the porpoise made another movement, she obtained the same reinforcement that was given the first time. This changing of contexts continued for fourteen sessions.

> The experience of being in the wrong was so disturbing to the porpoise that in order to preserve the relationship between porpoise and trainer ... it was necessary to give many reinforcements to which the porpoise was not entitled.... Each of the first fourteen sessions was characterized by many futile repetitions of whatever behavior had been reinforced in the immediately previous session. Seemingly only by "accident" did the animal provide a piece of different behavior. In the time-out between the fourteenth and fifteenth sessions, the porpoise appeared to be much excited, and when she came on stage for the fifteenth session she put on an elaborate performance including eight conspicuous pieces of behavior of which four were entirely new – never before observed in this species of animal. (Bateson, 1972, p. 277)

The case of the porpoise neatly illustrates the productive – and pathogenic – potential of the inner contradictions embedded in Learning II. However, it does *not* illustrate the breakthrough to Learning III. As Bateson states,

"Mammals other than man are probably capable of Learning II but incapable of Learning III" (Bateson, 1972, p. 306). What, then, does the case of the porpoise illustrate in terms of the mechanisms of learning? Certainly not the unconscious molding of habits. Also certainly not the reorganization of consciousness characteristic of Learning III.

In order to come to grips with this paradox, we must reinterpret Bateson's theory in terms of the concept of activity.

LEARNING AND DEVELOPMENT

Human activity is always a contradictory unity of production and reproduction, invention and conservation (see Moscovici, 1984, p. 60–62). The distinctive feature of human activity is that it is continuous *creation of new instruments* that in turn complicate and change qualitatively the very structure of the activity itself. It is essential that human activity cannot be reduced to the upper subtriangle of Figure 2.6 alone. Human activity is not only individual production. It is simultaneously and inseparably also social exchange and societal distribution. In other words, human activity always takes place within a community governed by a certain division of labor and by certain rules.

In Chapter 2, I discussed Leont'ev's (1978) hierarchy, consisting of three levels: the level of overall *activity,* the level of constituent *actions,* and the level of *operations* by means of which the actions are carried out. The corresponding regulative units are called *motives, goals,* and *conditions.* These three levels are not stable and fixed. Rather, activity is to be conceived of as "continuously proceeding transformations" between the levels (Leont'ev, 1978, p. 67).

> Activity may lose the motive that elicited it, whereupon it is converted into an action realizing perhaps an entirely different relation to the world, a different activity; conversely, an action may turn into an independent stimulating force and may become a separate activity; finally, an action may be transformed into a means of achieving a goal, into an operation capable of realizing various actions. (Leont'ev, 1978, p. 67)

Harré, Clarke, and DeCarlo (1985, p. 24–30) have proposed an analogous three-level hierarchy of the control of human actions. Their Level 1 is called "behavioural routines," Level 2 is "conscious awareness," and Level 3 is a dual formation of the "deep structure of mind" and "social orders." The otherwise convincing analysis suffers, however, from the authors' restrictive emphasis on language and "moral orders" (the lower-left-side subtriangle of Figure 2.6) with the corresponding neglect of the productive material aspects of activity.

In Bateson's Learning I, both the object/outcome and the instrument are given. Learning means repetitive corrections in the way the subject uses the instrument upon the object. There is a fixed correct way that is to be obtained. The movement is primarily one-way and nonconscious: from the object to the subject to the instrument to the object. Instruments at this level may be called tools or primary artifacts (Wartofsky, 1979, p. 201–202; Bunn, 1981, p. 23).

A tool is a generalized embodiment of operations that have become standardized through repetition: "The labor operations that have been given material shape, are crystallized, as it were, in it" (Leontyev, 1981, p. 216). A tool always implies more possible uses than the original operations that have given birth to it: The tool is the first "rational generalization" (Leontyev, 1981, p. 215). Phylogenetically, Learning I means extremely slow and gradual improvement of tools, due to the essentially nonreflective nature of their use: "for example, the 'natural retouching' of universal stone implements in the course of using them" (Leontyev, 1981, p. 237). Learning I is equivalent to the formation of nonconscious operations "in the course of simple adaptation to existing external conditions" (Leontyev, 1981, p. 237).

Learning II is actually an inseparable companion of Learning I. In its rudimentary or reproductive form, Learning II means that as the given tasks are repeatedly accomplished within Learning I, a tacit representation or image of the way of accomplishing the tasks is necessarily generated. It first takes the form of a habit, essentially unconscious and implicit. However, even such a reproductive habit or image is potentially a second-order instrument, a secondary artifact, "created for the purpose of preserving and transmitting skills, in the production and use of 'primary' artifacts" (Wartofsky, 1979, p. 201).

> Such representations, then, are reflexive embodiments of forms of action or praxis, in the sense that they are symbolic externalizations or objectifications of such modes of action – "reflections" of them, according to some convention, and therefore understood as images of such forms of action – or, if you like, pictures or models of them.... The modes of this representation may be gestural, or oral (linguistic or musical) or visual, but obviously such that they may be communicated in one or more sense-modalities; such, in short, that they may be perceived. (Wartofsky, 1979, p. 201)

Wartofsky speaks about "reflexive embodiments." Bunn, in making essentially the same distinction between tools and models (corresponding to primary and secondary artifacts, respectively), argues in a similar vein.

> The wider application of an exosomatic instrument to the world implies that the laws which had governed the working of a tool have become so useful at large that, by synecdoche, they come to substitute for the world. When a tool is "turned" from its intended use and contemplated instead of applied, the arbitrary connection between a tool and its referred function is transformed so that it is no longer a means to a different end. Seen as reflections of the end itself, the principles by which a tool is constructed may be construed as hieroglyphs, omens, signatures, symptoms, laws, or models of higher function. (Bunn, 1981, p. 24)

part stated for the whole [handwritten margin note]

At first sight, these notions are incompatible with the unconscious nature of the acquisition of habits within Learning II. How can something be unconscious and reflexive at the same time? Yet, this is exactly what Learning II is. It is best conceived of as oscillation between two ways of making models, two kinds of generalizations. These two ways were identified by Selz (1924) as "instrument actualization" and "instrument abstraction." Bartlett, coined these two ways "closed system thinking" and "adventurous thinking."

> Thinking, as a mental process, likes, so to speak, to go on in closed systems. For this gives it a wide apparent range, and especially rids it, as completely as possible, of all ultimate uncertainty.... But the thinker is more than a thinking machine. So there grows up a tremendous struggle between those forces which try to reduce all forms of human knowledge to the closed-system variety ... and those forces which lie behind the human zest for adventure and are continually revolting against and breaking out of the closed system. (Bartlett, 1958, p. 96)

A very illustrative experimental description of the oscillatory interaction of these two ways was provided by Karmiloff-Smith and Inhelder (1975). The essential precondition of any Learning II is a problem situation. The training of the porpoise moved the animal into the realm of Learning II because she was presented with a task in which uncertainty concerning the correct procedure prevailed. Similarly, Karmiloff-Smith and Inhelder presented young children with a relatively difficult block-balancing task. As in the case of the porpoise, the first approach taken by the subjects was that of seeking the immediate solution and concentrating on the outcome of one's effort – the "action response," as the authors named it.

The children were happy when they had the blocks balanced, unhappy when they failed. However, another approach emerged in the midst of the first one.

> Frequently, even when children were successful in balancing an item on one dimension ..., they went on exploring the other dimensions of each block. It was as if their attention were momentarily diverted from their goal of balancing to what had started as a subgoal, i.e., the search for means. One could see the children oscillating between seeking the goal and seeking to "question" the block. (Karmiloff-Smith & Inhelder, 1975, p. 201)

This latter approach was named "theory-response." Within that approach, the subject does not measure his or her success with the immediate outcome (balanced or not balanced), but rather with the verification or falsification of his or her hypothetical model. If the subject has formulated the hypothesis that, placed in a certain position, the block will not balance, he or she will rejoice when the block does not in fact balance. In Bruner's (1974, p. 218–238) words, the subject has entered "generic learning" or started "inventing a coding system."

> At this point we witness experimentation for the experimentation's sake; for attending to the means implies seeking knowledge of the approximate range of possible actions on an object. (Karmiloff-Smith & Inhelder, 1975, p. 207–208)

These two aspects of Learning II may be named (a) reproductive and (b) productive, for the sake of simplicity. In Learning IIa, the object/outcome is given and the instrument is found through trial and error, that is, through "blind search" among previously known means. In Learning IIb, the object/outcome is given and the instrument is found – or rather invented – through experimentation. The former leads to empirical generalizations; the latter is the prerequisite of theoretical generalizations (Dawydow, 1977). The latter, productive aspect cannot be totally eliminated from Learning II, even if it may well be subordinated to the point of invisibility.

Interestingly enough, the porpoise went through a learning process essentially similar to that of the children in the experiment of Karmiloff-Smith and Inhelder. As these authors point out, before a conscious theory construction can take place, the subject must gradually crystallize his or her previous mode of action into a model against which negative examples may be recognized as counterexamples. In a spontaneous process, this often takes a great number of attempts. This process of recognition is manifested in pauses.

> As long as the child is predominantly success-oriented, there are rarely any pauses in his action sequences. As his attention shifts to means, however, pauses become more and more frequent in the course of the sequence. Only when goal and means are considered simultaneously do pauses precede action. (Karmiloff-Smith & Inhelder, 1975, p. 208)

The classic treatment of the importance of pauses in problem solving is Köhler's (1925) study of Sultan the ape. The pauses are obviously a close relative to the excitation of the porpoise between the fourteenth and fifteenth sessions. The recent work of Schön (1983) testifies nicely that moments of productive experimentation or "reflection-in-action" appear in the daily work practice of professionals in various fields. Here again, pauses or momentary withdrawals from the interaction play a crucial role as the professional enters into a "framing experiment," a reformulation of the problem with the help of analogy based on a "generative metaphor" from his or her earlier experience (Schön, 1983, p. 268–269). Lopes (1981) reports similar findings from his research on therapy sessions.

In Learning I, the object presents itself as mere immediate resistance, not consciously separated from the subject and instrument by the learner. In Learning II, the object is conceived of as a problem, demanding specific efforts. The subject is no more a nonconscious agent but an individual under constant self-assessment stemming from the success or failure of his or her attempts at the solution. In other words, the whole triangle depicted in Figure 2.6 acquires a hierarchically higher second layer. This second layer corresponds to the formation and execution of goal-directed actions in Leont'ev's scheme. The operations formed on this basis, from the "top down," become automatic but not in the same way as in Learning I. These operations are in principle capable of becoming subjected to conscious elaboration when there is some departure from the normal conditions of performance.

> Labour operations ... thus acquire another genesis in connection with their complication: when the goal of the action is part of another action as a condition of its performance, the first action is transformed into a mode of realising the second, into a conscious operation.... From the aspect of the structure of man's consciousness the formation of conscious operations means a new step in its development, a step that consists in the rise of a "consciously controlled" content in addition to the content presented in consciousness, and the transition of the one to the other. (Leontyev, 1981, p. 237)

At the first glance, Learning IIb would seem to be true learning activity. However, Learning IIb is still typically restricted to the insightful, experimental solution of *discrete, given problems*. In this sense, Learning IIb is essentially discontinuous, limited to the level of actions. The creation of new instruments within Learning IIb is potentially expansive – but only potentially. Learning IIb does not in any automatic manner imply that the context of the given problem is broken and expanded.

Learning II represents a fundamental generalization of the outcomes of learning. In that sense, Learning II means development, going from the specific to the general (recall Brown's criterion). But the developmental step from Learning I to Learning II is not restricted to humans, and neither is it fundamental for the typically human brand of development. Learning II is a level open in principle to other higher mammals as well. In terms of human phylogenesis, it is dejà vu. "Put simply, a man may evolve, but how could he truly get beyond himself?" (Dell, 1982, p. 34)

The typically human type of development, not found in any other species, is transition to Learning III. This we know from Bateson. But what is the specific mechanism of Learning III?

Bateson offers some key hints. As we remember, Learning III is a product of double bind situations. The most well-known product of continuous double binds is schizophrenia. It is a deep restructuring of the subject's consciousness, caused by contexts where the subject is unable to comment in a metacommunicative way on the contradictory messages or commands he or she receives. But what if the subject is able to comment on the messages? "If you say the stick is real, I will strike you with it. If you say the stick is not real...." According to Bateson, the subject "might reach up and take the stick away from the master" (Bateson, 1972, p. 208). In other words, the subject may rise above the constraints of the context and break it, or put it into a wider context where it becomes relative and changeable.

> The question is explosive. The simple stylized experimental sequence of interaction in the laboratory is generated by and partly determines a network of contingencies which goes out in a hundred directions leading out of the laboratory into the processes by which psychological research is designed, the interactions between psychologists, the economics of research money, etc., etc. (Bateson, 1972, p. 305)

In Learning II, the subject is presented with a problem and tries to solve the problem. In Learning III, the problem or the task itself must be created.

> Problems do not present themselves to the practitioner as givens. They must be constructed from the materials of problematic situations which

are puzzling, troubling, and uncertain. (Schön, 1983, p. 40; see also Seidel, 1976)

If the problem is given, the subject asks: "What is the meaning and sense of this problem in the first place? Why should I try to solve it? How did it emerge? Who designed it, for what purpose and for whose benefit?" As Bateson notes, this kind of behavior is readily interpreted as disruptive.

> Even the attempt at Level III can be dangerous, and some fall by the wayside. These are often labeled by psychiatry as psychotic, and many of them find themselves inhibited from using the first person pronoun. (Bateson, 1972, p. 305–306)

Learning III is motivated by the resolution of the contradictions of Level II.

> The resolution of contraries reveals a world in which a personal identity merges into all the processes of relationship in some vast ecology or aesthetics of cosmic interaction.... Every detail of the universe is seen as proposing a view of the whole. (Bateson, 1972, p. 306)

Whereas in Learning II the object is seen as a problem possessing its own objective dynamics outside the subject, in Learning III the object system is seen as containing the subject within it. Furthermore, the quality of the subject itself changes radically. As Dell (1982, p. 34) notes, "All multi-individual interactional systems are capable of true discontinuous change ... because *coherence as an interactional system is fundamentally different from the coherence that constitutes the individual living members who constitute that system.*".

> Selfhood is a product or aggregate of Learning II. To the degree that a man achieves Learning III, and learns to perceive and act in terms of the contexts of contexts, his "self" will take on a sort of irrelevance. The concept of "self" will no longer function as a nodal argument in the punctuation of experience. (Bateson, 1972, p. 304)

This fundamental change in the character of the subject has been described by Raiethel (1983), following Hegel, as the progression from the initial "Urzentrierung" (Learning I) to "Dezentrierung" (Learning II) and finally to "Rezentrierung" (Learning III). The individual self is replaced – or rather qualitatively altered – by a search for a collective subject, capable of mastering the complexity of "contexts of contexts," that is, of societal practices with highly developed division of labor as well as multilevel technological and symbolic mediations.

What are the appropriate instruments of Learning III? Wartofsky suggests a concept of tertiary artifacts.

> We may speak of a class of artifacts which can come to constitute a relatively autonomous "world", in which the rules, conventions and outcomes no longer appear directly practical, or which, indeed, seem to constitute an arena of non-practical, or "free" play or game activity.... So called "disinterested" perception, or aesthetic perception, or sheer contemplation, then becomes a possibility; but not in the sense that it has no use. Rather, in the sense that the original role of the representation has been, so to speak, suspended or bracketed....
>
> I would characterize such artifacts, abstracted from their direct representational function, as "tertiary" artifacts, and suggest that they constitute a domain in which there is a free construction in the imagination of rules and operations different from those adopted for ordinary "this-worldly" praxis.... That is to say, just as in dreams our imagery is derived from our ordinary perception, but transcends or violates the usual constraints, so too in imaginative praxis, the perceptual modes are derived from and related to a given historical mode of perception, but are no longer bound to it. (Wartofsky, 1979, p. 208–209)

In discussing the means of scientific activity, Judin (1978, p. 323; see also Otte, 1984) proposes "theoretical substantiations" as the instruments of the tertiary level. They serve as the means of constructing and using "modeling conceptions" as second level instruments. In a similar vein, we may argue that Wartofsky's tertiary artifacts are actually methodologies or visions or world outlooks that serve as guidelines in the production and application of secondary artifacts, that is, models.

Learning III may now be characterized as the construction and application of world outlooks or methodologies – or ideologies, if you will. But it is not only a matter of imaginary production.

> The activity of the imagination is therefore a mode of alternative perceptual praxis, and is "off-line" *only* relative to a historically actual or dominant present mode of perceptual praxis. What the imagination is, as "internal representation", i.e., as a picturing "in the mind" of such alternatives, I take to be derivative from the actual making of imaginative artifacts. That is to say, in its genesis I take imaginative praxis to be praxis in the actual world, or the actual production of representations; the interiorization of these representations, as "mental" artifacts, I take to be a derivative process. (Wartofsky, 1979, p. 209)

In Learning III, the subject becomes conscious and gains an imaginative *and* thus potentially also a practical mastery of whole systems of activity

TABLE 3.1. *Characterizations of the hierarchical structure of activity*

Leont'ev (1978)	Harré & al. (1985)	Bateson (1972)	Raiethel (1983)	Wartofsky (1979)	Judin (1978)
Activity/ motive	Deep structure of mind/ social orders	Learning 3	Rezentri- erung	Tertiary artifacts	Theoretical substan- tiations
Action/ goal	Conscious awareness	Learning 2	Dezentri- erung	Secondary artifacts	Modeling concep- tions
Operation/ conditions	Behavioral routines	Learning 1	Urzentri- erung	Primary artifacts	Procedures

TABLE 3.2. *The proposed hierarchical structure of activity*

Subject	Instruments	Object	Community	Rules	Division of labor
Collective subject	Methodology, ideology	We in the world	Societal net- work of activities	Societal (state, law, religion)	Societal division of labor
Individual subject	Models	Problem task	Collective organiza- tion	Organiza- tional rules	Organiza- tional division of labor
Noncon- scious	Tools	Resistance	Immediate primary group	Interpersonal rules	Interpersonal division of labor

in terms of the past, the present, and the future. Individual manifestations of Learning III are commonly called "personal crises," "breaking away," "turning points," or "moments of revelation."

The triangle of learning activity (Figure 2.12) should now be depicted as a three-level hierarchy. Each corner of the triangle would thus have three qualitatively different levels: that of the overall activity, that of actions, and that of operations. Instead of attempting such a complex graphic presen- tation, I summarize the various characterizations of those three levels in Table 3.1.

I summarize my own characterization of the corners of the three-level triangular model of learning activity in Table 3.2.

Learning I and Learning II, in their interaction and contradictions, represent what is commonly understood as learning. Learning III represents what is often referred to as development. However, this kind of categorization is misleading. Learning I and Learning II are always embedded, in an altered form, in Learning III. Development can only take place as a "result" of learning. This was clearly realized by Vygotsky. He made a distinction between two kinds of (school) learning – bad and good. According to him, "The only 'good learning' is that which is in advance of development" (Vygotsky, 1978, p. 89). This distinction corresponds to my distinction between Learning IIa and Learning IIb.

> From this point of view, learning is not development; however, properly organized learning results in mental development and sets in motion a variety of developmental processes that would be impossible apart from learning. Thus, learning is a necessary and universal aspect of the process of developing culturally organized, specifically human, psychological functions. To summarize, the most essential feature of our hypothesis is the notion that developmental processes do not coincide with learning processes. Rather, the developmental process lags behind the learning process.... Our hypothesis establishes the unity but not the identity of learning processes and internal developmental processes. It presupposes that the one is converted into the other. (Vygotsky, 1978, p. 90–91)

In other words, productive experimentation of type IIb is a necessary precondition for the fruitful resolution of double binds. Expansive, nonpathological breaking out of the context of the double bind requires certain sophisticated learning actions, typical of the researchlike reflective model building and testing of Learning IIb. In the school context, this implies that pupils questioning the relevance of their school learning and seeking wider contexts of life activities will benefit from acquiring and applying actions of Learning IIb. However, this is only a stepping-stone toward learning activity, or Learning III. In learning activity, development itself becomes the object of learning.

But what about the criterion and direction of development? Brown's suggestion was that development is formation of general, context-free structures and skills. Nearly the same is said about Vygotsky's conception. According to Wertsch, Vygotsky's principle of development was the "decontextualization of mediational means."

> The decontextualization of mediational means is the process whereby the meanings of signs become less and less dependent of the unique spatiotemporal context in which they are used. (Wertsch, 1985c, p. 33)

The problem with this kind of criterion of development is its inherently ahistorical nature. Rather than being nonspecific or context-free, the cognitive structures and skills of competent modern Western adults are specific to a societal context saturated and dominated by the abstract bond of exchange value (see Chapter 2). The structures and skills of competent adults of an industrialized socialist society are likewise not decontextualized in any general, ahistorical manner. Beneath their seemingly universal surface, these structures and skills stem from a certain peculiar socioeconomic bond between people.

So the criterion of human psychological development is to be found in the historical development of the human society. But is there a direction to that development?

In their recent work on the historical development of human activity, Kuchermann and Wigger-Kösters (1985) argue that there is a direction: toward increased subjectivity or subjectness (*zunehmende Subjektwerdung*). This is manifested in the historical increase in the numbers and interconnections of human activities, and in the tremendous widening of the object field of those activities.

I prefer to say that *activities are becoming increasingly societal*. The German word for this is *Vergesellschaftung* – a corresponding convenient English phrase is lacking. To become increasingly societal means, first of all, that activity systems become gradually larger, more voluminous, and denser in their internal communication. Consequently, activity systems have impact on growing numbers of people. Second, it means that different activity systems, and people within them, become increasingly interdependent, forming ever more complex networks and hierarchies of interaction. Third, this interdependency is not just a formal affiliation. Activity systems are increasingly penetrated and saturated by the basic socioeconomic laws and by the corresponding contradictions of the given society. In other words, activities are less and less left in relative isolation from societal turbulences, as remnants from earlier socioeconomic formations.

These formulations do not coincide with a linear, mechanically deterministic conception of history. When I talk about contradictions, I mean that each socioeconomic formation has its own, qualitatively specific contradictions, which make simple quantitative comparisons and finalistic images of an ideal society senseless. Contradictions also imply zones of relative indetermination in the course of development. Yet, the formulations provide a basis for talking sensibly about more or less advanced forms, even about "higher" and "lower" levels of development. Such words are not taken here as synonyms for "better" and "worse," or for "desirable" and "objectionable."

INDIVIDUAL AND SOCIETAL DEVELOPMENT

I have covered one side of the contradictory unity of learning and development. The other side may be more unexpected. Learning is not only a necessary precondition of development – development is also a necessary and always present ingredient of learning. This contention resembles the traditional idea of defining development as a sum of learning experiences. But the resemblance is only external.

Learning III as the outcome and form of typically human development is basically collective in nature. The collective Learning III is perhaps not so dramatic as its individual manifestations. But the real production and application of world outlooks, restructuring of complex activity systems, is not conceivable in individual and drastically sudden terms alone. In periods of exceptional upheavals, such as revolutions, the collective and the individual, the profound and the sudden, the action and the activity, seem to merge, even to the point where the individual seems to take the leading role. But these are temporary phenomena. The bread and butter of human development is collective Learning III, gradual in form but profound in substantial effects.

In Learning II, in problem solving, there is always – whether conscious or not, planned or unplanned – the phase of the application and realization of the acquired instrument (be it a habit or a model) in real-life conditions, in societal practice. This phase, however, is rarely included in the object field of learning research.

> If we are to study the conditions under which generic learning occurs, the pattern of much of present learning research needs drastic change. The present approach is to study the speed of acquisition of new learning and, possibly, to study the conditions that produce extinction. When we have carried our experimental subjects through these steps, we either dismiss them or, if they are animal subjects, dispose of them. The exception, of course, is the clinician; but even his research on learning and cognition is of the cross-sectional type. We have been accustomed to speaking of maze wise rats and test wise human beings, but in the spirit of being annoyed by an inconvenience.... If we really intend to study the conditions of generic learning ..., then we shall have to keep our organisms far longer and teach them original tasks of greater diversity than we do now. (Bruner, 1974, p. 233)

If we follow Learning II after the laboratory phases described by Bruner, into the subject's activity outside the laboratory, we shall find out that the newly acquired instrument never stays exactly the same as it was in the phases of its original individual acquisition and internalization. It will change and produce surprises, new qualities, in its very integration into the wider context of the social life activity of the subject. It will be concretized and generalized in practice, which is necessarily richer than the abstraction originally acquired.

> Appearing in direct contiguity with objective reality and subordinate to it, activity is modified and enriched, and in that enrichment it is crystallized in a product. The realized activity is richer and truer than the consciousness that precedes it. Thus, for the consciousness of the subject, contributions that are introduced by his activity remain cryptic; from this it follows that consciousness may seem a basis of activity. (Leont'ev, 1978, p. 78)

This tacit transition from the sphere of initial internalization to the sphere of the often delayed externalization and objectification is actually a transition from Learning II to Learning III – from individual actions to the public or collective mode of activity.

> The ends of the actions are intended, but the results which actually follow from these actions are not intended; or when they do seem to correspond to end intended, they ultimately have consequences quite other than those intended. Historical events thus appear on the whole to be ... governed by chance. But where on the surface accident holds sway, there actually it is always governed by inner, hidden laws and it is only a matter of discovering these laws. (Engels, 1976, p. 366)

Blackboxed

The individual makes a contribution to the societal development and thus indirectly to his or her own individual development. This differs from the explosive mode of Learning III described by Bateson. Obviously both modes exist – the explosive and the tacit or gradual. The problem with the latter is that it takes place in the form of unrecognized innovations, "behind the back" of the subject, as it were. The subject remains merely a potential subject of the activity and development, effectively cut off from their collective mastery by the fragmented division of labor.

A proper example of this latter, gradual and tacit aspect of Learning III is the development of language. As the individual learns new models of using language, he or she and the teachers know that these models are not societally new; they are only new to this specific individual. But as the individual uses those models in life activities, he or she actually produces *societally new* variations of the models, though mostly nonconsciously. As Ushakova (1977, p. 533) notes, "Word invention, having the characteristics of an analogical process, takes place as a result of 'collision' of two generalized lexical structures." The individual's contribution quickly loses its individual identity and merges into a vast pool of similar contributions in the social exchange within communities. In the long run, it will participate in the formation of new compelling models of language use, models into which the individual may or may not "grow from below," without explosions. These models eventually mold his or her whole world outlook and methodology of dealing with the world, though often very slowly and marginally.

In this, admittedly indirect and even somewhat drab sense Learning II always entails Learning III. What is not so drab is that this view suggests a new approach for developmental and learning research. Instead of asking how the individual subject developed into what he or she is, the developmentalist might start by asking how the objects and structures of the life-world (themselves understood as activity systems) have been and are created by human beings, how something objectively new is developed all the time. The researcher would thus start with Bronfenbrenner's "train," but as a train that is continuously constructed and reconstructed by its passengers. On the other hand, this kind of constructivism does not mean seeing "individuals as producers of their own development." Rather, individuals are seen as coproducers of societal and cultural development and only indirectly as producers of their own development. Consequently, a learning researcher might not be satisfied with recording what is learned within the period of the initial acquisition of new knowledge or skills. Rather, he or she would concentrate on the practical application as an integral part of the process of learning and trace the mutations of the acquired contents as they become integrated into the life activities of the learner, that is, truly socialized and generalized.

Previously I have presented two alternative forms of Learning III from the point of view of the individual: development as personal crises and explosions and development as tacit, invisible contributions. Both these are very old forms of learning, perhaps as old as the human race. How does this fit with the conclusion of Chapter 2, namely, that learning activity or learning by expanding is an emerging, historically new and higher form of human learning?

The solution is that Learning III, or learning activity, or learning by expanding, is both old and new. The two old forms considered earlier (personal crises and invisible contributions) are preliminary and premature forms. In them, the Batesonian concept of Learning III does not yet reveal its full potential. They both fail to account for the most interesting phenomena of Learning III – for its new, emerging form.

Consider, for example, the Children's Campaign for Nuclear Disarmament, initiated by Maria Schumann (fifteen years), Becky Dennison (twelve years), Nessa Rabin (thirteen years), Hannah Rabin (sixteen years), Susie Dennison (sixteen years), Solveig Schumann (seventeen years), and Max Schumann (seventeen years), in the United States in June 1981. The movement started from the idea of writing personal letters to President Reagan, demanding nuclear disarmament.

> By word of mouth, sending information – describing the idea of the letter writing campaign – to schools and kids they had the addresses of, the seven friends received 2 832 letters written to President Reagan from children all over the country till October 1981. Until June of 1982 further 5 404 letters were received. On October 17th, 1981, and on June 19th, 1982, the letters were read aloud by a delegation of children standing in front of the White House, after a meeting with President Reagan could not be realized on both days. (Grünewald, 1985, p. 14)

In an interview, Hannah Rabin stressed the importance of kid groups working independently of adults.

> We do need adults' support in some way. We need adults to give us money, because we kids have no money, we need adults to drive us around and feed us when we have meetings and things like that, but it's very important that kids have their own groups, that kids are speaking directly to kids. If adults are involved there are too many just adult-kid-conflicts that come into play. And adults have their own movement, too. (Grünewald, 1985, p. 15)

The work of the planning committee and the centralized letter campaign stopped in 1982. Today the work is carried on by a number of local groups that develop various activity forms. The campaign spread to the former West Germany and some other European countries. Susie Denison writes.

> In working for the letter writing campaign we have gotten in touch with many kids and there are about 30 CCND chapters all over the country. We have also gone to lots of schools and had workshops with kids where we talk with them about the arms race, the threat of nuclear war, our fears that we may all be destroyed and what we can do to bring about nuclear disarmament. (Grünewald, 1985, p. 16)

The children who started the campaign did not experience explosive personal crises; nor were their contributions invisible, tacit, and nonconscious. Their small actions grew into an objectively new form of societal activity. The societal development to which the circle of seven children had given the impulse has undoubtedly had important effects on the individual development of those children. According to Leont'ev (1978, p. 133), the first basic parameter of personality development is "the richness of the connections of the individual with the world" – something that was multiplied for the initiators of the campaign. The second parameter is the degree to which activities and their motives are arranged hierarchically. In this respect, a highly developed personality is characterized by central, dominant motives that have become conscious "life goals." Such a "motive-goal" "merges his (man's) life with the life of people, with their good" (Leont'ev, 1978, p. 134). Something like this may be discerned in the interview of Hannah Rabin.

> There are adults who say we shouldn't do what we are doing because it's a grown-up issue. We really disagree with that. We think it's our future that is going to be destroyed and we have to take responsibility for it because the adults alone are not strong enough to get rid of the arms race. It's going to take every single person in the world I think to finally end this threat. (Grünewald, 1985, p. 18)

Compare this example with the effects of school learning, or with the effects of the regular campaigns against smoking, against traffic accidents, and so forth. In these cases, the initial impulses are massive, as measured with hours, manpower, or money. Yet the developmental effects in societal practice are meager, sometimes negligible.

This suggests that there are two basic types of development – development now understood as *transitions between the levels of learning*, as movement from operations to actions to activity. These two types may be compared with the consequences of throwing a stone into the water. Normally, the stone produces a series of circles of waves, where the innermost waves are highest and then get smaller while moving outward, until they die out completely. In human development, there appears not only this type of movement, but also another, opposite type, in which the waves grow while they move outward from the impulse, then turn back to mold the initial source of impulse, and finally create a new, higher-level structure or stability than the original.

This metaphor, used also by Ilya Prigogine (1985, p. 7) in a more general context, forces us to consider the crux of the problem. How is the objectively, societally new generated in human development?

HOW THE NEW IS GENERATED

Prigogine defines the essence of the emerging new scientific rationality as follows.

> Classical science is associated with the negation of time in the name of eternity. Nineteenth-century science is associated with a concept of time as decay. But the history of our world cannot be a succession of historical catastrophes only.... After all, if there was decay, there must also have been some moments of creation. Curiously enough, this simple truth seems to have been first perceived by artists.... At present, physics is in search of a third conception of time as reducible neither to repetition nor to decay. (Prigogine, 1985, p. 3)

In an impressive essay on the relations between the organism and the environment, the biologist Lewontin specifies this approach further.

> We cannot regard evolution as the "solution" by species of some predetermined environmental "problems" because it is the life activities of the species themselves that determine both the problems and solutions simultaneously.... So, too, our central nervous systems are not fitted to some absolute laws of nature but to laws of nature operating within a framework created by our own sensuous activity.... Organisms within their individual lifetimes and in the course of their evolution as a species do not *adapt* to environments; they *construct* them. They are not simply *objects* of the laws of nature, altering themselves to bend to the inevitable, but active *subjects* transforming nature according to its laws. (Lewontin, 1982, p. 162–163)

In developmental psychology, we find occasional discussions and puzzlements around the question "How is the new generated from the old?" The analysis presented so far suggests that this is an erroneous way of stating the question. The new is not generated from the old but from the *living movement* leading away from the old.

> "If you do not know what you are looking for, then why are you looking; if you know what you are looking for, then why are you looking for it?" For a creature with a mind, search and investigation, which involve this internal contradiction, are characteristic. This fundamental contradiction is the true source of the development of the mind of animals and man.... To look for something that does not yet exist but that is possible... this is the fundamental, cardinal aspect of the vital activity of every sentient and thinking being – a subject.... In light of this activity the paradox of search consists in the fact that it combines within itself the possible and the actual. (Davydov & Zinchenko, 1982, p. 24)

Davydov and Zinchenko, in line with Bernshtein, define the living movement as the genetically primary unit of analysis of mental reality. The
cultural prototype of living movement is work. The paradox of search is
embedded in the very first forms of human labor activity.

> Movement takes place as a necessary connective link between foreseeing
> and remembering. The disjunction between these two elements is over-
> come by the present, that is, intensive action in the present. (Davydov &
> Zinchenko, 1982, p. 31)

We may now return to the example of Children's Campaign for Nuclear
Disarmament and to the postulated two types of development. It seems
that the living movement demonstrated by the campaign contains one
distinctive feature. The paradox of the search has in this case become conscious to the searchers themselves; it has reached the quality of a genuine
double bind; and it has been resolved through collective, conscious action
in the present. In other words, the type of development we are concerned
with here – expansive generation of new activity structures – requires above
all an *instinctive or conscious mastery of double binds*. A double bind may
now be reformulated as a *social, societally essential dilemma that cannot be
resolved through separate individual actions alone – but in which joint cooperative actions can push a historically new form of activity into emergence*.

The mastery of double binds is first of all historical analysis or historical intuition of the inner contradictions of the activity system of which the
subject is a part. Here we go back to the instruments. To be inventive in a
dilemma is to invent a new instrument for the resolution of the dilemma.
This demands experimentation, borrowing, or "conquering" already existing artifacts (such as letters in the case of the children's campaign) for
new uses.

> The experimenter cannot move beyond the point for which methods and
> instrumentation are available. He may sometimes invent them; more
> often he adopts them from some source that may be well outside of his
> own immediate interest....
>
> One of the most important features of these turning-points in experi-
> mental development is that they very often introduce methods and
> instrumentation new to the field of research involved, but already devel-
> oped in some other region of investigation. But if the experimenter who
> does this has any original impact upon his science he always does more
> than this. He must adapt the new methods and instruments for use in his
> own field, and he must show that they can be used to reach a compelling
> answer to some current problems, and at the same time to lead on to a
> number of further problems. (Bartlett, 1958, p. 133–135)

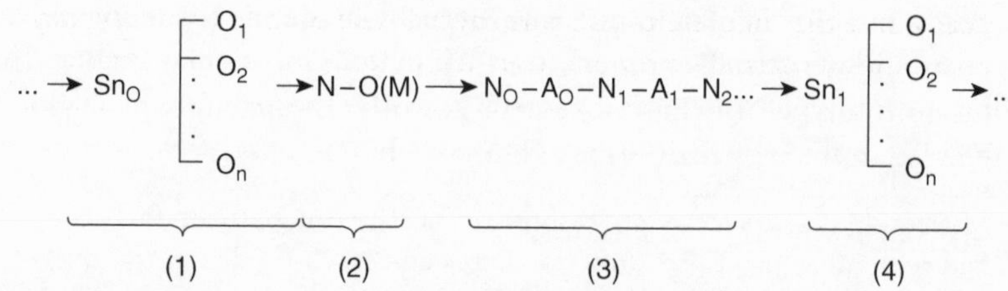

$$\ldots \to Sn_O \begin{bmatrix} O_1 \\ O_2 \\ \vdots \\ O_n \end{bmatrix} \to N{-}O(M) \longrightarrow N_O{-}A_O{-}N_1{-}A_1{-}N_2\ldots \to Sn_1 \begin{bmatrix} O_1 \\ O_2 \\ \vdots \\ O_n \end{bmatrix} \to \ldots$$

$$\underbrace{\hspace{3cm}}_{(1)} \quad \underbrace{\hspace{2cm}}_{(2)} \quad \underbrace{\hspace{3cm}}_{(3)} \quad \underbrace{\hspace{2cm}}_{(4)}$$

FIGURE 3.1. The emergence of activity according to Bratus & Lishin (1983, p. 44).

Bartlett's analysis of scientific experimentation is transferable to other societal activities. The problem in Kohlbergian moral dilemmas is that there is no field of activities and artifacts in which the dilemma would be embedded. Thus, there is nothing to experiment with in the first place.

The instruments are also what distinguishes the case of the porpoise from the case of the children's campaign. Though the porpoise went through an intensive dilemma and resolved it by producing genuinely new behavior, she never produced new instruments in the proper sense of the word. She did not produce implements or models that could be communicated about, preserved, and transmitted among her own species. These processes could possibly take place only through a kind of symbiosis with man. The actions of the porpoise could not by themselves push into emergence a new cooperative activity system in the "societies" of the porpoise species. They would remain individual achievements unless man chose try to transfer them to other individuals of that species.

Bratus and Lishin (1983) have presented an instructive discussion that has direct relevance to the problem of the double binds. On the basis of Leont'ev's (1978) theoretical work and their own clinical experiments, they describe the psychological phases of the emergence of a new activity with the diagram presented in Figure 3.1.

In the diagram, the symbol N refers to "need," the symbol A refers to "activity," the symbol O refers to "object," and the symbol M refers to "motive." Each new expanded need is produced in an activity that in turn is established on the basis of a previous need that, having met its object, has been transformed into a motive. But the exceptional point in these continuing cycles is something that is symbolized with S_n. This symbol refers to the concept of "need state."

A breakdown in the sequence of activity is possible at two points: either at the point N-A, when a need cannot be satisfied by the previous set of means of activities; or at the point A-N, when, on the contrary, the existing operational and technical means do not correspond to the previous needs. In either of these cases some special state of indeterminacy may arise in which desires, as it were, lose their object, and one may say that a person desires (sometimes very passionately) something he himself does not know and cannot clearly describe. This peculiar state of indeterminant, temporarily objectless desire may be called a need state. (Bratus & Lishin, 1983, p. 43)

This characterization immediately reminds us of the notion of the paradox of the search as formulated previously by Davydov and Zinchenko. Essential in the need state is that the subject faces competing alternatives and is unable to determine the direction of his or her efforts. The new activity emerges through three zones: (1) the zone of a need state, (2) the zone of motive formation, and (3) the zone of transformation of needs and activity (Bratus & Lishin, 1983, p. 44).

> However, a need state cannot last long. Sooner or later an encounter with, discovery, or active testing action of some object occurs; this object fits the particular need state, which places it in a qualitatively different rank, the rank of an objectified need, i.e., a need that has found its object or motive. Then, through the discovered motive, the need stimulates activity, during the course of which the need is reproduced and ... somewhat modified, impelling it on to a new cycle of activity that is different compared with the previous one, etc., i.e., a sequence of transformations emerges. (Bratus & Lishin, 1983, p. 43–44)

Two important critical comments are necessary here. First, it is never a question of arbitrary or accidental competing objects in the need state. Beneath the seemingly accidental surface of disconnected "alternatives" or "options," there lie the historically determined inherent contradictions of any object of the given socioeconomic formation. In capitalism, the inherent contradiction functioning in every single object is the double nature of commodities, being simultaneously abstract and concrete, exchange value and use value. Thus, the need state is grounded in the subject's bewilderment at the face of these two mutually excluding and mutually dependent sides of the same object.

The other critical comment concerns the "automaticity" of the emergence of new activities postulated by Bratus and Lishin. The authors claim that a need state "cannot last long" and that it will eventually be replaced by a new cycle of transformations. First, there are good grounds to argue that a need state often does indeed last long and produces various forms of deprivation, passivity, and withdrawal, not to mention "substitute activities" such as alcoholism, studied in depth by the authors themselves. But more important is the manner in which the need state is supposed to be resolved. Bratus and Lishin make it sound like a very easy and effortless process: "Sooner or later an encounter with, discovery, or active testing action of some object occurs." There is ample evidence that most of such "sooner or later" choices actually involve not generation of new activities but "rediscovery" of old, regressive activity forms. Life then moves in circles, not in an ascending spiral. Obviously invisible contributions to development are made in this form, too. But this is not really what we are looking for.

A need state contains no automatism. It may be "resolved" through regression or it may be resolved through expansion. To clarify the structure of the latter process, we now turn to the elaboration of the category of the zone of proximal development.

THE ZONE OF PROXIMAL DEVELOPMENT

Vygotsky's famous definition of the zone of proximal development reads as follows.

> It is the distance between the actual developmental level as determined by independent problem solving and the level of potential development as determined through problem solving under adult guidance or in collaboration with more capable peers. (Vygotsky, 1978, p. 86)

According to Vygotsky, the zone of proximal development defines those functions that will "mature tomorrow but are currently in an embryonic state," that is, the "buds" of development (Vygotsky, 1978, p. 86). Vygotsky claimed that primates and other animals cannot have a zone of proximal development. Human children, on the other hand, can "go well beyond the limits of their own capabilities"; they "are capable of doing much more in collective activity" (Vygotsky, 1978, p. 88).

Vygotsky saw instruction as a chief means to exploit the zones of proximal development.

> Therefore the only good kind of instruction is that which marches ahead of development and leads it; it must be aimed not so much at the ripe as the ripening functions.... Instruction must be oriented toward the future, not the past. (Vygotsky, 1962, p. 104)

Vygotsky refers to Montessori's idea of "sensitive periods" as optimal points of departure for instruction.

> She found, for instance, that if a child is taught to write early, at four and half or five years of age, he responds by "explosive writing", an abundant and imaginative use of written speech that is never duplicated by

children a few years older. This is a striking example of the strong influence that instruction can have when the corresponding functions have
not yet fully matured. (Vygotsky, 1962, p. 105)

The concept of the zone of proximal development has had quite a renaissance, especially in the United States. A common interpretation and application of this concept is to use it as a rationale for different versions of "dynamic
assessment of intelligence" (see Brown & French, 1979; Day, 1983).

Another common interpretation takes the zone of proximal development as a rationale for creating social situations or environments where
instructional support is given to children, thus enabling children to acquire
new skills in a new way, through joint problem solving and interaction. The
notion of "scaffolding" (see Wood, Bruner & Ross, 1976; Wood, 1980) is a
product of this line of interpretation, as is Cazden's (1981) work on children's
speech acquisition, and so are several contributions to the important volume edited by Rogoff and Wertsch (1984).

Neither one of these common interpretations does full justice to
Vygotsky's conception. In the case of the dynamic assessment interpretation, it is easy to notice that Vygotsky "does speak to broader issues" (Day,
1983, p. 164). But even the notion of "scaffolding" is unduly narrow. Peg
Griffin and Michael Cole point out two serious weaknesses in this interpretation. First, scaffolding (or creating "formats"; see Bruner, 1985) refers to
acquisition of discrete skills and actions, not to the emergence of long-last-
ing molar activities. It is a "largely spatial metaphor, in which the temporal
aspect of the construction of the whole remains as a residual, unanalyzed
aspect of the living process" (Griffin & Cole, 1984, p. 48). Second, the idea
of scaffolding is restricted to the acquisition of the given.

> The scaffold metaphor leaves open questions of the child's creativity. If
> the adult support bears an inverse relation to the child's competence,
> then there is a strong sense of teleology – children's development is cir-
> cumscribed by the adults' achieved wisdom. Any next-step version of the
> Zo-ped [zone of proximal development; Y. E.] can be of similar concern,
> including work that we have done. (Griffin & Cole, 1984, p. 47)

This self-critical formulation is exceptionally important. Griffin and Cole
try to sketch an expanded conception of the zone of proximal development.
In line with the analyses of Leont'ev (1981) and El'konin (1977), they see
the child's development as a series of transitions from one ontogenetically
leading or dominant activity to another: from play to formal learning, from
formal learning to peer activity, from peer activity to work. Furthermore,
they do not subscribe to a fixed universal order of automatically occurring

transitions. To the contrary, "it is possible to show changes in leading activities that follow development sequences within a single setting" (Griffin & Cole, 1984, p. 60). Play activity, for example, is often a mediating device that helps youngsters enter new activities (Griffin & Cole, 1984, p. 62).

> Adult wisdom does not provide a teleology for child development. Social organization and leading activities provide a gap within which the child can develop novel creative analysis.... A Zo-ped is a dialogue between the child and his future; it is not a dialogue between the child and an adult's past. (Griffin & Cole, 1984, p. 62)

Inspiring as this conclusion is, it is difficult to avoid the impression that the authors themselves, not to mention other researchers, have only started to consider its implications. This is evident in the inconsistency between the conclusion cited previously and Cole's formulations in other publications. An article in the fine volume edited by Wertsch (1985a) is a case in point. Here, Cole speaks of the zone of proximal development exclusively in terms of "acquiring culture," never in terms of creating it. He summarizes the article with the following statement.

> The acquisition of culturally appropriate behavior is a process of *interaction* between children and adults, in which adults guide children's behavior as an essential element in concept acquisition/acculturation/education. (Cole, 1985, p. 158)

In the same volume, Sylvia Scribner goes still further.

> The child is an assimilator of sign systems and develops higher functions through processes of internalization. Adults in the course of history are the inventors and elaborators of sign systems, as well as users. Assimilative and creative processes are not the same. (Scribner, 1985, p. 130)

Scribner supports her standpoint by referring to Vygotsky's discussion of the development of memory. But it is obscure how that relates to the question of children's potential to create new cultural means and forms. Probably more relevant are the findings of Davydov and Poddyakov (Dawydow, 1977; Poddjakow, 1981) according to which even preschool children can form real theoretical generalizations, though they do not yet appear in a verbal form but take other, object-bound and enactive as well as graphic forms of expression.

As a matter of fact, Vygotsky, too, said very little about creative processes (except in his early work on the psychology of art). Vygotsky's concept of the zone of proximal development is itself in need of development.

The cultural-historical school founded by Vygotsky has up to the present time concentrated on the acquisition, assimilation, and internalization of the tools and sign systems of the culture. How these tools and sign systems are created has mainly been treated as a problem for the future. One important exception is the theoretical work of V. S. Bibler, who reveals the creative potential in Vygotsky's conception of internalization as follows.

> The process of immersion of social relations in consciousness ... is ... a process of transforming expanded and relatively independent "cultural models," prepared cultural phenomena, into the culture of *thinking*, a dynamic culture, which is fused and condensed in the individual person. An objectively developed culture acquires a subjective determination in inner speech, i.e., a determination in which it is manifest as a future-oriented *form of creativity*, of new, as yet nonexisting, merely possible models of culture. The relationship is inverted, and inner speech must be understood as not so much a "phenomenon of internalisation" as the intention of the "externalization" of thought, as an embryo of a new, not yet objectively posited culture, not yet deployed in the external, social aspects of culture, an embryo concentrated in the concept. Social relations are not only immersed in inner speech: they are radically *transformed* in it; they acquire a new (as yet unrealized) sense, a new orientation toward external activity, toward their objective materialization.... But then, ... inner speech (and its elementary form of mono-dialogue) may be represented as the dialogue of those cultural-historical models of thinking (activity) that are internalized in the different voices of my own "I," the argument among these functioning as a kind of positing, the creation of new cultural phenomena (knowledge, ideas, works of art). (Bibler, 1984, p. 52–53)

The individual "mechanism" of transforming internalization into externalization may well follow the lines sketched by Bibler. But the relationship between individual and societal development remains the fundamental problem within the concept of the zone of proximal development. Griffin and Cole (1984, p. 48–49) stress that the zone of proximal development "includes models of a future, models of a past, and activities that resolve contradictions between them." But this temporal perspective seems to be understood in individual terms only: The individual moves from one activity to another in the course of his or her development. What is not discussed is whether and how *the activities themselves as societal systemic formations develop and change constantly.*

Old and new, regressive and expansive forms of the same activity exist simultaneously in the society. Children may play in a reproductive and repetitive manner, but they do also invent and construct new forms and structures of play, new tools and models for play activity. Their playing seems to become increasingly consumptive and prefabricated; the exchange-value aspect seems to dominate it more and more as the toys and games have become big business. But is it so simple and unidirectional? What are the inner contradictions and historical perspectives of the play activity of our children? Once in a while parents are astonished as they find their children playing something that does not seem to fit any preconceived canons: Something new has been produced "from below." Sometimes these inventions from below become breakthroughs that significantly change the structures of play activity.

Human development is real production of new societal activity systems. It is not just acquisition of individually new activities, plus perhaps individual creation of "original pieces of behavior" (recall the porpoise). Earlier, I have distinguished among three types of development: the *individual-explosive*, the *invisible-gradual*, and the *collective-expansive*. The third type is the one that requires intuitive or conscious mastery – the subjectification of the subject. The concept of the zone of proximal development as an *instrument of subjectification* is relevant in the context of this third type of development. To put it more precisely, the individual-explosive and invisible-gradual types of development can be purposefully affected and steered in a societally meaningful scale only indirectly, through the collective-expansive type.

A provisional reformulation of the zone of proximal development is now possible. It is the *distance between the present everyday actions of the individuals and the historically new form of the societal activity that can be collectively generated as a solution to the double bind potentially embedded in the everyday actions.*

Klaus Holzkamp, seemingly unaware of Vygotsky's conceptualization, has recently developed a somewhat similar idea of human development. According to him, embedded in every individually experienced existential threat and restriction in capitalism there is a "second alternative" of "*exceeding the limits of individual subjectivity* through immediate co-operation in the direction toward realizing *general interests of joint self-determination against dominating partial interests*" (Holzkamp, 1983, p. 373). Holzkamp speaks here of the principle of "double possibilities." He concretizes further this idea with the concepts of "possibility zone" and "possibility generalization." The former refers to a "relationship between general societal possibilities to act and my specific way of realizing, limiting, mystifying them" (Holzkamp, 1983, p. 548). The latter means that the individual grasps and realizes his or her individual possibilities to act in relation with other individuals within the same "typical possibility zone" and with the societal possibilities (Holzkamp, 1983, p. 549).

We still need a closer, if only tentative, analysis of the steps to be taken in traveling through the zone of proximal development. Recall the three subzones suggested by Bratus and Lishin: the zone of a need state, the zone of motive formation, and the zone of transformation of needs and activity. In the light of the preceding discussion, these three steps turn out to be insufficient. What is lacking, above all, is the *transformation of the need state into a double bind*, into a contradiction that uncompromisingly demands *qualitatively new instruments* for its resolution. To make the necessary steps concrete, I now turn to a literary example of the zone of proximal development.

THE ADVENTURES OF HUCKLEBERRY FINN AS A VOYAGE THROUGH THE ZONE OF PROXIMAL DEVELOPMENT

The example is Mark Twain's (1950) *The Adventures of Huckleberry Finn*. At the outset, Huckleberry Finn's dominant activity is that of vagabondism. It is a social kind of vagabondism, seeking communion with the adventurous middle-class boy Tom Sawyer, on the one hand, and with poor, downtrodden people like the black slave Jim, on the other hand. This social vagabondism takes place within a culture of slavery. Huck has been offered the opportunity to adapt himself to the safe middle-class family life – but he rejects that alternative after a while. The *primary contradiction* inherent *within* every component of this activity is that between the private freedom of the individual vagabond and the public nonfreedom prevailing in the vagabond's immediate cultural context. The latter is threatening Huck Finn, too – in the form of either soft middle-class taming or violent suppression by the authorities.

In its initial form, Huck Finn's life activity may be depicted with the help of the diagram in Figure 3.2.

The story begins with Huck's being harassed and threatened by his father. Huck gets away by staging his own death. He settles on an island in the Mississippi River. There he accidentally meets the runaway slave Jim, his old friend. Because of the friendship, Huck promises not to tell anybody about Jim. The two live on the island a while. Then things start to move.

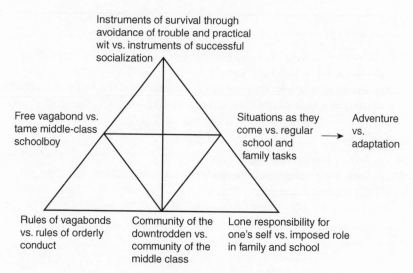

Instruments of survival through avoidance of trouble and practical wit vs. instruments of successful socialization

Free vagabond vs. tame middle-class schoolboy

Situations as they come vs. regular school and family tasks

Adventure vs. adaptation

Rules of vagabonds vs. rules of orderly conduct

Community of the downtrodden vs. community of the middle class

Lone responsibility for one's self vs. imposed role in family and school

FIGURE 3.2. The primary contradiction of Huckleberry Finn's life activity.

Next morning I said it was getting slow and dull, and I wanted to get a stirring up, some way. I said I reckoned I would slip over the river and find out what was going on. Jim liked that notion; but he said I must go in the dark and look sharp. (p. 54)

This is a signal of a *need state:* There seem to be lots of alternatives for the choosing.

Huck finds out that Jim is being intensively hunted. So they set off down the big river on a raft, floating during the nights and hiding during the days. But this is not yet "intensive action" to resolve the dilemma. Rather, it is *reaction,* forced by the circumstances and still relatively aimless. This goes on until they approach areas where slavery is abolished. Now, for the first time, Huck realizes that his activity of vagabondism has a qualitatively *new subject:* It is no more just he; it is he and Jim together. In his introduction to the book, T. S. Eliot points out that "Huck in fact would be incomplete without Jim" (Eliot, 1950, p. xi).

This new component represents a new kind of activity – it disturbs the old activity and aggravates its latent inner contradiction. Thus, the story enters the phase of the *secondary contradiction between* the introduced new component and the *old* components of the activity. The new collaborative subject component is in sharp conflict with the old secondary instrument, namely, the avoidance model of "Don't get mixed up with other people's troubles." It is Huck's uncompromising honesty that moves this secondary contradiction to the level of a genuine double bind.

Jim said it made him all over trembly and feverish to be so close to freedom. Well, I can tell you it made me all over trembly and feverish, too, to hear him, because I begun to get it through my head that he was most free – and who was to blame for it? Why, me. I couldn't get that out of conscience, no how nor way. It got to troubling me so I couldn't rest; I couldn't stay still in one place. It hadn't ever come home to me, before, what this thing was that I was doing. But now it did; and it stayed with me and scorched me more and more....

This is a beautiful description of the *double bind*. The contradiction is intensified until it becomes unbearable. Huck desperately tries to *analyze* the situation and find an acceptable solution.

I got to feeling so mean and so miserable I most wished I was dead. I fidgeted up and down the raft, abusing myself to myself, and Jim was fidgeting up and down past me. We neither of us could keep still. Every time he danced around and says. "Dah's Cairo!" it went through me like a shot, and I thought if it was Cairo I reckoned I would die of miserableness.

... My conscience got to stirring me up hotter than ever, until at last I says to it, "Let up on me – it ain't too late yet – I'll paddle ashore at the first light and tell." I felt easy, and happy, and light as a feather, right off. All my troubles was gone. I went to looking out sharp for a light, and sort of singing to myself. By and by one showed. (p. 87–88)

Now Huck really starts to paddle ashore. As he leaves, Jim says to him:

"Pooty soon I'll be a-shout'n for joy, en I'll say, it's all on accounts o' Huck; I's a free man, en I couldn't ever ben free ef it hadn' ben for Huck; Huck done it. Jim won't ever forgit you, Huck; you's de bes' fren' Jim's ever had; en you's de only fren' ole Jim's got now."

Here Huck first enters the phase of *hesitation and pause*. Then the *intensive action to solve the dilemma* starts. In a very short period, Huck finds the *first new instrument* (the lie about the sick family), which leads him to the new *object and motive*: joint freedom. The lie as the first new instrument is a specific tool, a springboard (like the letters in the children's campaign), not yet a general model of wide applicability.

I was paddling off, all in a sweat to tell on
him; but when he says this, it seemed to
kind of take the tuck all out of me. I went
along slow then, and I warn't right down
certain whether I was glad I started or
whether I warn't. When I was fifty yards
off, Jim says:
"Dah you goes, de ole true Huck; de on'y
white genlman dat ever kep' his promise
to oel Jim."
Well, I just felt sick. But I says, I got to do
it – I can't get out of it. Right then, along
comes a skiff with two men in it, with
guns, and they stopped and I stopped.
One of them says:
"What's that, yonder?"
"A piece of a raft," I says.
"Do you belong on it?"
"Yes, sir."
"Any men on it?" "Only one, sir." "Well,
there's five niggers run off
to-night, up yonder above the head of
the bend. Is your man white or black?"
I didn't answer up prompt. I tried to, but
the words wouldn't come. I tried, for a
second or two, to brace up and out with
it, but I warn't man enough – hadn't the
spunk of a rabbit. I see I was weakenin;
so I just give up trying, and up and
says: "He's white." "I reckon we'll go and
see for ourselves." "I wish you would,"
says I, "because it's pap that's there,
and maybe you'd help me tow the raft
ashore where the light is. He's sick – and
so is mam and Mary Ann'" "Oh, the
devil! we're in a hurry, boy. But I s'pose
we've got to. Come – buckle to your
paddle, and let's get along." I buckled to
my paddle and they laid to their oars.
When we had made a stroke or two,
I says: "Pap'll be mighty much obleeged
to you, I can tell you. Everybody goes
away when I want them to help me
tow the raft ashore, and I can't do it by
myself."

"Well, that's infernal mean. Odd, too.
Say, boy, what's the matter with your
father?" "It's the – a – the – well, it ain't
anything much." They stopped pulling.
It warn't but a mighty ways to the raft,
now. One says: "Boy, that's a lie. What
is the matter with your pap? Answer
up square, now, and it'll be the better
for you." "I will, sir, I will, honest – but
don't leave us, please. It's the – the –
gentlemen, if you'll only pull ahead,
and let me heave you the head-line,
you won't have to come a-near the
raft – please do"
"Set her back, John, set her back!" says
one. They backed water. "Keep away,
boy – keep to looard. Confound it, I
just expect the wind has blowed it to us.
Your pap's got the smallpox, and you
know it precious well. Why didn't you
come out and say so? Do you want to
spread it all over?"
"Well," says I, a-blubbering, "I've told
everybody before, and then they just
went away and left us." (p. 89–90)

After the intensive episode, Huck formulates in an inner dialogue ("conversation with the situation," as Schön [1983] calls it) the new general model for generating the new activity.

They went off and I got abroad the raft feeling bad and low, because I knowed very well I had done wrong, and I see it warn't no use for me to try to learn to do right; a body that don't get started right when he's little, ain't got no show – when the pinch comes there ain't nothing to back him up and keep him to his work, and so he gets beat. Then I thought a minute, and says to myself, hold on – s'pose you'd <u>a done right and give Jim up</u>: would you felt better than what you do now? No, says I, I'd feel bad – I'd feel just the same way I do now. Well, then, says I, what's the use

Huck's new general instrument is something like a pragmatic moral philosophy. It buttresses him against the attacks of the "bad conscience" stemming from the old societal norms of slavery. This model represents and anticipates the new activity *offered* to Huck, namely, that of a bourgeois-liberal way of life (let it be called the *given* new activity). But this model already contains the seeds of a new inner contradiction: that between

*you learning to do right, when it's
troublesome to do right and ain't no
trouble to do wrong, and the wages is just
the same? I was stuck. I couldn't answer
that. So I reckoned I wouldn't bother no
more about it, but after this always do
whichever come handiest at the time."*
(p. 91)

bourgeois liberalism and radical
moral anarchism.

The rest of the book is about the *practical application* of the model of the new activity. There occurs, in a miniature form, a *transformation of actions into a collective activity*, temporarily joined by a couple of common crooks (representing the old vagabondism in slavery) and finally joined by Tom Sawyer, too (representing the given new bourgeois-liberal pragmatism).

This practical application and generalization is not smooth and straightforward. The new liberatory actions accomplished within the process of drifting down the river are in general subordinated to the old form of vagabondist activity. The circumstances and the two crooks repeatedly disrupt the new liberatory actions: The communion of Huck and Jim is broken up, Huck has to act individually, and Jim is isolated or captured. This struggle between the old and the given new activity is resolved in favor of the latter only as Tom Sawyer finally enters the scene (and Twain ingeniously forces Huck to pretend he is Tom, thus personifying the transition to the given new activity).

But the struggle between the old and the given new activity is not the most essential tension in the application and generalization phase. The more important (and less noticeable) aspect is that *something entirely new* emerges beside these two societally already known activity forms. In certain problematic, ambivalent situations, Huck's actions produce results that exceed qualitatively the limits of both the old and the given new activity. These actions take the external form of severe disturbances, nearly catastrophes. Two such situations may be identified.

In the first one, Huck is accidentally separated from Jim and lives temporarily with the aristocratic family of the Grangerfords. The family has a feud with another aristocratic family. One day Sophia, a daughter of the Grangerfords, asks Huck to fetch her Testament from the church. Huck senses that this is illegitimate *but helps the girl anyway*. This action has no value either for the old activity of vagabondism or for the given new activity of bourgeois pragmatism. The Testament contains a note that launches the running off of two lovers, Sophia and a son of the rival family. A massacre ensues, but the lovers are rescued.

In the second situation, the two crooks, using Huck as their servant, steal the whole fortune of the newly orphaned Wilks girls. Huck follows the crooks and finds out where they hide the money. He takes it and hides it again. He then *risks his neck and informs one of the girls* of what has happened. Both the crooks and Huck are eventually caught, barely escaping a public beating – but the girls get their money back. Again, Huck's action is not a logical consequence of either the old or the given new activity. To the contrary, it clearly endangers both.

In both these situations (as in the original double bind situation on the river), Huck develops actions indicating the birth of a third activity, an emergent formation that I will call the *created new* activity. These actions remind us of the "liberated or unloosed action" mentioned by V. P. Zinchenko in Chapter 2 and of the loss of the "self" in Learning III as described by Bateson earlier in this chapter. Bateson (1978, p. 63–64) extends the notion of nonpathological double binds using as examples the actions of mountain climbers and musicians, "unrewarded and unbribed in any simple way." Shotter (1982, p. 47) points out that such actions contain a transformation of the subject "from a being who must first plan an action in thought before executing it in practice into someone who knows what to do in the course of doing it."

> While playing games it is not uncommon for people to have such experiences, if only briefly; they simply become momentarily a game-playing thing, describing the experience as that of "losing themselves in the game", or of playing "out of their minds". In such a state, players are clearly not unconscious as such, but they do not have to *try* to do what is required of them, they seem simply to know it in the course of doing it. (Shotter, 1982, p. 48)

These actions correspond to the aspect of radical moral anarchism, embedded in Huck's new general model. This radical moral anarchism makes Huck a personality of entirely different dimensions from those of Tom Sawyer. For Tom, freeing Jim is a safe, imaginary adventure – Tom knows that Jim has actually been granted freedom but does not tell this to Huck and Jim. For Huck, it is a deadly serious moral and existential struggle. Just before Tom enters, Jim is captured and Huck faces his double bind again.

> I studied a minute, sort of holding my breath, and then says to myself:
>
> "All right, then, I'll *go* to hell" ...
>
> It was awful thoughts, and awful words, but they was said. And I let them stay said; and never thought no more about reforming. I shoved the

whole thing out of my head; and said I would take up wickedness again,
which was in my line, being brung up to it, and the other warn't. And for a
starter, I would go to work and steal Jim out of slavery again; and if I could
think up anything worse, I would do that, too; because as long as I was in,
and in for good, I might as well go the whole hog. (Twain, 1950, p. 214)

It is this very quality, this going beyond the alternatives given, that makes
Huckleberry Finn a great classic.

And the *style* of the book, which is the style of Huck, is what makes it a
far more convincing indictment of slavery than the sensationalist propa-
ganda of *Uncle Tom's Cabin*. Huck is passive and impassive, apparently
always the victim of events; and yet, in his acceptance of his world and
of what it does to him and others, he is more powerful than his world,
because he is more *aware* than any other person in it. (Eliot, 1950, p. x)

It is almost as if Mark Twain had had a notion of the zone of proximal
development as he ended the book with Huck's words.

But I reckon I got to light out for the Territory ahead of the rest, because
Aunt Sally she's going to adopt me and civilize me, and I can't stand it.
I been there before. (Twain, 1950, p. 292)

THEORETICAL LESSONS

What can be learned from this case analysis?

First, the emergence of Leont'ev's (1981, p. 402–403) "only understood
motive" is a relatively late step in learning activity. It represents a phase
when the contradiction is already external, *between two activities* and
motives, the old one and the given new one. A forced early instructional
introduction of this "only understood motive" may effectively hide – perhaps also prevent – the unfolding of the initial phases of learning activity,
that is, the appearance of the primary contradiction (need state) and the
secondary contradiction (working out the double bind).

Second, there are two aspects in the new activity produced by learning
activity, namely, the *given new aspect* and the *created new aspect*. The given
new aspect is that which is offered by the advanced frontiers of culture (as
by the pragmatic bourgeois liberalism in Huck Finn's case). The created new
aspect is that which emerges *as the new actions produce richer results than
expected* and thus expand, transform, or even explode the constraints of the
given new, turning into something wider and uncontrollable. Thus, the new

activity realized is never qualitatively quite the same as the representatives of the advanced frontiers had planned. This means also that the modest terms of "application and generalization" bear the true essence of creation and surprise.

From the instructional point of view, my definition of the zone of proximal development means that teaching and learning are moving within the zone only when they aim at developing historically new forms of activity, not just at letting the learners acquire the societally existing or dominant forms as something individually new. To aim at developing historically new forms of activity implies an instructional practice that follows the learners into their life activities outside the classroom. It also implies the necessity of forming true expansive learning activity in and between the learners. The instructional task is thus twofold: to develop *learning activity* and to develop historically new forms of the *central activity* – work, for example (of course learning activity is itself the central target activity during the early school years).

Huck Finn traveled across the zone of proximal development *without* consciously constructing and employing the vehicle of expansive learning activity. However, the sequential structure of the travel remains basically similar when the new vehicle is introduced.

But how could instruction possibly bring about something even remotely resembling Huck Finn's travel?

Instruction operates with tasks. The instructor's task and the learner's perceived task are seldom the same. If this is not taken into account, the learners "are scored as doing poorly when they are not doing the task in the first place" (Newman, Griffin & Cole, 1984, p. 190). When this happens, "the activity in the school does not help me to orientate myself in the world, instead it becomes the part of the world where I must orientate myself" (Halldén, 1982, p. 138).

> A "whole task" thus becomes specifically a task considered in the context of the activity or higher-level goals that motivate it. Whenever there is a task, there is always a whole task. But in some settings, like the laboratory, the classroom, or wherever there is a hierarchical division of labor, the higher-level goals may not be under the actors' individual control.... In standard laboratory practice, where it is necessary to have as complete control as possible over the goals that the subjects are trying to accomplish, subjects are never called upon to formulate their own goals and so are confronted with only a part of the problem – the solution part.
> (Newman, Griffin & Cole, 1984, p. 191–192)

The "whole task" of the authors mentioned is essentially identical to the "open problem" of Seidel (1976). The open problem includes its own generation and justification. The closed problem contains only the operative solution part. Research on problem solving within cognitive psychology has been mainly concerned with the latter (see Chaiklin, 1985, for an exception).

Earlier in this chapter, problems, tasks, and goals were identified as belonging to Learning II, to the level of individual actions. Questioning and exploding given problems and tasks, as well as generating and formulating new tasks derived from "the context of the context," that is, from the overall activity, are processes indicating a transition from Learning II to Learning III.

> In other words, in order to arouse interest it is necessary not to indicate the goal and then try to motivationally justify the action and the direction of the given goal, but it is necessary, on the contrary, to create a motive and then to disclose the possibility of reaching the goal (usually a whole system of intermediate and 'indirect' goals) in one or another subject content. (Leont'ev, 1978, p. 182)
>
> Of course, in mastering school subjects (just as in mastering any kind of knowledge in general, as in mastering science), it is decisively important what kind of place cognition occupies in the life of man, whether it is a part of real life for him or only external, a condition coupled to it externally.... It is necessary that learning should enter into life, that it should have a *vital sense* for the learner. (Leont'ev, 1978, p. 185)
>
> Consequently, we must speak of the problems of nurturing the motives for learning in connection with the development of life, with the development of the content of actual vital relations of the child.... (Leont'ev, 1978, p. 186)

This demand differs deeply from the Piagetian idea of learning in natural action settings. Here we are concerned with sociohistorical activities as the proper forms of "actual vital relations." Halldén (1982, p. 139) points out that in the classes observed by him, in spite of varied "assimilative actions" of practical exploratory nature, instruction did not result in the pupils' "broadening their frame of reference." These actions remained dissociated from the life activities of the pupils. Or as Halldén (1982, p. 132) puts it, "It is practically impossible for the pupils to work with a given question because it runs into conflict with their total life situation."

Huck Finn's learning was based on his life activity, but not in the naive sense of "extending" or "combining." Developmentally effective learning, the "good learning" of Vygotsky, grew out of the inner contradictions of the old life activity.

In Huck Finn's case, the double bind was created "accidentally," as the inner contradictions of the societal life touched the individual in a bare, unmasked form. But this is not instruction. Can the teacher intentionally activate a double bind?

Obviously this is possible, provided that we stick to the concrete-historical, analyzable character of double binds. The prerequisite is that the teacher works his or her way *from the inside* of the activity to be developed. This means that the teacher takes as his or her point of departure the double nature and inner contradictions of the leading activity of the pupils. He or she works out the zone of proximal development of this activity, first analytically and historically, then as a hypothesis, and finally in the form of practical tasks. The teacher acts as the devil's advocate, confronting the learners with the contradictions of their own vital activity in a bare form.

This implies that the proper unit of developmentally effective, expansive instruction is not a discrete task, but a *whole cycle of activity generation*, of *learning activity*, corresponding to the phase structure of the zone of proximal development.

Davydov (1982, p. 42) identifies the following constituent learning actions within learning activity.

1) *transforming* the situation to find out the general relation of the system under consideration;
2) *modeling* the relation in question in a material, graphic and symbolic form;
3) *transforming* the model of the relation for studying its properties in their original form;
4) *deducing and constructing* a series of particular concrete practical problems having a general method of solution;
5) *controlling* the preceding operations;
6) *evaluating* the mastering of the general method.

It is relatively easy to notice the similarities between these learning actions and the phases of the zone of proximal development described in connection with Huck Finn's case. This phase structure of the zone of proximal development may now be depicted as the general cycle of expansion (Figure 3.3).

In the cycle, transforming 1 refers to the first learning action of Davydov, that is, to transforming the initial double bind by means of thought experiments, inner dialogue, or the like. However, this phase has a complex substructure: the emergence of a new conflicting element in the structure of the

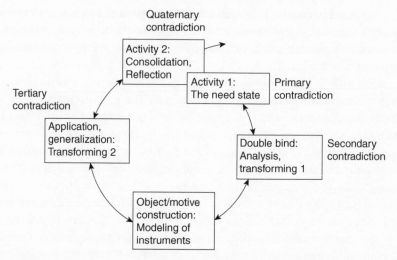

FIGURE 3.3. The phase structure of the zone of proximal development.

old activity, aggravation of this contradiction into a double bind, reflective analysis, and experimentation ("intensive action").

The phase of object/motive construction seems to begin with finding the first new specific instrument that functions as a "springboard" (Kedrov, 1972; see Chapter 4 of this book) for breaking the constraints of the double bind and for constructing a new general model for the subsequent activity. Object/motive construction is inseparable from modeling. The object is constructed through modeling it – and the model becomes a general instrument for handling the object. The model is that of a *given new* activity, but it contains a latent inner contradiction that will give rise to actions anticipating the *created new* activity. This phase contains also Davydov's third learning action when the model is transformed in order to study its properties in "pure form."

The phase of application and generalization means the transformation of actions into activity (transforming 2, in the sense of Bratus and Lishin). In effect, the subject starts to carry out certain actions that correspond to the model of the given new activity. These actions are initially more or less subordinated to the resistant form and motive of the old activity. The new actions are disturbed as the old activity breaks them down. But there is also another, less understandable and more significant type of disturbance, caused by precursors of the created new activity. Thus, transforming 2 is the place of birth of the societally new – of the outcomes unexpected by the instructor.

The phase of activity 2 signifies the consolidation of a new activity form, being a *contradictory unity of the given new and the created new.* This phase is essentially reflective, conscious of itself, and contains Davydov's two last learning actions. The consolidation of the new activity (activity 2) may be divided into three broad subphases. First the activity appears as systematic application, extension, and generalization of the newly created instruments (e.g., letters in the case of the children's campaign). This subphase is offensive but often somewhat repetitive. In a way, the basic idea of the new activity is reproduced and multiplied in an almost exhaustive manner – essentially within the confines of the uppermost "production" subtriangle of the structure of activity (Figure 2.6).

The second subphase may appear in the form of decreasing intensity and increasing decentralization – recall the circular waves created by the stone thrown into water. This subphase is essentially variation and creation of further new instruments. The new activity consolidates itself by diversification, starting to produce new means – often surprising or even foreign to the initiators. Certainly the new activity has to coexist and compete with resistant structures of the old one. The survival of the new activity becomes a question of whether or not it succeeds in creating its own social "infrastructure": rules, community, division of labor – resulting in triangles of exchange and distribution (the bottom part of Figure 2.6). If the new activity remains within the subtriangle of production only, it will soon run out of energetic and material resources. In other words, in order to survive, the new activity must become a *life activity* for the subjects, and a truly *societal* activity system for the neighbor activities.

In the third subphase of the consolidation, the new activity system is no more new. The focus is on the external relations of the activity. Paradoxally, this implies also that the activity system begins to defend and encapsulate itself. But the new activity is not a closed system. It must, among other things, produce outcomes for its object activity and implement means produced by its instrument-producing activities. In short, it must coexist and interact within a network of activities (recall Figures 2.7 and 2.11).

As I pointed out in Chapter 2, these transactions are characterized by *quaternary contradictions: The new central activity has to compete with and adjust to the dynamics of its neighbor activities.* In the course of this outward interaction, the latent primary inner contradiction of the new activity is transformed into a new need state. The interaction of the new activity with its neighbor activities (like the interaction of Huck's vagabondism with Jim's slavery) sooner or later introduces some qualitatively new, disturbing element into the system of the new central activity – which eventually may

TABLE 3.3. *The sequential structure of Huckleberry Finn's zone of proximal development*

Contradiction	Phase	Content in *Huckleberry Finn*
Primary *within* the components of the old activity	Need state	Social vagabondism: individual private freedom vs. cultural norm of public nonfreedom
	Double bind	Emerging new subject: Huck and Jim vs. old instrument (avoidance model: "Don't get mixed up with other people's business")
Secondary *between* the components of the old activity	Object/motive construction	Springboard: lie; new object: joint freedom New general model: "I'll do whatever is handy at the moment" (bourgeois pragmatism vs. radical moral anarchism as inner contradiction of this new model of activity)
Tertiary between the old and the *given* new activity/motive (between the only understood and the effective motive)	Application, generalization; component actions of the given new activity	Vagabondism in slavery (represented by the two crooks) vs. bourgeois-liberal pragmatism (represented by Tom Sawyer); the bourgeois-liberal actions are *disturbed* by the old activity form but also (as they produce more than expected) by precursor actions of the *created new* activity
Quaternary – *between* the new activity and its neighbor activities	Activity 2: reflection, consolidation	

lead to a new double bind. In that sense, the arrow pointing forward from activity 2 implies the continuous character of the cycle.

To define the entire cycle as the *basic unit of expansive learning*, and consequently of developmental instruction, means that we are dealing with learning processes of considerable length. The intensive formation of a historically new activity system within a limited community or collective (e.g., workplace, school, family, trade union) is typically a matter of months and years. During such a period of creation, there appear iterative transitions back and forth among the phases of the cycle. *Huckleberry Finn's* zone of proximal development may now be condensed into a sequential systematization (Table 3.3).

For my present purpose, certain shortcomings of the case of Huck Finn may also be pointed out. First, Huck Finn is a loner and remains so. The case only hints at the problems and possibilities of the collective dimension in zones of proximal development. Second, intentional instruction plays no part in Huck Finn's case – a fact that somewhat restricts speculations on the relevance of instruction. Third, the phase of activity 2 (consolidation and reflection) is left practically untouched by Twain.

In the next section, I shall extend my analysis of the zone of proximal development. The material of the analysis is another novel, namely, *Seven Brothers* by Aleksis Kivi, the greatest classic of Finnish literature.

THE ANALYSIS OF THE ZONE EXTENDED: THE CASE OF *SEVEN BROTHERS*

Aleksis Kivi published his *Seven Brothers* in 1870. It was the true break-through of Finnish literature written in the native language. Its unconventional realism was met with devastating criticism from the leading authorities of literary criticism. The author never became a celebrity in his lifetime. *Seven Brothers* begins with a description of the physical and social setting.

> Jukola Farm, in the south of the province of Häme, stands on the northern slope of a hill, near the village of Toukola. Around it the ground is bestrewn with boulders, but below this stony patch begin fields, where, before the farm fell into decay, heavy-eared crops used to wave. Below the fields is a meadow, rimmed with clover and cleft by a winding ditch; and richly it has yielded hay before becoming a pasturage for straying village cattle. In addition to these, the farm owns vast forests, bogs and backwoods, most of which the founder of the farm, with admirable foresight, succeeded in adding to it at the first great settlement of boundaries in former days. On that occasion the master of Jukola, with an eye more to the benefit of his descendants than his own best, had accepted as his share a forest ravaged by fire and by this means received seven times the area given his neighbours. But all signs of this fire had long ago disappeared from his holding and dense forests had replaced them.

> Such is the home of the seven brothers whose fortunes I am about to relate. Their names, in order of age, are: Juhani, Tuomas, Aapo, Simeoni, Timo, Lauri and Eero. Tuomas and Aapo are twins, and so are Timo and Lauri. Juhani, the eldest, is twenty-five, while Eero, the youngest, is barely eighteen. In build they are sturdy and broad of shoulder: all of middling height except Eero, who is still very short....

Their father, a passionate hunter, met a sudden death in the prime of his life while fighting an enraged bear. Both were found dead, the shaggy king of the woods and the man, lying side by side on the bloodstained ground. The man was terribly mangled, but the bear, too, displayed the marks of a knife in its throat and side, while the keen ball of a rifle had pierced its breast. Thus perished a sturdy fellow who had killed in his time over fifty bears. But for the sake of these hunting trips he neglected the care of his farm, and bereft of a master's guidance, it had gradually fallen into ruin. Nor were the boys better inclined towards sowing and ploughing; from their father they had inherited his keen longing for the chase. They laid traps, set gins and snares, and dug grouse-pits, to the undoing of wildfowl and hares. In such pursuits they spent the days of their boyhood, until they could handle fire-arms and dared approach the bear in its wilds.

Their mother tried, indeed, with scoldings and the rod, to turn their thoughts to work and diligence, but the brothers' obstinacy proved equal to all her efforts. (Kivi, 1929, p. 3–4)

The primary contradiction in the existing dominant activity of the brothers is that between nature and culture, between free hunting and domesticated farming, between life in the woods and life among people (Figure 3.4).

The need state is manifested in a variety of latent threats and conflict situations. The boys' mother dies, leaving the brothers to steer the farm clear of total ruin. The rector of the parish demands that they learn to read, which is also a legal precondition for marriage. The conversation between the boys records their elaboration of the need state.

> AAPO. What I say is that this wild life isn't right, and is sure to end in ruin and destruction. Brothers! Other works and other habits, if we wish for peace.
>
> JUHANI. What thou sayest is true, it can't be denied.
>
> SIMEONI. God ha' mercy! Wild and unbridled has our life been unto this day.
>
> TIMO. This life's as good as another, and so's this world. It's all right, even if it does tell on a man. Oho!
>
> JUHANI. The wildness, or to use the right word, the carelessness of our life cannot be denied. Let us remember though, "youth and folly, old age and wisdom."
>
> AAPO. It's time now for us to grow wiser, time to put all our lusts and passions under the yoke of our brains and do chiefly that which brings profit, and not that which tastes best. Let us begin without delay to work up our farm into respectable shape again.
>
> ...

[handwritten margin note: Contradition]

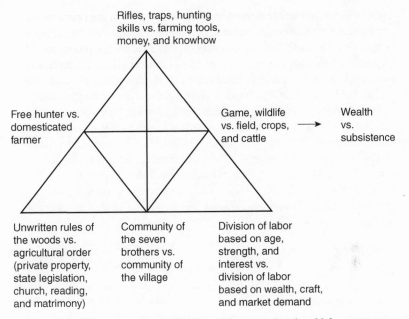

Rifles, traps, hunting skills vs. farming tools, money, and knowhow

Free hunter vs. domesticated farmer

Game, wildlife vs. field, crops, and cattle   →   Wealth vs. subsistence

Unwritten rules of the woods vs. agricultural order (private property, state legislation, church, reading, and matrimony)

Community of the seven brothers vs. community of the village

Division of labor based on age, strength, and interest vs. division of labor based on wealth, craft, and market demand

FIGURE 3.4. The primary contradiction of the seven brothers' life activity.

JUHANI. What dost thou, Lauri, always a man of few words, say?

LAURI. I'd say something. Let us move into the forest and say farewell to the racket of this world.

JUHANI. Ey?

AAPO. The man is raving again.

JUHANI. Move into the forest? What foolishness!

AAPO. Never mind him. Listen, this is how I have thought out the matter....

LAURI. Another and better plan is this. Let us move far into the forest and sell wretched Jukola, or rent it to the tanner of Rajaportti.... Let us do as I say and move with horse, dogs and guns to the foot of Impivaara's steep fell. There we can build ourselves a merry cabin on a merry, sunny hillside, and there, hunting game in the forests, live in peace far away from the din of the world and its crabby people. – This is what I have dreamed of night and day for many years.

JUHANI. Has the Devil turned thy brains, boy?

...

EERO. There's an idea for you: say goodbye to salt and bread and instead suck meat, gorge flesh like mosquitos or Lapland wizards. Would we eat fox and wolf, too, out there in Impivaara's caves, like hairy ogres?

LAURI. Foxes and wolves would give us skins, the skins money, and with money we could buy salt and bread.

EERO. The skins will do for clothing, but let meat, bloody, smoking meat, be our only food; salt and bread are no use to apes and baboons in the forest.

LAURI. That is what I think of and what I shall yet do.

TIMO. Let us take and weigh over the matter from the roots upwards. Why shouldn't we be able to munch bread and salt in the forest? Why? It's Eero who is a mocker, always in our way, always the cross stick in our pile. Who can prevent a man of the woods from drawing near to a village now and again, once in awhile, as his needs drive him? Or wouldst thou hit me on the head with a stick if I did, Eero?

EERO. No, brother, I would even "salt give to him who berries doth bring." – Move, boys, move, I won't forbid you, but will even cart you there, carry you off at a wolf's trot. (Kivi, 1929, p. 12–16)

The hesitation and uncertainty typical of a need state here take the form of a debate within the group. The inner contradiction of the activity is personified in Eero. He is the youngest and smartest of the brothers, always casting doubt and mocking. He first ridicules Lauri's idea. But a few moments later he takes on ridiculing the authority and godliness of Juhani and Simeoni, respectively. They are going to punish Eero with a spanking.

SIMEONI. Strike, but wisely and not with all thy strength.

JUHANI. I know how.

LAURI. Not a single swipe, say I.

TUOMAS. Leave the boy alone!

JUHANI. He needs a little something on his tail.

LAURI. Thou wilt not lay a finger on him.

TUOMAS. Let the boy go! This minute!

TIMO. May he be forgiven, Eero-boy, this once at least.

SIMEONI. Forgiven, forgiven, until he tares and thorns choke the wheat.

LAURI. Don't touch him.

AAPO. Let us forgive him; and in so doing we can try to heap coals of fire on his head.

JUHANI. Go now and thank thy luck. (Kivi, 1929, p. 26)

The brothers finally decide to submit to being taught how to read. The teaching is done by the parish clerk.

Very slowly the brothers' learning has proceeded, the fear-inspiring strictness of their teacher tending rather to damp their zeal and their spirits than to carry them onward. Juhani and Timo hardly knew more than the letter A; the others' knowledge has progressed a few letters further. Only

Eero had proved a great exception to the rest, and having left the alphabet behind him, worked nimbly at spelling. (Kivi, 1929, p. 52)

Today, the parish clerk has not let the boys eat before evening, "trying the effect of hunger on their willingness to learn" (Kivi, 1929, p. 52). When they finally are allowed to eat, Juhani refuses in protest.

> AAPO. Such spite would make the old man laugh heartily.
> JUHANI. Let him laugh! I'm not going to eat. – Eero spells already, oh ay. – I'm not going to eat.
> TUOMAS. Neither am I here, but on Sonninmäki Heath yonder. There I'll soon be sitting on a bolster of heather.
> JUHANI. Right! There we'll soon be tumbling.
> EERO. I agree to your plan, boys.
> AAPO. What madness now?
> JUHANI. Away out of captivity!
> AAPO. Brains ahoy!
> JUHANI. Sonninmäki's pines ahoy!
> EERO. Just so! And our brains answer: ahoy! (Kivi, 1929, p. 53–54)

The boys break the window and flee to the woods. Notice that Eero is learning well – but actively supports the idea of fleeing. This episode is the first preamble to the double bind. A new element, representing the given new activity and the only understood motive (*agricultural life*), has entered the structure of the dominant activity (*hunting life*). This new element appears in the form of *new rules*: Reading is required as a rule of civilized agricultural life (not as an instrument, to be sure). This secondary contradiction is not, however, worked out and sharpened. It is rather resolved regressively. The boys rent out their home and build a new cabin in the backwoods of Impivaara. But the unresolved secondary contradiction keeps haunting the brothers.

> AAPO. The path of our lives has taken a sharp turn today.
> JUHANI. That's what makes me so uneasy, so very uneasy in my mind.
> SIMEONI. Dark is the state of my heart. What am I? A prodigal son.
> JUHANI. Hm. A lost sheep in the wilderness.
> SIMEONI. Leaving our neighbours and Christian fellows like this.
> TUOMAS. Here we are and here we stay as long as the forest yields fresh meat.
> AAPO. All will turn out well if only we always set to with common-sense.
> SIMEONI. The owl is hooting in yonder wilds and its cry never bodes any good. Doesn't it foretell fire, bloody battle and murder, like the old folks say.

TUOMAS. To hoot in the forest is its job and has no meaning.

EERO. Here we are in our village, on Impivaara's turf-roofed farm. (Kivi, 1929, p. 122)

The contradiction is aggravated as the brothers, during a hunting trip, are chased by the forty raging bulls of the neighboring mansion of Viertola. The boys escape on the top of a large rock in the forest. But they are surrounded by the bulls for four days. Yelling and shouting do not help. Finally the brothers decide to shoot down the bulls with their rifles. The boys now again face the rules of the agricultural civilization. How to repay Viertola for the damage? The juryman threatens the boys with cossacks. The situation comes close to a double bind. Juhani desperately suggests that the brothers start boiling tar and selling that to get money. Aapo points out that tar will not earn enough money.

JUHANI. Boy! how are we to appease the fiery master of Viertola and pay for his bulls?

AAPO. Pitch won't be enough for that, nor tar nor game, which grows less at an alarming rate. But look now, how one thought springs from another and one word from another. When thou spokest of tarry stumps, there came into my mind the boundless backwoods of Jukola, its dense birch-woods, pine-woods, and spruce-woods. In a few days seven men could fell many acres of forest for sowing. We could burn the undergrowth and branches and sow the ground, and later reap and take the harvest to Viertola as the price of his bulls, leaving, however, a part in the storeroom for our own needs.... And to come back to Viertola, if the first crop is not enough to pay for the bulls, why a second will do it, and in any case a third. But until the grain waves in our new clearing, we can squeeze mother nature with all our might.... We can go on thus for two years; but when a heavy-eared harvest stands in our clearing, then we can build frames for our ricks and hammer together a threshing-barn, and well, that'll be like working on a real farm. But if we decide to begin such a task, one or two of us must go quickly to talk over the matter with Viertola, and I do believe he'll be appeased and agree to await the harvest from our clearing; for they say he is a somewhat worthy fellow.

TUOMAS. That's advice worth thinking over.

JUHANI. Sure, 'tis worth it. (Kivi, 1929, p. 253–254)

Notice how the idea of tar, close to the forest-bound old activity of the boys, functions here as the springboard, comparable to the lie of Huckleberry Finn. "One thought springs from another and one word from another," says Aapo. The new general model is also embedded in Aapo's suggestion: "That'll be like working on a real farm." Intensive action ensues.

> Whereafter they began the felling of the forest; axes clashed, the forest rang, and with a great crashing pine fell on pine. Always in the van hastened Eero, cutting down the tough pliant shoots with his hook. So fell many an acre of luxuriant forest, and all around spread the fresh scent of shavings and of green, coniferous branches. And soon on the sunny slope, Impivaara clearing lay ready, enormously large, so that its like had hardly been seen before. And the work had been accomplished within five September days. (Kivi, 1929, p. 255)

The debt is paid, but the new activity does not last. The boys fall back to the ways of living in the woods, now adding to that the distilling and drinking of spirits. One of the brothers, Simeoni, gets lost in the forest. The others search for him desperately, finally finding him in poor condition. Simeoni tells them he has seen Luciferus himself in the woods.

JUHANI. Pitiful this is, ah, oh!

TIMO. Don't cry, Juhani.

JUHANI. I would weep blood if I could; here we have lived like Kalmucks, drunk spirits like Mahomets and Turks. But now may a new chapter follow that verse, a different life, or soon the awful anger of Heaven will fall on us like a mountain and press us down to Hell. Ay, we lads have been warned by signs and miracles, and it's the worst of devils for us if we don't heed these signs in time.

LAURI. It's the very worst we have to expect; for I too have something to relate. Listen: once while you were hitting the disc on the clearing, I walked in the forest, looking for useful bits of wood for tools, and while I slept on yonder heath I had a marvellous dream. I watched as though from the top of a tall pine you playing fast and furiously with the disc on the clearing here along fresh ox-hides. And guess with whom? Brothers, it was with our own hot-tempered rector you hammered away. But what happened? The rector noticed at last that it was no ordinary disc, but a red-backed a-b-c book you were hitting. This made him fearfully angry, and waving his sword he shouted in aloud voice: "Iiyah, iiyah!" and at once a terrible hurricane arose which sucked you up like chaff into the power of the winds. This I dreamed and this dream must mean something too.

JUHANI. Surely it means something, foretells some Hell's polka for us; that we needn't doubt. We have been warned from two quarters, and now if we give no heed, fire, pitch and little stones will soon rain down on us as they once did on the towns of Sodom and Gomorrah.

AAPO. Don't let us be too terrified, all the same.

TUOMAS. I won't say for certain, but what Simeoni has seen is perhaps all sprung from a drink-ridden brain. (Kivi, 1929, p. 278–279)

The brothers decide to destroy their apparatus for distilling spirits. They then take off for church, to pray. But on their way, they meet the final obstacle, which will eventually aggravate their double bind to the utmost. The brothers' old rivals, the young men of the Toukola village, start mocking the brothers, who, in their isolation, have mistaken Monday for Sunday. A fight breaks out, and many men are wounded. After the fight, the brothers desperately ponder their coming punishment.

SIMEONI. Brothers, brothers! say a word. What are we to do to escape the clutches of the law?

AAPO. Ah! there is not a single road of escape left to us out of this fix, not one.

JUHANI. We're trapped now, trapped! All is lost, all hope and happiness!

TUOMAS. The Devil'll get us without any mercy; so let us take what we have earned with eyes shut. We disturbed a Crown Servant in the midst of his hurry, and that's a serious thing; we made men into cripples perhaps, and that's a worse thing. Ha! maybe we even knocked the dear life out of someone, and then all's well; we'll be shut up and can eat the Crown's carefree bread.

SIMEONI. Oh we poor boys!

TIMO. Poor sons of Jukola! And seven of them! What shall we do now?

LAURI. I know what I'll do.

JUHANI. I do too. Knife to throat, every man of us!

TIMO. For God's sake!

JUHANI. My knife, my shining knife! I'll let blood in waves!

AAPO. Juhani!

JUHANI. Let the blood of seven men flow into one single pool and let us drown together in this Red Sea, like every man-jack in the Old Testament once did. Where's my birch-handled knife that atones for all, the atoner of all?

AAPO. Calm thyself!

JUHANI. Away out of my way, thou, and away out of this accursed life! My knife!

SIMEONI. Hold him!

AAPO. To me, brothers!

JUHANI. Out of the way!

TUOMAS. Steady, my lad!

JUHANI. Let go, brother Tuomas!

TUOMAS. Thou sittest down quietly.

JUHANI. What good will quietness do us when all is lost? Art thou
   minded to take forty brace of fresh birch-rods quietly?
TUOMAS. I'm not.
JUHANI. What wilt thou do?
TUOMAS. I'll hang myself, but not before.
JUHANI. Let's do now what we shall have to do in the end.
TUOMAS. Let's think it over first.
JUHANI. Ha-ha! It's all no use.
TUOMAS. We don't know yet exactly.
JUHANI. The law's waiting to lay its gloves on us.
SIMEONI. Let's leave Finland and go as herds to Ingermanland!
TIMO. Or as doorkeepers to St. Petersburg town.
AAPO. These are childish ideas.
EERO. Away off to sea to cleave the waves like our grand old uncle used to!
   Once we get away from the Finnish coast we are free from the hand of
   the law, and can then try to reach the Englishman; a man's worth some-
   thing in the masts of his ships.
AAPO. There is advice worth thinking over.
TUOMAS. It might perhaps be that, but remember: before we could reach
   the coast, we'd most likely have the Crown's engagement-rings on our
   wrists.
TIMO. Aah! Even if we get away from Finland with whole skins, when
   should we be in England? It's millions and thousands of millions miles
   there. Aa!
AAPO. Listen to a word: let's join the wolves ourselves, and it's little we
   need fear their teeth. Let's march to the army and enlist for a few years.
   Ah! it's a hard way out, but still perhaps the best in this mess. Ay, let us
   set out for that famous and great big battalion at Heinola, that marches
   and drills all summer on Parola Plain. This is an idea worth weighing,
   seeing that the Crown looks after its own.
JUHANI. I'm afraid, brother, thou hast found the only way. (Kivi, 1929,
   p. 288–290)

This is what the brothers decide to do. Notice, however, the content of
Eero's suggestion. He tries to combine nature and civilization, freedom and
social adjustment, in a unique way: off to sea (freedom, nature), then to the
Englishman (sociality, civilization). The *created new* aspect in this solution
is its intellectually expansive nature: "Let us go and see the world" seems
to be Eero's real message. This does not correspond either to the old or to
the new activity; it goes beyond both. But this solution is still immature – it
would rather escape than solve the contradiction.

So would the accepted solution. That is why it is never realized. The
brothers set off to Heinola barracks. But on the road they soon meet

the sheriff. They are on the point of running away, but then step forward, sure in the belief that the sheriff alone would not be able to arrest them. It turns out that nobody has been killed in the fight and there are no charges against the brothers. Even the parish rector has ceased to haunt the brothers, regarding their case as hopeless. The brothers refuse to believe the sheriff, thinking that this might be a trick to appease them before more troops arrive to make the arrest. The brothers hide in the woods for three days, watching the cabin in suspicion. Then Aapo is sent to the village to confirm their safety. As the truth finally becomes clear to the brothers, they vigorously take up the given new activity of civilized agricultural life.

TUOMAS. And now to reading, now a-b-c-book in hand and the alphabet in our heads even if it has to be hammered there with a mallet.

AAPO. Now thou has said something which, if we carry it out, will bring us new happiness. Ah! what if we were to start this great work together, without resting until it is done!

...

JUHANI. Hard work conquers even the worst of luck. Ay, if we once start on the job, we'll stick to it with clenched teeth. But the matter needs thinking over, wisely and from the roots upward.

AAPO. We're going to try, for it is a mighty matter. Note: If we cannot read, even a lawful wife is forbidden fruit for us.

TIMO. What! Is that so too? Well rot me! Then it's worth trying is this trick is perhaps going to help me to get a good wife, if I should ever be so mad as to want one. But who knows what'll come into a lad's head. Only God knows that.

...

JUHANI. . . . But where can we get a good and gentle teacher?

AAPO. I've thought that out too. I look to thee, Eero. Ay, ay, thou hast a sharp head, that can't be denied. But thank God for this gift and go out for a few weeks into the world, with food on thy back and thy a-b-c-book on thy bossom. Go to the Sheriff's Man, that fine wolf-catcher will teach thee.... Then when thou hast learned the chief points of ordinary reading, thou canst return and teach us.

JUHANI. What? Is Eero to teach us? Hm! Eero! Well, see that it doesn't make thee proud, Eero; that I say.

EERO. Never! A teacher must always set a good example to his pupils, remembering the day of stern reckoning when he will have to say: "Here, Lord, am I and those Thou gavest me."

JUHANI. Hark, hark, did it prick thee? But this is what is going to happen: thou wilt teach me when I want, and I learn from thee only when I want.

That's that. We'll keep thee in order all right, that thou knowest. But
maybe this plan will do.

...

AAPO. Eero, what is thou own idea of the matter?

EERO. I'm willing to think it over. (Kivi, 1929, p. 302–304)

This plan was followed. Eero's instruction and the brothers' learning themselves were not much more modern than the first attempt in the parish clerk's house. But these low-level learning actions gain a new quality
because of their overall activity context. It is no more school going. This
time, the context is that of conquering a new central activity with the help
of certain – albeit mechanical – learning actions. The whole long process of
traveling across the zone of proximal development has not been characterized by conscious mastery, or expansive learning activity. But at this point
of decisive transition (application and generalization of the new model), the
brothers are *subjects* of their specific learning actions.

Eero sat as teacher and his brothers as pupils, all shouting as with one
mouth the names of the letters as the youngest brother called them
out.... Hard and agonizing was this work to them, full of agony especially in the beginning; sorely they all sighed and sweated. Hardest of all
worked Juhani; for very zeal his jaw would shake, and dozing Timo who
sat beside him received many an angry poke of his fist whenever his poor
head drooped. An added trial was that Eero did not always take his high
calling with due gravity, but frequently allowed stinging little remarks to
pass his lips. For this he had received many warnings from his brothers,
but the game was dear to him.

Once on a winter day, when a biting frost prevailed outside and an
almost rayless sun shone over the southern rim of the world, the brothers
sat hard at work in their cabin, a-b-c-books in their hands. The devoted,
but monotonous sound of their reading might have been heard afar; it
was the second time they were going through the alphabet.

EERO. A.

THE OTHERS. A.

EERO. B.

THE OTHERS. B.

EERO. Ay, A is the first letter of the alphabet and Z the last. "A and Z,
the beginning and the end, the first and the last," as it says somewhere
in the Bible. But have you ever happened to see the last as the first, Z
as A? It certainly looks a bit funny to see that little thing, the one that
always used to be at the tail end, suddenly cock on the dunghill and all

the others looking up to him with honour and respect, as at something fatherly, even though they do it with somewhat bulging eyes. But why do I turn to matters with which we have nothing to do just now. Ay, go on reading.

JUHANI. Do I catch thy meaning? I'm afraid I do. But teach us nicely now, or the Devil'll get you.

EERO. Go on nicely with your lesson now. C.

THE OTHERS. C.

EERO. D.

THE OTHERS. D, E, F, G.

JUHANI. Wait a bit; I, poor boy, have lost my place. Let's start again at the beginning.

EERO. A.

THE OTHERS. A.

EERO. A, B, C, "the cow ran up the tree." What does this sentence tell us, Juhani. Canst thou explain it?

JUHANI. I will try to discover its meaning. Come out with me a little, you others; there is something important we must talk over.

So saying, he went out into the yard, and the others followed him; and with beating heart Eero began guessing what this withdrawal might portend. But in the yard the brothers discussed the best way of keeping down Eero's cruel way of bent for joking, which caused him to jest with the a-b-c-book in his hand and thus mock not only them, but also God and His word. And they concluded that he had earned a good whipping. They entered the cabin again, and the fresh birch-rod in Juhani's hand struck the soul of Eero with dread. Tuomas and Simeoni seized the lad firmly; and then Juhani's rod did its best. Eero yelled, kicked and raved, and when at last he was free, looked around him with terrible, murderous glance.

Juhani. Now then, take the book in thy hand and teach us properly, thou rascal, and remember this hiding whenever thy blackguard tongue feels like talking mockingly. Ah indeed! Did it hurt? Ay, ay, thous hast got what I prophesied thee years ago. For "evil is the mocker's reward in the end," that thou now knowest. Take the book, say I, and teach us in a sensible and proper way, thou rascal. (Kivi, 1929, p. 308–310)

This incident exemplifies how the given new actions are disturbed as the created new breaks into the open. Eero's acting does not correspond to either the old activity (isolated hunting life) or the given new activity (civilized agricultural life). And it certainly gains no reward for him, rather to the contrary.

There are other kinds of disturbances, too. Frost destroys the broth-ers' crops, and a hard winter threatens them with a famine. The disaster is avoided as the brothers once more succeed in bear hunting. Temporarily, the old activity takes over once more. But this disturbance is regressive or nostalgic, fundamentally different from the one described previously.

Now what is the essence of the created new activity manifested in Eero's actions? What is the inner contradiction embedded in the new model of agricultural life?

Eero's joke cited previously hits the heart of the matter: "It certainly looks a bit funny to see that little thing, the one that always used to be at the tail end, suddenly cock on the dunghill and all the others looking up to him with honour and respect, as at something fatherly, even though they do it with somewhat bulging eyes." The message is clear: The stable hierarchies based on wealth, age, and physical power are turned upside down. The last becomes the first. The smallest and youngest takes the power, which is sud-denly based on knowledge, wit, and intellect.

This perspective is real and objective, not just Eero's subjective fancy. The very stability and unity of the Lutheran agricultural order required the ability to read. But this ability was a double-edged sword. It could be turned into an *instrument* instead of a *rule*. Eero's actions anticipate just this: a created new activity in which reading and intellect are used as instruments of power, implying an essentially dynamic and fluid social and economic order – that which was to take the shape of industrial capitalism.

In the last chapter of the book, Kivi sketches the future destinies of each of the brothers, Eero the last.

> On Sundays and holidays he either studied his newspaper, or wrote the news or described parochial happenings from his own parish for the same newspaper. And gladly the editor accepted these writings of his, whose contents were always to the point, their style pithy and clear, often showing genius. And with these interests his outlook on life and the world broadened. The country of his birth was to him no lon-ger a vague part of a vague world, of which he knew neither the site nor the character. He knew well where lay the country, that dear corner of the earth, where the Finns dwelt in toil and struggle, and in whose bosom the bones of his fathers rested. He knew its frontiers, its seas, its secretly-smiling lakes and the pine-clad ridges that run like stake-fences throughout its breadth. The whole picture of the land of his birth, its friendly mother-face, had sunk for ever into the depths of his heart. And from it was born in him the desire to help the happiness and prosperity of his country. Through his sturdy and unresting endeavours a kind of

elementary school was built in the parish, one of the first in Finland. And other useful institutions, too, he brought into the district. And in all his work in the house his eye dwelt constantly on his eldest son, whom he had decided to educate into a man of knowledge and skill. (Kivi, 1929, p. 402–403)

Aleksis Kivi himself was an Eero of the Finnish nation, only with a less happy and harmonious end. His book disturbed the given new way of life, the stable hierarchy of authority. The leading literary critic crushed *Seven Brothers*, accusing it of low naturalism. Kivi lived in constant financial anguish. His mental health was shattered, and he died in oblivion in 1872.

I'll now summarize the brothers' voyage across the zone of proximal development in the following table (Table 3.4). Just as in Huck's case, the case of the brothers represents a developmental sequence structurally *similar* to learning activity but occurring essentially nonconsciously, *without* learning activity. A comparison between the voyages of Huckleberry Finn and the seven brothers also discovers an interesting difference. In the case of Huck Finn, the double bind situation was a singular conflict taken to the extreme and solved expansively because of Huck's personal honesty and strength. In the case of the brothers, the double bind appears four times, each time in a more aggravated form.

The reading instruction in the house of the parish clerk produces the first premature form of the double bind. The second appearance of the double bind ensues from the incident with the bulls. The third time it is faced after the drinking period, as the boys find Simeoni in the woods and hear about the visions of Simeoni and Lauri. Very soon follows the fourth and decisive appearance, as the boys consider the consequences of their fight with the men of Toukola. The solution is not found as a momentary revelation, manifested as an exceptional action in the pressing situation. Rather, the solution is ripened stepwise, and the release of tension demands more calming down and relaxing than extreme effort.

This is probably one real type of the double bind. Bateson (1978, p. 63–64) seems to hint at something like this as he speaks of double binds as "taking pains," as "recursive and reflexive trains of phenomena." In one type of double bind, a singular unexpected action is decisive for the expansive solution. In the other type, the solution is reached through a series of more or less incomplete and unsatisfactory attempts leading to the final point where withdrawal from regressive action may be the decisive element after which the solution appears as something self-evident and easy.

TABLE 3.4. *The sequential structure of seven brothers' zone of proximal development*

Contradiction	Phase	Content In *Seven Brothers*
Primary *within* the components of the old activity	Need state	Hunting life in the woods: freedom in nature vs. social interaction with people
Secondary *between* the components of the old activity	Double bind	Intruding new rules (reading, economic responsibility, physical restraint) vs. old instruments (isolation model, direct recourse to physical action)
	Object/motive construction	(a) The idea of cultivating land as a solution to the payment of the bulls (springboard: the idea of making tar)
		(b) The taking up of reading and agriculture as reactions to the release of tension after the fight (springboard: the idea of wife) New object: land, stable prosperity; new general model: civilized life (stable agricultural hierarchy vs. dynamic movement stimulated by reading and intellect as inner contradiction of this new model of activity)
Tertiary between the old and the *given new* activity/motive (between the only understood and the effective motive)	Application, generalization; component actions of the given new activity	Hunting (made necessary by frost and famine) vs. agriculture and reading; new actions of reading are *disturbed* by Eero's precursor actions of the *created new* activity
Quaternary *between* the new activity and its neighbor activities	Activity 2: reflection, consolidation	Agricultural life of the brothers, including Eero's work for enlightenment in the community

THE SECOND INTERMEDIATE BALANCE

In the preceding chapter, learning activity was characterized as "learning by expanding." In this chapter, learning activity has been characterized as a *voyage across the zone of proximal development,* and a sequential model of this voyage has been worked out. In the course of this voyage, elements of an *objectively and societally new activity form* are produced simultaneously with qualitative change in the subject of activity.

The model put forward in this chapter as well as the concrete literary cases may give a picture of an essentially spontaneous process, largely independent of interventions and instructional efforts from the outside. The literary cases are actually examples of spontaneous forbears of learning activity. Their sequential structure is basically similar to that of learning activity, but they lack the *specific instrumentality* of the latter.

In Chapter 4, I will turn to this specific instrumentality, representing the complex psychic formation of theoretical thinking or theoretical relation to reality.

4

The Instruments of Expansion

In the preceding chapters, I have formulated the object of my investigation in terms of expansion from the level of prevalent individual actions to the level of novel collective activity. Such transitions have commonly taken place as if above the heads of the affected individuals and groups, in the form of historical tragedies and puppet shows of varying scales.

I have argued that a new type of "learning by expanding" is emerging in the current phase of human history. This implies that the transitions mentioned previously are becoming potential objects of conscious or intuitive mastery.

Conscious goal-directed processes are situated at the level of actions, or secondary instruments. This level is the homestead of thinking. Thinking is most typically described as a series of relatively discrete actions of "gap filling" or problem solving. The emergence of thoughtfully mastered learning activity or "learning by expanding" implies the extension of thinking into an activity, and the merger of learning and thinking into one unified process at this level.

The problem is to identify the specific instruments of this new type of expansive learning and thinking. For this purpose, I shall first critically examine certain dominant modes of theorizing about thinking.

THE FIRST DICHOTOMY: "PRIMITIVE" VERSUS "ADVANCED" THOUGHT

In his book *The Foundations of Primitive Thought*, C. R. Hallpike (1979) defines the characteristics of "primitive" and "advanced" thinking as follows (Table 4.1; compiled by Atlas 1985, p. 336).

Hallpike uses the Piagetian cognitive stages as his analytical framework. According to him, inhabitants of "primitive" societies are for the most part

TABLE 4.1. *Characteristics of "primitive" and "advanced" thought after Hallpike (1979)*

Domain of thought	Type of thought	
	"Primitive"	"Advanced"
Symbolism	Image-based, affective	Linguistic
Classification	Associational	Taxonomic
Number and measurement	Concrete, absolute	Abstract, relative
Space	Perceptual	Conceptual
Time	Qualitative, incommensurable	Quantitative, capable of comparison
Conceptions and representations of the person	Fusion of the psychical and physical; private states not verbally elaborated	Mind/body duality; distinction between private and public awareness
Causality	Essentialist	Impersonal, probabilistic

characterized by preoperational thought, not reaching the level of concrete operational thinking typical of children of seven years and older living in "advanced" societies.

For Hallpike, life in "primitive" societies is cognitively less demanding than life in "advanced" societies. One source of higher cognitive demands in "advanced" societies is the presence of mechanical devices and complex technical implements. Substitutability of labor, impersonal productive relations, and the rationalization of activity are the features of civilization celebrated by Hallpike. As Atlas (1985, p. 335) notes in his review, Hallpike's book echoes old mainstream ideas on "primitive" mentality. The novelty is his wedding of Piaget to this tradition.

The form of theorizing demonstrated by Hallpike is deeply rooted in our psychological reasoning. It is salient in many current discussions of the psychology of human thinking, including attempts with aims opposite to those of Hallpike. This general form of theorizing is the pervasive use of *dichotomies* as explanatory constructs.

In his pioneering study of the cultural foundations of cognition, A. R. Luria (1976) distinguished between two broad types of thinking: one concrete, situational, and "graphic-functional"; the other abstract, categorical, and logical. The protocol of a subject called Rakmat, produced as a response to a classification task, is a famous example of the former type.

Subject: Rakmat, age thirty-nine, illiterate peasant from an outlying district; has seldom been in Fergana, never in any other city. He was shown drawings of the following: *hammer – saw – log – hatchet.*

"They are all alike. I think all of them have to be here. See, if you're going to saw, you need a saw, and if you have to split something you need a hatchet. So they're *all* needed here."

Employs the principle of "necessity" to group objects in a practical situation.

...

Which of these things could you call by one word?

"How's that? If you call all three of them a 'hammer,' that won't be right either."

Rejects use of general term.

But one fellow picked three things – the hammer, saw, and hatchet – and said they were alike.

"A saw, a hammer, and a hatchet all have to work together. But the log has to be there, too."

Reverts to situational thinking.

Why do you think he picked up these three things and not the log?

"Probably he's got a lot of firewood, but if we'll be left without firewood, we won't be able to do anything."

Explains selection in strictly practical terms.

True, but a hammer, a saw, and a hatchet are all tools.

"Yes, but even if we have tools, we still need wood – otherwise, we can't build anything."

Persists in situational thinking despite disclosure of categorical term"
(Luria, 1976, p. 55–56)

Luria's schooled subjects behaved differently. To them, the task of isolating a particular attribute as a basis of categorization seemed "a natural, self-evident procedure" (Luria, 1976, p. 78). These schooled subjects actually represented a historical phase entirely different from that represented by Rakmat. Rakmat was a man of a preindustrial and preliterate age. The schooled subjects were men and women of both socialism and industrialization in the takeoff.

Luria's conclusions imply that concrete situational thinking is lower or less developed than abstract categorical thinking. This has prompted Cole and Griffin (1980, p. 352) to note that the qualitative changes in cognition that Luria sought to demonstrate led him into comparisons "that were distressingly quantitative in their implications."

The problem is, Can development be conceived of as a linear process in which certain valuable ingredients (such as the "abstractness" of thinking) gradually or abruptly increase while other, restrictive ingredients (such as the "concreteness" of thinking) decrease? The answer given by Cole and Griffin is negative. While being forced to admit that technologies have evolved from the simple to the complex and more powerful, they point out that in spheres such as politics or family life such linear evolutionary schemes are inappropriate (Cole & Griffin, 1980, p. 362).

The justified opposition to linear schemes easily leads to a denial of all logic or lawfulness in history. The result may be a pluralistic ahistorical constructivism along the lines of Nelson Goodman's (1978) "worldmaking." The idea that anything may be constructed from what is given and that no constructed world is instrinsically more true than any other is refreshing and spiritually liberating. But it is not very powerful in the face of the overwhelming movement of societal reality. And it helps us very little in our attempts to understand how our societies have evolved.

So Luria's weakness is not the same as that of Hallpike, who presents his dichotomy in essentially ahistorical terms. Luria's dichotomy is an attempt to understand historically the transformation of thinking. It is precisely this that makes Luria's study a pathbreaking classic. Luria's trouble is on a different level. It is the question *What is the logic of history – if it is not linear?*

THE SECOND DICHOTOMY: EXPERIENCE VERSUS ANALYSIS

Hallpike's dichotomy sees the concrete thought of the "primitive" societies as essentially lower than the abstract thought of the "advanced" societies. Some recent treatises take a different standpoint, actually praising the neglected virtues of various forms of concrete, tacit, and nonanalytical thought (though not necessarily connecting these forms to so-called primitive societies).

In their book *Mind over Machine* (1986) Hubert and Stuart Dreyfus discuss the nature and acquisition of expertise in the era of the computer. Their argument is that we cannot explain human expertise as behavior based on explicable principles and rules. A true expert makes decisions on an intuitive basis. The psychological mechanism behind intuition is *experience-based holistic recognition of similarity,* producing deep situational understanding and fluid, rapid behavior. Through experience, we store in our memories large amounts of typical situations that bear no names and defy complete verbal description: "Experience seems immeasurably more important than any form of verbal description" (Dreyfus & Dreyfus, 1986, p. 23).

TABLE 4.2. *The five stages of skill acquisition after Dreyfus and Dreyfus (1986)*

Skill level	Components	Perspective	Decision	Commitment
1. Novice	Context-free	None	Analytical	Detached
2. Advanced beginner	Context-free and situational	None	Analytical	None
3. Competent	Context-free and situational	Chosen	Analytical	Detached understanding and deciding; involved in outcome
4. Proficient	Context-free and situational	Experienced	Analytical	Involved understanding; detached deciding
5. Expert	Context-free and situational	Experienced	Intuitive	Involved

> While most expert performance is ongoing and nonreflective, when time permits and outcomes are crucial an expert will deliberate before acting. But ... this deliberation does not require calculative problem-solving, but rather involves critically reflecting on one's intuitions. (Dreyfus & Dreyfus, 1986, p. 31–32)

The authors describe the process of becoming an expert as consisting of five stages of skill acquisition (Table 4.2).

The acquisition process is depicted as a linear sequence from the analytical to the intuitive, from the rule-guided "knowing that" to the experience-based knowhow. It is essentially a process of internalization.

> An expert's skill has become so much a part of him that he need be no more aware of it than he is of his own body. (Dreyfus & Dreyfus, 1986, p. 30)

The process is not only linear. For the authors it also seems to be automatic and self-evident in every case of expertise acquisition. Experience is the golden key to the consequent steps of this path.

This assumption fails to explain why so many people never become fluid intuitive experts in spite of years and years of experience. Somehow the authors seem to forget all about the rigidity associated with extensive routinization.

The Dreyfus brothers' singular praise of experience may be contrasted with the findings produced over the years by research on learning from experience in probabilistic situations (see Brehmer, 1980; Kahneman, Slovic & Tversky, 1982). Brehmer (1980, p. 224–227) points out the weakness of the psychological research supposedly demonstrating how people learn from experience. The tasks used in that kind of research, such as paired associates and classification tasks, typically employ materials in which the truth is manifest. In the word lists of paired associates *the subject immediately knows what he or she is supposed to learn.* Similarly, in the classification tasks the common components of the stimuli, such as color and form, are already well-formed concepts and the experimenter is certain that the subjects already have the hypotheses relevant to the task. Thus, the guarantee of the validity of the solution in these tasks does not result from experience. It results from the experimenter through his or her choice of materials.

> The paradigm may thus very well model the situation in teaching, where the teacher decides for the pupil what the truth should be in a given case, but it certainly does not model the situation in which a person is learning from experience. (Brehmer, 1980, p. 225)

The situation is different when subjects face complex probabilistic tasks, such as diagnostic decision making. The truth is not manifest. Nobody tells the practitioner what there is to learn, or even whether there is anything for him or her to learn. The fact that the chosen treatment leads to recovery does not mean that the decision was correct, for (a) the recovery may have had other causes, (b) other kinds of treatment may have been equally or more effective, and (c) the chosen treatment may eventually have other unwanted effects, which are, however, difficult if not impossible to trace back to their cause with full certainty. Even if the chosen treatment works, the explanation for *why* it works may be very different from what the practitioner thinks it is. But the practitioner learning from experience learns mainly from the outcomes of his or her actions. As Dreyfus and Dreyfus (1986, p. 28) put it, "The proficient performer has experienced similar situations in the past and memories of them trigger plans similar to those that worked in the past."

> When we learn from outcomes, it may, in fact, be almost impossible to discover that one really does not know anything. This is especially true when the concepts are very complex in the sense that each instance contains many dimensions. In this case, there are too many ways of explaining why a certain outcome occurred, and to explain away failures of predicting the correct outcome. Because of this, the need to change may not be apparent to us, and we may fail to learn that our rule is invalid,

not only for particular cases but for the general case also. (Brehmer, 1980, p. 228–229)

Mere experience, even of probabilistic tasks, seems only to strengthen the subjects' nonprobabilistic thinking. Subjects prefer to assume that there is a deterministic causal rule behind every task. When their assumed deterministic rules fail, they tend to assume that there is no rule at all, rather than seriously consider the possibility that the rule may be probabilistic in character.

These results, then, support the earlier results on clinical inference in that they show that people do not learn optimal strategies from experience even if they are given massive amounts of practice. The reason why the subjects fail to improve in these tasks seems to be that they lack the necessary basic schemata to help them understand and use the information provided by their experience. Rather than using the appropriate statistical schemata, subjects use an inappropriate causal or deterministic schema.... The characteristic of probabilism is, of course, not manifest, but it has to be inferred.... For a person with a firm belief in the deterministic character of the world, there is nothing in his experience that would force him to discover that the task is probabilistic and to give up the notion of determinism.... In short, probabilism must be invented before it can be detected. (Brehmer, 1980, p. 233–235)

The problem with learning from experience is actually the classical problem of induction. According to the classical theory of induction, we make generalizations on the basis of experiencing many things of a similar kind. Dreyfus and Dreyfus (1986, p. 22) seem to subscribe to the classical position: "Through practical experience in concrete situations with meaningful elements, which neither the instructor nor the learner can define in terms of objectively recognizable context-free features, the advanced beginner starts to recognize those elements when they are present." And this happens "thanks to a perceived similarity with prior examples."

This kind of empirical generalization seems to work reasonably well when we are dealing with simple stimuli and well-established conventions. But when the cases we observe are complex and novel, how do we know that things are really similar and instances of the same general class? For that, we need to know what the relevant characteristics are in the first place. We have to define what we are to learn before we can learn it. Pure induction turns out to be a fallacy, as Nelson Goodman demonstrated long ago.

To say that valid predictions are those based on past regularities, without being able to say which regularities, is thus quite pointless. Regularities are where you find them, and you can find them anywhere. (Goodman, 1983, p. 82)

What we commonly think is pure experience are actually sense data selected and interpreted by our culturally molded but not necessarily modern schemata and mental models. Probability calculus was invented in the seventeenth century, perhaps because "it was only at this point in time that the notion of causality had reached such a level that it could provide a suitable contrast against which to evaluate disorder" (Brehmer, 1980, p. 235). In individual practitioners, the old cultural model of linear causality has tremendous persistence. This illuminates the conservative bias of experience. Recalling the Dreyfus brothers' unreserved belief in the power of experience, Brehmer's (1980, p. 224) conclusion that we have come to have "a perverse conception of the nature of experience" is not unfounded.

The Dreyfus brothers' dichotomy is *experience-based intuitive expertise versus rule-based analytical expertise.* Employing Brehmer's critique of experience, we obtain a further dichotomy: *experience as casual growth of holistic intuition versus experience as strengthening of rigid and biased routines.* So we are still stuck with a dichotomy.

THE THIRD DICHOTOMY: NARRATIVE VERSUS PARADIGMATIC THOUGHT

One final version of the dichotomy deserves our attention. It is the split between scientific and artistic, or paradigmatic and narrative thought, recently revitalized by Jerome Bruner (1986).

According to Bruner (1986, p. 12), the paradigmatic or logicoscientific mode of thought attempts to fulfill the ideal of a formal, mathematical system of description and explanation. It employs categorization or conceptualization and the operations by which categories are established, instantiated, idealized, and related one to the other to form a system. Propositions are extracted from statements in their particular contexts. The logicoscientific mode deals in general causes, and in their establishment. It makes use of procedures to assure verifiable reference and to test for empirical truth. Its language is regulated by requirements of consistency and noncontradiction.

The narrative type of thought has opposite characteristics.

The imaginative application of the narrative mode leads instead to good stories, gripping drama, believable (though not necessarily 'true') historical accounts. It deals in human or human-like intention and action.... It strives to put its timeless miracles into the particulars of experience, and to locate the experience in time and place.... The paradigmatic mode, by contrast, seeks to transcend the particular by higher and higher reach for abstraction, and in the end disclaims in principle any explanatory value at all where the particular is concerned. (Bruner, 1986, p. 13)

Bruner's book is a continuation of a distinguished series on essentially analogous dichotomies: science versus humanities, nomothetic versus idiographic, concepts versus images, positivism versus phenomenology. In psychology, the same basic division was championed already by Wundt.

Many recent efforts to deal with these dichotomies aim at balancing or combining the two sides. In his important book *Imagery in Scientific Thought*, Arthur I. Miller (1984, p. 312) concludes that "when scientists hold a theory, they hold a particular mode of imagery as well." Herbert Simon (1983, p. 28) supports the credo by stating that there is no contradiction between the intuitive model and the behavioral model of thinking, since "all serious thinking calls on both modes, both search-like processes and the sudden recognition of familiar patterns." In his theory of fantasy, Roset (1984) presents the two sides as alternating phases of intuitive production and analytical control, or "an axiomatization" and "hyper-axiomatization." These combinations leave us with constructions of the type "both-and" instead of mere "either-or." But the abstract dichotomous structure remains at the heart of the argument.

REACHING BEYOND THE DICHOTOMIES: DEWEY, WERTHEIMER, AND BARTLETT

The problem with the dichotomies is that they depict movement as mechanical opposition, summation, or oscillation between two fixed poles, thus effectively excluding the dimension of concrete historical development.

"Either-or" and "both-and" are closed and timeless structures. Within them, there is no room for something qualitatively new emerging first as a subordinated mediator between the two poles and being transformed into a determining factor that will eventually change the character of the whole structural configuration. There is no room for thirdness.

In classical treatises on the psychology of thinking one finds, however, intriguing attempts to overcome the dichotomous structure. My first example is John Dewey's (1910) *How We Think*. In this book, Dewey takes up the problem of experience. He first criticizes our belief in experience much as Brehmer did seventy years later.

> But even the most reliable beliefs of this type fail when they confront
> the *novel*. Since they rest upon past uniformities, they are useless when
> further experience departs in any considerable measure from ancient
> incident and wonted precedent....
>
> Mental inertia, laziness, unjustifiable conservatism, are its probable
> accompaniments. Its general effect upon mental attitude is more seri-
> ous than even the specific wrong conclusions in which it has landed.
> Wherever the chief dependence in forming inferences is upon the con-
> junctions observed in past experience, failures to agree with the usual
> order are slurred over, cases of successful confirmation are exaggerated.
> Since the mind naturally demands some principle of continuity, some
> connecting link between separate facts and causes, forces are arbitrarily
> invented for that purpose. (Dewey, 1910, p. 148)

But Dewey is not satisfied with this. He realizes that people may also
become truly flexible and inventive experts. This kind of development is
based on experimentation and hypothesis testing. But that in turn cannot
be explained as given from above, mechanically separated from experience.
Thus, experience acquires a deeper double meaning.

> In short, the term *experience* may be interpreted either with reference to
> the *empirical* or the *experimental* attitude of mind. Experience is not a
> rigid and closed thing; it is vital, and hence growing. When dominated
> by the past, by custom and routine, it is often opposed to the reason-
> able, the thoughtful. But experience also includes the reflection that
> sets us free from the limiting influence of sense, appetite, and tradition.
> Experience may welcome and assimilate all that the most exact and pen-
> etrating thought discovers. Indeed, the business of education might be
> defined as just such an emancipation and enlargement of experience.
> (Dewey, 1910, p. 156)

The external opposition of experience versus analysis has thus been transformed into an internal contradiction within experience itself. But the
mediating thirdness is still lacking. To find the way out, we must take a critical look at the logic implicitly attributed to both components of experience,
or to both intuitive and analytical thinking. Max Wertheimer's *Productive
Thinking* (1945) is a classic work that provides us with this critique.

> There are several objects. (The way in which they are segregated, and
> why just so, how an object constitutes itself in separation from other
> objects, is a question neglected in traditional logic, is taken for granted
> without real investigation.) I compare them. In their qualities of their
> parts I find similarities and differences. Abstracting from the differences,
> and concentrating on common qualities or parts in the objects, I get a

general concept. The content is given by these common parts. This is the "intension." The "extension" is the manifold of objects embraced by the class concept.

If we call the common element *m,* and the other elements *x,* an exact expression for the class (or for any object as conceived under the class concept) is

$$m + x.$$

Between the *m* and the *x* is an "and." The *m* is what is common in the contents of the objects; the *x* is what there is besides the *m* and may vary in the contents of the various objects. The conceived datum, *m,* is independent of its setting to the left and right, and apparently must be so for the sake of exact use of the concept in inference, syllogisms, etc. There is no reference to whatever else there may be in the object besides, no references to the role which *m* plays in this object, no reference to its meaning as a part among the other parts of the same entity, no reference to the structure of this entity. This abstraction is substractive; it simply isolates the *m.* For the *m* it does not matter what the *x* is....

In the historic development difficulties have arisen as to the adequacy of the procedure. .... The problem was whether such a procedure, although exact, does not easily combine objects which are basically different in nature and, on the other hand, sharply separate objects which belong to each other in fact. The logician seeks help in the term "essential." There always was emphasis on this point; but although for common sense the meaning of "essential" is often clear enough, unfortunately it was and has remained extremely controversial in logic. It has served to name the problem rather than to solve it. It has consequently been rejected again, excluded in newer developments of logic. (Wertheimer, 1945, p. 207–208)

Another grave feature in traditional logic is its insistence that the items of discourse – concepts, propositions, and others – must remain rigidly identical if repeated. In real thinking processes, items do not remain identical. To the contrary, precisely their change is required. Their functional and structural meaning changes, and blindness to such change impedes productive processes. Formal logic is incapable of grasping development because it disregards "the intense directedness of live thought processes as they improve a given situation" (Wertheimer, 1945, p. 215).

This fundamental insight has long been neglected in cognitive and anthropological studies of classification. A study of the conceptual organization of practicing blacksmiths indicates that the emphasis may be changing. "What leads to highly effective means of blacksmithing is flexibility in classification. There is no one basic structure to which we can turn as the key to the practice of blacksmithing. Blacksmithing, like other behavior, is characterized by productivity" (Dougherty & Keller, 1985, p. 170–171; see also Gatewood, 1985).

Wertheimer (1945, p. 10) concludes that in comparison with actual thought processes, the rules and examples of traditional logic look "dull, insipid, lifeless." If one tries to describe processes of productive thinking in terms of formal logic, one may have a series of correct operations, but the sense of the process, what is vital and creative in it, is lost.

One factor behind the persistence of formal-logical conceptions of thinking is their correspondence to certain deep-seated modes of real thought processes. The outstanding instance is our habit of proceeding only successively, step by step, in an "and-summative" fashion. According to Wertheimer (1945, p. 88), this may be due to the fact that "we cannot write down two propositions simultaneously, that in reports we have to proceed one thing after the other." In other words, the concrete-historical instrument of written language enters as a structural determinant of thinking. Unfortunately Wertheimer does not continue this line of analysis. It remains an intriguing hint, a sidetrack without consequence.

For Wertheimer, there *is* something essential behind the endless multitude of external properties of objects. This essential includes the following aspects:

- the wholeness or whole-quality of the object or situation, as opposed to a mere additive listing of its parts;
- the clear, complete, and consistent structure of the object, as opposed to an incomplete or shallow structure;
- the inner relatedness of the parts of the whole, as opposed to their separation or discreteness;
- the center, core or radix of the whole, as opposed to a structure without center.

The essential is thus the "good gestalt," and productive thinking is transition from a bad gestalt to a good one. Wertheimer summarizes his idea in the following description.

> Thinking consists in envisaging, realizing structural features and structural requirements; proceeding in accordance with, and determined by, these requirements; thereby changing the situation in the direction of structural improvements, which involves:
>
> that gaps, trouble-regions, disturbances, superficialities, etc., be viewed and dealt with structurally;

that inner structural relations – fitting or not fitting – be sought among such disturbances and the given situation as a whole and among its various parts;

that there be operations of structural grouping and segregation, of centering, etc.; that operations be viewed and treated in their structural place, role, dynamic meaning, including realization of the changes which this involves;

realizing structural transposability, structural hierarchy, and separating structurally peripheral from fundamental features – a special case of grouping; looking for structural rather than piecemeal truth. (Wertheimer, 1945, p. 190–191)

For a modern cognitive scientist, characterizations like the one cited are aggravating, if not totally meaningless. It is hard to find tangible operational, not to mention measurable, counterparts or indices for Wertheimer's concepts. For Wertheimer, this kind of reaction would rather prove his point, as another example of the dominant piecemeal, and-summative way of thinking.

It is not justified to nullify Wertheimer's work on account of its lacking concreteness. Wertheimer does present a very convincing series of concrete examples, ranging from the famous parallelograms to the unique account of Einstein's way to the discovery of relativity. In these examples, he demonstrates how productive thinking proceeds. But he does not demonstrate *what primary and secondary instruments could be used to enhance this type of thinking.* Obviously this is why gestalt theory was overrun by the many variants of behaviorism. Skinner offered the world concrete tools with which one could do something practical. Wertheimer did not.

This criticism could be interpreted as crude utilitarianism. But there is more at stake here. The question of instruments is above all a theoretical weakness in Wertheimer's work. As I noted earlier, he only accidentally touched the role of cultural instruments – namely, written language – as determinants of the development of thinking. He did not seek the expansive perspective by way of a historical analysis of the emerging new instrumentalities of thought. His conception was presented as an unhistorical, eternal solution. Productive thinking, aimed at the "good gestalt," was for him a moral imperative, stemming from inside, already planted deeply in the human nature: "In humans there is at bottom the desire, the craving to face the true issue, the structural core, the radix of the situation" (Wertheimer, 1945, p. 191). Thus, at least implicitly, the emergence of productive thinking was to be realized by individual willpower.

And yet, in spite of this critical weakness, there is something prophetic in Wertheimer's vision of thinking as expansion.

> In such processes of thinking the solution of an actual task, "Problem solved, task finished," is not the end. The way of solution, its fundamental features, the problem with its solution function as parts of a large expanding realm. Here the function of thinking is not just solving an actual problem, but discovering, envisaging, going into deeper questions. Often in great discoveries the most important thing is that a certain question is found....
>
> Often such a process takes a long time; it is drama with setbacks and struggles. There are fine cases in which the process proceeds irresistibly, through months, through years, never losing sight of the deeper issue, never getting lost in petty details, in detours, bypaths. (Wertheimer, 1945, p. 122–123)

So Wertheimer gives us prophecy, but not instruments. To get some idea of the latter, I will consult a third classic, namely, Sir Frederic Bartlett's book *Thinking* (1958).

According to Bartlett (1958, p. 182), much of what is called inductive generalizing is "no more than the acceptance, with biased selection, of already formed social conventions." These generalizations "have little to do with transfer of practice or training save that they make it more difficult" (Bartlett, 1958, p. 184).

There is, however, also an exploratory or experimental type of generalization, which may lead to genuinely new discoveries and concepts. But even this is not accomplished by "purifying" the sensory data from cultural conventions. To the contrary.

> However "pure" his aims may be he has to be able to practise a technique and to handle a technology. Far the most important aspect of the experimenter's need to master method and to handle apparatus is that in the majority of cases ... the method and the instrumentation are brought into his field of work from the outside. (Bartlett, 1958, p. 133)

Why are instruments so important in experimental thinking? Successful experimenting requires that the experimenter know where to look for new crucial findings. This step becomes possible when apparatus, methods, hints, or established findings are taken over from some field different from that in which they are applied. They subsequently function as "lenses" that allow for a novel perspective (Bartlett, 1958, p. 134).

Bartlett's insight has been restated by Tweney, Doherty, and Mynatt (1981, p. 411–412).

Scientists self-consciously bring a store of knowledge to bear on the task at hand, as well as a highly developed set of intellectual tools. They may use extensive note-taking, carefully organized records of data, files, and libraries, as "external memories." They use blackboards, mathematics, even formal logic. Latour and Woolgar (1979) noted that nearly all of the behavioral activity in a major laboratory consisted of manipulation of symbols, and only a tiny fraction involved direct contact with the phenomena under investigation. Cognitive psychologists have typically studied "prescientific man." The typical subject in a psychological laboratory has access only to presented stimuli and almost never to memory aids or other heuristics. The intent has been to study basic cognitive processes, unencumbered by cultural artifacts or aids. A cognitive psychology of science will have to focus instead on *aided* cognition, on the psychology of scientists when all the tools of the trade are at their disposal.

However, the preceding statement falls short of grasping the gist of Bartlett's idea. For Bartlett, the specific instrumentality of exploratory thinking also implies its specific *sociality*. The sociality of experimental thinking is not of an immediate, face-to-face nature (though it may certainly include that, too). The necessity of *taking over instruments from other, overlapping fields* means that experimental thinking is "fundamentally co-operative, social, and cannot proceed far without the stimulus of outside contacts" (Bartlett, 1958, p. 123).

This is a specific *extended* kind of sociality. It indicates the expansive, cyclic nature of experimental thinking. According to Bartlett (1958, p. 136), when any experimental science is ripe for marked advance, a mass of routine thinking has come near to wearing itself out by exploiting a limited range of technique to establish more and more minute and specialized detail.

> However, at the same time, perhaps in some other branch of science, and perhaps in some hitherto disconnected part of what is treated as the same branch, there are other techniques generating their own problems, opening up their own gaps. An original mind, never wholly contained in any conventionally enclosed field of interest, now seizes upon the possibility that there may be some unsuspected overlap, takes the risk whether there is or not, and gives the old subject-matter a new look.

This passage takes us back to Figure 3.2. The phase of repetitive production of more and more specialized detail precedes the phase of the need state, or the primary contradiction. The phase when a new instrument is seized upon and taken over from an overlapping field corresponds to the emergence of the secondary contradiction in which a foreign element is introduced into the prevalent activity structure.

In Chapter 3, I used the metaphor of a voyage to characterize the zone of proximal development. Bartlett (1958, p. 137) describes the course of experimental thinking in much the same manner.

> The experimental thinker is in the position of somebody who must use whatever tools may be available for adding to some structure that is not yet finished, and that he himself is certainly not going to complete. Because the materials that he must use have properties of their own, many of which he cannot know before he uses them, and some of which in all likelihood are actually generated in the course of their use, he is in the position of an explorer rather than that of a spectator.

Notice the expression "he himself is certainly not going to complete." Here Bartlett hints at the social dimension of the expansion. The qualitatively new scientific concept – or the qualitatively new form of scientific activity – is going to be a collective formation that goes beyond all the individual actions that gave rise to it.

At the end of his book, Bartlett discusses artistic thinking. He notices that when an artist has his work well under way, "it very often appears to him that something outside himself has taken charge and is now settling everything that happens" (Bartlett, 1958, p. 192). This experience is not foreign to scientists either. The phenomenon is due to the anticipation of the essentially collective and societal, tertiary character embedded within a work of art (or science) under creation (recall Zinchenko's "liberated actions" and Bateson's loss of the "I"). The double nature of this expansion is evident in a work of art in that "it is at once convincing and satisfying, and yet question-making and disturbing" (Bartlett, 1958, p. 196). In other words, it requires simultaneously accepting a convention – *the given new* – and passing beyond it "towards whatever standard it serves" (Bartlett, 1958, p. 193) – *the created new*.

THE COMPLEMENTARITY OF INSTRUMENTS

When is the artifact an instrument? In the realm of primary artifacts, we speak of objects of consumption, raw materials of production, and instruments of production. There are rapidly and slowly renewed objects of consumption: A loaf of bread belongs to the former; a television set belongs to the latter. A piece of wood and a bag of flour are raw materials of production. A hammer is supposedly an example of instruments of production.

One hesitates to make sharp distinctions like those suggested. The differences between these types of artifacts are relative, and the same artifact may have different meanings depending on the context. For a television critic, the TV set is an instrument of production. For a collector of old tools, the hammer may be an object of consumption.

In the realm of secondary artifacts, similar types may be tentatively distinguished. First, the continuously changing flow of information, consisting of specific opinions, news, descriptions, advertisements, and so forth, may be identified as the rapidly renewed objects of consumption at the secondary level.

Second, the relatively stable and general representations with which we filter and modulate our daily information flow may be identified as the slowly renewed objects of consumption on the secondary level.

Third, both of the types mentioned may be turned into objects or raw materials of production, to be molded and transformed into something new.

Fourth, sign systems such as gestures, spoken and written language, or mathematical and musical notation may be identified as typical, continuously available instruments of production at the secondary level.

The relations between the types of artifacts are not "and-summative" but genuinely complementary (see Otte, 1980; 1984). They both presuppose and struggle with each other. In the course of development, the different types are truly transformed into each other.

Expansive thinking requires that relatively stable *objects* of consumption and production be transformed into *instruments* of production. Cycles of expansion, or zones of proximal development, activate the "complementarity of representational and instrumental aspects" (Otte, 1980, p. 64) of such conceptual objects. *The representational concept, as a static and uncritically accepted frame, must be transformed into an instrumental concept, critically reflected, molded, and applied, and back to a new representational frame.*

COGNITIVE THEORIES OF CONCEPTS – ONCE AGAIN AT THE LIMITS OF COGNITIVISM

According to the standard view, a concept is a verbal label that encompasses an array of diverse instances deemed to be related. The array must have coherence or family resemblance. Concepts are formed by comparing particular objects with one another and finding their common features. Concepts are thus memoranda of identical features in objects perceived. They are means for bunching together objects scattered in experience. The process necessary and sufficient to generate concepts is classifying (Sigel,

1983, p. 242–245). This standard view has been remarkably persistent in psychology and education. Within the mainstream cognitive psychology, it has been seriously challenged only quite recently.

The first challenge arises from the Piagetian impulse. Katherine Nelson is a well-known representative of this challenge. According to her, "The child's *initial* mental representations are in the form of scripts for familiar events involving social interaction and communication" (Nelson, 1983, p. 135). A script is a structured whole, a generalized representation of a sequence of activity that has occurred more than once. Therefore, the basic and initial form of conceptual representation is that of event representation. Concepts of particular objects are later achievements. In other words, paradigmatic categories are extracted from syntagmatic representations. Finally context-free categories are formed.

> Note that what is not involved in any of the operations outlined thus far is an analysis in terms of the *similarity* of object types independent of their functional relations. The analysis assumes instead that the child operates for a very long time with a conceptual representation that defines object categories in terms of their relationships and not in terms of their internal qualities.... The establishment of similarity relations is assumed to be a more advanced cognitive operation that takes place only after the basic categories have been formed. (Nelson, 1983, p. 141; italics in the original)

Nelson's critique of the standard view is that the abstraction and generalization of similarity features are assumed to be initial. For Nelson, this type of concept formation becomes dominant only later.

Nelson's view leaves the old belief in induction intact. According to her, children acquire their scripts through the same kind of induction the standard view attributes to the acquisition of similarity features – only the unit is more holistic, namely, a social event script. In other words, Nelson's critique accepts the basic logic of the standard view. This point has been made very clearly by Ivana Marková (1982, p. 59; italics added).

> We can thus conclude that although "scripts" and "plans" and perhaps some other terms introduce "context" and "experience" into the understanding of language and events, the conceptual framework has not changed. We may say that the theory of "scripts" and "plans" is an example of the attempts to save the collapsing Cartesian paradigm.... scripts and plans exist only because a person has been in that particular situation before and is simply matching the pre-stored representations to his new experience. People can cope with new situations because they can

understand them in terms of their previous experience, because they can re-organize the pieces of information they already have in their internal representations. *No actual development is taking place:* the apparent development of plans and scripts is really only a regrouping of static and predetermined elements of information.

This very logic has been partially questioned in two contributions to the problem of conceptual thinking. These are Susan Carey's (1985) monograph *Conceptual Change in Childhood* and the paper *The Role of Theories in Conceptual Coherence* by G. I. Murphy and D. L. Medin (1985).

Not surprisingly, the authors of both contributions take their philosophical stance from Nelson Goodman's critique of induction. They point out that any two entities can be found arbitrarily similar or dissimilar by changing the criterion of what counts as a relevant attribute. There is always an infinity of features in terms of which two objects may be compared. There is no ontologically given, theory-neutral arbiter of projectability. Thus, there is no pure induction. Abstraction and concept formation are always theory-driven.

Accordingly, concepts must be identified by the roles they play in theories (Carey, 1985, p. 198). Representations of concepts are best thought of as theoretical knowledge or, at least, as embedded in knowledge that embodies a theory about the world (Murphy & Medin, 1985, p. 298).

So what is a theory? And how do theories emerge in the first place? Carey (1985, p. 201) points out that explanation is at the core of theories. Explanatory mechanisms distinguish theories from other types of conceptual structures, such as scripts. The cognitive psychologists' famous restaurant script tells us what happens and in which order when we go to a restaurant. But it does not explain why we pay for our food, for example.

Murphy and Medin also see explanatory relations and causal connections – "underlying principles" in their choice of words – as the essence of theories. They note that "one might have a theory that could connect (to some degree) objects that seem to share very few features" (Murphy & Medin, 1985, p. 298). But they disagree with Carey in that they also accept scripts as theories. After all, "scripts may contain an implicit theory of the entailment relations of mundane events" (Murphy & Medin, 1985, p. 290). Indeed, even the restaurant script contains one kind of explanation for Carey's "why" question: We pay because we are expected or asked to do that.

In other words, the presence of explanation does not seem to be a sufficient criterion of a theory. What is more important, we will probably never find a clear and sufficient criterion by following the approach taken by Carey, Murphy, and Medin. These authors try to define theory by looking at knowledge and mental representations as self-sufficient bodies or things stored within the head of the individual. They fall prey to the cognitivist or Cartesian fallacy, exhibited by Nelson Goodman, too. Theory is conceived as an entity the individual "has." When a theory emerges or is acquired, it may be stored and begins to function as a filter or lens, constraining the individual's inductive projections. Such a constructivism is mere mental constructivism, world making in the mind only.

This cognitivist conception is unable to say anything interesting about how theories actually emerge in the first place. Carey (1985, p. 200) has recourse to a moderate innatism: "My guess is that the 'initial state' of human children can be described by saying that they are innately endowed with two theoretical systems: a naive physics and a naive psychology." Murphy and Medin (1985, p. 311) are even more vague: "It is certainly possible that children's prototheories of the functions, relations, and importance of objects have effects quite early" – but "exactly when they do is an empirical question."

In this respect, Nelson's contention that event scripts are the initial form of conceptual representation is much more advanced than the conceptions of Carey, Murphy, and Medin. It avoids the dead end of innatism by acknowledging a simple but powerful idea: In the beginning there was an act.

At one point in their paper, however, Murphy and Medin step beyond the cognitivist confines. They take up Bulmer's (1967) anthropological study of the Karam of New Guinea who do not consider a cassowary a bird. Bulmer argued that that this is not merely because the cassowary does not fly, but because of its special role as a forest creature and its resulting participation in an antithesis in Karam thought between forest and cultivation. This antithesis is further related to basic concerns with kinship roles and rights. Murphy and Medin (1985, p. 305) correctly note that "apparently, the Karam's theories about forest life and cultivation produce different classifications than do our culture's biological theories."

This conclusion implies that theory is no more seen as a self-sufficient entity within the individual mind but rather as *a social activity system in itself.* In this view, theories and concepts can only be understood as the representational, secondary aspect of sensuous, material activity systems. This has nothing to do with the mechanical idea of theories as somehow direct copies of material objects. But theories live and develop only integrally embedded in activities. Theories may be separated from activities – forgotten and hidden in obscure books, for example – but contrary to Popper's view, this means that they are in effect dead or frozen, barren of life and development at least temporarily.

VYGOTSKY AND THE PROBLEM OF CONCEPTS

In Vygotsky's late work *Thinking and Speech*, the problem of concepts was central. Vygotsky rejected the traditional inductivist notion of concepts. He pointed out that for the traditional view concept formation is similar to Galton's composite "family portraits." These are made by taking pictures of different members of a family on the same plate, so that the traits common to several people stand out vividly while differing individual traits are blurred by the superimposition. For the traditional view, the totality of the common traits is the concept.

> One cannot depict the real process of concept formation in a more mistaken way than this logified picture. It was found already long ago, and our experiments have shown in clearly, that *concept formation in adolescents never conforms to the logical process which traditional psychology describes*. (Wygotski, 1977, p. 160–161; italics in the original)

Vygotsky cites Vogel's and Bühler's findings according to which children do not start with mere particulars but use general concepts from the beginning. The child acquires the word "flower" earlier than the names of various particular flowers. Or if it acquires first the name of a particular flower, say "rose," it uses this word not only for roses but for all flowers (Wygotski, 1977, p. 162).

Vygotsky concludes that concept formation is a two-way movement within a pyramid of concepts: from the particular to the general and from the general to the particular at the same time. This fundamental idea is further elaborated in an analysis of the relationship of everyday and scientific concepts.

> From the standpoint of dialectical logic, our everyday concepts are not concepts in the proper sense of the word. They are rather general notions of objects. (Wygotski, 1977, p. 150)

This important statement implies that we have to work out and apply a logic qualitatively different from the traditional formal logic if we are to grasp the nature of genuine scientific concepts. This demand was, however, never met in Vygotsky's own analysis. As a matter of fact, later in his book he states that "one can say that the logical side of this question has been fully treated and investigated" while the genetic and psychological aspect remains open (Wygotski, 1977, p. 263). Thus, Vygotsky did not work out an alternative logic of genuine concepts.

According to Vygotsky, scientific concepts work their way downward from the general to the particulars. Everyday concepts develop the opposite way. As the two meet, they penetrate and transform each other.

There are three characteristics that make scientific concepts distinctive. First, scientific concepts are always included in a *conceptual system*. Second, scientific concepts require that the learner be *conscious* of them; their formation begins with the word, with the definition, and the learner is required to work on the concepts themselves. Third, scientific concepts are thus not acquired spontaneously but *through instruction*.

V. V. Davydov points out the weakness of this definition. First of all, even empirical concepts possess a system that may take the form of elaborate classificatory dependencies of the "genus-species" type. Furthermore, such descriptive concepts, or "general notions," are systematically transmitted in school instruction. As a matter of fact, they dominate the subject matter of primary school instruction. The two-way movement in a conceptual pyramid is fully possible within a purely empirical or descriptive structure of concepts.

> The acquisition which begins with the "general" verbal definition by no means characterizes the scientific nature of a concept; also arbitrary everyday notions, empirical general notions can be transmitted this way in instruction. (Dawydow, 1977, p. 162–163)

In other words, Vygotsky could not solve the problem of the specific *contents* of scientific concepts. His definitions remained formal – a little like those put forward by Carey and by Murphy and Medin more than fifty years later. Surely Vygotsky was right when he wrote that scientific concepts are systemic – but what is the specific quality of their systems? In a like manner, Carey and Murphy and Medin are right in stating that theories contain explanatory mechanisms or principles – but what distinguishes a theoretical explanatory mechanism from an empirical one?

DIALECTICAL LOGIC AND CONCEPTS

Within the cultural-historical school, V. V. Davydov was the first psychologist who broke out of the confines of traditional formal logic in the problem of concept formation. The importance of this step has not been widely understood, and Davydov's foundational work was translated into English only in 1990 although it appeared in Russian in 1972. The far-reaching instructional implications of Davydov's work have often met with aggressive resistance and misinterpretation, both in his own culture and in the West.

But Davydov's achievement was made possible by certain advances in the philosophy and epistemology of dialectical materialism. The two works that had the strongest effect on Davydov seem to have been E. V. Ilyenkov's (1982 [in Russian 1960]) book *The Dialectics of the Abstract and the Concrete in Marx's Capital* and the volume *Analysis of the Developing Concept* written jointly by A. S. Arsen'ev, V. S. Bibler, and B. M. Kedrov (1967). As philosophical works, both books are exceptional in that they are based on detailed analysis of important developments in the history of science. The former investigates the formation of the concept of value in Marx's research in political economy. The latter analyzes the development of central concepts in mechanics and chemistry.

The point of departure in Ilyenkov's work is a redefinition of the meaning of "concrete" and "abstract." Contrary to the common notions, dialectics does not see "concrete" as something sensually palpable and "abstract" as something conceptual or mentally constructed. "Concrete" is rather the holistic quality of systemic interconnectedness.   *Ilyenkov*

> If consciousness has perceived an individual thing as such, without grasping the whole *concrete chain of interconnections* within which the thing actually exists, that means it has perceived the thing in an extremely abstract way despite the fact that it has perceived it in direct concrete sensual observation, in all the fullness of its sensually tangible image.
>
> On the contrary, when consciousness has perceived a thing in its *interconnections* with all the other, just as individual things, facts, phenomena, if it has grasped the individual through its universal interconnections, then it has for the first time perceived it concretely, even if a notion of it was formed not through direct contemplation, touching or smelling but rather through speech from other individuals and is consequently devoid of immediately sensual features. (Ilyenkov, 1982, p. 87–88)

General notions are formal abstractions since they separate arbitrary features of objects from their interconnections. Genuine concepts are concrete abstractions since they reflect and reconstruct the systemic and interconnected nature of the objects. This systemic nature is not of the static classificatory "genus-species" type but of a *genetic and dynamic* type. Ilyenkov uses Marx's concept of the proletariat to illustrate this.

When Marx and Engels worked out the concept of the proletariat as the most revolutionary class of bourgeois society, as the gravedigger of capitalism, it was in principle impossible to obtain this concept by considering an abstractly general trait inherent in each separate proletarian and each particular stratum of the proletariat. A formal abstraction which could be made in the mid-19th century by comparing all individual representatives of the proletariat, by the kind of abstracting recommended by non-dialectical logic, would have characterised the proletariat as the most oppressed passively suffering poverty-ridden class capable, at best, only of a desperate hungry rebellion.

This concept [better: general notion; Y. E.] of the proletariat was current in the innumerable studies of that time, in the philanthropic writings of the contemporaries of Marx and Engels, and in the works of utopian socialists. This abstraction was a precise reflection of the empirically general. But it was only Marx and Engels who obtained a *theoretical* expression of these empirical facts....

The concept of the proletariat, as distinct from the empirical general notion of it, was not a formal abstraction here but a theoretical expression of the objective conditions of its development containing a comprehension of its objective role and of the latter's tendency of development....

The truth of this concept was shown, as is well known, by the real transformation of the proletariat from a "class in itself" into a "class for itself". The proletariat developed, in the full sense of the term, towards a correspondence with "its own concept." (Ilyenkov, 1982, p. 130–131)

In other words, the systemic nature of the genuine concept is essentially temporal, historical, and developmental. The concept expresses the origin and the developmental tendency of the totality it reconstructs.

To *comprehend* a phenomenon means to discover the mode of its origin, the rule according to which the phenomenon emerges with necessity rooted in the concrete totality of conditions, it means to analyse the very conditions of the origin of phenomena. That is the general formula for the formation of a *concept*. (Ilyenkov, 1982, p. 177)

Moreover, the concept "expresses a reality which, while being quite a particular phenomenon among other particular phenomena, is at the same time a genuinely universal element, a 'cell' in all the other particular phenomena" (Ilyenkov, 1982, p. 79). The task of genuine concept formation is thus to find out the developmental "germ cell," the initial genetic abstraction, of the totality under investigation and to develop it into its full concrete diversity. Herein lies the kernel of the "other logic" Vygotsky pleaded for but could never formulate. *"The logical development of categories ... must coincide with the historical development of the object"* (Ilyenkov, 1982, p. 215–216; italics added). In other words, we are not talking of an eternal and content-indifferent logic but of a developmental logic of the object itself. This logic is stored nowhere in the form of ready-made formulas to be imposed upon the object. To the contrary, "the concrete history of a concrete object should be considered in each particular case rather than history in general" (Ilyenkov, 1982, p. 215).

In dialectical logic, the concrete is an interconnected systemic whole. But the interconnections are not of any arbitrary kind. At the core of the interconnections there are *internal contradictions.*

> Concreteness is in general *identity of opposites*, whereas the abstract general is obtained according to the principle of bare identity, identity without contradiction. (Ilyenkov, 1982, p. 272)

Contradictions become central if we are to handle movement, development, and change conceptually.

> Any utterance expressing the very moment, the very act of transition (and not the *result* of this transition only) inevitably contains an explicit or implicit contradiction, and a contradiction "at one and the same time" (that is, during transition, at the moment of transition) and "in one and the same relation" (precisely with regard to the transition of the opposites into each other). (Ilyenkov, 1982, p. 251)

The struggle and mutual dependency of opposite forces or elements constitute the developmental driving force within objective systems. To create a genuine concept is to grasp and fixate this inner contradiction of the object system and to derive the system's subsequent developmental manifestations from that initial contradiction.

> The dialectical materialist method of resolution of contradictions in theoretical definitions thus consists in tracing the process by which the movement of reality itself resolves them in a new form of expression. Expressed objectively, the goal lies in tracing, through analysis of new empirical materials, the emergence of reality in which an earlier established contradiction finds its relative resolution in a new objective form of its realisation. (Ilyenkov, 1982, p. 262–263)

For Arsen'ev, Bibler, and Kedrov, a genuine scientific-theoretical concept is always the simple, initial germ of a whole complex theory. The characteristic of a genuine concept is its expansive "potency of concretization, tendency of developing into a theory" (Arsen'ev, Bibler & Kedrov, 1967, p. 15). It tends to generate a multitude of successive developmental elaborations

and conceptual offshoots out of itself. This view is actually opposite that of
Carey and Murphy and Medin, who see concepts as products generated by
initial theories.

But if concept is the initial form of a theory, how does the concept emerge
in the first place? Here Arsen'ev, Bibler, and Kedrov disagree with Nelson's
inductivist view, according to which the initial scripts emerge as mental
recollections of repeated familiar events. Arsen'ev, Bibler, and Kedrov argue
that the initial concepts emerge out of the interplay of two psychic processes
constitutive of any practical productive activity: (1) the continuous construction of the anticipated future object (outcome) of the activity through
active material and mental *experimentation* and (2) the equally continuous
sensuous or contemplative experiencing and *observation* of the object "as it
is." In other words, the initial concepts are not just reproductions of events
as experienced. Already from the very beginning they also possess the tendency of creating something not yet observed and experienced.

Arsen'ev, Bibler, and Kedrov do not ascribe this potency solely to the
concepts developed and used within the historically formed activity called
science. "From our standpoint, any thinking and any concept is in its poten-
tiality, i.e., in its essence, scientific-theoretical" (Arsen'ev, Bibler & Kedrov,
1967, p. 14). Thus, so-called everyday concepts have in principle the same
expansive quality as the consciously elaborated concepts of science. A similar point is made by Ilyenkov.

> It stands to reason that the universal laws of thought are the same both
> in the scientific and so-called everyday thinking. But they are easier to
> discern in scientific thought for the same reason for which the universal
> laws of the development of the capitalist formation could be easier estab-
> lished, in mid-19th century, by the analysis of English capitalism rather
> than Russian or Italian. (Ilyenkov, 1982, p. 100)

DAVYDOV AND THE PROBLEM OF CONCEPTS

Davydov characterizes the theoretical concept as follows.

> This type of concept functions as a completely specified and concrete
> *means of connecting* the general and the specific, a *means of deducing*
> particular and specific phenomena from their general basis. Due to this,
> *the development* of an object functions as the content of the theoretical
> concept.

> The concept is a procedure of realizing a substantial generalization, a
> means of transition from the essence to the phenomena. It fixates the

conditions and means of such transformation, such deduction of the individual from the universal. (Dawydow, 1977, p. 305)

Genuine concept formation and conceptual thinking ascend first from the perceptually concrete phenomena to the substantial abstraction, the "germ cell" that expresses the genetically original inner contradiction of the system under scrutiny. They then proceed to concrete generalization by deducing the various particular manifestations from this developmental basis. Following Hegel and Marx, this procedure is called *ascending from the abstract to the concrete*. Davydov points out that outside this process the concept becomes "a mere word" (Dawydow, 1977, p. 308).

> To have a concept of an object means that one is able to use the general method of its construction, the knowledge of its *origination*. This method is a specific thinking activity of human beings which itself is formed as a derivative of object-oriented action reproducing its object of cognition....
>
> Thus, behind every concept there is a specific hidden object-oriented action (or a system of such actions), the discovery of which is a special research task. (Dawydow, 1977, p. 309)

Davydov summarizes the qualities of empirical and theoretical knowledge and thought in six points.

1. Empirical knowledge is produced by *comparing* objects and their representations which makes is possible to discern in them common general traits. Theoretical knowledge arises on the basis of an *analysis* of the role and function of a certain relation of things inside a structured system.
2. Comparison discerns the *formally* common trait which makes it possible to classify separate objects under a certain formal class irrespective of their being interconnected. By means of the analysis, the *real*, specific relation of things is found which is the genetic foundation of all other manifestations of the system. This relation functions as the *general* form or essence of the mentally reproduced totality.
3. Empirical knowledge, based on *observation*, reflects only *external* traits of objects and relies on perceptual notions. Theoretical knowledge, based on the *transformation* of objects, reflects their *internal* relations and interconnections. In the reproduction of an object, theoretical thinking *exceeds the limits* of perceptual presentations.
4. The formally common trait is *separated* from the particular features of the objects. In theoretical knowledge, the *connection* between the real general relation and its various manifestations, i.e., the connection of the general and the specific, is fixated.

5. The concretization of empirical knowledge consists in the gathering of illustrations or examples which belong to a formally derived category. The concretization of theoretical knowledge presupposes its conversion into a developed theory by *deducing* and explaining the specific manifestations from their general foundation.

6. The necessary means of fixating empirical knowledge is the word, the term. Theoretical knowledge is primarily expressed in the *methods* of intellectual activity and subsequently in various systems of signs and symbols, especially in artificial and natural languages. The theoretical concept may exist as a method of deducing the specific from the general before it has acquired a terminological formulation. (Dawydow, 1977, p. 310–312)

Davydov's argumentation suffers here from a dichotomous structure. Empirical thinking and theoretical thinking are presented as mutually exclusive alternatives. Their mutual dependency and mutual penetration are temporarily set aside. However, Davydov discusses this problem of complementarity earlier in his book.

> Man's sensuousness as objective-practical activity is inherently *contra-dictory*. Sensation and perception in themselves reflect things as immediately given. But through the *practical action* which brings things purposefully into contact with each other (object and tool), another content "penetrates" into sensuousness – the mediated and interconnected character of things, their inner substance. The practical action as *sensuous-objective* action unifies in itself contradictory contents – the external and the internal, the immediately given and the mediated, the specific and the general. (Dawydow, 1977, p. 261–262)

Later, both phylogenetically and ontogenetically, these original moments of practical action are differentiated into separately identifiable fundamental modes of thought, the empirical and the theoretical, or the classificatory and the experimental. Still, neither of these can be conceived of as fully independent of the other. Both modes contain latent forms or seeds of the other. This does not mean that they are developmentally on the same level. To the contrary, it is theoretical thought that contains the instrumentality necessary for expansive development, for the production of the new.

Davydov's central point is theoretically compelling. And it leads to practical consequences.

> From a logico-psychological point of view, a person's true understanding of a subject can be shown by the ability to reproduce and demonstrate to another person the entire process of its origin. In the case of the concept

of number, this means that a student should be able to demonstrate independently to a teacher, using appropriate actions upon objects, why it is both possible and necessary to form this concept. Further, the student should also be able to utilize the numerical properties of *any* quantifiable set for *any* specified purpose. For example, whether or not a child understands the concept of number can be shown by the proper execution of tasks like the following:

1. Require the child to pour into a second container the same amount of water provided in a first container that differs is form from the second. (The first container is a narrow, graduated cylinder, the second a wide-mouthed glass.) A child who can really isolate the conditions for obtaining a number, that is, who really understands its meaning, should use some intermediate measure, such as a small glass, to determine the amount of water the narrow cylinder contains (for example, five small glasses) and then pour the same number of glasses into the wide-mouthed glass.

2. Require a child to determine how many large glasses of water are contained in a series of three large and four small glasses if a small glass is equal to one half of a large one. Here, the child must count two small glasses as one large one and obtain the result of five.

3. Using a single set of blocks, require the child to determine various conditions under which several different numerical attributes would be defined. In this task, the child must construct equal groups of blocks and then use those groups as a unit of measure to determine different numbers. For instance, if 24 blocks are grouped by twos, then the number 12 will be expressed; if grouped by fours, then the number will be six; and so on.

4. Require a child to show how, using a single volume of water in a glass, different numerical descriptions of that same volume of water can be expressed. This task is similar to Task 3 but uses a continuous quantity instead of discrete objects. Different measures (for example, different sized small glasses) must be used to determine several different numbers.

For each of these tasks, the child must recognize the multiple relationships that can exist between a continuous or discrete object (as expressed by its numerical measure) and some part of that object that has been used as the unit of measure. In so doing, it is of particular importance that the child realizes the arbitrary nature of the size of the part (the unit of measure) that is used to determine the measure of the entire object. When measuring, the child should be able to exchange one unit size for another and thereby determine different measures for the same object. In this exercise, the child needs a clear understanding of the *origin* of numerical measure to generate various concrete numerical representations of the object. Only when a child can carry out these fundamental steps can one speak of the child's *understanding* of number as a general mathematical method of expressing quantitative relationships within and between objects....

Initially, we found that a majority of children enrolled in traditional programs could not carry out these tasks. For instance, in the first and fourth tasks they had no idea of how to proceed. In the second task they counted each glass, large or small, as a separate unit and thus obtained an answer of seven rather than the correct response of five. In the third task they counted the blocks singly to obtain 24 and were not able to group out any other unit of counting. (Davydov, 1982, p. 225–227)

Although these children were able to use a limited notion of number to deal with day-to-day and school problems, they really did not exhibit a true mathematical understanding of the number concept. This was due to the teachers' use of "familiar" numbers as the starting point for instruction within the traditional program. On this basis first-grade children quickly proceeded to addition and subtraction of numbers known to them only on an experiential basis. Davydov cites the famous mathematician Kolmogorov (1960, p. 10): "Divorcing mathematical concepts from their origins in teaching results in a course with a complete absence of principles and with defective logic."

MODELS AS INSTRUMENTS OF EXPANSIVE THINKING

In cognitive psychological research, interest in so-called mental models has increased notably. Alone in 1983, two major volumes appeared under the title *Mental Models* (Gentner & Stevens, 1983; Johnson-Laird, 1983). In their review, Rouse and Morris (1985, p. 7) propose the following definition of mental models: They are mechanisms whereby humans are able to generate descriptions of system purpose and form, explanations of system functioning and observed system states, and predictions of future system states. Norman (1983, p. 7) adds an important point.

Mental models are naturally evolving models. That is, through interaction with a target system, people formulate mental models of that system.

Norman distinguishes mental models from conceptual models. The latter are consciously invented by teachers, designers, scientists, and engineers. But it remains unclear whether conceptual models are also mental – or perhaps nonmental. The difference seems to be merely one of the degree of consciousness and presentational rigor.

In many ways, the recent discussion on mental models is a new version of the "model muddle" prevalent in philosophy during the 1960s. Wartofsky summarizes the muddle as follows.

> In much of model-talk, models inhabit a limbo between worlds. On the one hand, they are not citizens of the blood-and-guts world of real objects and processes; or at best have only a derived citizenship by way of their reference to such a world. On the other hand, they are denied full equality in the cognitive world of purported truths, assigned only the function of instruments of such cognition: crutches, aids to the imagination, inference-machines, heuristic devices, data-ordering frameworks and whatnot. (Wartofsky, 1979, p. 3)

The problem with the cognitive psychological notion of mental models is that it is *static, dead* in a twofold sense.

First, mental models are conceived of as something evolving spontaneously within individual heads, on the basis of individual experience. This evolution consists of two basic processes (De Kleer & Brown, 1983, p. 156): constructing or *envisioning* the mental model and simulating the result of this construction or *running* the model. However, both these processes are *cut off from the construction and use of external, material, sociocultural models*. How these external, objectified models are generated and how they interact with individual mental models remain a mysterious sphere outside the interest of mainstream cognitive psychology. This isolationist mode of inquiry renders the mental models of cognitive psychology mere filters, slowly renewed objects of consumption. Models are deprived of their productive and instrumental aspect.

Second, in consequence of the first delimitation, there seem to be no satisfactory ways of assessing the qualitative level or type of a mental model. A host of different classifications and typologies have been offered, but all of them seem to be equally arbitrary. The reason is that the classifications and typologies have *no historical basis*. As long as the historical steps of the societal production of models remain obscure, psychologists are bound to keep inventing their private favorite typologies ad nauseam. They will also remain incapable of foreseeing and enhancing the necessary future qualities of models.

Earlier in this chapter I noted that expansive thinking demands that the consumptive objects of thought be transformed into productive instruments of thought. Representational concepts must be transformed into instrumental concepts. This transformation requires a specific type of objectivity-instrumentality. Models are specifically simplified and "purified" reconstructions of the perceptual-concrete object, created for the purpose of gaining unexpected information or working out unforeseen potentialities of the object. Models are an integral moment of experimentation. Being transparent and compact at the same time, models function both as projections and as means of constructing and realizing the projections (Dawydow, 1977, p. 260–261).

Wartofsky sees models in much the same way. For him, a model is not simply the *entity* we take as a model but, potentially, rather the *mode of action* that such an entity itself represents. In this sense, "models are embodiments of purpose and, at the same time, instruments for carrying out such purposes" (Wartofsky, 1979, p. 142).

Models are the specifically theoretical or expansive mode of *ideality*. The ideal exists only in man. But man is to be understood not as one individual with a brain, but as a real aggregate of people collectively realizing their human life activity, as the aggregate of social relations arising between people around the process of the social production of their life. Only in this sense is the ideal *inside man.*

> "Inside" *man thus understood* are *all the things* that "mediate" the individuals that are socially producing their life: *words, books, statues, churches, community centres, television towers* and (above all!) *the instruments of labour....*
>
> The ideal form is a form of a thing, but a form that is outside the thing, and is to be found in man as a form of his dynamic life activity, as *goals and needs.* Or conversely, it is a form of man's life activity, but outside man, in the form of the thing he creates. "Ideality" as such exists only in the constant succession and replacement of these two forms of its "external embodiment" and does not coincide with either of them taken separately. It exists only through the unceasing process of the transformation of the *form of activity – into the form of a thing and back – the form of a thing into the form of activity* (of social man, of course). (Ilyenkov, 1977, p. 98)

I suggest that models as the specifically theoretical type of ideality may be fruitfully analyzed from two angles: the functional and the historical.

THE FUNCTIONING OF MODELS IN THEORETICAL THINKING – PRESENTED AND QUESTIONED

From the functional angle, three general steps of model construction and application may be identified. Theoretical thinking starts with the constitution of its object. The object of inquiry is delineated with the help of

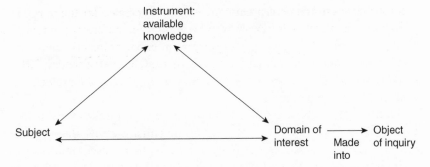

FIGURE 4.1. Object constitution as the first step of theoretical thinking.

available previous knowledge concerning the problem domain. This constitution of the object often takes place in a tacit fashion, without the individual's conscious effort, as an unreflecting projection of the social conventions and relations in which the individual is embedded. However, the object is never just there, without constitutive actions of the subject – without being identified and named. This first step of object constitution or problem identification may be depicted diagrammatically as follows (Figure 4.1).

Now this, often tacit or implicit, step does not discriminate between theory construction and any everyday problem solving. Theoretical thinking differs from other types of thinking in that it constructs a model of the object, attempting to uncover and make visible the hidden relations or regularities behind the observable behavior of the object. This model construction is achieved with the help of analogy: "Thus, at the heart of a theory are various modelling relations which are types of analogy" (Harré, 1970, p. 35).

Analogy as an instrument is closely related to play and imagination. In both, the subject is making the "rules of the game" or the hidden relations of the object transparent and visible through various forms of practical and mental experimentation.

This second step of theory construction is a step to the realm of "secondary processes" in Bateson's (1972, p. 185) terminology, that is, a step to consciously externalized and objectified abstractions. This step is diagrammatically depicted in Figure 4.2.

A model is not yet a full-blown theory. The theoretical model may be considered as an instrument for developing and applying the theory at the same time. The model invites and provokes thought experiments and concretizations. As Wartofsky (1979, p. 142) says, it is "a creation of something working toward the future." In this working toward the future, the subject

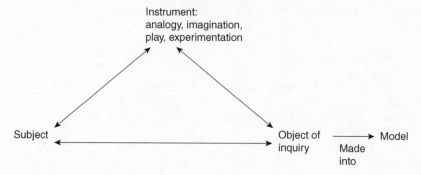

FIGURE 4.2. Model construction as the second step of theoretical thinking.

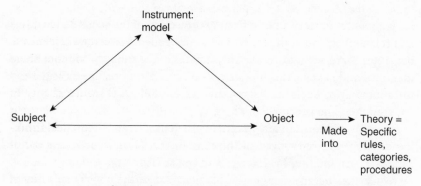

FIGURE 4.3. Ascending to the concrete as the third step of theoretical thinking.

not only elaborates the object with the help of the model. He or she also elaborates the model, modifies it into new, more complex developmental forms and variations. In other words, he or she builds a theory on the basis and with the help of the model. This is the third step of theory construction proper (Figure 4.3). In this view, a theory is an active, evolving relationship of the model to the things the model is supposed to represent. In its embodiments, it takes the form of statements, categories, rules, and procedures.

The stepwise process described previously is neat and compact. It corresponds to the manner in which the process of ascending from the abstract to the concrete is often depicted in Marxist literature: as an essentially individual and mental process of expansion. However, it is too clean and regular to account for the cognitive-instrumental aspect of the ruptures involved in the creation of societally new activity structures.

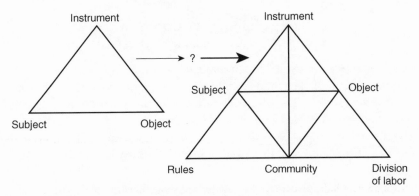

FIGURE 4.4. Transition from individual actions to collective activity.

A glance at Figures 4.1 to 4.3 reveals that thinking is here restricted to a *solitary* process. The subject remains individual. No community is involved. Similarly, the *object remains the same* from the beginning to the end. There is no structural expansion in these corners. Furthermore, theory as the end product of the process consists of *new representations* of reality; change in the reality itself is not implied.

To summarize, the steps described previously depict theoretical thinking as a series of individually situated mental actions. The process corresponds to that of Learning IIb, as described in Chapter 3.

What remains to be explained is the *qualitative transition* from series of individual, mental actions to a new collective, material activity system: in diagrammatic terms, Figure 4.4.

The *general* cyclic model of this expansive transition, or zone of proximal development, has been presented in Figure 3.3 in the preceding chapter. However, we are now dealing with the *specific* cognitive instruments needed for the conscious or intuitive mastery of the transition. So far, I have indicated that a new conception of concepts is required. I have also indicated that models play a special role within this new conception of concepts. But in order to characterize the cognitive instruments and their functioning more concretely, the successive *dominant historical forms of the transition* have to be analyzed. In other words, my functional analysis will necessarily acquire a historical dimension. The strict boundary between functional and historical analysis must be tendentially overcome.

To enter this kind of functional-historical analysis, I shall reinterpret B. M. Kedrov's (1966–1967; 1972) famous historical account of the discovery of the periodic law of the elements by D. I. Mendeleev in 1868.

THE DISCOVERY OF THE PERIODIC LAW AS AN
INSTANCE OF EXPANSIVE TRANSITION

D. I. Mendeleev discovered the periodic law in 1869. As an extraordinarily accurate person, he kept and stored without exception all documents and rough notes related to his work, even relatively minor and insignificant ones. From the late 1940s, Kedrov conducted intensive investigations in the D. I. Mendeleev Museum at what was then called the University of Leningrad to reconstruct the course of the great discovery on the basis of these archive materials.

Mendeleev's discovery can be divided into four periods. First, there was a preparatory period of about fifteen years (1854–1869). Second, the discovery itself took shape within one day, February 17, 1869. Third, the discovery was elaborated and refined during a period of approximately three years (February 1869–December 1871). Finally, Mendeleev used the remaining thirty-five years of his life for the less intensive and condensed tasks of proving and completing the theory and pushing it through in the scientific community.

The activity system under our scrutiny here is that of the "invisible college," or community of chemical researchers, in the second half of the nineteenth century. Typically of science as universal labor, this activity system consisted of extremely distributed parallel working units. But these were still relatively autonomous and independent of each other.

> The first level, on which the overwhelming majority of chemists of this time stood, amounted to sorting the elements into natural groups ("specific") without relating them in a single unity. The second level involved laying bare the general law relating all of the elements ("general"), hence relating the groups in which they were already classified. (Kedrov, 1966–1967, p. 33)

The *barrier* preventing this expansive breakthrough from the specific to the general level consisted of the relative encapsulation of the standard procedure.

> The grouping of elements according to their specific features became a tradition and stabilized itself in the consciousness of chemists. It finally became the strongest hindrance to the further development of the science.... In fact, the grouping of elements according to the specific features requires that only chemically similar elements are compared and associated with each other, while chemically dissimilar and especially chemically opposite elements are not compared and definitely not associated with each other.

> Contrariwise, the transition to the general level, i.e., the discovery of a general natural law covering *all* elements, … necessarily requires the association of not only similar but importantly also of *dissimilar* elements. (Kedrov, 1972, p. 88)

The inductive tradition made it impossible to use the atomic weight, at that time the only known feature common to all elements, as the unifying basis for constructing a comprehensive system of the elements. It would have placed chemically dissimilar, even polar opposite elements beside each other.

As the knowledge of the elements and their specific natural groups increased and became technically easier to obtain (electrolysis, spectroscopy), the disadvantages resulting from the lack of a general principle for arranging the elements gradually became visible.

> By the sixth decade of the nineteenth century, chemistry had reached such a stage that chemists *ought to* have discovered and brought about, by some means, a shift from the first level to the second. This was the task placed before chemistry by the objective line of development of the science itself. (Kedrov, 1966–1967, p. 33)

As a matter of fact, at least two other scientists, Newlands in England and De Shancourt in France, were very close to making the discovery at the same time as Mendeleev. This general *need state* within the activity of chemical research was specifically aggravated in the case of Mendeleev. At the time of the discovery, he was writing his major textbook *Fundamentals of Chemistry*.

> The first part of this work was completed at the end of 1868, its final chapters being devoted to the group of very strong non-metallic haloids (halogens). Directly after the haloids followed the group of very strong metals – alkaline metals – to which the author allotted the first two chapters of the second part of his work.
>
> It can be assumed that by the middle of February 1869 both chapters were finished, and the task confronted the author, with all insistence, of deciding which group of elements should follow the alkaline metals in the book. But to decide this it was necessary to elucidate which metals adjoined the alkaline closest of all…. To answer it, it was necessary to find some general principle according to which the elements should be arranged in their groups in a definite order. (Kedrov, 1966–1967, p. 19)

Mendeleev's chemical research activity may be characterized with the help of the triangle model developed in Chapter 2 (Figure 4.5).

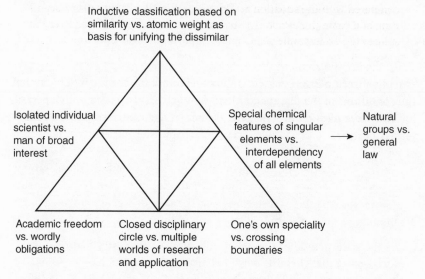

FIGURE 4.5. The primary contradiction of Mendeleev's chemical research activity.

Now this personal aggravation of the general need state was not enough. A *foreign element* entered the system of research activity and intensified the conflict into a *secondary contradiction*. Parallel with his research, Mendeleev was passionately involved in cooperative programs of practical agricultural development. He had planned to carry out an inspection trip to some dairy *artels* in central Russia between February 17 and February 28, 1869. However, having just finished the two first chapters mentioned earlier, Mendeleev was intensely preoccupied with the problem of the continuation of the book. At the same time, the departure for the inspection trip was becoming closer.

> Thanks to these purely accidental coincidences, on the 17th of February, unexpectedly for Mendeleev, both lines of his activity during this period came in conflict and crossed: first, writing the *Fundamentals of Chemistry* and, second, his trip to the dairy co-op. Since the trip was agreed upon with the interested organizations, Mendeleev could not avoid his obligation to go on a specific day. This circumstance strictly limited the time he could set aside for solving the problem confronting him.... In other words, Mendeleev achieved the discovery of the periodic law under conditions of the most severe *Zeitnot* [time pressure], which gave rise to a very distinctive character and path in its development. The general psychological situation of Mendeleev on the day of the discovery can be

compared with the situation of a chess master, caught at the very beginning of a game in *Zeitnot,* but striving at all costs to achieve a victory in spite of the unfavorable conditions. (Kedrov, 1966–1967, p. 20)

Thus, the foreign element that entered the research activity was a new *rule,* namely, that of a time limit. This, however, is still an insufficient picture of the conditions of the discovery. Mendeleev actually quickly found a partial, half-intuitive solution to the particular problem concerning the next chapter of his book.

When Mendeleev found the answer to the question that had interested him – what group of metals should be treated after the alkaline metals in the *Fundamentals of Chemistry* – he did not regard his work as finished.... The concern was now with carrying out to the end the discovery of the lawfulness, already found in the first approximation....

However, the method initially selected for constructing the table of elements by entering elements in it successively (one after the other), although it was successful in the first stage of discovery, turned out to be inapplicable for the whole set. The point is: while Mendeleev was operating on the well-known elements, all of them, with few exceptions, took their places in the table; even if their places had to be changed subsequently, such failures were few and did not obscure the whole picture of the organization of the elements which at any moment were included in the table. But when Mendeleev tried by these same means to find a basis for including in the table the poorly studied elements, the number of necessary corrections, transpositions, and deletions became so great that it began to interfere with the progress of the discovery. To recopy from the beginning in every case the incomplete table ... was practically impossible. This would have taken so much time that one could not think of completing the whole work in a single day (for he was still to go out to the cooperatives on the following day). The *Zeitnot* ... required finding a more convenient method for quickly carrying to completion the developing discovery. (Kedrov, 1966–1967, p. 23–24)

This situation, the aggravated contradiction between an emerging idea and the lack of instruments for its formulation and elaboration, was sharpened to a point where symptoms of a *double bind* appeared.

Calling on Mendeleev, it would seem, at just this moment, his friend A. A. Inostrantzev found Mendeleev in a gloomy, depressed state. According to Inostrantzev, Mendeleev began to speak of what was subsequently the embodiment of the periodic system of elements. But at this moment the law was still not formulated and the table still not completed. "It's all formed in my head," said Mendeleev with bitterness, "but I can't express it in the table." ...

Mendeleev himself ... wrote in his diary that after a period of enthusiasm he sometimes fell into a sudden slump, or even depression, ending some-times in tears. (Kedrov, 1966–1967, p. 24)

How did Mendeleev break the double bind? Here quite an interesting, seemingly accidental, analogy functioned as the *springboard*.

It should be mentioned that Mendeleev loved to play the game of patience, where the thoroughly shuffled cards must then be rearranged according to definite rules, resulting in a definite pattern of disposing them by suit and denomination. The analogy with the distribution of elements turns out to be nearly complete; for at the moment when he considered this problem, two incomplete tables of elements were already written down on paper, and in them was already clearly charted a distribution of ele-ments in two dimensions: horizontally, according to their general chem-ical properties or chemical similarity (which corresponds to arranging the playing cards according to suit), and vertically, according to the closeness of their atomic weights (which corresponds to arranging the playing cards by denomination). (Kedrov, 1966–1967, p. 24)

The springboard thus consisted of a technique and an image taken from a recreational activity quite remote from research work but thoroughly familiar to the subject. This kind of association may look purely accidental and arbitrary. But that is not the whole truth. Basically the same analogy had earlier been used in another problem by the famous scientist Gerhardt. Gerhardt drew the parallel between arranging cards by suit and denomi-nation, on the one hand, and arranging organic substances in homolo-gous and genetic series, on the other. Mendeleev counted himself one of Gerhardt's convinced adherents and of course was acquainted with this ear-lier application.

With the help of this springboard, Mendeleev constructed his famous "chemical patience," which quickly "grew into a general picture of the future system of elements in its completeness" (Kedrov, 1966–1967, p. 26). In other words, the new *general model of the object* of chemical research activity was formulated.

The course of the discovery may now be summarized with the help of a table (Table 4.3) similar to those presented in the cases of *Huckleberry Finn* (Table 3.3) and *Seven Brothers* (Table 3.4).

Table 4.3 graphically reveals the problem peculiar not only to Kedrov's account but to most descriptions of scientific discoveries. The transition

TABLE 4.3. *The sequential structure of the discovery of the periodic law*

Contradiction	Phase	Content according to Kedrov
Primary *within* the components of the old activity	Need state	Generally, the inductive classificatory tradition vs. the need to master the growing amount and complexity of the elements; individually, the choice of the group of elements for the next chapter of the book
Secondary *between* the components of the old activity	Double bind	The intruding new rule (time limit) vs. old instruments (inductive classification, serial one-by-one procedure)
	Object/motive construction	The idea of patience as the springboard; new object *all* elements in a comprehensive system New general model: the periodic law, embodied in the periodic table
Tertiary between the old and the *given new* activity	Application, generalization	?
Quaternary *between* the new activity and its neighbor activities	Activity 2: reflection, consolidation	?

from the singular and specific to the general is followed only halfway, to the point of the formulation and modeling of the new law or principle. But this is not yet the true level of generality. How does the new general model transform the structure and content of the practical scientific research activity in question? What is the nature of the tertiary and quaternary contradictions? These questions are left open, as if they were considered nonessential for the understanding of scientific creativity. In my analysis, these questions should be recognized as all-important.

There is a reason for the general omission of these phases from the accounts of discoveries. A "classical" discovery, such as that of Mendeleev, is typically made by an ingenious *craftsmanlike individual scientist*. Such a discovery, at least its intensive course, actually seems to terminate at the point where the individual craftsman-scientist publishes his revolutionary findings and, metaphorically speaking, hands them over to the scientific community (and indirectly to the society in general) for judgment and eventual application. The discontinuous nature of this historical type of transition makes it hard to realize the tremendous potential embedded in the emergence of the *created new* through the tertiary contradictions.

But does it make any sense to talk about the *given new* in the case of a great scientific discovery? Is not it all created new?

My contention is that scientific discoveries just like expansive developmental transitions in more mundane activity systems are to a large extent achievements of synthesizing and crystallizing elements that were already "there." In Mendeleev's case, atomic weights were already known. Surely in this case the given new is different from that of the Seven Brothers, for example. Science as *universal labor* produces strong generalizations. But the most dynamic and revolutionary aspect of scientific discoveries resides in the unexpected questions and ideas they evoke while being assimilated, argued against, generalized, and applied. The psychologist or historian studying scientific creativity is usually interested in the creative individual. He or she thus loses track of the expansive development as soon as the subject of the process is no more just the individual genius but a collective or several collectives.

As Mendeleev's creative process reached its intensive phases, a *new rule* – the time limit – entered the lower left corner of the triangle in Figure 4.3. To facilitate the solution of the contradiction between the new rule and the old instruments, a provisional *new instrument,* namely, the patience, appeared in the uppermost corner in the function of a springboard. These new prerequisites led to an expansive transition when there was a qualitatively *new outcome* of Mendeleev's actions: not just new specific classificatory knowledge about the elements but a totally new general principle for the understanding of their relations – the periodic law. This outcome was transformed into a *new kind of general instrument,* eventually giving rise to a qualitatively new developmental form of chemical research activity.

This historical type of activity and expansive transition corresponds to the classical ideal of university research. The ingenious individual scientist and his selfless striving after pure truth seem to be the prime movers behind great discoveries. In modern days, Michael Polanyi (1964) has turned this type of transition into the eternal model of all research work. Polanyi's conception of science as activity may be summarized with the help of Figure 4.6. The noteworthy feature of this model is the lack of internal contradictions. Pressures toward change are seen as external threats, not as manifestations of the inner dynamics of research activity.

Drawing directly upon Polanyi, Jerome Ravetz (1971, p. 103; emphasis added) concludes that "in every one of its aspects, *scientific inquiry is a craft activity,* depending on a body of knowledge which is informal and partly tacit."

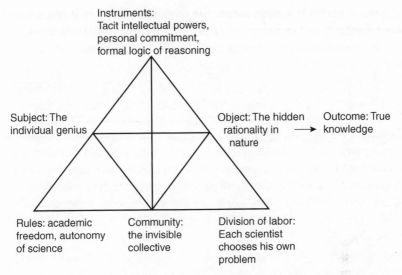

FIGURE 4.6. Polanyi's conception of science (adapted from Miettinen, 1986)

ANOTHER INSTANCE: FROM NUCLEAR FISSION
TO MANHATTAN PROJECT

The ahistorical craft position renders Polanyi and Ravetz pitifully helpless when they face the fact of the industrialization of science. The tool they offer to scientists is heightened moral awareness. Especially in Ravetz's work, there is a striking contradiction between the quite accurate description of the industrialization of research and the insistence on the eternal craft quality of scientific work.

> In recent years, the vision of "science" as the pursuit of the Good and the True has become seriously clouded, and social and ethical problems have accumulated from all directions.... This means, in the first place, the dominance of capital-intensive research, and its social consequences in the concentration of power in a small section of the community. It also involves the interpenetration of science and industry, with the loss of boundaries which enabled different styles of work, with their appropriate codes of behaviour and ideals, to coexist. Further, it implies a large size, both in particular units and in the aggregate, with the consequent loss of networks of informal, personal contacts binding a community. Finally, it brings into science the instability and sense of rapid but uncontrolled change, characteristic of the world of industry and trade in our civilization. (Ravetz, 1971, p. 31)

The industrialization of science means the breakthrough of "big science" (Price, 1963; Weinberg, 1967), of large-scale research projects and research institutes with costly equipment and complex organization.

> This change is as radical as that which occurred in the productive economy when independent artisan producers were displaced by capital-intensive factory production employing hired labour. The social consequences of the Industrial Revolution were very deep, and those of the present change in science, while not comparable in detail, will be equally so. With his loss of independence, the scientist falls into one of three roles: either an employee, working under the control of a superior; or an individual outworker for investing agencies, existing on a succession of small grants; or he may be a contractor, managing a unit or an establishment which produces research on a large scale by contract with agencies. (Ravetz, 1971, p. 44)

If the historical type of research work exemplified by Mendeleev's discovery (and idealized by Polanyi and Ravetz) is *craft*, then this new type may be called *rationalized* research. Its primary inner contradiction is that of any wage labor in capitalism.

> There then develops a research business, making its profit by the production of results in the fulfillment of contracts. The director of such an establishment is then truly an entrepreneur, who juggles with a portfolio of contracts, prospective, existing, extendable, renewable or convertible, from various offices in one or several agencies. In such a research factory, conditions are usually not conductive to the slow, painstaking and self-critical work which is necessary for the production of really good scientific results. Hence much, most, or even all the work can be shoddy; but the entrepreneur does not operate in the traditional market of independent artisan producers who evaluate work by consensus. So long as he can keep his contacts happy, or at least believing that they personally have more to lose by exposing themselves through the cancellation or non-renewal of contracts than by allowing them to continue, his business will flourish. (Ravetz, 1971, p. 55–56)

The most salient new components of research activity may be listed as follows: (a) Expensive and intricate technological *instruments* make state, military, or industrial financing necessary. (b) The instruments make it possible to find unexpected practical applications of newly discovered natural laws, and this creates a demand for new kinds of research *objects and outcomes*. (c) As a consequence, the *community* of research is no more the invisible college of free scientists but a large project, institute, or conglomerate, consisting of researchers and entrepreneurs, often also of state administrators and military officials. (d) This community rapidly reorganizes the *subject* of research – the ingenious individual is replaced by the managers of the project or institute (leaving the individual researcher a more or less anonymous role). (e) The community is subjected to new kinds of *rules,* notably secrecy and pressing time limits (recall Mendeleev's *Zeitnot:* now it is an institutionalized feature). (f) The community is also subjected to a new inner *division of labor,* including, above all, horizontal compartmentalization and vertical hierarchization (separation of planning and execution) within the research organization.

The first and most famous example of rationalized research work is naturally the Manhattan Project. It involved altogether 150,000 people and cost around U.S.$2 billion. The history of the project is documented and analyzed in many publications. One of the most concrete and detailed among the histories is Robert Jungk's (1956) *Heller als Tausend Sonnen: Das Schicksal der Atomforscher.* It is based on interviews and letters of an impressive array of persons who were central in the process that led from the discovery of nuclear fission to the development and use of atom and hydrogen bombs. I shall briefly go through this process of expansive transition and summarize it with the help of the means already employed in the preceding case analyses.

Let us first depict the late craftwork form of atomic physical research that existed and bloomed during the 1920s and 1930s (Figure 4.7).

It is easy to notice that the activity of Figure 4.7 represents a late developmental form of science as craft. The subject is no more just an individual but a laboratory – though strongly identified and led by a prominent individual. The division of labor is becoming dominated by an international competition among the laboratories. And what is most important, the instruments are rapidly becoming more costly and complex.

Within this activity system, the *need state* was experienced as tremendous uncertainty and excitement. It was caused by the collapse of the worldview of classical physics through a series of revolutionary discoveries that culminated in Einstein's theory of relativity. The Curies, Rutherford, and Bohr were showing that the indivisible could indeed be divided. Among leading physicists, there emerged a growing but still vague awareness that their research was dealing with unprecedented powers, the release of which might eventually have great societal consequences. Jungk (1956, p. 16) quotes the German physicist and Nobel laureate Walter Nernst, writing in 1921.

> We live so to speak on an island made of guncotton, for which we thank God have not yet found the igniting match.

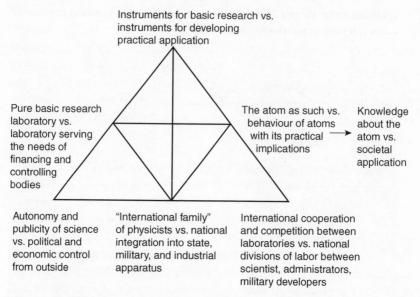

Instruments for basic research vs. instruments for developing practical application

Pure basic research laboratory vs. laboratory serving the needs of financing and controlling bodies

The atom as such vs. behaviour of atoms with its practical implications → Knowledge about the atom vs. societal application

Autonomy and publicity of science vs. political and economic control from outside

"International family" of physicists vs. national integration into state, military, and industrial apparatus

International cooperation and competition between laboratories vs. national divisions of labor between scientist, administrators, military developers

FIGURE 4.7. The primary contradiction of the activity of atomic-physical research at the end of its innocence.

One could say that the primary internal contradiction of this type of research activity was that between the basically individual-autonomous form of scientific work *and* the increasingly societal dependencies and consequences of the instruments, objects, and outcomes of that work. As Jungk (1956, p. 12) points out, already World War I had actually shattered the basis of the innocent isolation of the laboratories from the bloody reality of the rest of society. But the extraordinary creative ferment among the family of physicists during the 1920s and 1930s seemed temporarily to strengthen their autonomy.

The secondary contradiction and the eventual double bind ensued through a twofold process. First, Chadwick's discovery of the neutron in 1932 and a series of experimental advances following it led the researchers to the threshold of splitting the atom. Second, at the same time a very different activity system, namely, politics, intervened in the research activity. The strongest intervention was by the Nazis, first as persecution against numerous Jewish scientists, later as subordination of basic research to military purposes.

But what an extraordinary coincidence it was that within twelve months, the neutron was discovered (February 1932), Roosevelt was elected

(November 1932), and Hitler became the head of the German government (January 1933)! (Jungk, 1956, p. 61)

The secondary contradiction was created, sharpened into a double bind, and resolved expansively in two waves. The first wave resulted in the discovery of nuclear fission by Otto Hahn late in 1938. The second wave resulted in the launching of the Manhattan Project in 1942.

The barrier to be overcome in the first wave was still "purely scientific," reminiscent of Mendeleev's barrier.

> According to the prevailing conceptions of physics, only shots of as yet unreachable penetrating power would be able to enter into the core of a heavy atom and split it.... The idea that neutrons with a diminishing small voltage would succeed in doing what had not been accomplished by heavy shots was too fantastic to believe. (Jungk, 1956, p. 72–73)

In Mendeleev's case, the foreign (and seemingly accidental) element that aggravated the problem into a double bind was the rule of *Zeitnot*. In the case of atomic physics, the foreign element was also a rule – the rule of Nazi racial politics.

The background was a rivalry between the two leading female scientists in the field, Irène Joliot-Curie of Paris and Lise Meitner of Berlin, the latter having been for years the closest collaborator of Otto Hahn. The barrier characterized earlier could in effect be overcome only if the findings and procedures of the two laboratories, Paris and Berlin-Dahlem, were put together. The rivalry made that impossible, to the point that Hahn refused to read Joliot-Curie's scientific publications. But in 1938, the Nazi government was about to arrest Meitner because of her Jewish origin. Meitner emigrated from Germany in a hurry. Hahn's new right hand, Strassmann, read Joliot-Curie's new paper and literally forced Hahn to assimilate it by going through it aloud.

> "That struck Hahn like a lightning", his collaborator recollects. "He did not not even finish his cigar, left it burning on the desk and ran with me down into the laboratory." (Jungk, 1956, p. 77)

Hahn now pursued the new track of experimentation and discovered the basic mechanism of the splitting of the atom, which he immediately sent for publication on December 22, 1938. Hahn's own theoretical generalizations were, however, still hesitant. Lise Meitner had moved to Sweden, where she lived in isolation. She had just invited a young relative, the physicist O. R. Frisch from Niels Bohr's laboratory, to spend Christmas with her. She then received Hahn's letter that contained the revolutionary findings of the new experiments. Meitner, in her turn, literally forced Frisch to listen to her reflections on these findings. This conversation and the ensuing ones resulted in a joint article by Meitner and Frisch (in the February 1939 issue of *Nature*) where an adequate theoretical interpretation was made on the basis of Hahn's experimental findings. The concept of nuclear fission was born.

In this first wave, the double bind seems to have been experienced as the irreparable termination of most fruitful collaborative research work. Meitner's emigration seriously weakened the Berlin laboratory (whose efforts had been on a wrong track at the decisive point, anyway), and collaboration with the competing Paris laboratory was unthinkable. In this apparent dead end, *the new social constellation* (the two novel dyads, Hahn-Strassmann and Meitner-Frisch, in only indirect communication with each other) *functioned as a springboard.*

In other words, it seems that there may be not only instrumental but also social springboards, consisting of novel intersubjective formations or recombinations.

The contradiction of the second wave was caused by the foreign political and military element (Hitler administration) that had entered the community of physicists and, using Hahn's discovery as instrument, now threatened to convert the object and outcome of the activity into an evil force: an atomic bomb. In other words, the contradiction was formed between the prevailing subject (relatively autonomous laboratory researchers) and the emerging new community (physicists embedded in a pool of politicians and military officials). The paradox is that the old subject tried to defeat the intruders by inviting other, at least equally powerful intruders. The attempt was to stop the atom bomb by preparing an atom bomb.

The ensuing double bind consists of the well-known struggle of Leo Szilard and his companions (beginning in April 1939) to convince the American government of the necessity to take practical action against the danger of the possible manufacture of an atom bomb in Hitler's Germany.

Szilard, Wigner, Teller and Weisskopf had to overcome an internal and external barrier before they could contact the American government. As former continental Europeans, they had, at the most, meager trust basically in any government, but especially in military officials. None of them was a native American, and with the exception of Wigner they had not even stayed long enough in the country to become citizens.

While Szilard and his friends were still having headache about how they could get into conversation with some really influential American official, they received the trustworthy news that in the Third Reich work was already in progress on the "Uranium problem", with the awareness and support of the administration. Thus, the worst fears of the emigrated atomic scientists seemed to be confirmed. (Jungk, 1956, p. 89)

In July 1939, Szilard and Wigner went to meet Einstein – another pacifist – in order to persuade him to use his authority to wake up the American government. After driving quite a while looking in vain for Einstein's house, Szilard began to hesitate and suggested that they give up – the whole idea was perhaps a grave mistake. His friend Wigner wanted to continue, and soon a little boy helped them to find the right house. The conversational contact with Einstein wiped out all doubt for the moment.

The episode bears the familiar characteristics of a double bind situation. Again, the springboard was social and conversational. The contradiction was solved through intensive action: The fatal letter to President Roosevelt was written.

What happened then is well known. The new military-scientific-industrial activity of nuclear research and development was indeed proposed and planned – or modeled – and practically established. The modeling was initiated in two successive steps. First, in July 1942, Robert J. Oppenheimer was appointed to head a small group of scientists to sketch the best theoretical model of the new *object,* then called the "fast fission bomb." Second, in the autumn of 1942, a group consisting of Professor Oppenheimer, General Groves, and Colonels Nichols and Marshall met in a train called the *Twentieth Century Limited* to work out a plan for a centralized "superlaboratory" – the coming *community* of the new activity. In fact, the group sitting in the train could itself be conceived of as a *social model* or *microcosm,* a precursor of the community of Los Alamos.

Leaders of the huge sites of Los Alamos, Oak Ridge, and Hanford became the true subjects of the activity – General Groves much more so than Robert J. Oppenheimer. The work was done under the rules of extreme time pressure and secrecy, and the division of labor was compartmentalized to the utmost.

> They elevated invisible walls around each small partial field, so that one department did not know anymore what the other one was working at. Hardly a dozen of the altogether 150 000 people who were finally employed by the "Manhattan Project" could have a view of the whole. In fact, only a very small portion of the personnel knew even that they worked at an atom bomb. (Jungk, 1956, p. 122)

Table 4.4 summarizes the sequential structure of the discovery of nuclear fission, and eventually of the atom bomb.

TABLE 4.4. *The sequential structure of the discovery of nuclear fission*

Contradiction	Phase	Content according to Jungk
Primary *within* the components of the old activity	Need state	Generally the autonomous form of research vs. its increasing societal dependencies and consequences Individually: rivalry between Hahn and Meitner and Joliot-Curie, resulting in a scientific dead end
Secondary *between* the components of the old activity	Double bind	First wave: intruding new rule (Nazi racial policy) vs. old community (Hahn-Meitner group); second wave: new political and military element (Hitler administration) intruding into the community (family of physicists) vs. old object and outcome (atoms and knowledge of them as such)
	Object/motive construction	First wave: new socioconversational constellation (Hahn-Strassmann; Meitner-Frisch) as springboard; second wave: new socioconversational constellation (Szilard-Wigner- Einstein) as springboard; new object: the bomb; new general model: first the theory of the fission reaction, then model of the optimal bomb and of the "superlaboratory"
Tertiary between the old and the *given new* activity/motive	Application, generalization	Traditional autonomous craft research vs. rationalized research in the nuclear establishment (plus *created new* actions going beyond both)
Quaternary *between* the new activity and its neighbor activities	Activity 2	Rationalized nuclear research and development

In the phase of application and generalization, the physicists' struggle against the subordination of research to destructive purposes, to secrecy and rationalization, has obviously not only been defensive. It has also produced elements of the *created new*.

However, I shall not go further into the historical development of the inner contradictions of the new activity system of rationalized nuclear

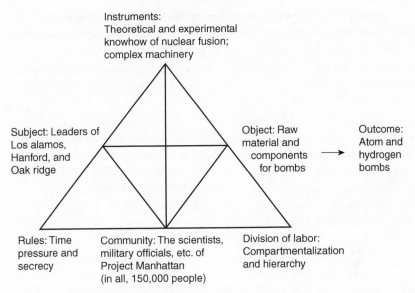

Instruments:
Theoretical and experimental
knowhow of nuclear fusion;
complex machinery

Subject: Leaders of
Los alamos,
Hanford, and
Oak ridge

Object: Raw
material and
components
for bombs

Outcome:
Atom and
hydrogen
bombs

Rules: Time
pressure and
secrecy

Community: The scientists,
military officials, etc. of
Project Manhattan
(in all, 150,000 people)

Division of labor:
Compartmentalization
and hierarchy

FIGURE 4.8. The idealized structure of the new activity of nuclear arms research and development.

research. Here, the main point is that the Manhattan Project was not a historical accident but rather a prototype of the coming projects of rationalized big science.

The structure of the resulting new activity system is depicted in Figure 4.8. It presents the idealized anatomy of the first major formation of rationalized science. No doubt, it was still science. The world's foremost theoretical physicists, such as Niels Bohr and Enrico Fermi, worked in Los Alamos. In Figure 4.8, the new activity system looks harmonious and free of contradictions. This is in fact how it appeared in the eyes of its leading subjects at the peak of the creative enthusiasm, before Germany's surrender and the actual explosion of the first bombs.

HISTORICAL TYPES OF ACTIVITY AND EXPANSIVE TRANSITION

As a historical activity type, rationalized science differs greatly from science as craft. In science as craft, the individual scientist produces a new general model (a law of nature, a theory), which he or she "gives up" into the hands of the scientific community. There is a marked break between the phase of object/motive construction and the phase of application and generalization (see Table 4.3). This break may even take the form of a long standstill: The new discovery is first rejected and perhaps only after the death of the individual subject is finally applied and generalized.

In rationalized science, the time factor becomes essential. The new scientific product must be quickly put out into the market (whatever that is as a system of object-activity; recall Figure 2.7).

Furthermore, in rationalized science, the object and outcome of the activity become fixed in advance. The basic idea is to produce what has been ordered. However, this does not mean that rationalized science is somehow automatically more conscious of the consequences of that new product, of the transformations it may bring about in the structure of the scientific activity itself and in its object activity. To the contrary, the compartmentalized and hierarchical division of labor effectively prevents the participants – including the leaders – of rationalized science from foreseeing and influencing these transformations. Thus, even though the transition from individual actions to a qualitatively new form of activity may take place rapidly and dramatically, as if in a compressed period, the events proceed to a large extent behind the backs or above the heads of the actors. Robert J. Oppenheimer's personal tragedy testifies to this in an exemplary manner.

However, within rationalized science, there were from the very beginning certain more urgent and practically pressing problems.

> Thus, for example the majority of the staff of the Los Alamos computing centre had for a long time no idea of the purpose of the complex calculations carried out with their computing machines. Since they did not know what the aim of their calculations was, they worked without real interest. Feynman, one of the young theoretical physicists, finally accomplished to get the approval to tell these people what was actually supposed to be made in Los Alamos. After that, the output of the department increased noticeably and some people even did voluntarily extra hours. (Jungk, 1956, p. 122)

This was clearly breaking the rules of the activity. Jungk reports a further incident from Los Alamos, this time concerning Edward U. Condon, one of the pioneers of American experimental physics.

> As a consultant of big industrial companies, Condon had practical experience in problems of production which the academician Oppenheimer could not have. On the basis of this very experience, Condon immediately saw that the "compartmentalization" would not work without harmful consequences in Los Alamos. Therefore he worked out a decree

of his own, tearing apart the artificially constructed walls between the individual departments. Groves regarded this as severe disobedience and accomplished to transfer Condon to another post. (Jungk, 1956, p. 129)

The history of rationalized science – and rationalized labor in general – is full of <u>similar conflicts</u>, endangering the motivation and productivity of the work. The preceding quotations demonstrate how a parallel historical type of activity emerged out of these inner conflicts of rationalized science almost as soon as the former was born. This parallel type may be called *humanized* science.

In humanized research, above all, the *division of labor* is revised. Instead of extreme hierarchization and compartmentalization, an organization or suborganization of relatively autonomous production groups is formed. A production group is given a meaningful, often challenging task that has a holistic character. The group is mainly responsible for the quantity and quality of its total output. Its procedures are not closely supervised from above. Therefore, within the group the hierarchy is minimized while cooperation and open communication are supported. Members of the group may be highly specialized individuals, but measures are taken to reach and uphold a shared consciousness of the total task and overall progress of the work. Subtasks are flexibly combined and redelegated in the process of the project's work.

Also the *subject* of the activity changes. In rationalized science, the compartmentalized individual researcher may find it very hard to identify him- or herself as a subject of the activity. In humanized science, the management strongly strives for this identification. Personal commitment of each participant is a key element of this type of activity. Thus, the subject acquires two distinct layers: the management of the overall activity and the semiautonomous group as a functional unit of that activity.

On the other hand, the object, the outcome, the instruments, and the community of the activity are in principle not qualitatively different from those of rationalized science. Even the rules normally change only within the group. In the context of the overall activity, secrecy and competition between groups often prevail. And the time pressure may become harder than it could ever be in rationalized research.

Humanized research – and humanized work in general – obviously has a double function. It is a competing, hostile alternative to rationalized research. Simultaneously, it is a balancing or compensating factor, living in symbiosis with the rationalized type of research.

In *The Soul of a New Machine,* Tracy Kidder (1981) vividly describes the process of developing the new computer MV/8000 by a semiautonomous group of engineers at Data General. Though not an example from the sphere of basic research, the process nicely fulfills the requirements of the humanized type of activity characterized previously.

Kidder's account also demonstrates the fatal barrier common to both rationalized and humanized research. The group produces the prototype of the qualitatively new machine (the new model) in record time. But the group, including its leaders, is all but helpless when the process enters the phase of application and generalization. The sales and marketing people take over. The group suddenly has no identity – it disintegrates and vanishes. There is an unavoidable feeling of loss at the end of the book. Somehow the subjects were only fake subjects, unable to foresee even the near-future of their own group, not to mention the future transformation of the overall activity of the company. Even though the transition was fast, it was no less beyond human mastery than the craft type of transition.

I have now sketched three broad *historical activity types:* the *craft* type, the *rationalized* type, and the *humanized* type. At the same time, these are historical types of expansive transition. Within each historical activity type, the expansive transition from one form of activity to another, more advanced form bears the historical characteristics of the given activity type. There may be several successive expansive transitions within one and the same historical activity type. But there are also revolutionary expansive transitions that lead from one activity type to another.

In Chapter 2, I have indicated that a fourth historical activity type is currently emerging. In the conceptual context of Chapter 2, I talked about expansive learning activity or learning by expanding. In the conceptual context of Chapter 3, I talked about expansive Learning III. Such a new type of transition implies an emerging *collectively* and *expansively mastered activity type.*

I feel tempted to use the term "consciously mastered" or even "theoretically mastered." On the other hand, those labels sound foolhardy. It is safer to acknowledge the potential importance of intuitive forms of collective and expansive mastery, especially since the concept of consciousness is usually restricted to individual awareness alone. The "loss of the I" or the "liberated action" is indeed difficult to include in our common conceptions of consciousness.

Why have I used so much space for the discussion of science as activity? Because it is *universal* labor, containing in a relatively pure form the tendency toward the creation of novel general use values. This tendency is, though mostly in disguised forms, embedded in any human activity system. Science (along with art) makes expansive transitions its own main business, being supposedly conscious of what it is doing.

But what is the relationship between the literary examples of Chapter 3 and these examples from the development of science? First, *Huckleberry Finn* and *Seven Brothers* both are historically about the craft type of transition. Second, in both those stories we are dealing with transitions in which the given and created new is mainly objectified in the changed lifestyle of the subjects themselves. In other words, the new models are not easily separable from the subjects and hence the discontinuity of craft transition remains invisible (it becomes visible only when we consider it in terms of social and geographical isolation). In science, the new models are objectified entities that "live their own lives" separate from their creators – hence the visible discontinuity. Third, and for this very reason, in science we are more visibly dealing not only with the transformation of the central research activity itself but also with the – nowadays often nearly simultaneous – transformation of the object activity for which the given research activity provides new general instruments.

The central features of the four historical activity types, and of the corresponding types of expansive transition, are summarized in Figure 4.9.

The collectively mastered type of transition in Figure 4.9 refers to a *mastery over the entire cycle of expansion* depicted in Figure 3.3. After the presentation of such awesome transitions as the one behind the Manhattan Project, it is only reasonable to doubt that this fourth type of transition will ever be reality.

Jungk (1956, p. 91) quotes Heisenberg's saying that in the summer of 1939, twelve leading physicists could have prevented the construction of the atom bomb through joint discussions. According to Jungk, those twelve men had morally and politically not matured to meet the challenge of the great discovery. "The suspicion was stronger than the 'family ties' between the atomic scientists." Jungk (1956, p. 91) further quotes Heisenberg's friend von Weizsäcker saying that "it was not enough that we were a family, perhaps we ought to have been an international brotherhood with powers of disciplinary coercion over its members." In effect, von Weizsäcker is here ex post facto groping after a *social model* or *microcosm* that might have worked as an instrument for mastering and directing the transition in an alternative manner.

No doubt there is a kernel of truth in Heisenberg's statement. Those twelve men could at least have influenced the development much more

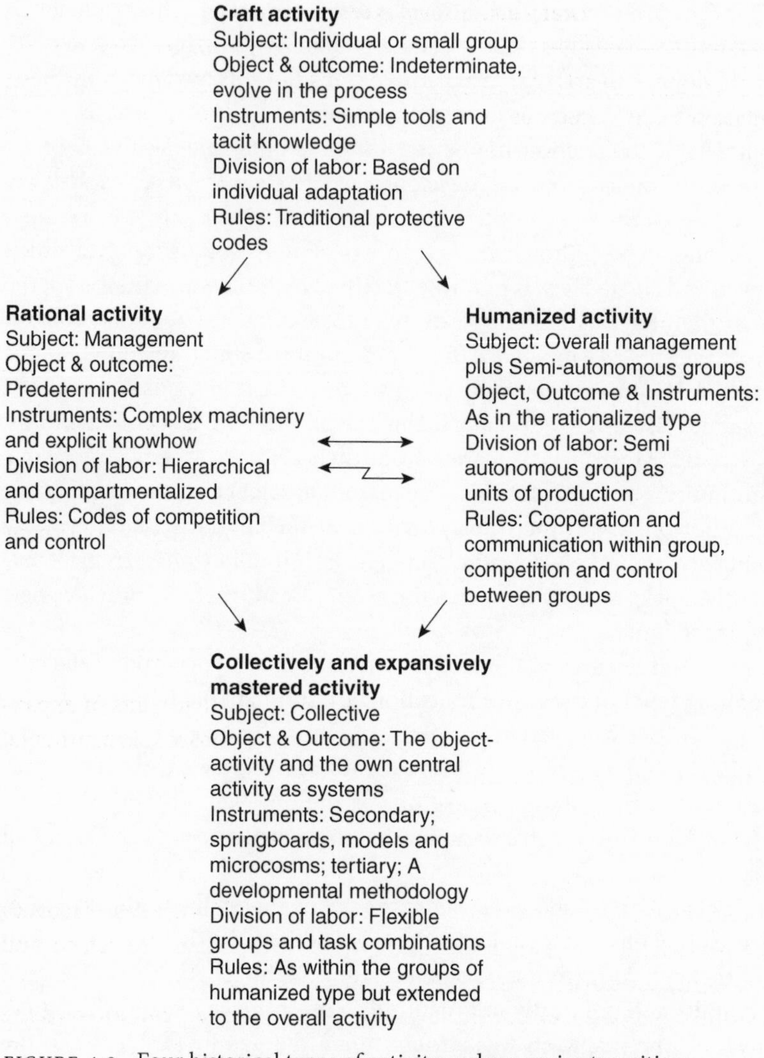

Craft activity
Subject: Individual or small group
Object & outcome: Indeterminate,
evolve in the process
Instruments: Simple tools and
tacit knowledge
Division of labor: Based on
individual adaptation
Rules: Traditional protective
codes

Rational activity
Subject: Management
Object & outcome:
Predetermined
Instruments: Complex machinery
and explicit knowhow
Division of labor: Hierarchical
and compartmentalized
Rules: Codes of competition
and control

Humanized activity
Subject: Overall management
plus Semi-autonomous groups
Object, Outcome & Instruments:
As in the rationalized type
Division of labor: Semi
autonomous group as
units of production
Rules: Cooperation and
communication within group,
competition and control
between groups

**Collectively and expansively
mastered activity**
Subject: Collective
Object & Outcome: The object-
activity and the own central
activity as systems
Instruments: Secondary;
springboards, models and
microcosms; tertiary; A
developmental methodology
Division of labor: Flexible
groups and task combinations
Rules: As within the groups of
humanized type but extended
to the overall activity

FIGURE 4.9. Four historical types of activity and expansive transition.

than they actually did. Indeed, there seems to have been a marked lengthy period of ambivalence and indetermination between Hahn's discovery and the actual commencement of the Manhattan Project.

Here, I will not to try to prove that such unexploited possibilities are a lawlike regular ingredient of any expansive transition. That can only be demonstrated through historically informed developmental research in concrete activity systems. My task here is to work out conceptual instruments

TABLE 4.5. *Examples of springboards*

Huckleberry finn	Seven brothers	Periodic law	Manhattan project
Technique of lying	Image of making tar	Image and technique of patience	a) Novel socio-conversational constellation: Hahn-Strassman; Meitner-Frisch b) Novel socio-conversational constellation: Szilard-Wigner-Einstein

for such research. These research instruments are necessarily also means for the *practical* accomplishment of collectively mastered transitions.

Thus, I will now systematize the central secondary instruments of expansion found so far.

SECONDARY INSTRUMENTS SYSTEMATIZED

In the preceding analysis, three types of secondary instruments of expansive transition have been identified. These are springboards, instrumental models, and social models or microcosms.

Springboards

In the cases of *Huckleberry Finn, Seven Brothers,* Mendeleev's discovery of the periodic law, and the emergence of the Manhattan Project, several examples of springboards were found (Table 4.5).

On the basis of the examples summarized previously, I put forward the following definition of the springboard.

The springboard is a facilitative image, technique or socioconversational constellation (or a combination of these) misplaced or transplanted from some previous context into a new, expansively transitional activity context during an acute conflict of a double bind character. The springboard has typically only a temporary or situational function in the solution of the double bind.

Is there any difference between the concept of the springboard and the concept of experience, as advocated by Polanyi and the Dreyfus brothers?

TABLE 4.6. *Examples of general models*

Huckleberry finn	Seven brothers	Periodic law	Manhattan project
"I'll do whatever is handy at the moment"	Civilized agricultural life	The periodic law, embodied in the periodic table	a) Physical theory of nuclear fission b) Theoretical model of the optimal bomb *and* the model of the "superlaboratory"

Experience is supposed to be functioning in the form of smooth, tacit, and automatic similarity recognition. Springboards do not come about smoothly and automatically. They appear in times of distress, almost as life-buoys. Little is known about the psychological mechanism of their appearance, but intense mental struggle seems to be a necessary precondition. Moreover, experience is supposed to provide solutions on the basis of earlier similar occasions. Springboards are not solutions. They are starters or hints toward a path leading to an expansive solution. In their appearance, their concrete contents often have little or nothing to do with the substance of the eventual solution.

These differences are usually neglected in cognitive theories of metaphoric and analogical reasoning. Donald Schön's (1983) work is exceptional in its emphasis on context and developmental continuity. He uses the concept of "generative metaphor," which is based on the mechanism of "seeing-as." In other words, even he restricts his theory to more or less direct *relations of visual similarity*. The cases presented earlier demonstrate that a springboard may indeed be a visual image (e.g., the image of making tar). But it can also be an entirely nonvisual, almost motor technique (e.g., the technique of lying). And it can be a socioconversational constellation in which the verbal interaction is decisive. Thus, the modality of the springboard varies, and direct similarity relations are an exception rather than the rule.

Models

In the four cases analyzed in this book, a number of general models were found (Table 4.6).

There are obvious qualitative differences in the modality of the models found. For Huck Finn and for the Seven Brothers, the new general model remained a *verbal expression of external or internal speech* (for the concept of inner or private speech, see Zivin, 1979). For Mendeleev, the new general model took the shape of a *written* theory, crystallized in graphic form in the periodic *table*. For Hahn and Meitner and Frisch, the model was expressed in the form of *written* theory and *mathematical formulae*. For Oppenheimer and Groves, the model of the bomb and the model of the superlaboratory appeared in the form of *written* theory, *mathematical formulae*, and technical *drawings*.

However, there is a more important dimension along which the models should be compared. I shall call it the *structural quality* or *type of rationality* exhibited by the model. This dimension is intimately connected with the conception of *causality* behind the model.

The most primitive models are *exemplars* or *prototypes* chosen or made to represent something general within a broader class of things or phenomena. The concept of model within the fashion industry still carries this meaning: an individual representing the broader class of "beauty" or "style." Such a primitive model is originally *spontaneous;* it is not constructed with the help of conscious analysis but rather through intuition and habituation. This type of a model implies a *magic or animistic conception of causality*: Things and phenomena are seen as being driven by forces or even intentions of their own. Perhaps more importantly, this rationality type seeks explanations in history and in the holistic nature of the universe.

> In place of a common causal background conditioning the properties and events of nature, "historical" grounds are adduced.... This inclination to evolve a *concrete causality* expresses itself in advanced mythical thought in the conception of an epoch removed from any historical duration. The mythical period is conceived as creative, as containing the forces of genesis governing the appearance of this world. (Werner, 1961, p. 304–305)

> The world is seen as a visible whole whose parts are of material, thing-like nature. It is interpreted as a unity, but this unity is that of a concretely represented, mytho-sociological organism. (Werner, 1961, p. 312)

> The psyche in a culture innocent of writing knows by a kind of empathetic identification of knower and known, in which the object of knowledge and the total being of the knower enter into a kind of fusion, in a way which literate cultures would typically find unsatisfyingly vague and garbled and somehow too intense and participatory. (Ong, 1977, p. 18)

Writing entails a worldview characterized by closure: fixed definitions and nomenclature, stable order and classification. The static, eternal hierarchies of the medieval conception of universe are most typical models of this type.

These may be called *nominalistic* and *classificatory* models. The conception of causality behind them is that of *predetermination* from above. As Koestler (1964, p. 640) points out, such models are "hierarchic *par excellence* but rigid; they resemble stone pyramids in the mental landscape."

Classificatory models reached one of their peaks in the work of Peter Ramus (1515–1572) on textbooks.

> Textbooks for virtually all arts subjects (dialectic or logic, rhetoric, grammar, artihmetic, etc.) that proceeded by cold-blooded definitions and divisions leading to still further definitions and more divisions, until every last particle of the subject had been dissected and disposed of. A Ramist textbook on a given subject had no acknowledged interchange with anything outside itself.... Moreover, the material in each of the Ramist textbooks could be presented in printed dichotomized outlines or charts that showed exactly how the material was organized spatially in itself and in the mind. (Ong, 1982, p. 134–135)

(margin handwritten note: What ?)

Among my four cases, the model of the Seven Brothers exemplifies this classificatory type. The picture of civilized agricultural life in the village is deeply anchored in ideals of stable order, harmony, and hierarchy.

The emergence of modern natural science produced a rationality type that gradually surpassed the nominalistic and classificatory type.

> The higher craftsmen of the 16th century, the artists and military engineers were not only used to experimenting but also to expressing their results in empirical rules and quantitative concepts. The substantial forms and occult qualities of the learned were of little use for them. They sought *usable and if possible quantitative rules of procedure* when they were to construct levers, machines and guns. In the manuscripts of Leonardo da Vinci (around 1500), such quantitative prodedural rules are given time and again. Normally they are formulated in the manner of cooking recipes: "If you want to know," so says Leonardo in the explanation to a drawing of a balance beam, "how much more MB weighs than AM, observe how many times CB goes into AD", etc. (Zilsel, 1976, p. 82; italics added)

Models of this type are *procedural*, whether *algorithms* or *heuristic rules*. If nominalistic and classificatory models answer the question "what?" these procedural models answer the question "how?" They no longer try to capture fixed, immovable hierarchies – they are constructed to facilitate practical achievements. The conception of causality behind this type of model is *linear* and *sequential*. This rationality type reaches its peak in the design and manufacture of machines.

(margin handwritten note: How ?)

Among our four cases, Huckleberry Finn's model is an example of heuristic rules. Typically, it has the form of a command or recipe: "After this always do whichever comes handiest at the time."

The limits of procedural models become visible when something goes wrong, when the object or instrument no more acts according to the steps prescribed in the algorithm. They also become visible when the situation is novel and there is uncertainty about which procedure to select or design. Finally, the limits become visible when the object or instrument becomes so complex that the sheer multitude of possible specific rules and procedures becomes overwhelming. In such contexts, general heuristic rules are offered as a solution. However, the more general the heuristic, the more empty of content and void of explanatory power it becomes.

In the nineteenth century, conceptions of holism, systemic interdependency, and probabilism gained momentum in various branches of science (von Bertalanffy, 1968, p. 45). The background conception is *retroactive causality,* in which "a whole system is seen to be involved in a closed retroactive causal relation" (Wartofsky, 1968, p. 306).

> Modern physics, particularly the physics of elementary particles, cogently demonstrates the restricted nature of the causal conception viewed as a unilateral action of one body on another and shows its failure to account for microprocesses. The idea of cause as an interaction of fields, particles, which gives rise to various microprocesses is of essential significance in substantiating the physical ideas of modern quantum field theory. Twentieth-century physics has a marked tendency to combine the causality principle with the systemic-structural approach to phenomena. Essentially speaking, a cause is in the nature of an interaction of the various elements, parts, tendencies of a system that governs the behaviour of that system. (Svechnikov, 1971, p. 241–242)

Models of this rationality type are *systemic models*. If classificatory models answer what questions and procedural models answer how questions, systemic models aim at answering questions of the why type. Such models function as aids for diagnosing and predicting the behavioral states and changes of complex systems. They are typically probabilistic in nature (for a discussion of the social construction of systemic models, see Bloomfield, 1986).

Among my four cases, Mendeleev's model of the periodic system of elements seems to lie between a classificatory model and a systemic model. It is no more a simple hierarchy. It was constructed through uncovering interdependencies between the whole system and its elements. However, the tabular form of the model does not directly depict dynamic transitions and movements within the system.

On the other hand, when Oppenheimer, Groves, and their staff designed the bomb as a complex technical device and the superlaboratory of Los Alamos as a complex organization, they were bound to use systemic models. For one thing, the probabilistic uncertainty before the first successful test explosion testifies to that.

The very successes of systems thinking and systems engineering have prompted doubts about the final adequacy of the systemic rationality type. The growing awareness of global and universal interdependencies evokes questions like "Where are we all going?" and "How did all this begin?" But the dimension of time is very restricted in the closed systems view behind most of the cybernetic efforts. Time is seen as a continuum in which the *given* system moves between different behavioral *states*. But there is no conceptualization for the dynamics of the qualitative development, or expansive transformation, of the *system itself.* This is particularly evident in the pessimistic world models, or "simulations of doom" (Bloomfield, 1986, p. 167), produced by systems analysts since the early 1970s.

> Global modeling projects typically begin by looking at the past and using it as a basis for describing the present. Once a model has been developed, it is used to generate a "baseline" scenario from the present into the future, assuming no fundamental change. (Richardson, 1984, p. 126)

In the natural sciences, this restricted conception of reversible time has been most strikingly challenged by Ilya Prigogine's notions of irreversible time and self-organization (see Prigogine, 1984; Prigogine & Stengers, 1985).

Moving along somewhat similar lines, David Bohm (1981) tries to reconceptualize causality using the notion of "formative cause."

> In the Ancient Greek philosophy, the word form meant, in the first instance, an inner *forming activity* which is the cause of the growth of things, and of the development and differentiation of their various essential forms.... In more modern language, it would be better to describe this as *formative cause,* to emphasize that what is involved is not a mere form imposed from without, but rather *an ordered and structured inner movement that is essential to what things are.* (Bohm, 1981, p. 12)

Attempts like Prigogine's and Bohm's indicate the emergence of a new rationality type. This rationality type is essentially historical and holistic – features in common with the most primitive rationality type described previously. But where primitive historicism and holism are essentially *immediate* or spontaneous, the new historicism and holism are highly reflective and *mediated* by a specific type of model.

Neither Prigogine nor Bohm elaborates on the question of the instrumental models of this new rationality type. As Prigogine acknowledges, there is another tradition of thought that has struggled with this problem.

> We have described ... a nature that might be called "historical" – that is, capable of development and innovation. The idea of a history of nature as an integral part of materialism was asserted by Marx and, in greater detail, by Engels. Contemporary developments in physics, the discovery of the constructive role played by irreversibility, have thus raised within the natural sciences a question that has long been asked by materialists. For them, understanding nature meant understanding it as being capable of producing man and his societies. (Prigogine & Stengers, 1985, p. 252–253)

The lineage from Hegel to Marx and Engels, and further to Ilyenkov and Davydov (see the sections Dialectical Logic and Concepts and Davydov and the Problem of Concepts), suggests that the models needed here are of the *germ cell* type, expressing the genetically original inner contradiction of the system under scrutiny. Such models function not just as devices for diagnosing the behavioral state of the given closed system but as means for tracing and projecting the genesis and expansive transitions, or "fluctuations," of an open system.

I suggest that the triangle models of activity developed and used in this book may be considered as an attempt at such modeling. Moreover, among my four cases, the theory of nuclear fission, discovered by Hahn and further formulated by Meitner and Frisch, is an obvious candidate to represent this type of model. The problem with this model is, however, that it was restricted to representing the expansive and irreversible process of nuclear fission *in terms of a natural phenomenon only,* being totally unable to model it as a sociohistorical phenomenon. The latter aspect, the sociohistorical modelling of nuclear fission, was thus left to people like Groves and Oppenheimer who could only produce closed systemic models suited for technical optimization but not for mastery of the sociohistorical process.

I shall now summarize what has been said about the five historical types of models (Table 4.7).

In expansive transitions, in voyages through zones of proximal development, general models are primarily needed to *envision and project the evolving object and motive of the new activity.* Such models are instrumental in the strict sense of the word. However, another type of vehicle is also often found to play an important part in expansive transitions. In the analyses of the four cases, I have called these vehicles *social models* or *microcosms.*

TABLE 4.7. *Five historical types of models*

Type of Model	Conception of Causality	Case Example
1. Spontaneous prototype	Magic, animistic	–
2. Nominalistic and classificatory	Predetermined from above	*Seven Brothers*
3. Procedural	Linear and sequential	*Huckleberry Finn*
4. Systemic	Retroactive	Periodic table? Manhattan Project
5. Germ cell	Historical, formative	Nuclear fusion?

TABLE 4.8. *Examples of microcosms*

Huckleberry finn	*Seven brothers*	Periodic law	Manhattan project
The raft and its people	The farmhouse of Impivaara	–	a) – b) Oppenheimer, Groves, and the two colonels in the train

Microcosms

In my four cases, also some microcosms were found (Table 4.8).

Microcosms are miniatures of the community upon which the new form of activity will be based. They are social test benches of the new activity. It is common to all the three examples in Table 4.8 that the microcosm is physically and socially a relatively isolated formation: a raft on the river, a lonely house in the backwoods, a train car. It is also a temporary formation – a vehicle to be abandoned after the time is ripe for the decisive step of social and organizational generalization.

On the other hand, the examples of Table 4.8 do not cover the emerging collectively mastered type of expansive transition. Features like relative isolation may be radically altered as we enter transitions of that type.

IN SEARCH OF A TERTIARY INSTRUMENT OF EXPANSION

I have now proposed a set of secondary instruments of expansive transition. However, expansive transition in its emerging collectively and expansively mastered form is to be understood as *learning activity*. A whole molar activity can only be mastered with the help of a tertiary instrument (recall Tables 3.1 and 3.2). In other words, it requires an *overall methodology* for making and using the secondary instruments described previously.

The classical candidate for such an instrument is formal logic, or its close relative, the Piagetian formal operations. As has been argued earlier in this chapter, formal logic is not suitable for mastering processes in which irreversible time and qualitative development are central.

> Formal-operational adults supposedly live in a hermetically sealed ahistorical universe where life is a matter of necessities deriving from the natural, non-manmade laws of equilibration. Such individuals have no life histories, much as they have no memories. The elimination of the historical dimension ... is conductive to the kind of technological rationality that underlies the most profound problems of modernized life, including the nuclear threat. (Broughton, 1984, p. 408)

Feeling uncomfortable with formal operations as the penultimate stage of cognitive development, a number of researchers are today entertaining the idea that there must be one or more *developmental stages beyond Piaget's stage of formal operations.*

The volume *Beyond Formal Operations* (Commons, Richards & Armon, 1984) contains a representative collection of papers from this broad approach. In his vehemently critical closing paper, Broughton (1984) lists nine variations of this approach. He characterizes the theorists behind these attempts as "liberal revisionists," trying to "humanize" the Piagetian formal-logical apparatus. They exhibit little quarrel with the orthodoxy of Piaget's stage theory and most of them support the reality and significance of formal thought. For them, formal logic applies in one sphere, but in some other sphere or developmental period an alternative or more advanced mode of thought appears. The basic Piagetian sequence remains intact. Thus, Broughton argues, the proposed stages beyond formal operations are built on a false foundation.

Broughton's critique might be interpreted to suggest that no formal-operational type of thought actually exists. I agree with this conclusion if formal operations are understood as a universal, in the final analysis biologically determined mode of thought. However, in sociohistorical reality formal logic and formal operational thought (in various approximations to the ideal type) no doubt do exist. In my analysis, formal-operational thought, like any thought form, is a human-made artifact, a tertiary instrument of a certain historical period. It exists but it has only a limited life cycle.

Thus, the question is not what follows formal operations in the (ahistorically understood) ontogenesis but what follows it sociohistorically. The analyses presented in this book point to one requirement: The new tertiary instrument must facilitate the mastery of expansion in irreversible time.

Among the theoreticians writing in *Beyond Formal Operations,* only Patricia Arlin takes up the notion of expansion as a central problem. She points out that the hypotheticodeductive model of formal-operational thought requires that problems be presented to subjects for solution. Possibilities and hypotheses are constrained by the nature of the problem presented; they are confined within the given system (Arlin, 1984, p. 262). Arlin suggests that there are two basic mechanisms operating in postformal thought: contraction and expansion. Contractions imply purposeful subordination of the thought to the limited constraints of the problem. Expansions imply purposeful ascending above the confines of the given problem. The expansive form of thought analyzed by Arlin is called *problem finding.* It represents "the ability to raise general questions from many ill-defined problems" (Arlin, 1984, p. 264; see also Getzels & Csikszentmihalyi, 1976).

> The argument for a fifth stage [formal operations being the fourth; Y. E.] is based on this definition of problem finding and on the observations that "general questions" are uncommon in adolescent thought. (Arlin, 1984, p. 265)

Arlin's notion of expansion thus remains at the individual-psychological and empirical-observational levels. It is more a hunch than a concrete methodological instrument.

In fact, the representatives of the postformal approach do not discuss their proposed higher stages in terms of instruments. Among them, development seems to be considered in a rather traditional fashion – as something that can be observed and explained but not touched and mastered. Interventions are curiously absent in *Beyond Formal Operations.*

Understandably this stance leaves a vacuum within the field of education. This vacuum is currently filled by numerous programs for teaching "general thinking skills" (for an overview, see Nickerson, Perkins & Smith, 1985). The promising word "general" hints at something on the order of tertiary instruments. However, the dominant tenor within this movement is that creative and critical thinking are to be divided into separate skills. Some of these skills are further analyzed into steps. These stepwise procedures are then taught, either in separate courses or embedded in various school subjects. A typical "general thinking skill" may look like one of the following three examples.

EXAMPLE 1

1. Refocusing phase – 2. Awareness phase – 3. Responsibility phase – 4. Goal-setting phase – 5. Task engagement phase – 6. Task completion phase (Marzano & Arredondo, 1986, p. 21)

EXAMPLE 2

Rule 1. Identify/state purpose for analysis. – Rule 2. Identify clues or questions to guide your analysis. – Step 1. Separate the "whole" into its parts. – Step 2. Compare one part to your clues or questions. Record your findings (make a list). Repeat this step for every identified part from Step 1. – Step 3. Draw inference/make generalization to satisfy goal stated in Rule 1. (Jackson, 1986, p. 35)

EXAMPLE 3

1. Define the situation. – 2. State the goal. – 3. Generate ideas. – 4. Define the new situation. – 5. Prepare a plan. – 6. Take action. (Wales, Nardi & Stager, 1986, p. 40)

These "general thinking skills" are actually algorithms or heuristic rules for carrying out certain commonplace actions that our cultures are accustomed to calling "problem solving" or "analysis" or "decision making." Compared even with Piaget's elaborate structure of formal operations, the separate "thinking skills" are specific and arbitrary. They certainly have little to do with an overall mastery of expansive transitions. From the point of view of people's life activities, the term "general" is here used perversely, as if life consisted of heaps or puzzles of discrete pieces that could be put together in a haphazard "and-summative" manner.

Then again, that is how life often does look. The perversion is itself an adequate reflection of the subjective consequences of an alienating division of labor.

FORMAL DIALECTICS AS A CANDIDATE

Before the current wave of interest in postformal operations, Klaus Riegel (1973) proposed that the "fifth stage" of cognitive development consists of "dialectical operations." Riegel's conception of dialectics is summarized in his *Foundations of Dialectical Psychology* (1979). Parallel to that effort, the social scientist Ian Mitroff and his colleagues started a research program on what they called "dialectical inquiring systems" (for an overview, see Mitroff & Mason, 1981). Though stemming from different disciplinary traditions, the epistemological and psychological conceptions of these two strands of research are essentially similar. The most thorough empirical investigation along these lines so far is presented in *Dialectical Thinking and Adult Development* by Michael Basseches (1984). Riegel's characterization of dialectical thinking goes as follows.

> Each thing is itself and, at the same time, many other things. For example, any concrete object, such as a chair, is itself but, at the same time, is of many different properties. By selecting some and disregarding others, we might develop one or another abstract notion (theory) about the chair. But only when we see all of these properties in their complementary dependencies do we reach an appropriate, concrete comprehension.... *Dialectical thinking* (Vernunft) comprehends itself, the world, and each concrete object in its multitude of contradictory relations. (Riegel, 1979, p. 39)

Riegel then takes up Hegel's (1966) famous discussion of "master and slave." He points out that to consider either one, the master or the slave, separated from the other, would be abstract and nondialectical.

> Only a description of both in their mutual relation provides a concrete representation of the totality without covering up one or the other. Such a description represents dialectical thought with its intrinsic contradictions. (Riegel, 1979, p. 39)

This sounds reasonable. However, a closer look reveals deep problems. First of all, Riegel systematically reduces his systems into *dyadic* formations. The mother-child dyad and the author-reader dyad are among his favorite examples.

> The minimal condition for an analysis that searches not only for answers but also for the questions includes two individuals (for example, a mother and her child), both operating interactively over time and thus growing and developing together. (Riegel, 1979, p.1)

> The load for the reader as well as for the child should neither be too heavy or too light. Information has to be given at the right moment, in the right amount, and of the right kind.... The topic of coordination and synchronization of two time sequences is ... the most central issue in dialectical theory. (Riegel, 1979, p. 8)

There is no expansive mediating *thirdness* here (recall my discussion of Peirce and Popper in Chapter 2). Instead of the creation of new contexts, synchronization within the given context is taken as the central task of dialectics.

In Riegel's dialectics, very little attention is paid to the historically formed objects and instruments of human interactive systems. Dialectics becomes ahistorical analysis of relations and interactions.

> But by presenting these isolated relations, the abstract interaction, as the whole, as the totality of man-world relationship, the "dialectical psychologists" reify the relationships. They replace psychology with systems thinking.... Human beings as well as things are only exchangeable carriers, only material for the system of relations. (Grüter, 1979, p. 162)

Riegel's dialectics is a reflection of societal relations from the viewpoint of circulation and exchange only. Within the spheres of circulation and exchange of the bourgeois society, people and things appear in their abstract relations, mediated and regulated by the invisible substance of exchange value. No new values seem to be produced; no material substance seems to be worked upon and given form. Symptomatically, Riegel's dialectics knows no dialectics of nature and no dialectics embedded in the objects of human labor. Charles Tolman (1981) calls it "the metaphysics of relations."

Ian Mitroff and his collaborators take a slightly different angle. For them, dialectics is a procedure for exposing, challenging, and synthesizing competing positions and interpretations. As Mitroff and Kilmann (1978, p. 73) put it, "The purpose of the procedure is to make ... implicit assumptions explicit and line them up side by side with their counter assumptions from the opposing viewpoint." One conclusion from the research is the following.

> The message is that subjects *can* be taught to appreciate that on complex issues they are wise to listen to the stories of competing experts, if only for the reason that this is extremely helpful in better understanding the assumptions which underlie the positions of experts. (Mitroff & Mason, 1981, p. 36)

Here, dialectics is reduced to a form of discourse and debate. It is cut off from any historical analysis of the objects of discourse. The task is to understand and synthesize competing views, not to grasp and exploit practically the objective dynamics and expansive contradictions of systems of societal reality.

Work by Basseches (1984) completes this excursion into the realm of formal dialectics. The author tries to identify "dialectical schemata" in interview protocols of college students and professors. He lists four groups of such schemata, namely, "motion-oriented schemata," "form-oriented schemata," "relationship-oriented schemata," and "meta-formal schemata."

But he never seriously considers the content and history of the topic dealt with in the interviews (the topic being, for convenience, the nature of college education!). Thus, the thought forms and conceptions displayed by the subjects may be coined "dialectical" quite independently of their topics. A conception based on sheer ignorance or misinformation may still be deemed "motion-oriented" or "relationship-oriented." Subjects could very well develop a specific skill of producing "dialectical" humbug to please the researcher or to amuse themselves. At the end of his book, Basseches (1984, p. 366–367) nearly admits this.

> From a philosophical perspective, perhaps the most striking tension in this book comes from the fact that dialectical thinking has been described in a relatively formalistic, content-free way.... An attempt to describe dialectical thinking formalistically, though potentially useful, is necessarily limited and potentially distorting.

The present wave of formal dialectics is actually not novel. Recollecting his student years at the Sorbonne, Claude Lévi-Strauss (1961, p. 54–55) provides a poignant characterization of this form of thought.

> It was then that I began to learn how any problem, whether grave or trivial, can be resolved. The method never varies. First you establish the traditional "two views" of the question. You then put forward a commonsense justification of the one, only to refute it by the other. Finally you send them both packing by the use of a third interpretation, in which both the others are shown to be equally unsatisfactory. Certain verbal maneuvers enable you, that is, to line up the traditional "antithesis" as complementary aspects of a single reality.... Before long, the exercise becomes the merest verbalizing, reflection gives place to a kind of superior punning.

Here, one has a kind of "thirdness." But it is an "and-summative" thirdness, not an expansive one.

DIALECTICS OF SUBSTANCE

Proponents of formal dialectics justly refer to Hegel as the founder of scientific dialectics. Their interpretations, however, fail to do justice to the quality of Hegel's thinking. Grasping the essence of Hegel is a necessary prerequisite of substantive, content-bound dialectics.

It is well known that reason, thought, was for Hegel the prime mover and infinite power through which and in which all reality finds its being. But reason or thought was *not* something purely mental, taking place within the individual's head and manifesting itself in words only. Hegel demanded that thought should be investigated in all the forms in which it was realized, above all in human actions and activities, in the creation of things and events outside the head of the individual.

On this basis, Hegel correctly saw the logical forms of the individual consciousness as being objectively determined by things outside the individual psyche, by the entire spiritual and material culture, collectively created and transformed by people, surrounding the individual and interacting with him or her from the cradle. This collective process, the intellectual development of humanity, could be objectively traced in the history of science and technique. According to Hegel, this process also included, as a phase, the act of realizing thought in object activity, and through activity in the forms of things and events outside consciousness. Here Hegel "came *very close* to materialism," as Lenin (1963, p. 278) noted.

Thought had to be investigated as collective, cooperative activity in which the individual performed only partial functions. In really taking part in common work, the individual was subordinating him- or herself to the laws and forms of universal thought, though not conscious of them as such.

For Hegel, dialectics was the form and method of thought that included the process both of elucidating contradictions and of concretely resolving them at a more profound level of understanding the object. In other words, the contradictions could be solved only in the course of developing science, industry, and all the spheres Hegel called the "objective spirit." The practical outcome of dialectical thought was not individual adjustment but collective societal development and qualitative change of material human culture.

Hegel's essential superiority to the modern proponents of formal dialectics lies in two facts: (1) Hegel pointed out and defended the *objectivity* of logical forms of thought, their origination in the universal forms and laws of development of human culture – science, technique, and morality; (2) Hegel introduced *practice,* the process of activity on sense objects that alters things in accordance with a concept, into our conception of thought and logic.

But where did the universal forms and patterns of logic and thought begin? How did universal spirit originate? In order to understand Hegel's view, one has to realize that he did not take any easy answers from religion. Rather, his conception was an accurate reflection of the real conditions under the spontaneously developing division of social labor, the separation of mental work from physical labor in particular. Under these conditions, science was transformed into a special profession, above and opposed to the majority of human beings, to practical physical labor.

Registering and reproducing this condition, Hegel counterposed man and his real thought to impersonal, "absolute" thought as an eternal force that had actually created man and the world of man. Logic became an absolute form, in relation to which the material world and real human activity were something derivative, secondary, and created. The scientist, the mental worker, appeared as the representative of the universal thought, approaching and formulating its categories. The sensuously objective activity of physical labor appeared only as the "prehistory" and "application" of thought. Logically, the word (or speech) appeared as the primary tool of the externalization and objectification of thought.

According to Engels, dialectics is "nothing more than the science of the general laws of the motion and development of nature, human society, and thought" (Engels, 1975, p. 168–169). In other words, dialectical logic is not only the science of the laws and patterns of thought but also, and above all, the science of the development of all things, both material and "spiritual."

Hegel was also interested in the world around him, in human culture and labor. But he considered them as derivatives of the universal thought. This rendered him unable to study the different forms of nature and culture *in their own right,* independently of the eternal universal spirit. Even so, Hegel never reduced dialectics to pure "dialogic interactions" or "procedures of debate," void of objective contents. Hegel may have seen the relation between thought and external material world upside down, but he certainly did not exclude the world from his eyesight: "Thinking is not an activity which treats the content as something alien and external; it is not reflection into self away from the content" (Hegel, 1966, p. 113).

Hegel directed devastating criticism against abstract formalism.

> If the knowing subject carries round everywhere the one inert abstract form, taking up in external fashion whatever material comes his way, and dipping it into this element, then this comes about as near to fulfilling what is wanted – viz. a self-origination of the wealth of detail, and a self-determining distinction of shapes and forms – as any chance fantasies about the content in question. It is rather monochrome formalism, which only arrives at distinction in the matter it has to deal with, because this is already prepared and well known. (Hegel, 1966, p. 78)

In contradistinction to formalism, Hegel defined the proper nature of dialectics.

> The abstract or unreal is not its element and content, but the real, what is self-establishing, has life within itself, existence in its very notion.

> It is the process that creates its own moments in its course, and goes through them all; and the whole of this movement constitutes its positive content and its truth. This movement includes, therefore, within it the negative factor as well, the element which would be named falsity if it could be considered one from which we had to abstract. (Hegel, 1966, p. 105)

In other words, dialectics deals with real substantive contents. Moreover, dialectics deals with the movement of objects. This movement is characterized by two essential features: It is self-movement, not externally caused but internally generated (*causa sui*), and it is movement in the form of inner contradictions. Dialectical thinking "should sink into and pervade the content, should let it be directed and controlled by its own proper nature, i.e., by the self as its own self, and should observe this process taking place" (Hegel, 1966, p. 117).

The process of dialectical thought is compared with the process of formal understanding.

> Instead of making its way into the inherent content of the matter in hand, (formal) understanding always takes a survey of the whole, assumes a position above the particular existence about which it is speaking, i.e., does not see it at all. (Hegel, 1966, p. 112)

Not reducible to what was already known, the outcome of dialectical thought emerges as if through an intense adventure or detective story.

> True scientific knowledge, on the contrary, demands abandonment to the very life of the object, or, which means the same thing, claims to have before it the inner necessity controlling the object, and to express this only. Steeping itself in its object, it forgets to take that general survey, which is merely a turning of knowledge away from the content back into itself. Being sunk into the material in hand, and following the course that such material takes, true knowledge returns back into itself, yet not before the content in its fullness is taken into itself, is reduced to the simplicity of being a determinate characteristic, drops to the level of being one aspect of an existing entity, and passes over into its higher truth. By this process the whole as such, surveying its entire content, itself emerges out of the wealth wherein its process of reflection seemed to be lost. (Hegel, 1966, p. 112–113)

This process unifies the content and the form, the theory and the method.

> The concrete shape of the content is resolved by its own inherent process into a simple determinate quality. Thereby it is raised to logical form,

and its being and essence coincide; its concrete existence is merely this
process that takes place, and is *eo ipso* logical existence. It is therefore
needless to apply a formal scheme to a concrete content in an external
fashion; the content is in its very nature a transition into a formal shape,
which, however, ceases to be formalism of an external kind, because
the form is the indwelling process of the concrete content itself. (Hegel,
1966, p. 115)

According to Hegel, the truth is the whole. "The whole, however, is merely
the essential nature reaching its completeness through the process of its
own development" (Hegel, 1966, p. 81). The whole "comes to the stage to
begin with in its immediacy, in its bare generality. A building is not finished
when its foundation is laid; and just as little is the attainment of a general
notion of a whole the whole itself" (Hegel, 1966, p. 75). Theoretical thought
has to find the initial and truly general essence of the complex whole; it has
to reduce the whole to its abstract foundation.

But the actual realization of this abstract whole is only found when those
previous shapes and forms, which are now reduced to ideal moments of
the whole, are developed anew again, but developed and shaped with
this new medium, and with the meaning they have thereby acquired.
(Hegel, 1966, p. 76)

The dialectical method is a method of grasping the essence of the object
by reproducing theoretically the logic of its development, of its historical
"becoming." The dialectical method is thus a historical method. But it is
also a unity of the historical and the logical. The history of the object is
purified of its arbitrary details; it is elevated to the level of logical succession from which the details in their full richness may again be derived, now
"with the meaning they have thereby acquired."

Earlier in this chapter, this method was named ascending from the
abstract to the concrete. It offers no shortcuts. With each object, the logic
of development has to be found anew, by "sinking into the material at
hand."

I am searching for a tertiary instrument of expansive transitions.
Dialectics as it was conceived of by Hegel and by many of Hegel's materialist
followers is here problematic in two respects. First, dialectics as a method
of thought is commonly pictured as a *solitary* endeavor. Second, dialectics
is commonly pictured as a method of *thought* only.

In my analysis, dialectics is the logic of expansion. And expansion is
essentially a social and practical process, having to do with collectives of
people reconstructing their material practice.

SOCIALITY AND EXPANSION: FROM
APPRENTICESHIP TO POLYPHONY

Hegel was aware of the superindividual nature of thought. As noted, in really taking part in common work, the individual was subordinating him- or herself to the laws and forms of universal thought, though not conscious of them as such. For Hegel, the superindividual nature of thought could not be adequately realized by human beings made of flesh and blood. The absolute spirit had to be posited as its subject.

Hegel was witnessing the dissolution of precapitalist social structures, characterized by collectivism without conscious reflection. Such structures are exemplified in medieval systems of apprenticeship. They may still be studied in vivo, for example, in traditional Japanese forms of performance.

> Japanese traditional performance forms ... have been construed so that they can not be taught scientifically and learners can master them only through imitating and repeating what the teachers do. We sometimes call that way of learning "stealing action". What a novice of Japanese dancing begins first, for example, is just to imitate the teacher's form of performance. Continuing repeating it for many years, he finally reaches the point where he knows Japanese dancing and is called a master. (Hiromatsu, 1986, p. 1–2)

The performance is practiced in a specific social formation called "world." Sumo wrestling is a case in point.

> In Sumo world, there is an established stable system (Heya system), and any wrestler is obliged to get into one of the "heya" and to live with the teacher and other wrestlers. The purpose of this stable system is to train young wrestlers into senior champions while inculcating them with the strict etiquette, discipline and special values which are the foundations of Sumo's world-apart society. Physically, a stable (heya; literally "room") is a self-contained unit complete with all living-training facilities....
>
> A stable is managed under the absolute control of a single boss (oyakata). All oyakata are ex-senior wrestlers and members of the Japanese Sumo Association. Oyakata are generally married and live in special quarters with their wives, who are known by the title of "okamisan," the only woman to live in heya. Okamisan plays an important behind-the-scenes role in the smooth operation of a stable, but their duties never include cooking or cleaning for the wrestlers. These and all other housekeeping chores outside the oyakata's quarters are performed by apprentices and low-rank wrestlers who receive no pay at all for all their pains and must

in addition serve as tsukebito (servant) for senior wrestlers.... In living in heya with oyakata and other senior wrestlers, young wrestlers not only practise Sumo performance but also learn the whole atmosphere of Sumo world. (Hiromatsu, 1986, p. 11–13)

Hiromatsu (1986, p. 15) concludes that the traditional performance has to be considered not from the point of view of a "spot" but of a "space" as a whole. This is obviously correct, but the spatial dimension is here inseparably united with the temporal one. History in the form of tacit tradition is present in all actions within the "world," and the *oyakata* is essentially a representative or embodiment of tradition.

Industrial capitalism is the triumph of individualism. Here, the mature form of learning is obligatory school going. In the obligatory school, the dominant unit of functioning is the individual spatially and temporally discrete task.

The basic pattern is this. Learning is presented (1) in the form of discrete primary learning tasks (put a peg in a hole, where is the cat, spell dog, how much are two and two); (2) tasks are separated out of the flow of events as special episodes, with a beginning, an end, and some sort of a marker signaling "this is a special situation"; (3) tasks are carefully calibrated during the years when the secondary learning pattern is being established to be comfortably within the perceptual-motor and cognitive capabilities of the child; (4) tasks end at a point of resolution; (5) the point of resolution is so structured that it has two digitally opposed outcomes, "success" or "failure" (that is, the point of resolution is equivalent to the point at which the "solution" is provided); (6) tasks are all amenable to "successful solution"; (7) such a solution is reached in short period of time (within the attention span or, later, "motivational span" of the child); (8) the "solution" is rewarded (the non-reward for "failure" comes to be perceived as punishment), which reward is clearly differentiated from a secondary minor reward for "trying"; (9) the usual reward in the stage of the establishment of the learning pattern is praise associated with increased tenderness or lovingness; (10) and this reward is from a figure of major emotional importance to the child. (Levy, 1976, p. 179–180)

Levy (1976, p. 183) points out that "the content of the task is trivial, except as it is related to greater or lesser success markers." This type of learning is intimately connected with the dominance of narrow specialization (recall "compartmentalization") and of a situational approach to life. The former represents the spatial, the latter the temporal dimension of sociality, both in learning and in wage labor.

Marx takes up these two aspects of sociality in a famous short passage on universal labor.

> Incidentally, a distinction should be made between universal labour and co-operative labour. Both kinds play their role in the process of production, both flow one into the other, but both are also differentiated. Universal labour is all scientific labour, all discovery and all invention. This labour depends partly on the co-operation of the living, and partly on the utilisation of the labours of those who have gone before. Co-operative labour, on the other hand, is the direct co-operation of individuals. (Marx, 1971, p. 104)

Cooperative labor, the direct cooperation of individuals, is the spatial dimension of sociality. But truly universal labor always presupposes also the temporal dimension, indirect "cooperation" with those who have gone before and those who will follow later. Previously I have sketched these dimensions of sociality in apprenticeship and in school going. What kind of sociality would correspond to learning by expanding? The most promising elements toward an answer may be found in the work of the Soviet literary theorist Mikhail Bakhtin (1973; 1982) on the nature of the novel.

As Michael Holquist (1982, p. xxvi) notes, "The enormous success of the novel in the 19th century has obscured the fact that for most of its history it was a marginal genre, little studied and frequently denounced." Bakhtin compares the novel with the epic. According to him, "The epic world knows only a single and unified world view, obligatory and indubitably true for heroes as well as for authors and audiences" (Bakhtin, 1982, p. 35). Moreover, "Outside his destiny, the epic and tragic hero is nothing; he is, therefore, a function of the plot fate assigns him; he cannot become the hero of another destiny or another plot" (Bakhtin, 1982, p. 36).

There is a deep affinity between the epic as the dominant form of literary consciousness and the apprenticeship as the dominant form of learning. The "world" of apprenticeship corresponds to the "fate" and the "plot" of the epic. As industrial capitalism and obligatory schooling replace apprenticeship, the novel replaces the epic.

> The destruction of epic distance and the transferral of the image of an individual from the distanced plane to the zone of contact with the inconclusive events of the present (and consequently of the future) result in a radical re-structuring of the image of the individual in the novel – and consequently in all literature. Folklore and popular-comic sources for the novel played a huge role in this process. Its first and essential step was the comic familiarization of the image of man. Laughter destroyed

epic distance; it began to investigate man freely and familiarly, to turn him inside out, expose the disparity between his surface and his center, between his potential and his reality. A dynamic authenticity was introduced into the image of man, dynamics of inconsistency and tension between various factors of this image; man ceased to coincide with himself, and consequently men ceased to be exhausted entirely by the plots that contain them. (Bakhtin, 1982, p. 35)

It is precisely the zone of contact with an inconclusive present (and consequently with the future) that creates the necessity of this incongruity of man with himself. There always remains in him unrealized potential and unrealized demands. The future exists, and this future ineluctably touches upon the individual, has its roots in him. (Bakhtin, 1982, p. 37)

Bakhtin reveals here that capitalist individualism has not only the face of alienation, compartmentalization, and situationalism; it also has the face of contemporaneity, open-endedness, and fluidity; of freedom from fixed authorities and absolute traditions. It has the potential of "ever questing, ever examining itself and subjecting its established forms to review" (Bakhtin, 1982, p. 39).

But Bakhtin does not stop here. His ideas are not restricted to revealing the optimistic aspect of individualism. To the contrary, his main finding is the potential new quality of sociality emerging from amid individualism. He found this new potential anticipated in the novel.

The novel can be defined as a diversity of social speech types (sometimes even diversity of languages) and a diversity of individual voices, artistically organized. The internal stratification of any single national language into social dialects, characteristic group behavior, professional jargons, generic languages, languages of generations and age groups, tendentious languages, languages of the authorities, of various circles and of passing fashions, languages that serve the specific sociopolitical purposes of the day, even of the hour (each day has its own slogan, its own vocabulary, its own emphases) – this internal stratification present in every language at any given moment of its historical existence is the indispensable prerequisite for the novel as a genre. The novel orchestrates all its themes, the totality of the world of objects and ideas depicted and expressed in it, by means of the social diversity of speech types and by the differing individual voices that flourish under such conditions. Authorial speech, the speeches of narrators, inserted genres, the speech of characters are merely those fundamental compositional unities with whose help heteroglossia can enter the novel; each of them permits a multiplicity of social voices and a wide variety of their links and interrelationships (always more or less dialogized). These distinctive links and interrelationships between utterances and languages, this movement of the theme through different languages and speech types, its dispersion into the rivulets and droplets of social heteroglossia, its dialogization – this is the basic distinguishing feature of the stylistics of the novel. (Bakhtin, 1982, p. 262–263)

The new sociality envisioned here is one of heteroglossia and polyphony, orchestrated and organized around a common object. Borrowing from cognitive science, one could perhaps speak of parallel distributed processing systems. An evolving activity system socially based on such parallel distributed modules could be conceived of as a local or global *paradigmatic network* of groups and individuals sharing a common object/motive and common instruments.

But how would such a social structure differ from the classical idea of a community of scholars, or from an invisible college of related research groups? We get advice from Bakhtin: "The novel must represent all the social and ideological voices of its era, that is, all the era's languages that have any claim of being significant; the novel must be a microcosm of heteroglossia" (Bakhtin, 1982, p. 411). Applied to expansive learning and research, this means that *all the conflicting and complementary voices of the various groups and strata in the activity system under scrutiny shall be involved and utilized.* As Bakhtin shows, this definitely includes the voices and nonacademic genres of the common people. Thus, instead of the classical argumentation within the single academic speech type, we get clashing fireworks of different speech types and languages.

The metaphor of parallel distributed systems or paradigmatic networks typically refers to the spatial dimension of sociality. The temporal dimension, the cooperation with those who have gone before, is exemplified in Darwin's "conversation" with Humboldt (see Gruber, 1984, p. 13–14) and in Einstein's "conversation" with Newton (see Glazman, 1972, p. 209–212). However, these are still examples of dialogues carried out by great individuals, operating very much within uniform speech types. The necessity of heteroglossia alters the nature of this indirect cooperation. Instead of an individual scientist arguing with his or her predecessor from the past, we have a heterogeneous community of parallel distributed units conversing with a variety of pasts, ranging from published classical theories to practical experiences preserved only in scattered remnants and personal memories.

THE THIRD INTERMEDIATE BALANCE

In this chapter I have argued that learning by expanding (intimately connected with the emerging historical type of collectively and expansively mastered activity) requires its own instruments of theoretical thinking.

In general terms, such expansive thinking requires a new conception of *concepts* as procedures for *ascending from the abstract to the concrete*. This is the logical essence of dialectical thinking.

Within this general instrument, three types of secondary instruments may be discerned: *springboards, models,* and *microcosms.* Among models, the historically most advanced type is that of *germ cell models,* expressing the initial simple contradictory relation giving rise to the development and transformation of the system in question.

Ascending from the abstract to the concrete corresponds to the logic of expansive transition from the individual actions to the qualitatively new collective activity. This means that dialectics as the tertiary instrument of expansive transitions is not understandable in terms of solitary thought. The specific form of sociality connected with this instrument is characterized by Bakhtin as heteroglossia or orchestrated polyphony.

The obvious question pointing toward the final chapter of this book is, What are the rules of expansive orchestration? How is unity created in diversity?

5

Toward an Expansive Methodology

THE CYCLE OF CULTURAL-HISTORICAL METHODOLOGY: VYGOTSKY, SCRIBNER, AND COLE

In her brilliant paper *Vygotsky's Uses of History,* Sylvia Scribner (1985) describes the four moments of Vygotsky's methodology as follows.

1. Vygotsky begins with observations about the behavior of *contemporary,* not primitive, adults. His starting points were little noticed but everyday cultural forms of behavior. Vygotsky called these phenomena "rudimentary forms." Each reveals the tripartite structure of cultural forms of behavior, consisting of environmental stimulus and response and a human-created symbolic stimulus mediating between the two. Each form reveals the "key to higher behavior."

2. To determine how rudimentary forms change to new forms requires a shift away from observations of everyday contemporary behavior to the historical transformation of structures. Historical and ethnopsychological information permits the reconstruction of the phases through which rudimentary forms pass on the way to becoming higher systems.

3. The historical sequence can serve as a model for an artificially evoked process of change in children, a process created through experimental means. The experiments will reveal in "pure and abstract form" how cultural development proceeds in ontogeny. The experimental-genetic method thus constitutes the third methodological moment and the source of the richest and most vital evidence.

4. Observations about the actual developmental progress of contemporary children constitute the fourth moment of theory building.

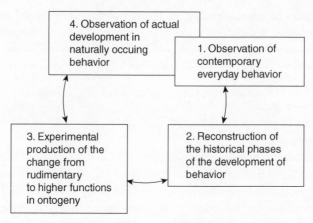

FIGURE 5.1. The four moments of Vygotsky's methodology (adapted after Scribner, 1985).

Vygotsky believed that models emerging from experimental studies are, of necessity, schematic and simplified. The experiment fails
to inform us about how higher systems are actually realized by the
child; an experimentally induced process never mirrors genetic
development as it occurs in life. Nor do experiments capture the
rich variety of child behavior in the many settings in which children grow up. Although the experiment models the process, concrete research is required to make the observations harmonious with
observations of naturally occurring behavior. Thus, Vygotsky begins
with and returns to observations of behavior in daily life to devise
and test models of the history of higher systems.

(Scribner, 1985, p. 135–137; see also Wertsch, 1985c, chapter 2.) Scribner's
reconstruction of Vygotsky's methodology may be summarized with the
help of Figure 5.1.

Scribner herself adds important considerations to Vygotsky's original
scheme.

In Vygotsky's theory, ... history appears as a single unidirectional course
of sociocultural change. It is a world process that informs us of the genesis of specifically human forms of behavior and their changing structures and functions in the past.... For purposes of concrete research, and
for theory development in the present, such a view seems inadequate.
Societies and cultural groups participate in world history at different
tempos and in different ways. Each has its own past history influencing

the nature of current change.... Individual societal histories are not independent of the world process, but neither are they reducible to it. To take account of this plurality, the Vygotskian framework needs to be expanded to incorporate ... the history of individual societies. (Scribner, 1985, p. 138–139)

Scribner also points out the insufficiency of focusing on child development alone. She proposes that "child history" be replaced with "life history" (Scribner, 1985, p. 140).

In another paper, Michael Cole (1986) goes a step further in the elaboration of the cultural-historical methodology. He analyzes the research efforts of the Soviet cultural-historical school and their later counterparts carried out by him and his colleagues, especially in the field of cross-cultural psychology. After that, he draws the following conclusion.

> The Soviet tradition ... emphasized broad historical changes in the nature of mind somewhat at the expense of synchronic variability arising from differences across concrete activity settings. Empirical research came late in the experience of the Soviet socio-historical scholars, and that research, when it at last became possible, followed the early tendency to concentrate on major historical shifts in political economic formations in place of detailed studies of particular activity systems and the functional psychological systems to which they give rise.

> The American tradition began from an applied-empirical demand to explain synchronic, culturally conditioned differences in quite specific domains of cognition in connection with equally specific domains of socio-cultural practice. It generated a great deal of research with relatively shallow, ahistorical, and eclectic underpinnings but a strong methodological, interdisciplinary base as a warrant for claims about the factors controlling different levels of performance across contexts within cultural groups.

> ... Overall, I see current progress in the development of the socio-historical school growing out of its cross-cultural research program as a process of combining the American emphasis on cultural context and the study of concrete activity systems with the Soviet emphasis on the mediated structure of higher psychological functions and the importance of history and political economy. (Cole, 1986, p. 19–21)

The methodological extensions put forward by Scribner and Cole are fully in line with the original intentions of Vygotsky, Luria, and Leont'ev, intentions that remained "imperfectly implemented in their research" (Cole, 1986, p. 21).

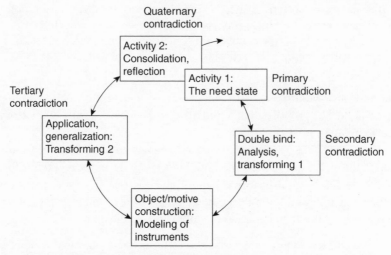

FIGURE 5.2. The cycle of expansive transition.

THE CYCLE OF EXPANSIVE METHODOLOGY

It is instructive to compare Vygotsky's methodological moments with the cycle of expansive transition put forward in Chapter 3. For this purpose, the cycle is once again depicted in Figure 5.2.

In Vygotsky's methodological cycle, the final object of investigation is the *higher functional system* or the higher form of behavior in its *ontogenetic* development. General cultural history as well as the history of particular societies and activity settings serve as sources of hypotheses for understanding and reconstructing ontogenesis. Ontogenesis, in turn, is basically understood in terms of interiorization. The general direction of investigation proceeds *from the socioculturally given to the individually acquired and interiorized.* The papers of Scribner and Cole are consistent with this basic direction.

What is left unexplained is how the socioculturally mediated forms of behavior, or the activity settings, or even societies, are generated or created in the first place. The fourth moment in Vygotsky's cycle provides for variation but not for creation.

The cycle of expansive transition addresses this very question. It traces the generation of socioculturally new activity systems by collectives of concrete human beings. Here, individually manifested doubt, hesitation, and disturbance constitute the starting point. The direction is *from the individual to the societal.* However, *the individual point of departure is itself understandable only as a cultural-historical product.*

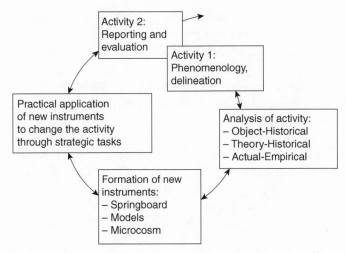

FIGURE 5.3. The methodological cycle of expansive developmental research.

Obviously both cycles express their own aspect of reality, or better, their own aspect of the cyclic movement of history. History is both interiorization and expansion. As was shown in Chapter 2, in connection with *The Psychology of Art,* the aspect of expansive transition was not foreign to Vygotsky. But it remained unintegrated into his general methodology. In Leont'ev's work, expansion appears as the phenomenon of actions growing into activities. But again, this remains a sidetrack.

Though the general directions of the two cycles are opposite, their inner structures are remarkably similar in terms of steps of concrete research. This similarity becomes even more visible when the cycle of expansive transition is transformed into a cycle of developmental research (Figure 5.3).

In the following, each step of the methodological cycle depicted in Figure 5.3 will be briefly elaborated. It will be a methodological sketch or outline, not a comprehensive presentation of expansive research methodology. The latter can only be made in connection with and saturated by concrete empirical research. That remains a task for the future.

PHENOMENOLOGY AND DELINEATION
OF THE ACTIVITY SYSTEM

The first step of expansive developmental research consists of (a) gaining a preliminary *phenomenological insight* into the nature of its discourse and problems as experienced by those involved in the activity and of (b) *delineating* the activity system under investigation.

As to (a), the researcher's task is to gain a grasp of the need state and primary contradiction beneath the surface of the problems, doubts, and uncertainties experienced among the participants of the activity. This may be accomplished through comprehensive reading of the internal and public discussion concerning the activity, through participant on-site observations, discussions with people involved in the activity or having expertise about it, and the like.

As to (b), expansive research is not dealing with activities "in general" but with real activities realized by identifiable persons in identifiable locations. Delineation is this very act of identifying the personal and geographical locus and limits of the activity. The reason for putting delineation after phenomenology is obvious. Often the locus and limits of activity can be properly defined only after a relatively extensive "dwelling" in it.

ANALYSIS OF ACTIVITY

The second step consists of rigorous analyses of the activity system. These analyses may be divided into three (see Holzkamp, 1983): (a) the *object-historical analysis,* (b) the *theory-historical analysis,* and (c) the *actual-empirical analysis.*

(a) The object-historical analysis implies identifying and analyzing the successive developmental phases of the activity system. However, it aims not only at periodization but especially at uncovering the secondary contradictions giving rise to the transitions from one developmental phase to another. The analysis is carried out with the help of the general models of activity (presented in Figures 2.6 and 2.7), as well as with the help of techniques for describing the sequential structure of transitions (such as those used earlier in the four cases).

As Leont'ev stressed, the identity of any activity is primarily determined by its object. Thus, the analysis takes as its point of departure the qualitative transformations of the object, itself understood as an activity system. However, the system of object activity cannot be regarded as external to the central activity, only to be "connected" with it. To the contrary, the object is to be analyzed above all as an integral component of the central activity while acknowledging it as a relatively independent activity system of its own. This procedure, moving "from within" the central activity out to the object activity and back into the central activity, is essential if the researcher is to preserve his or her grasp of the self-movement, the self-organizational dynamics of the activity under investigation. In other words, the object-historical analysis cannot be reduced to the self-contained object. The object becomes an object *(Gegenstand)* only as a component of the developing central activity.

(b) The theory-historical analysis is motivated by the fact that an activity system in any of its developmental phases utilizes a set of shared secondary artifacts, that is, concepts and models. These cultural artifacts are embodied in different modalities (i.e., handbooks, working instructions, fixed procedures for classification and diagnosis, etc.), but all they are in principle public knowledge and function as general conceptual instruments of the practical activity. The degree to which these conceptual instruments are acknowledged as theoretical or theory-based is immaterial here. What is essential is that they are partly constructed within the central activity, partly imported into it from without. The latter aspect requires a special analysis of the development of the theories introduced into the central activity and eventually of the instrument-producing activities behind those theories. Here again, though a descriptive periodization may be the necessary beginning, the main aim of the analysis is to identify and trace the formation of the secondary contradictions initiated by or connected to the secondary instruments of the successive developmental periods.

(c) Publicly available objectified instruments are powerful constraints, but, being generalizations, they are always interpretable and applicable in multiple ways, for a multitude of purposes. Therefore, object-historical and theory-historical analyses are not enough. They need to be complemented by actual-empirical analysis of the internalized and invented models professed and actually used or upheld by the participants in the activity.

Three tenets may be put forward for the actual-empirical analysis. *First,* the models actually applied in the activity should if possible be analyzed on all the three levels of activity/motive, action/goal, and operation/conditions (recall Tables 3.1 and 3.2). *Second,* the models should be analyzed as declarative conceptions, as procedural performances, as social discourses or interactions, as communicational networks, and as organizational structures. *Third,* the models should be evaluated with the help of the results of the historical analyses ([a] and [b]) and with the help of the five general historical types of models presented earlier (prototypes, classificatory models, procedural models, systemic models, germ cell models).

One essential outcome and instrument of the three complementary types of analyses presented is the definition of the *object unit* of the given developmental phase of the activity under investigation. By object unit I mean the typical slice or chunk of the object handled and molded by the subject at a time. Such a unit enables us to follow the "life span" of the object from raw material to finished product. Being handled directly or indirectly by all compartments and hierarchical levels within the community of the activity, it also enables us to study in a compact form the breaches and links between individual actions and the overall activity. Once identified, the object unit thus provides a strategic lens or magnifying glass through which the inner movement of the activity system becomes visible.

Another outcome of the analyses is a hypothetic picture of the next, more advanced developmental form of the activity system. Such a provisional model, however, is not yet a sufficient general instrument for accomplishing the expansive transition. Rather, it is a necessarily sketchy general device for guiding the process further.

The ultimate aim of the analysis is not just to reveal the inner contradictions and developmental logic of the activity to the researcher. The aim is to make the participants, the potential subjects of the activity themselves, face the secondary contradiction. In other words, the analysis functions as the midwife for *bringing about the double bind,* or at least an anticipatory grasp of the double bind in the form of an intense conceptual conflict. This can be achieved by letting the participants reconstruct the analysis through their own actions. Such a reconstruction typically takes place on the basis of selected and condensed materials as well as tasks involving debate between the participants. Much as in the case of *Seven Brothers,* the emergence and aggravation of the double bind may occur in several successive steps, each being at first only partially or temporarily resolved.

FORMATION OF NEW INSTRUMENTS

The third main step is easily recognized as the most dramatic one in the expansive methodology. The participants of the activity system under investigation are pushed into formulating qualitatively new models as genuine keys for resolving the double bind. As was shown earlier in this chapter, this step consists of three main elements: (a) finding a *springboard,* (b) formulating the *general instrumental model* and its derivative models, and (c) constructing a *microcosm* for taking over the responsibility of elaborating further the instrumental models and turning them into new forms of practice.

(a) How is a springboard found? Is it an intuitive event that cannot be purposefully facilitated and directed? I will use the work of G. S. Altshuller (1984) on "creativity as an exact science" to formulate an alternative conception. For Altshuller, the crucial problem of technical inventions is how to overcome the object-indifferent search typical of the various methods of brainstorming, syncetics, and so on.

> For instance, the focal object method consists in transposing features of a few objects chosen at random to an object needing improvement as a result of which one can come up with unusual combinations and overcome psychological inertia. Thus if a "tiger" is taken as an accidental object and "pencil" as the (focal) object to be improved, then one obtains a combination such as "striped pencil", "rapacious pencil", "fanged pencil". By examining these combinations and developing them one can sometimes come up with original ideas. (Altshuller, 1984, p. 13)

Needless to say, such an object-indifferent method may require thousands of chance combinations before it "hits the jackpot." Altshuller characterizes such methods with the help of metaphor. "Imagine that we are studying the actions of a helmsman aboard ship on a meandering river. We want to know nothing about the river itself but only try to explain the actions of the helmsman in purely psychological terms" (Altshuller, 1984, p. 8).

Altshuller's own solution is that creative solutions require specific, *object-typical notational systems* with the help of which one can represent, analyze, and elaborate the problem. On the basis of painstaking analysis of thousands of patents and historical inventions, Altshuller has developed a complex apparatus of complementary notational systems for technical problems. First of all, he emphasizes that technical problems have to be transformed into technical contradictions and further into physical contradictions. "In physical contradictions [PC] the conflict of demands is intensified to the maximum. Therefore at first glance the PC seems absurd, inadmissible by definition" (Altshuller, 1984, p. 29).

To represent the problem, Altshuller applies what he calls "S-Field Analysis." "In any inventive problem there is an object.... This object cannot realize the required action on its own but has to interact with its environment or with another object. In so doing any change is accompanied by the discharge, absorption or conversion of energy. The two substances and a field can be completely dissimilar, but they are necessary and sufficient for the formation of a minimal technical system which has been given the name S-Field (from Substance and Field)" (Altshuller, 1984, p. 52). There is an elaborate notational system for constructing simple graphic S-Field representations out of complex problems. "There are rules which permit one to build an exact model of the problem. Thus, into a pair of conflicting elements it is necessary to introduce the artefact.... If one does not include the artefact in the conflicting pair, the model of the problem breaks down and we are back to square one" (Altshuller, 1984, p. 79; recall the problem of thirdness).

There is still a more specific system of notation, namely, the Method of Little Men, as Altshuller calls it. This is a related to the use of empathy by the inventor's "becoming the object," looking for a solution from the position and viewpoint of the object. This method has disadvantages. "In identifying himself with a particular machine (or a part of it) and examining possible alterations to it, the inventor involuntarily selects those which are acceptable to man and rejects any which are unacceptable to the human organism, such as dissecting, splintering, dissolving in acid, etc. The indivisibility of the human organism prevents one from successfully employing empathy in solving many problems" (Altshuller, 1984, p. 108). Representing and modeling parts of the object graphically in the form of groups of little men preserve the power of empathy without its inherent shortcomings.

Altshuller's notational systems are actually constructed languages for gaining a liberating *holistic but at the same time analytic view* of the overall structure and dynamics of the contradictory situation. In the four cases analyzed in this book, the springboard was invented as if by a lucky accident because the language in which it was potentially embedded remained invisible and unrecognized. Expansive research and intervention proceed the opposite way. The participants are provided with a language (or several complementary languages) for working out the springboard. These languages are not arbitrary. Their power depends on their ability to penetrate and organize the object. Thus, they are *constructed on the basis of the object-historical, theory-historical, and actual-empirical analyses.*

(b) In expansive research, the transition from a provided language to a springboard and over to a new general model is seldom clear-cut and unidirectional. Moreover, it would be fallacious to expect and demand that each step and substep be taken by the participants as if through their own discovery. Certainly it is important to let the participants proceed through tasks of problem solving and problem finding, so that the new general model is not acquired only mechanically and superficially at the outset. But no matter how cleverly such tasks are designed, the new model represents the *given new* and thus includes the aspect of guided or even imposed acquisition.

This aspect is related to the fact that the springboard – as a personal experience of revelation – does not necessarily appear *before* the formulation of the new general model. To many an individual participant in a process of expansive transition, the gist of the transition may be personally experienced, acquire a *personal sense* in Leont'ev's terminology, only in a postponed fashion, as the new general model is studied in an objectified form or even applied in practice. This is the meaning of the double-headed arrows in Figures 5.2 and 5.3. They imply the possibility of "returning," for example to the step of finding a personal springboard when the overall transition has reached the step of model formulation or application.

Such a postponement in itself is not necessarily a danger to be avoided. This implies that the formation of new instruments, though outwardly the most dramatic step of the transition, is in fact *not* the decisive step from the point of view of the resolution of the contradictions. In this phase, there is generally much enthusiasm among the participants: Keys are being found. But the awareness of obstacles, uncertainty, and struggle is heightened in the phases of analysis and application.

Previously I pointed out that the analysis of the activity produces a sketchy hypothetical model of the next, more advanced developmental form of the activity system. To make this sketchy hypothesis a real general instrument of expansion it is necessary to elaborate the *strategic component(s)* of the activity system (strategic "corners" of the triangle) into novel models. Most typically, the strategic component is the *object* of the activity.

For example, in order to find an expansive solution to the mounting contradictions of the work activity of general practitioners or family physicians (recall the example in Chapter 2), it may be necessary to create a new model of the object of their work. Traditionally the object is conceived of as "a sickness" or as "a patient," understood as an individual with certain symptoms and illnesses to be cured. Today, the symptoms have become increasingly complex and subtle, including psychic and social factors intertwined and not reducible to the classified biomedical illnesses. A reconceptualization of the object may require a model of the patient as situated in his or her life activity, embedded in a model for conducting "community diagnosis" (see e.g., Haglund, 1983). Such models would be general instruments with which the practitioners could reorganize their diagnostic procedures.

On the other hand, the strategic component may also be the *instrument* of the activity. This is typically the case when the research is dealing with an activity faced with the incorporation and implementation of a major new complex technology. Toikka's (1986) analysis of the implementation of a FMS (Flexible Manufacturing System) in a machine engineering factory is a case in point. On the basis of collective modeling of the historical development and inner contradictions of the production process in question (germ cell models), systemic models for planning and mastering the implementation were developed with the workers.

The system model of FMS consists of two main parts: on the one hand of the *process* model (layout + material flow), on the other hand of the *control system* model (units and hierarchy of control functions as a graphical model). Actually the system model is a paper simulator with which we analyzed the process and control events needed for manufacturing a certain gear. On the basis of the system model it was possible to develop concrete models for special problem situations. So far we have developed the procedures for both a change of batch and restarting after breakdown in the turning cell. (Toikka, 1986, p. 4)

An acquisition process based on historical insight and leading to real application is far from mechanical and unidirectional.

The final models produced in working groups and plenary discussions increasingly often exceed the quality of the model solutions made by the researchers. This also means that the collective modeling process is a valuable method of obtaining new information about the system. An interesting thing, too, is that there is no qualitative difference between the results of the worker and management groups.... The training increasingly includes elements of planning. The more concrete the analysis of the system has become, the more open questions have entered the discussion. For instance, while simulating the operations required in the breakdown situation of the turning cell, the workers found out a more elegant and simple procedure for restarting the cell than that planned by the designer of the central control system. (Toikka, 1986, p. 4)

(c) For the formation of microcosms, the developmental nature of intersubjectivity is of essential importance. Fichtner (1984) has suggested a developmental sequence of three basic forms of intersubjectivity.

The first and most rudimentary form of intersubjectivity is called *coordination*. Individuals are gathered together to act upon a common object, but their individual actions are only externally related to each other. They still act as separate individuals, each according to his or her individual task. Interaction is not reflected upon; it occurs mainly in the form of spontaneous reactions and attachments.

The second, intermediate form is that of *cooperation*. "Each individual has to relate an over-individual task to the individual aim of the action and he has to maintain the relationship. With regard to the common task, he has to balance both actions and action results of his partner with his own actions and their results. In addition to this, he must influence actions and results of his partner if necessary, again with regard to the common task" (Fichtner, 1984, p. 217). These are conscious, goal-directed sequences of interaction, aiming at successful joint completion of given tasks or successful joint solution of given problems.

The third form of intersubjectivity is called *reflective communication*. The living knowledge of personal subjects here develops in spoken and other symbolic processes. It becomes concrete as collective reflectiveness, or collective subjectivity. "The collective subject manifests itself and the laws of its functioning not so much through the inner structures of the individual's consciousness as through external practical activity involving objects and through collective cognitive activity with systems of objectified knowledge" (Lektorsky, 1984, p. 241). In this most advanced form of intersubjectivity, the interaction system as a whole, in its spatial and temporal-historical dimensions, becomes the focus of reflection and self-regulation.

Fichtner's three forms of intersubjectivity correspond to the three levels of operation, action, and activity, as presented in Tables 3.1 and 3.2. In Fichtner's argument, the developmental forms of intersubjectivity are not regarded as ontogenetic stages but as *phases of any cycle of genuine learning activity*. This corresponds very well to the idea of expansive cycles. Each expansive transition is a transition from the individual to the collective, or from coordination to reflective communication.

A microcosm is a social test bench and a spearhead of the coming culturally more advanced form of the activity system. The conscious formation of a microcosm as a substep of expansive research corresponds to the *formation of a vehicle for transition from cooperation to reflective communication*. In other words, the microcosm is supposed to reach within itself and propagate outward reflective communication while expanding and therefore eventually dissolving into the whole community of the activity.

PRACTICAL APPLICATION OF NEW INSTRUMENTS

The new instruments can only be implemented in selected *strategic tasks*. Such tasks represent the points of probable breakthroughs into the qualitatively more advanced form of practice. In carrying out these tasks with the help of the new instruments, the participants of the activity system face intense conflicts between the old and the given new ways of doing and thinking – the tertiary contradiction.

These conflicts take various forms. They may be struggles between the old rules and the new instruments, or between the old division of labor and the new communication emerging in the microcosm. They may also be clashes between the traditional and the novel instruments, often experienced as fear, resistance, stress, and other intense psychic conflicts within individuals and collectives.

The task of research is not only to register and support this drama. The most demanding task is to trace and analyze the *solutions* to the conflicts produced by the participants in their daily actions. The *created new* resides in such practical solutions. The practical solutions that represent the unexpected, the unrecognizable, are actually *initial forms of new theories.* Most likely they are uneasily incorporated into the given new, somehow rebelling against it but still indispensable for it as its most dynamic ingredients – as Eero was indispensable to the Seven Brothers in spite of his arrogance.

For the researchers, this step of expansive research is the most difficult and the most rewarding one. The difficulty is twofold. First, the application and generalization of the new instrument constitute a lengthy process requiring patient on-site data collection. Second, in the preceding phase the researchers and key participants in the expansive transition have strongly committed themselves to the given new general model and derivative instruments. Now the researchers suddenly have to give up the advocacy of those instruments and open their eyes to record events and ideas that are all but foreign to the models or sometimes make the models look outright ridiculous.

The reward awaits in the careful analysis of such data. The researchers face the fact that all their skillful efforts to make the participants acquire and apply the culturally more advanced models according to a plan have been partially futile. A genuine expansive cycle inevitably produces not only civilization but also an ingredient of wilderness. To gain a theoretical grasp of this wilderness, to find and understand something unexpected as a piece of the history of the future is the reward.

REPORTING

Reporting and assessing outcomes of expansive research are not easy. The voyage through the zone of proximal development is best followed and recorded by employing a set of multiple methods, ranging from phenomenological and anthropological observation and historical analysis to rigorous cognitive analysis of performances, conceptions, and discourse processes. The sheer amount and variety of data collected make new types of reporting necessary.

There is a simple rule for such reporting. One should apply the historico-genetic method in the presentation of the research findings. In other words, one should reproduce the actual course of the expansive transition, following its basic temporal structure. This does not exclude seemingly atemporal excursions and digressions into conceptual, descriptive, statistical, experimental, and comparative terrains.

This type of reporting has ancestors and relatives in the genres of the diary, the expedition report, the travel story, and the developmental novel. On the other hand, the chronicle, the biography, and the historical novel are not its closest relatives. There is an important difference between these two groups. The former group is characterized by committed quest for new visions and conquests. The latter group is characterized by a kind of outsider's wisdom, easy to profess after the events have ended.

THE TERMINAL BALANCE

What is the historical mission of expansive developmental research? Against the background of the analysis presented in this book, the task may be defined as follows.

Expansive developmental research aims at making cycles of expansive transition collectively mastered journeys through zones of proximal development. In other words, it aims at furnishing people with tertiary and secondary instruments necessary for the mastery of qualitative transformations of their activity systems.

6

Epilogue

What are the main findings of this study? In a simplified and condensed manner, the findings may be presented as the following set of categories.

1. The category of activity, expressed in the form of the triangular models depicted in Figures 2.4–2.7.
2. The category of learning activity, or learning by expanding, expressed in the form of the triangular models depicted in Figures 2.11 and 2.12.
3. The reinterpreted and extended category of the zone of proximal development, corresponding to the sequential structure of learning by expanding, expressed in the cyclic model depicted in Figure 3.3.
4. The categorical framework for identifying and analyzing historical types of activity systems and expansive transitions, depicted in Figure 4.9.
5. The categorical framework for identifying and analyzing instruments of learning by expanding, elaborated in Tables 4.5–4.8.
6. The outline of a methodology for expansive developmental research, summarized in Figure 5.3.

It is the nature of theoretical research that the categories found do not corroborate, verify, or falsify themselves. This kind of research resembles an expedition. When Columbus returned from his expedition, he claimed he had found India. The categorical content of this claim was erroneous, yet his findings initiated an unforeseen expansive cycle of practical and conceptual development.

Analogously, I am sure the contents of the categories found in this study will be proven inadequate many times over. The real question is, Will they become instrumental in bringing about and mastering expansive cycles at different levels and in different branches of theoretical and practical activity?

REFERENCES

Alt, R. (1975). *Erziehung und Gesellschaft*. Berlin: Volk und Wissen (in German).

Altshuller, G. S. (1984). *Creativity as an exact science: The theory of the solution of inventive problems*. New York: Gordon and Breach.

Anthony, G., Hunter, R. & Thompson, Z. (2014). Expansive learning: Lessons from one teacher's learning journey. *ZDM: The International Journal on Mathematics Education, 46(2)*.

Argyris, C. & Schön, D. A. (1974). *Theory in practice: Increasing professional effectiveness*. San Francisco: Jossey-Bass.

(1978). *Organizational learning*. Reading, MA: Addison-Wesley.

Arlin, P. K. (1984). Adolescent and adult thought: A structural interpretation. In M. L. Commons, F. A. Richards & C. Armon (Eds.), *Beyond formal operations: Late adolescent and adult cognitive development*. New York: Praeger (pp. 258–271).

Arsen'ev, A. S., Bibler, V. S. & Kedrov, B. M. (1967). *Analiz razvivajuchegosja poniatia*. Moskva: Nauka (in Russian).

Atlas, J. A. (1985). A re-opening of the question of primitive mentality. *New Ideas in Psychology, 3*, 335–339.

Bakhtin, M. M. (1973). *Problems of Dostoyevsky's poetics*. Ann Arbor, MI: Ardis.

(1981). *The dialogic imagination: Four essays by M. M. Bakhtin*. Edited by M. Holquist. Austin: University of Texas Press.

(1982). *The dialogic imagination*. Austin: University of Texas Press.

(1986). *Speech genres and other late essays*. Austin: University of Texas Press.

Bakhurst, D. (1991). *Consciousness and revolution in Soviet philosophy: From the Bolsheviks to Evald Ilyenkov*. Cambridge: Cambridge University Press.

(2009). Reflections on activity theory. *Educational Review, 61(2)*, 197–210.

Baltes, P. B., Reese, H. W. & Nesselroade, J. R. (1977). *Life-span developmental psychology: Introduction to research methods*. Monterey, CA: Brooks/Cole.

Bartlett, F. (1941). Fatigue following highly skilled work. *Proceedings of the Royal Society of London, B*, 131, 247–257.

(1958). *Thinking: An experimental and social study*. London: George Allen & Unwin.

Basseches, M. (1984). *Dialectical thinking and adult development*. Norwood, NJ: Ablex.

Bateson, G. (1972). *Steps to an ecology of mind*. New York: Ballantine Books.

(1978). The birth of a matrix or double bind and epistemology. In M. M. Berger (Ed.), *Beyond the double bind*. New York: Brunner/Mazel (pp. 39–64).

Bereiter, C. (1985). Toward a solution of the learning paradox. *Review of Educational Research*, 55, 201–226.

Berger, M. M. (Ed.) (1978). *Beyond the double bind*. New York: Brunner/Mazel.

von Bertalanffy, L. (1968). *General system theory: Foundations, development, applications*. New York: Braziller.

Bibler, V. S. (1983–84). Thinking as creation (Introduction to the logic of mental dialogue). *Soviet Psychology*, XXII(1), 33–54.

Bibler, W. S. (1970). Hegel, Marx und das Problem der Wandlungen des logischen Aufbaus der wissenschaftlichen Tätigkeit. In T. I. Oiserman (Hrg.), *Karl Marx und die moderne Philosophie*. Moskau: Progress (S. 129–168; in German).

Bloomfield, B. P. (1986). *Modeling the world: The social constructions of systems analysts*. Oxford: Basil Blackwell.

Blunden, A. (2010). *An interdisciplinary theory of activity*. Chicago: Haymarket Books.

Bohm, D. (1980). *Wholeness and the implicate order*. London: Routledge & Kegan Paul.

Bolgar, R. R. (1969). The training of elites in Greek education. In R. Wilkinson (Ed.), *Governing elites: Studies in training and selection*. New York: Oxford University Press (pp. 23–49).

Borras, Jr., S. M. (2008). La Vía Campesina and its global campaign for agrarian reform. *Journal of Agrarian Change*, 8(2–3), 258–289.

Bratus, B. S. (1986). The place of fine literature in the development of a scientific psychology of personality. *Soviet Psychology*, XXV(2), 91–103.

Bratus, B. S. & Lishin, O. V. (1983). Laws of the development of activity and problems in the psychological and pedagogical shaping of the personality. *Soviet Psychology*, XXI(1), 38–50.

Braverman, H. (1974). *Labor and monopoly capital: The degradation of work in the twentieth century*. New York: Monthly Review Press.

Brehmer, B. (1980). In one word: Not from experience. *Acta Psychologica*, 45, 223–241.

Broadbent, D. E. (1977). Levels, hierarchies, and the locus of control. *Quarterly Journal of Experimental Psychology*, 29, 181–201.

Brödner, P. (1985). *Skill-based production – the superior concept to the "unmanned factory."* Paper presented at the 8th International Conference on Production Research: Towards the Factory of the Future. Stuttgart, West Germany, August 20–22, 1985.

Bronfenbrenner, U. (1977). Toward an experimental ecology of human development. *American Psychologist*, 32, 513–532.

(1979). *The ecology of human development: Experiments by nature and design*. Cambridge: Harvard University Press.

(1983). The context of development and the development of context. In R. M. Lerner (Ed.), *Developmental psychology: Historical and philosophical perspectives*. Hillsdale: Lawrence Erlbaum (pp. 147–184).

Bronkhorst, L. H., Meijer, P., Koster, B., Akkerman, S. F. & Vermunt, J. D. (2013). Consequential research designs in research on teacher education. *Teaching and Teacher Education*, 33, 90–99.

Bronowski, J. (1978). *The visionary eye: Essays in the arts, literature, and science.* Cambridge, MA: The MIT Press.

Broughton, J. M. (1984). Not beyond formal operations but beyond Piaget. In M. L. Commons, F. A. Richards & C. Armon (Eds.), *Beyond formal operations: Late adolescent and adult cognitive development.* New York: Praeger (pp. 395–412).

Brown, A. L. (1978). Knowing when, where, and how to remember: A problem of metacognition. In R. Glaser (Ed.), *Advances in instructional psychology.* Vol. 1. Hillsdale, NJ: Lawrence Erlbaum.

(1982). Learning and development: The problems of compatibility, access and induction. *Human Development*, 25, 89–115.

(1992). Design experiments: Theoretical and methodological challenges in creating complex interventions in classroom settings. *The Journal of the Learning Sciences*, 2(2), 141–178.

Brown, A. L. & DeLoache, J. S. (1978). Skills, plans, and self-regulation. In R. Siegler (Ed.), *Children's thinking: What develops?* Hillsdale, NJ: Lawrence Erlbaum.

Brown, A. L., Campione, J. C. & Day, J. D. (1981). Learning to learn: On training students to learn from texts. *Educational Researcher*, 10, 14–21.

Brown, A. L. & French, L. A. (1979). The zone of proximal development: Implications for intelligence testing in the year 2000. *Intelligence*, 3, 255–277.

Bruner, J. S. (1962). Introduction. In L. S. Vygotsky, *Thought and language.* Cambridge: The MIT Press (pp. v–x).

(1974). Going beyond the information given. In J. S. Bruner, *Beyond the information given.* London: George Allen & Unwin (pp. 218–238).

(1976). Nature and uses of immaturity. In J. S. Bruner, A. Jolly & K. Sylva (Eds.), *Play: Its role in development and evolution.* New York: Basic Books (pp. 28–64).

(1985a). On teaching thinking: An afterthought. In S. F. Chipman, J. W. Segal & R. Glaser (Eds.), *Thinking and learning skills.* Vol. 2. *Research and open questions.* Hillsdale, NJ: Lawrence Erlbaum (pp. 597–608).

(1985b). Vygotsky: A historical and conceptual perspective. In J. V. Wertsch (Ed.), *Culture, communication, and cognition: Vygotskian perspectives.* Cambridge: Cambridge University Press (pp. 21–34).

Bruner, J. (1986). *Actual minds, possible worlds.* Cambridge, MA: Harvard University Press.

Bullowa, M. (Ed.) (1979). *Before speech: The beginnings of human communication.* Cambridge: Cambridge University Press.

Bulmer, R. (1967). Why is the cassowary not a bird? A problem of zoological taxonomy among the Karam of the New Guinea highlands. *Man*, 2, 5–25.

Bunn, J. H. (1981). *The dimensionality of signs, tools and models.* Bloomington: Indiana University Press.

Buss, A. R. (1979). Dialectics, history, and development: The historical roots of the individual-society dialectic. In P. B. Baltes & O. G. Brim, Jr. (Eds.), *Life-span development and behavior.* Vol. 2. New York: Academic Press (pp. 313–333).

Carey, S. (1985). *Conceptual change in childhood*. Cambridge, MA: The MIT Press.

Cazden, C. B. (1981). Performance before competence: Assistance to child discourse in the zone of proximal development. *The Quarterly Newsletter of the Laboratory of Comparative Human Cognition*, 3(1), 5–8.

Chaiklin, S. (1985). *Beyond inferencing: Some cognitive processes that affect the direction of student reasoning in applying physical-science beliefs*. Paper presented at the conference "Cognitive Processes in Student Learning," Lancaster, England, July 18–21, 1985.

Cherns, A. (1980). Work and work organizations in the age of the microprocessor. In K. D. Duncan, M. M. Gruneberg & D. Wallis (Eds.), *Changes in working life*. Chichester: Wiley (pp. 253–268).

Cole, M. (1983). Introduction to V. V. Davydov & A. K. Markova, A concept of educational activity for schoolchildren. *Soviet Psychology*, XXI(2), 50–51.

(1985). The zone of proximal development: Where culture and cognition create each other. In J. V. Wertsch (Ed.), *Culture, communication, and cognition: Vygotskian perspectives*. Cambridge: Cambridge University Press (pp. 146–161).

(1986). *Cross-cultural research in the socio-historical tradition*. Paper presented at the First International Congress on Activity Theory, West Berlin, October 3–5, 1986.

(1988). Cross-cultural research in the sociohistorical tradition. *Human Development*, 31, 137–151.

Cole, M. & Griffin, P. (1980). Cultural amplifiers reconsidered. In D. R. Olson (Ed.), *The social foundations of language and thought*. New York: Norton (pp. 343–364).

Cole, M. & Scribner, S. (1978). Introduction. In L. S. Vygotsky, *Mind in society: The development of higher psychological processes*. Cambridge, MA: Harvard University Press (pp. 1–14).

Commons, M. L., Richards, F. A. & Armon, C. (Eds.) (1984). *Beyond formal operations: Late adolescent and adult cognitive development*. New York: Praeger.

Coulmas, F. & Ehlich, K. (Eds.) (1982). *Writing in focus*. The Hague: Mouton.

Cuban, L. (1984). *How teachers taught*. New York: Longman.

Cussins, A. (1992). Content, embodiment and objectivity: The theory of cognitive trails. *Mind*, 101, 651–688.

Damerow, P. (1980). Handlung und Erkenntnis in der genetischen Erkenntnistheorie Piagets und in der Hegelschen "Logik." In H. Furth (Ed.), *Arbeit und Reflexion*. Köln: Pahl-Rugenstein (pp. 159–187; in German).

Damerow, P., Furth, P., Heidtmann, B. & Lefèvre, W. (1980). Probleme der materialistischen Dialektik. In P. Furth (Ed.), *Arbeit und Reflexion*. Köln: Pahl-Rugenstein (pp. 234–282; in German).

Davis, L. E. (1980). Changes in work environments: The next 20 years. In K. D. Duncan, M. M. Gruneberg & D. Wallis (Eds.), *Changes in working life*. Chichester: Wiley (pp. 197–216).

Davydov, V. V. (1982). The psychological structure and contents of the learning activity in school children. In R. Glaser & J. Lompscher (Eds.), *Cognitive and motivational aspects of instruction*. Berlin: Deutscher Verlag der Wissenschaften (pp. 37–44).

(1990). *Types of generalization in instruction: Logical and psychological problems in the structuring of school curricula*. Reston, VA: National Council of Teachers of Mathematics.

(2008). *Problems of developmental instruction: A theoretical and experimental psychological study*. New York: Nova.

Davydov, V. V. & Radzikhovskii, L. A. (1985). Vygotsky's theory and the activity-oriented approach in psychology. In J. V. Wertsch (Ed.), *Culture, communication, and cognition: Vygotskian perspectives*. Cambridge: Cambridge University Press (pp. 35–65).

Davydov, V. V. & Zinchenko, V. P. (1982). The principle of development in psychology. *Soviet Psychology*, XX(1), 22–45.

Davydov, V. V., Markova, A. K. & Shumilin, E. A. (1980). Psihologicheskie problemy formirovanija potrebnosti i motivov uchebnoi dejatel'nosti. In *Morivy uchebnoi i obschestvenno poleznoi dejatelnosti skolnikov i studentov*. Moskva: MOPI (pp. 3–23; in Russian).

Dawydow, W. W. (1977). *Arten der Verallgemeinerung im Unterricht*. Berlin: Volk und Wissen (in German).

Dawydow, W. W., Lompscher, J. & Markowa, A. K. (1982). *Ausbildung der Lerntätigkeit bei Schülern*. Berlin: Volk und Wissen (in German).

Day, J. D. (1983). The zone of proximal development. In M. Pressley & J. R. Levin (Eds.), *Cognitive strategy research: Psychological foundations*. New York: Springer (pp. 155–175).

De Kleer, J. & Brown, J. S. (1983). Assumptions and ambiguities in mechanistic mental models. In D. Gentner & A. L. Stevens (Eds.), *Mental models*. Hillsdale, NJ: Lawrence Erlbaum (pp. 155–190).

Dell, P. F. (1980). Researching the family theories of schizophrenia: An exercise in epistemological confusion. *Family Process*, 19, 321–335.

(1982). Beyond homeostasis: Toward a concept of coherence. *Family Process*, 21, 21–41.

Dewey, J. (1910). *How we think*. Boston: Heath.

Dougherty, J. W. D. & Keller, C. M. (1985). Taskonomy: A practical approach to knowledge structures. In J. W. D. Dougherty (Ed.), *Directions in cognitive anthropology*. Urbana: University of Illinois Press (pp. 161–174).

Dreyfus, H. & Dreyfus, S. (1986). *Mind over machine: The power of human intuition and expertise in the era of the computer*. New York: The Free Press.

Edwards, D. & Middleton, D. (1986). Conversation with Bartlett. *Quarterly Newsletter of the Laboratory of Comparative Human Cognition*, 8, 79–89.

Eisenstein, E. (1985). On the printing press as an agent of change. In D. R. Olson, N. Torrance & A. Hildyard (Eds.), *Literacy, language, and learning: The nature and consequences of reading and writing*. Cambridge: Cambridge University Press (pp. 19–33).

El'konin, D. B. (1977). Toward the problem of stages in the mental development of the child. In M. Cole (Ed.), *Soviet developmental psychology*. White Plains, NY: Sharpe (pp. 538–563).

Eliot, T. S. (1950). Introduction. In M. Twain, *The adventures of Huckleberry Finn*. London: The Cresset Press (pp. vii–xvi).

Engels, F. (1975). *Anti-Dühring*. Moscow: Progress.

(1976). Ludwig Feuerbach and the end of classical German philosophy. In K. Marx & F. Engels, *Selected works in three volumes*. Vol. 3. Moscow: Progress (pp. 335–376).

Engelsted, N., Hedegaard, M., Karpatschof, B. & Mortensen, A. (Eds.) (1993). *The societal subject*. Aarhus: Aarhus University Press.

Engeström, R. (1995). Voice as communicative action. *Mind, Culture, and Activity*, 2, 192–214.

Engeström, Y. (1987). *Learning by expanding: An activity-theoretical approach to developmental research*. Helsinki: Orienta-Konsultit.

(1989). The cultural-historical theory of activity and the study of political repression. *International Journal of Mental Health*, 17(4), 29–41.

(1989). The cultural-historical theory of activity and the study of political repression. *International Journal of Mental Health*, 17(4), 29–41.

(1991a). *Activity theory and individual and social transformation. Multidisciplinary Newsletter for Activity Theory*, No. 7/8, 14–15.

(1991b). Developmental work research: A paradigm in practice. *The Quarterly Newsletter of the Laboratory of Comparative Human Cognition*, 13, 79–80.

(1991c). Developmental work research: Reconstructing expertise through expansive learning. In M. I. Nurminen & G. R. S. Weir (Eds.), *Human jobs and computer interfaces*. Amsterdam: Elsevier Science.

(1991d). Non scolae sed vitae discimus: Toward overcoming the encapsulation of school learning. *Learning and Instruction*, 1, 243–259.

(1993). Developmental studies of work as a testbench of activity theory: Analyzing the work of general practitioners. In S. Chaiklin & J. Lave (Eds.), *Understanding practice: Perspectives on activity and context*. Cambridge: Cambridge University Press.

(1994). The working health center project: Materializing zones of proximal development in a network of organizational learning. In T. Kauppinen & M. Lahtonen (Eds.) *Action research in Finland*. Helsinki: Ministry of Labour.

(1995). Innovative organizational learning in medical and legal settings. In L. M. W. Martin, K. Nelson & E. Tobach (Eds.), *Sociocultural psychology: Theory and practice of doing and knowing*. Cambridge: Cambridge University Press.

(1996a). Development as breaking away and opening up: A challenge to Vygotsky and Piaget. *Swiss Journal of Psychology*, 55, 126–132.

(1996a). Developmental work research as educational research: Looking ten years back and into the zone of proximal development. *Nordisk Pedagogik/Journal of Nordic Educational Research*, 16, 131–143.

(1996b). Interobjectivity, ideality, and dialectics. *Mind, Culture and Activity*, 3, 259–265.

(1996c). The tensions of judging: Handling cases of driving under the influence of alcohol in Finland and California. In Y. Engeström & D. Middleton (Eds.), *Cognition and communication at work*. Cambridge: Cambridge University Press (pp. 199–232).

(1999a). Activity theory and individual and social transformation. In Y. Engeström, R. Miettinen & R-L. Punamäki (Eds.), *Perspectives on activity theory*. Cambridge: Cambridge University Press.

(1999b). Expansive visibilization of work: An activity-theoretical perspective. *Computer Supported Cooperative Work*, 8, 63–93.

(1999c). Innovative learning in work teams: Analyzing cycles of knowledge creation in practice. In Y. Engeström, R. Miettinen & R-L. Punamäki (Eds.), *Perspectives on activity theory.* Cambridge: Cambridge University Press (pp. 377–404).

(2000a). Activity theory as a framework for analyzing and redesigning work. *Ergonomics,* 43(7), 960–974.

(2000b). From individual action to collective activity and back: Developmental work research as an interventionist methodology. In P. Luff, J. Hindmarsh & C. Heath (Eds.), *Workplace studies.* Cambridge: Cambridge University Press.

(2003). The horizontal dimension of expansive learning: Weaving a texture of cognitive trails in the terrain of health care in Helsinki. In F. Achtenhagen & E. G. John (Eds.), *Milestones of vocational and occupational education and training.* Vol. 1. *The teaching-learning perspective.* Bielefeld: Bertelsmann.

(2005a). *Developmental work research: Expanding activity theory in practice.* Berlin: Lehmanns Media.

(2005b). Knotworking to create collaborative intentionality capital in fluid organizational fields. In M. M. Beyerlein, S. T. Beyerlein & F. A. Kennedy (Eds.), *Collaborative capital: Creating intangible value.* Amsterdam: Elsevier.

(2007a). Enriching the theory of expansive learning: Lessons from journeys toward coconfiguration. *Mind, Culture, and Activity,* 14(1–2), 23–39.

(2007b). Putting Vygotsky to work: The Change Laboratory as an application of double stimulation. In H. Daniels, M. Cole & J. V. Wertsch (Eds.), *The Cambridge companion to Vygotsky.* Cambridge: Cambridge University Press (pp. 363–382).

(2008). *From teams to knots: Activity-theoretical studies of collaboration and learning at work.* Cambridge: Cambridge University Press.

(2009a). The future of activity theory: A rough draft. In A. Sannino, H. Daniels & K. D. Gutiérrez (Eds.), *Learning and expanding with activity theory.* Cambridge: Cambridge University Press (pp. 303–328).

(2009b). Wildfire activities: New patterns of mobility and learning. *International Journal of Mobile and Blended Learning,* 1(2), 1–18.

(2011). From design experiments to formative interventions. *Theory and Psychology,* 21(5), 598–628.

Engeström, Y. & Blackler, F. (2005). On the life of the object. *Organization,* 12, 307–330.

Engeström, Y. & Engeström, R. (1986). Developmental work research: The approach and the application of cleaning work. *Nordisk Pedagogik,* 6, 2–15.

Engeström, Y. & Escalante, V. (1996). Mundane tool or object of affection? The rise and fall of the Postal Buddy. In B. A. Nardi (Ed.), *Context and consciousness: Activity theory and human-computer interaction.* Cambridge, MA: The MIT Press.

Engeström, Y. & Middleton, D. (Eds.) (1993). *Cognition and communication at work.* Cambridge: Cambridge University Press.

Engeström, Y. & Sannino, A. (2010). Studies of expansive learning: Foundations, findings and future challenges. *Educational Research Review,* 5, 1–24.

Engeström, Y. & Sannino, A. (2011). Discursive manifestations of contradictions in organizational change efforts: A methodological framework. *Journal of Organizational Change Management,* 24(3), 368–387.

Engeström, Y. & Sannino, A. (2012). Whatever happened to process theories of learning? *Learning, Culture and Social Interaction*, 1(1), 45–56.

Engeström, Y. & Sannino, A. (2013). La volition et l'agentivité transformatrice: Perspective théorique de l'activité. *Revue Internationale du CRIRES: Innover dans la tradition de Vygotsky*, 1(1), 4–19.

Engeström, Y., Engeström, R. & Kärkkäinen, M. (1995). Polycontextuality and boundary crossing in expert cognition: Learning and problem solving in complex work activities. *Learning and Instruction*, 5, 319–336.

Engeström, Y., Engeström, R. & Vähäaho, T. (1999). When the center does not hold: The importance of knotworking. In S. Chaiklin, M. Hedegaard & U. J. Jensen (Eds.), *Activity theory and social practice: Cultural-historical approaches*. Aarhus: Aarhus University Press.

Engeström, Y., Kerosuo, H. & Kajamaa, A. (2007). Beyond discontinuity: Expansive organizational learning remembered. *Management Learning*, 38, 319–336.

Engeström, Y., Lompscher, J. & Rückriem, G. (Eds.) (2005). *Putting activity theory to work: Contributions from developmental work research*. Berlin: Lehmanns Media.

Engeström, Y., Miettinen, R. & Punamäki, R-L. (Eds.) (1999). *Perspectives on activity theory*. Cambridge: Cambridge University Press.

Engeström, Y., Nummijoki, J. & Sannino, A. (2012). Embodied germ cell at work: Building an expansive concept of physical mobility in home care. *Mind, Culture, and Activity*, 19(3), 287–309.

Engeström, Y., Puonti, A. & Seppänen, L. (2003). Spatial and temporal expansion of the object as a challenge for reorganizing work. In D. Nicolini, S. Gherardi & D. Yanow (Eds.), *Knowing in organizations: A practice-based approach*. Armonk: Sharpe.

Engeström, Y., Rantavuori, J. & Kerosuo, H. (2013). Expansive learning in a library: Actions, cycles and deviations from instructional intentions. *Vocations and Learning*, 6, 81–106.

Engeström, Y., Virkkunen, J., Helle, M., Pihlaja, J. & Poikela, R. (1996). Change laboratory as a tool for transforming work. *Lifelong Learning in Europe*, 1(2), 10–17.

Eri, T. (2013). The best way to conduct intervention research: Methodological considerations. *Quality and Quantity*, 47(5), 2459–2472.

Falmagne, R. J. (1995). The abstract and the concrete. In L. M. W. Martin, K. Nelson & E. Tobach (Eds.), *Sociocultural psychology: Theory and practice of doing and knowing*. Cambridge: Cambridge University Press.

Fichtner, B. (1984). Co-ordination, co-operation and communication in the formation of theoretical concepts in instruction. In M. Hedegaard, P. Hakkarainen & Y. Engeström (Eds.), *Learning and teaching on a scientific basis*. Aarhus: Aarhus Universitet, Psykologisk institut (pp. 207–228).

(1985). Learning and learning activity. In E. Bol, J. P. P. Haenen & M. Wolters (Eds.), *Education for cognitive development*. Den Haag: SVO/SOO (pp. 47–62).

Flavell, J. H. (1976). Metacognitive aspects of problem solving. In L. B. Resnick (Ed.), *The nature of intelligence*. Hillsdale, NJ: Lawrence Erlbaum.

Gagné, R. M. (1970). *The conditions of learning*. 2nd ed. London: Holt, Rinehart & Winston.

Gallagher, J. M. (1978). Reflexive abstraction and education: The meaning of activity in Piaget's theory. In J. M. Gallagher & J. A. Easley, Jr. (Eds.), *Knowledge and development*. Vol. 2. *Piaget and education*. New York: Plenum (pp. 1–20).

Gatewood, J. B. (1985). Actions speak louder than words. In J. W. D. Dougherty (Ed.), *Directions in cognitive anthropology*. Urbana: University of Illinois Press (pp. 199–219).

Geertz, C. (1973). *The interpretation of cultures: Selected essays*. New York: Basic Books.

Gentner, D. & Stevens, A. L. (Eds.) (1983). *Mental models*. Hillsdale, NJ : Lawrence Erlbaum.

Getzels, J. W. & Csikszentmihalyi, M. (1976). *The creative vision: A longitudinal study of problem finding in art*. New York: Wiley.

Giddens, A. (1982). Labour and interaction. In J. B. Thompson & D. Held (Eds.), *Habermas: Critical debates*. London: Macmillan (pp. 149–161).

Gladwin, H. (1985). In conclusion: Abstraction versus "how it is." *Anthropology & Education Quarterly*, 16, 207–213.

Glazman, M. S. (1972). Wissenschaftliches Schöpfertum als Dialog. In G. Kröber & M. Lorf (Eds.), *Wissenschaftliches Schöpfertum*. Berlin: Akademie-Verlag (pp. 199–212; in German).

Goodman, N. (1978). *Ways of worldmaking*. Indianapolis: Hackett.

    (1983). *Fact, fiction, and forecast*. Cambridge, MA: Harvard University Press.

Greeno, J. G. & Engeström, Y. (2014). Learning in activity. In R. K. Sawyer, *The Cambridge handbook of the learning sciences*. 2nd ed. Cambridge: Cambridge University Press.

Griffin, P. & Cole, M. (1984). Current activity for the future: The Zo-ped. In B. Rogoff & J. V. Wertsch (Eds.), *Children's learning in the 'zone of proximal development'*. San Francisco: Jossey-Bass (pp. 45–64).

Grimshaw, A. D. (1981). *Language as social resource*. Stanford, CA: Stanford University Press.

Gruber, H. E. (1974). *Darwin on man: A psychological study of scientific creativity*. New York: Dutton.

    (1984). The emergence of a sense of purpose: A cognitive case study of young Darwin. In M. L. Commons, F. A. Richards & C. Armon (Eds.), *Beyond formal operations: Late adolescent and adult cognitive development*. New York: Praeger (pp. 3–27).

Grünewald, G. (Ed.) (1985). *Children's campaign for nuclear disarmament*. Helsinki: International Peace Bureau – Peace Union of Finland.

Grüter, B. (1979). "Dialektische Psychologie" – eine amerikanische Variante kritischer Psychologie? *Forum Kritische Psychologie*, 5, 157–175 (in German).

Gutiérrez, K., Baguedano-López, P. & Tejeda, C. (1999). Rethinking diversity: Hybridity and hybrid language practices in the third space. *Mind, Culture, and Activity*, 6(4), 286–303.

Gutiérrez, K., Rymes, B. & Larson, J. (1995). Script, counterscript, and underlife in the classroom – Brown, James versus Brown v. Board of Education. *Harvard Educational Review*, 65, 445–471.

Haapasaari, A., Engeström, Y. & Kerosuo, H. (in press). The emergence of learners' transformative agency in a Change Laboratory intervention. *Journal of Education and Work*.

Habermas, J. (1981). *Theorie des kommunikativen Handelns. Bände 1–2*. Frankfurt am Main: Suhrkamp.

(1984). *The theory of communicative action. Vol. 1. Reason and the rationalization of society*. London: Heinemann.

Haglund, B. J. A. (1983). Community diagnosis: A theoretical model for prevention in primary health care. *Scandinavian Journal of Primary Health Care*, 1, 12–19.

Halldén, O. (1982). *Elevernas tolkning av skoluppgiften*. Stockholm: Pedagogiska institutionen, Stockholms Universitet (in Swedish).

Halliday, M. (1975). *Learning how to mean*. London: Edwin Arnold.

Hallpike, C. R. (1979). *The foundations of primitive thought*. New York: Oxford University Press.

Harré, R. (1970). *The principles of scientific thinking*. London and Basingstoke: Macmillan.

Harré, R., Clarke, D. & DeCarlo, N. (1985). *Motives and mechanisms: An introduction to the psychology of action*. London: Methuen.

Hasu, M. (2000). Blind men and the elephant: Implementation of a new artifact as an expansive possibility. *Outlines*, 2, 5–41.

Hasu, M. & Engeström, Y. (2000). Measurement in action: An activity-theoretical perspective on producer-user interaction. *International Journal of Human-Computer Studies*, 53(1), 61–90.

Haug, F. (1977). *Erziehung und gesellschaftliche Produktion: Kritik des Rollenspiels*. Frankfurt am Main and New York: Campus (in German).

Havelock, E. A. (1976). *Origins of western literacy*. Toronto: OISE.

Hegel, G. W. F. (1966). *The phenomenology of mind*. Translated by J. B. Baillie. 7th impression. London: George Allen & Unwin – Humanities Press.

Helenius, A. (1982). *Roolileikki ja lasten suhteet (Role play and the relations of children)*. Jyväskylä: University of Jyväskylä. Reports from the Department of Psychology 246 (in Finnish).

Hiromatsu, K. I. (1986). *"Habitus" as a key concept for understanding performance*. Paper presented at the SSRC and JSPS Conference on Cognition and the Arts, Harvard (Project Zero), March 27–30, 1986.

Hirschhorn, L. (1982). The soul of a new worker. *Working Papers for a New Society*, 9(1), 42–47.

Hoetker, J. & Ahlbrand, W. A. (1969). The persistence of recitation. *American Educational Research Journal*, 6, 145–167.

Hoffman, L. (1981). *Foundations of family therapy: A conceptual framework for systems change*. New York: Basic Books.

Holland, D. & Reeves, J. R. (1996). Activity theory and the view from somewhere: Team perspectives on the intellectual work of programming. In B. A. Nardi (Ed.), *Context and consciousness: Activity theory and human-computer interaction*. Cambridge, MA: The MIT Press.

Holquist, M. (1982). Introduction. In M. M. Bakhtin, *The dialogic imagination*. Austin: University of Texas Press (pp. xv–xxxiv).

Holzkamp, K. (1983). *Grundlegung der Psychologie.* Frankfurt am Main and New York: Campus (in German).

(1993). *Lernen: Subjektwissenschaftliche Grundlegung.* Frankfurt am Main: Campus.

Hundeide, K. (1985). The tacit background of children's judgments. In J. V. Wertsch (Ed.), *Culture, communication, and cognition: Vygotskian perspectives.* Cambridge: Cambridge University Press (pp. 306–322).

Ilyenkov, E. V. (1977). *Dialectical logic: Essays in its history and theory.* Moscow: Progress.

(1982). *The dialectics of the abstract and the concrete in Marx's "Capital."* Moscow: Progress.

Ingold, T. (2007). *Lines: A brief history.* Oxon: Routledge.

Jackson, R. M. (1986). Thumbs up for direct teaching of thinking skills. *Educational Leadership*, 43(8), 32–36.

Jensen, U. J. (1978). Über das Verhältnis zwischen Philosophie und Wissenschaft. In P. Plath & H. J. Sandkühler (Eds.), *Theorie und Labor.* Köln: Pahl-Rugenstein (S. 10–35; in German).

(1981). Introduction: Preconditions for evolutionary thinking. In U. J. Jensen & R. Harré (Eds.), *The philosophy of evolution.* Brighton: The Harvester Press (pp. 1–22).

Joas, H. (1980). *Praktische Intersubjektivität. Die Entwicklung des Werkes von G. H. Mead.* Frankfurt am Main: Suhrkamp (in German).

Johnson-Laird, P. N. (1983). *Mental models.* Cambridge: Cambridge University Press.

Judin, E. G. (1978). *Sistemnyj podchod i princip dejatel'nosti. Metodologiceskie problemy sovremennoj nauki.* Moscow: Nauka (in Russian).

Jung, C. G. (1966). *Two essays on analytical psychology.* London and Henley: Routledge & Kegan Paul.

Jungk, R. (1956). *Heller als Tausend Sonnen: Das Schicksal der Atomforscher.* Stuttgart: Scherz & Goverts (in German).

Kahneman, D., Slovic, P. & Tversky, A. (Eds.) (1982). *Judgment under uncertainty: Heuristics and biases.* Cambridge: Cambridge University Press.

Kärkkäinen, M. (1996). Comparative analysis of planning trajectories in Finnish and American teaching teams. *Nordisk Pedagogik*, 16, 167–190.

Karmiloff-Smith, A. & Inhelder, B. (1975). "If you want to get ahead, get a theory." *Cognition*, 3, 195–212.

Kedrov, B. M. (1966–1967). On the question of the psychology of scientific creativity (on the occasion of the discovery by D. I. Mendeleev of the periodic law). *Soviet Psychology*, V(1), 18–37.

(1972). Zur Theorie der wissenschaftlichen Entdeckung. In G. Kröber & M. Lorf (Eds.) *Wissenschaftliches Schöpfertum.* Berlin: Akademie-Verlag, (S. 34–116; in German).

Keiler, P. (1981). Natural history and psychology: Perspectives and problems. In U. J. Jensen & R. Harré (Eds.), *The philosophy of evolution.* Brighton: The Harvester Press (pp. 137–154).

Keiler, P. & Schurig, V. (1978). Einige Grundlagenprobleme der Naturgeschichte des Lernens. *Forum Kritische Psychologie*, 3, 91–150 (in German).

Kelly, A. E., Lesh, R. A. & Baek, J. Y. (Eds.) (2008). *Handbook of design research methods in education: Innovations in science, technology, engineering, and mathematics learning and teaching.* New York: Routledge.

Kern, H. & Schumann, M. (1984). *Das Ende der Arbeitsteilung?* München: Beck (in German).

Kerosuo, H. Mäki, T. & Korpela, J. (2013). Knotworking: A novel BIM-based collaboration practice in building design projects. In *Proceedings of the 5th International Conference on Construction Engineering and Project Management,* Orange County, California, January 9–11, 2013.

Kidder, T. (1981). *The soul of a new machine.* Boston: Little Brown.

Kivi, A. (1929). *Seven brothers.* New York: Coward – MacCann.

Klix, F. (1982). Are learning processes evolutionary invariant? An unproved assumption in psychology of learning revisited. *Zeitschrift für Psychologie,* 190, 381–391.

Koestler, A. (1964). *The act of creation.* London: Hutchinson.

Köhler, C., Schultz-Wild, R. & Lutz, B. (1983). *Flexible manufacturing systems: Manpower problems and policies.* Paper presented at the World Congress on the Human Aspects of Automation, Ann Arbor, Michigan, August 8–11, 1983.

Köhler, W. (1925). *The mentality of apes.* New York: Harcourt, Brace.

Kolmogorov, A. N. 1960. Introduction in H. Lebesque, *The measurement of quantities.* 2nd Russian ed. Moscow: Uchpedgiz (in Russian).

Kozielecki, J. (1986). A transgressive model of man. *New Ideas in Psychology* 4, 89–105.

Krigman, A. (1985). Bhopal: The unanswered questions. *InTech,* May 1985, 9–20.

Krinsky, J. (2007). *Free labor: Workfare and the contested language of neoliberalism.* Chicago: The University of Chicago Press.

(2008). Changing minds: Cognitive systems and strategic change in contention over Workfare in New York City. *Social Movement Studies,* 7(1), 1–29.

Krinsky, J. & Barker, C. (2009). Movement strategizing as developmental learning: Perspectives from cultural-historical activity theory. In H. Johnston (Ed.), *Culture, social movements, and protest.* Farnham: Ashgate.

Kruger, A. C. & Tomasello, M. (1998). Cultural learning and learning culture. In D. R. Olson & N. Torrance (Eds.), *The handbook of education and human development.* Malden, MA: Blackwell (pp. 369–387).

Kuchermann, R. & Wigger-Kösters, A. (1985). *Die Waren laufen nicht allein zum Markt…: Die Entfaltung von Tätigkeit und Subjektivität in der Geschichte.* Köln: Pahl-Rugenstein (in German).

de Lange, T. (2011). Formal and non-formal digital practices: Institutionalizing transactional learning spaces in a media classroom. *Learning, Media and Technology,* 36(3), 251–275.

Langley, P. & Simon, H. (1981). The central role of learning in cognition. In J. R. Anderson (Ed.), *Cognitive skills and their acquisition.* Hillsdale, NJ: Lawrence Erlbaum (pp. 361–380).

Latour, B. & Woolgar, S. (1979). *Laboratory life: The social construction of scientific facts.* Beverly Hills, CA: Sage.

Lave, J. (1985). Introduction: Situationally specific practice. *Anthropology & Education Quarterly,* 16, 171–176.

(1988). *Cognition in practice: Mind, mathematics and culture in everyday life.* Cambridge: Cambridge University Press.

Leadbetter, J. (2004). The role of mediating artefacts in the work of educational psychologists during consultative conversations in schools. *Educational Review*, 56(2), 133–145.

Leakey, R. E. & Lewin, R. (1983). *People of the lake: Mankind and its beginnings.* New York: Avon Books.

Lefèvre, W. (1978). *Naturtheorie und Produktionsweise.* Darmstadt: Luchterhand (in German).

Lektorsky, V. A. (1984). *Subject, object, cognition.* Moscow: Progress.

Lenin, V. I. (1963). Philosophical notebooks. In V. I. Lenin, *Collected works.* Vol. 38. Moscow: Progress.

Leontjew, A. A. (1980). Tätigkeit und Kommunikation. *Sowjetwissenschaft. Gesellschaftswissenschaftliche Beiträge*, 33, 522–535.

Leont'ev, A. N. (1978). *Activity, consciousness, and personality.* Englewood Cliffs, NJ: Prentice-Hall.

Leontiev, A. N. & Luria, A. R. (1968). The psychological ideas of L. S. Vygotskii. In B. B. Wolman (Ed.), *Historical roots of contemporary psychology.* New York: Harper & Row (pp. 338–367).

Leontyev, A. N. (1981). *Problems of the development of the mind.* Moscow: Progress.

Lerner, R. M. & Busch-Rossnagel, N. A. (Eds.) (1981). *Individuals as producers of their development: A life-span perspective.* New York: Academic Press.

Leroi-Gourhan, A. (1980). *Hand und Wort. Die Evolution von Technik, Sprache und Kunst.* Frankfurt am Main: Suhrkamp (in German).

Lévi-Strauss, C. (1961). *A world on the wane.* London: Hutchinson.

Levy, R. I. (1976). A conjunctive pattern in middle class informal and formal education. In T. Schwartz (Ed.), *Socialization as cultural communication.* Berkeley: University of California Press (pp. 177–188).

Lewontin, R. C. (1982). Organism and environment. In H. C. Plotkin (Ed.), *Learning, development, and culture.* New York: Wiley (pp. 151–169).

Lock, A. (Ed.) (1978). *Action, gesture and symbol: The emergence of language.* London: Academic Press.

Lomow, B. F. (1980). Die Kategorien Kommunikation und Tätigkeit in der Psychologie. *Sowjetwissenschaft. Gesellschaftswissenschaftliche Beiträge*, 33, 536–551 (in German).

Lopes, L. M. (1981). Problem solving in a human relationship: The interactional accomplishment of a "zone of proximal development" during therapy. *The Quarterly Newsletter of the Laboratory of Comparative Human Cognition*, 3(1), 1–5.

Luria, A. R. (1976). *Cognitive development: Its cultural and social foundations.* Cambridge, MA: Harvard University Press.

Malinowski, B. (1923). The problem of meaning in primitive languages. In C. K. Ogden & I. A. Richards, *The meaning of meaning.* London: Kegan Paul, Trench, Trubner. (pp. 296–336).

(1944). *A scientific theory of culture and other essays.* Chapel Hill: The University of North Carolina Press.

Marková, I. (1982). *Paradigms, thought, and language.* Chichester: Wiley.

Marx, K. (1909). *Capital*. Vol. 1. London: William Glaisher.

(1971). *Capital*. Vol. 3. Moscow: Progress.

(1973). *Grundrisse: Foundations of the critique of political economy* (rough draft). Harmondsworth: Penguin Books.

(1976). Theses on Feuerbach. In K. Marx & F. Engels, *The German ideology*. Moscow: Progress (pp. 615–617).

Marzano, R. J. & Arredondo, D. E. (1986). Restructuring schools through the teaching of thinking skills. *Educational Leadership*, 43(8), 20–26.

Maschewsky, W. (1977). *Das Experiment in der Psychologie*. Frankfurt am Main: Campus (in German).

McCarthy, T. (1984). Translator's introduction. In J. Habermas, *The theory of communicative action*. Vol. 1. *Reason and the rationalization of society*. London: Heinemann (pp. v–xxxvii).

McNeill, D. (1985). So you think gestures are nonverbal? *Psychological Review*, 92, 350–371.

Mead, G. H. (1934). *Mind, self, and society*. Chicago: The University of Chicago Press.

Meshcheryakov, A. (1979). *Awakening to life*. Moscow: Progress.

Miettinen, R. (1986). *The craftwork conception of science*. Paper presented at the 1st International Congress of Activity Theory, West Berlin, October 3–5, 1986.

Mikhailov, F. T. (1980). *The riddle of the self*. Moscow: Progress.

Miller, A. I. (1984). *Imagery in scientific thought: Creating 20th century physics*. Boston: Birkhäuser.

Mitroff, I. I. & Kilmann, R. (1978). *Methodological approaches to social science*. San Francisco: Jossey-Bass.

Mitroff, I. I. & Mason, R. O. (1981). Dialectical pragmatism: A progress report on an interdisciplinary program of research on dialectical inquiring systems. *Synthese*, 47, 29–42.

Morss, J. R. (1985). Old Mead in new bottles: The impersonal and the interpersonal in infant knowledge. *New Ideas in Psychology*, 3, 165–176.

(1986). Old Mead in new battles: A reply to Shotter. *New Ideas in Psychology*, 4, 85–88.

Morton, T. (2013). *Hyperobjects: Philosophy and ecology after the end of the world*. Minneapolis: University of Minnesota Press.

Moscovici, S. (1984). *Versuch über die menschliche Geschichte der Natur*. Frankfurt am Main: Suhrkamp (in German).

Mukute, M. & Lotz-Sisitka, H. (2012). Working with cultural-historical activity theory and critical realism to investigate and expand farmer learning in Southern Africa. *Mind, Culture, and Activity*, 19, 342–367.

Murphy, E. & Rodriguez-Manzanares, M. A. (2008). Using activity theory and its principle of contradictions to guide research in educational technology. *Australasian Journal of Educational Technology*, 24(4), 442–457.

Murphy, G. L. & Medin, D. L. (1985). The role of theories in conceptual coherence. *Psychological Review*, 92, 289–316.

Nardi, B. (Ed.) (1996). *Context and consciousness: Activity theory and human-computer interaction*. Cambridge: The MIT Press.

Nelson, K. (1979). The role of language in infant development. In M. C. Bornstein & W. Kessen (Eds.), *Psychological development from infancy: Image to intention.* Hillsdale, NJ: Lawrence Erlbaum (pp. 307–337).

(1983). The derivation of concepts and categories from event representations. In E. K. Scholnik (Ed.), *New trends in conceptual representation: Challenges to Piaget's theory?* Hillsdale, NJ: Lawrence Erlbaum (pp. 129–149).

Newman, D., Griffin, P. & Cole, M. (1984). Social constraints in laboratory and class-room tasks. In B. Rogoff & J. Lave (Eds.), *Everyday cognition: Its development in social context.* Cambridge, MA: Harvard University Press (pp. 172–193).

Nickerson, R., Perkins, D. N. & Smith, E. (1985). *The teaching of thinking.* Hillsdale, NJ: Lawrence Erlbaum.

Nonaka, I. & Tackeuchi, H. (1995). *The knowledge-creating company: How Japanese companies create the dynamics of innovation.* Oxford: Oxford University Press.

Norman, D. A. (1982). *Learning and memory.* San Francisco: Freeman.

(1983). Some observations on mental models. In D. Gentner & A. L. Stevens (Eds.), *Mental models.* Hillsdale, NJ: Lawrence Erlbaum (pp. 7–14).

Nummijoki, J. & Engeström, Y. (in preparation). Defensive and virtuous cycles of learning: A study of home care encounters.

Ogden, C. K. & Richards, I. A. (1923). *The meaning of meaning.* London: Kegan Paul, Trench, Trubner.

Olson, D. R., Torrance, N. & Hildyard, A. (Eds.) (1985). *Literacy, language, and learning: The nature and consequences of reading and writing.* Cambridge: Cambridge University Press.

Ong, W. J. (1977). *Interfaces of the word: Studies in the evolution of consciousness and culture.* Ithaca, NY: Cornell University Press.

(1982). *Orality and literacy: The technologizing of the word.* London: Methuen.

Otte, M. (1980). On the question of the development of theoretical concepts. *Communication & Cognition,* 13(1), 63–76.

(1984). The work of E. G. Judin (1930–1976) on activity theory in the light of recent tendencies in epistemological thinking. In M. Hedegaard, P. Hakkarainen & Y. Engeström (Eds.), *Learning and teaching on a scientific basis.* Aarhus: Aarhus Universitet (pp. 43–86).

Ottomeyer, K. (1980). Marxistische Psychologie gegen Dogma und Eklektizismus. *Forum Kritische Psychologie,* 7, 170–207 (in German).

Parmentier, R. J. (1985). Signs' place in medias res: Peirce's concept of semiotic medi-ation. In E. Mertz & R. J. Parmentier (Eds.), *Semiotic mediation: Sociocultural and psychological perspectives.* Orlando, FL: Academic Press (pp. 23–48).

Peirce, C. S. (1931–1935). *Collected papers of Charles Sanders Peirce.* Edited by C. Hortshorne & P. Weiss. Cambridge, MA: Harvard University Press.

Pharies, D. A. (1984). *Charles S. Peirce and the linguistic sign.* Amsterdam: John Benjamins.

Piaget, J. (1977). The role of action in the development of thinking. In W. F. Overton & J. M. Gallagher (Eds.), *Knowledge and development.* Vol. 1. *Advances in research and theory.* New York: Plenum (pp. 17–42).

Pihlaja, J. (2005). *Learning in and for production: An activity-theoretical study of the historical development of distributed systems of generalizing.* Helsinki: University of Helsinki, Department of Education.

Poddjakow, N. (1981). *Die Denkentwicklung beim Vorschulkind.* Berlin: Volk und Wissen (in German).

Polanyi, M. (1964). *Personal knowledge: Towards a post-critical philosophy.* New York: Harper & Row.

Popper, K. R. (1972). *Objective knowledge: An evolutionary approach.* Oxford: Clarendon Press.

Popper, K. R. & Eccles, J. C. (1977). *The self and its brain.* Berlin: Springer.

Price, D. J. de S. (1963). *Little science, big science.* New York: Columbia University Press.

Prigogine, I. (1984). A new model of time, a new view of physics. In J. Richardson (Ed.), *Models of reality: Shaping thought and action.* Mt. Airy, MD: Lomond (pp. 303–316).

(1985). *Science, civilization and democracy.* Keynote presentation at the 6th Parliamentary and Scientific Conference of the Council of Europe, Tokyo/ Tsukuba, 3–6 June, 1985.

Prigogine, I. & Stengers, I. (1985). *Order out of chaos: Man's new dialogue with nature.* London: Fontana.

Projekt Automation und Qualifikation (1980). *Automationsarbeit: Empirische Untersuchungen.* Teil 1. Argument-Sonderband 43. West-Berlin: Argument-Verlag (in German).

(1981). *Automationsarbeit: Empirische Untersuchungen.* Teil 2. Argument-Sonderband 55. West-Berlin: Argument-Verlag (in German).

Puonti, A. (2004). *Learning to work together: Collaboration between authorities in economic-crime investigation.* Vantaa: National Bureau of Investigation.

Radzikhovskii, L. A. (1984). Activity: Structure, genesis, and units of analysis. *Soviet Psychology,* XXII, 35–53.

Raiethel, A. (1983). *Tätigkeit, Arbeit und Praxis.* Frankfurt am Main and New York: Campus (in German).

Rao, H., Morrill, C. & Zald, M. N. (2000). Power plays: How social movements and collective action create new organizational forms. *Research in Organizational Behavior,* 22, 239–282.

Rasmussen, J. (1980). What can be learned from human error reports? In K. D. Duncan, M. M. Gruneberg & D. Wallis (Eds.), *Changes in working life.* Chichester: Wiley (pp. 97–114).

Rasmussen, J., Duncan, K. & Leplat, J. (Eds.) (1987). *New technology and human error.* Chichester: Wiley.

Ravetz, J. R. (1971). *Scientific knowledge and its social problems.* Oxford: Clarendon Press.

Reynolds, P. C. (1981). *On the evolution of human behavior.* Berkeley: University of California Press.

(1982). The primate constructional system: The theory and description of instrumental object use in humans and chimpanzees. In M. von Cranach & R. Harré (Eds.), *The analysis of action: Recent theoretical and empirical advances.* Cambridge: Cambridge University Press (pp. 343–386).

Richards, F. A., Armon, C. & Commons, M. L. (1984). Perspectives on the development of thought in late adolescence and adulthood: An introduction. In M. L. Commons, F. A. Richards & C. Armon (Eds.), *Beyond formal opera-*

tions: Late adolescent and adult cognitive development. New York: Praeger (pp. xiii–xxviii).

Richardson, J. M. (1984). Global modeling in the 1980's. In J. Richardson (Ed.), *Models of reality: Shaping thought and action.* Mt. Airy, MD: Lomond Books (pp. 115–129).

Riegel, K. (1973). Dialectic operations: The final period of cognitive development. *Human Development,* 16, 346–370.

Riegel, K. F. (1979). *Foundations of dialectical psychology.* New York: Academic Press.

Rogoff, B. & Lave, J. (Eds.) (1984). *Everyday cognition: Development in social context.* Cambrdige, MA: Harvard University Press.

Rogoff, B. & Wertsch, J. V. (Eds.) (1984). *Children's learning in the "zone of proximal development."* San Francisco: Jossey-Bass.

Roset, I. (1984). *The psychology of fantasy.* Moscow: Progress.

Rouse, W. B. & Morris, N. M. (1985). *On looking into the black box: Prospects and limits in the search for mental models.* Center for Man-Machine Systems Research. Georgia Institute of Technology. Report no. 85-2.

Ruben, P. (1978). *Dialektik und Arbeit der Philosophie.* Köln: Pahl-Rugenstein (in German).

——— (1981). From moralization to class society or from class society to moralization: Philosophical comments on Klaus Eder's hypothesis. In U. J. Jensen & R. Harré (Eds.), *The philosophy of evolution.* Brighton: The Harvester Press (pp. 120–136).

Saarelma, O. (1993). Descriptions of subjective networks as a mediator of developmental dialogue. *The Quarterly Newsletter of the Laboratory of Comparative Human Cognition,* 15, 102–112.

Sannino, A. (2011). Activity theory as an activist and interventionist theory. *Theory and Psychology,* 21(5), 571–597.

Schmandt-Basserat, D. (1978). The earliest precursor of writing. *Scientific American,* 238(6), 50–59.

Schön, D. A. (1983). *The reflective practitioner: How professionals think in action.* London: Temple Smith.

Schurig, V. (1976). *Die Entstehung des Bewusstseins.* Frankfurt am Main and New York: Campus.

Scribner, S. (1985). Vygotsky's uses of history. In J. V. Wertsch (Ed.), *Culture, communication, and cognition: Vygotskian perspectives.* Cambridge: Cambridge University Press (pp. 119–145).

Scribner, S. & Cole, M. (1981). *The psychology of literacy.* Cambridge, MA: Harvard University Press.

Seidel, R. (1976). *Denken – psychologische Analyse der Entstehung und Lösung von Problemen.* Frankfurt am Main/New York: Campus (in German).

Selz, O. (1924). *Gesetze der produktiven und reproduktiven Geistestätigkeit.* Bonn: Cohen (in German).

Sharp, D. W., Cole, M. & Lave, C. (1979). Education and cognitive development: The evidence from experimental research. *Monographs of the Society for Research in Child Development,* 44(1–2, Serial No. 178).

Shotter, J. (1982). Consciousness, self-consciousness, inner games, and alternative realities. In G. Underwood (Ed.), *Aspects of consciousness*. Vol. 3. *Awareness and self-awareness*. London: Academic Press (pp. 27–62).

(1986). Realism and relativism, rules and intentionality, theories and accounts: A response to Morss. *New Ideas in Psychology*, 4, 71–84.

Sigel, I. E. (1983). Is the concept of the concept still elusive or what do we know about concept development? In E. K. Scholnick (Ed.), *New trends in conceptual representation: Challenges to Piaget's theory?* Hillsdale, NJ: Lawrence Erlbaum (pp. 239–273).

Simon, H. A. (1983). *Reason in human affairs*. Oxford: Basil Blackwell.

Sluzki, C. E. & Ransom, D. C. (Eds.) (1976). *Double bind: The foundation of the communication approach to the family*. New York: Grune & Stratton.

Snyder, B. R. (1971). *The hidden curriculum*. New York: Knopf.

Soule, S. A. (2012). Social movements and markets, industries and firms. *Organization Studies*, 33(12), 1715–1733.

Suchman, L. (1987). *Plans and situated actions: The problem of human-machine communication*. Cambridge: Cambridge University Press.

Svechnikov, G. A. (1971). *Causality and the relation of states in physics*. Moscow: Progress.

Toikka, K. (1986). *Development of work in FMS – case study on new manpower strategy*. Paper presented in the IFAC Workshop "Skill Based Automated Manufacturing," Karlsruhe, FRG, September 3–5, 1986.

Toikka, K., Engeström, Y. & Norros, L. (1985). Entwickelnde Arbeitsforschung: Theoretische and methdologische Elemente (Developmental work research: Theoretical and methodological elements). *Forum Kritische Psychologie*, 15, 5–41 (in German).

Toikka, K., Hyötyläinen, R. & Norros, L. (1986). Development of work in flexible manufacturing. *Nordisk Pedagogik*, 6(1), 16–24.

Toiviainen, H. (2007). Inter-organizational learning across levels: An object-oriented approach. *Journal of Workplace Learning*, 19(6), 343–358.

Tolman, C. (1981). The metaphysic of relations in Klaus Riegel's "dialectics" of human development. *Human Development*, 24, 33–51.

Tomasello, M. (1999). *The cultural origins of human cognition*. Cambridge, MA: Harvard University Press.

Toulmin, S. (1982). *The return to cosmology: Postmodern science and the theology of nature*. Berkeley: University of California Press.

Trân Duc Thao (1984). *Investigations into the origin of language and consciousness*. Dordrecht: Reidel.

Trevarthen, C. & Hubley, P. (1978). Secondary intersubjectivity: Confidence, confiding and acts of meaning in the first year. In A. Lock (Ed.), *Action, gesture and symbol: The emergence of language*. London: Academic Press (pp. 183–230).

Tsuckerman, G. A. (2011). Developmental education: A genetic modeling experiment. *Journal of Russian and East European Psychology*, 49(6), 45–63.

Tuomi-Gröhn, T. & Engeström, Y. (Eds.) (2003). *Between school and work: New perspectives on transfer and boundary crossing*. Amsterdam: Elsevier.

Twain, M. (1950). *The adventures of Huckleberry Finn*. London: The Cresset Press.

Tweney, R. D., Doherty, M. E. & Mynatt, C. R. (1981). Epilogue. In R. D. Tweney, M. E. Doherty & C. R. Mynatt (Eds.), *On scientific thinking*. New York: Columbia University Press (pp. 399–417).

Ushakova, T. N. (1977). Causes of children's word invention (A psychophysiological model of the genesis of the syntactically structured verbal utterance). In M. Cole (Ed.), *Soviet developmental psychology: An anthology*. White Plains, NY: M. E. Sharpe (pp. 516–537).

van der Veer, R. & Valsiner, J. (1991). *Understanding Vygotsky: A quest for synthesis*. Oxford: Blackwell.

Virkkunen, J. (2006). Dilemmas in building shared transformative agency. *Activités*, 3(1), 44–66.

(2009). Two theories of organizational knowledge creation. In A. Sannino, H. Daniels & K. D. Gutiérrez (Eds.), *Learning and expanding with activity theory*. Cambridge: Cambridge University Press (pp. 144–159).

Virkkunen, J. & Newnham, D. S. (2013). *The Change Laboratory: A tool for collaborative development of work and education*. Rotterdam: Sense.

Vygotsky, L. S. (1962). *Thought and language*. Cambridge, MA: The MIT Press.

(1971). *The psychology of art*. Cambridge, MA: The MIT Press.

(1978). *Mind in society: The development of higher psychological processes*. Cambridge, MA: Harvard University Press.

(1981). The instrumental method in psychology. In J. V. Wertsch (Ed.), *The concept of activity in Soviet psychology*. Armonk, NY: Sharpe (pp. 134–143).

(1987). Lectures on psychology. In *The collected works of L. S. Vygotsky*. Vol. 1. *Problems of general psychology*. New York: Plenum (pp. 289–358).

(1997a). The historical meaning of the crisis in psychology: A methodological investigation. In *The collected works of L. S. Vygotsky*. Vol. 3. *Problems of the theory and history of psychology*. New York: Plenum (pp. 223–343).

(1997b). The history of the development of higher mental functions. In *The collected works of L. S. Vygotsky*. Vol. 4. *The history of the development of higher mental functions*. New York: Plenum (pp. 1–251).

(1997c). The instrumental method in psychology. In *The collected works of L. S. Vygotsky*. Vol. 3. *Problems of the theory and history of psychology*. New York: Plenum (pp. 85–89).

(1999). Tool and sign in the development of the child. In *The collected works of L. S. Vygotsky*. Vol. 6. *Scientific legacy*. New York: Kluwer/Plenum (pp. 1–68).

Wales, C. E., Nardi, A. H. & Stager, R. A. (1986). Decision making: New paradigm for education. *Educational Leadership*, 43(8), 37–41.

Wartofsky, M. (1968). *Conceptual foundations of scientific thought: An introduction to the philosophy of science*. New York: MacMillan.

(1979). *Models: Representation and scientific understanding*. Dordrecht: Reidel.

(1983). From genetic epistemology to historical epistemology: Kant, Marx, and Piaget. In L. S. Liben (Ed.), *Piaget and the foundations of knowledge*. Hillsdale, NJ: Lawrence Erlbaum (pp. 1–18).

Weinberg, A. M. (1967). *Reflections of big science*. Cambridge, MA: The MIT Press.

Werner, H. (1961). *Comparative psychology of mental development*. New York: Science Editions.

Wertheimer, M. (1945). *Productive thinking*. New York: Harper & Brothers.

Wertsch, J. V. (Ed.) (1985a). *Culture, communication, and cognition: Vygotskian perspectives*. Cambridge: Cambridge University Press.

(1985b). The semiotic mediation of mental life: L. S. Vygotsky and M. M. Bakhtin. In E. Mertz & R. J. Parmentier (Eds.), *Semiotic mediation: Sociocultural and psychological perspectives*. Orlando: Academic Press (pp. 49–72).

(1985c). *Vygotsky and the social formation of mind*. Cambridge, MA: Harvard University Press.

(1991). *Voices of the mind: A sociocultural approach to mediated action*. Cambridge, MA: Harvard University Press.

Wilde, L. (1989). *Marx and contradiction*. Aldershot: Avebury.

Wilhelmer, B. (1979). *Lernen als Handlung*. Köln: Pahl-Rugenstein (in German).

Wood, D. J. (1980). Teaching the young child: Some relationships between social interaction, language, and thought. In D. R. Olson (Ed.), *The social foundations of language and thought*. New York: Norton (pp. 280–298).

Wood, D., Bruner, J. S. & Ross, G. (1976). The role of tutoring in problem solving. *Journal of Child Psychology and Psychiatry*, 17, 89–100.

Wood, S. (Ed.) (1982). *The degradation of work?* London: Hutchinson.

(1987). The deskilling debate, new technology and work organization. *Acta Sociologica*, 30, 3–24.

Wygotski, L. S. (1977). *Denken und Sprechen*. Frankfurt am Main: Fischer (in German).

Zilsel, E. (1976). *Die sozialen Ursprünge der neuzeitlichen Wissenschaft*. Frankfurt am Main: Suhrkamp (in German).

Zinchenko, P. I. (1983–84). The problem of involuntary memory. *Soviet Psychology*, XXII, 55–111.

Zinchenko, V. P. (1985). Vygotsky's ideas about units for the analysis of mind. In J. V. Wertsch (Ed.), *Culture, communication, and cognition: Vygotskian perspectives*. Cambridge: Cambridge University Press (pp. 94–118).

Zivin, G. (Ed.) (1979). *The development of self-regulation through private speech*. New York: Wiley.

INDEX

Printed in the United States
By Bookmasters